D1479335

THE ABOLITIONIST CIVIL WAR

ANTISLAVERY, ABOLITION, AND THE ATLANTIC WORLD

R. J. M. Blackett and Edward Rugemer, Series Editors
James Brewer Stewart, Editor Emeritus

THE
ABOLITIONIST CIVIL WAR

IMMEDIATISTS AND THE STRUGGLE
TO TRANSFORM THE UNION

FRANK J. CIRILLO

LOUISIANA STATE UNIVERSITY PRESS
BATON ROUGE

Published by Louisiana State University Press
lsupress.org

DESIGNER: Barbara Neely Bourgoyne
TYPEFACE: Garamond Premier Pro

COVER PHOTOGRAPH: *Wendell Phillips, William Lloyd Garrison, and
George Thompson;* daguerreotype by Southworth & Hawes, 1851.
Courtesy of the Boston Public Library.

LIBRARY OF CONGRESS CATALOGING-IN-PUBLICATION DATA
Names: Cirillo, Frank J., author.
Title: The abolitionist Civil War : immediatists and the struggle to transform the Union /
  Frank J. Cirillo.
Other titles: Immediatists and the struggle to transform the Union
Description: Baton Rouge : Louisiana State University Press, [2023] | Series: Antislavery,
  abolition, and the Atlantic World | Includes bibliographical references and index.
Identifiers: LCCN 2023004007 (print) | LCCN 2023004008 (ebook) | ISBN
  978-0-8071-7915-4 (cloth) | ISBN 978-0-8071-8066-2 (pdf) | ISBN 978-0-8071-8065-5
  (epub)
Subjects: LCSH: Antislavery movements—United States—History—19th century. |
  Abolitionists—United States—History—19th century. | Abolitionists—Political
  activity—United States—History—19th century. | Slaves—Emancipation—United
  States—History—19th century. | United States—History—Civil War, 1861–1865—
  Participation, African American. | United States—History—Civil War, 1861–1865—
  Moral and ethical aspects. | American Anti-Slavery Society.
Classification: LCC E449 .C575 2023 (print) | LCC E449 (ebook) | DDC
  973.7/114—dc23/eng/20230223
LC record available at https://lccn.loc.gov/2023004007
LC ebook record available at https://lccn.loc.gov/2023004008

Per mio babbo e per i miei nonni

CONTENTS

ACKNOWLEDGMENTS

This book began at the University of Virginia's Corcoran Department of History, and its completion owes to the help and support of countless people in my life. I would like to thank Elizabeth Varon and Gary Gallagher for their incredible generosity at every stage of this project. Over many years, their advice helped shape the form and content of my ever-evolving work. I count myself lucky to have learned from these exemplary scholars.

Jim Stewart, the dean of abolitionist scholarship, began advising my project in its earliest stage. Over the ensuing years, his countless detailed insights proved invaluable as I revised the manuscript. And as a series editor emeritus at LSU Press, Jim shepherded my project to publication in more ways than one. I thank him profusely.

I would like to thank LSU Press as well for publishing my work. Rand Dotson and my series editors, Richard Blackett and Edward Rugemer, proved extremely helpful as I wrangled my project into a publishable form over the last few years. I owe them a great debt of gratitude.

In the course of my research and writing, I have received the invaluable assistance of librarians and administrators at a number of institutions where I have researched and held fellowships. From my time as a graduate student at the University of Virginia, I would like to thank Jimmy Wright and the Jefferson Scholars Foundation, the New England Regional Fellowship Consortium, the Gilder Lehrman Institute of American History, and the William L. Clements Library at the University of Michigan. And for their succor over the ensuing years, I would like to thank Michael Ryan and the New-York Historical Society, The New School, Caroline Janney and the University of Virginia's Nau Center for Civil War History, the John W. Kluge Center at the Library of Congress, the American Historical Association, David Blight and Yale University's Gilder

Lehrman Center for the Study of Slavery, Abolition, and Resistance, the Winterthur Museum, Sarah Dusend and the Bonn Center for Dependency and Slavery Studies, and Kanisorn Wongsrichanalai and the Massachusetts Historical Society.

I would be remiss without mentioning the scholars who cultivated my interest in history. As a high schooler, I became drawn to this field by my teacher, the late Bob Steel. His lessons opened up a world of possibilities to me. As an undergraduate, my burgeoning interest in history was advanced by my professors, including Richard Huzzey and David. And in graduate school, Professors Varon and Gallagher made me into the professional historian I am.

Finally, I would like to thank my friends and family for their boundless patience at every turn. I owe my heartfelt gratitude to my good friends from Charlottesville to Bonn, from Phoenix to Limassol, from Texas to Washington, and from San Francisco to St. Paul for keeping me sane all these years. I offer my especial thanks to my parents and to my much-missed grandparents, Joseph and Ada Cirillo. Their unwavering love and pride have always kept me going through everything. Above all, this book is a testament to them.

THE ABOLITIONIST CIVIL WAR

Introduction

n March 1862, the abolitionist orator Wendell Phillips received an urgent flurry of letters from his wife, Ann. Over the past year, he and the majority of American abolitionists had endeavored to mold the Union war into a holy crusade for emancipation by embarking upon a stunning metamorphosis. Upending decades-old tactics and norms, they had refashioned their moral reform movement into a political interest group, steeping themselves in the once-anathema rhetoric of political expediency and cementing pacts with an ever wider array of political figures. These abolitionists had accrued increasing influence, eventually prompting Republican leaders to invite some of their most prominent representatives, including Phillips, to lecture and lobby in Washington. After a moment of hesitation, Phillips had accepted their invitation, recognizing the progress it signified for the abolitionist cause—the fruits of these reformers' political labors.

Yet in the weeks preceding the trip, Ann Phillips beseeched Wendell to forego his plans. Invoking the couple's inseparable relationship as fervent abolitionists, she warned of the dangers of her husband's political reinvention: the imperiling of his moral identity as an upright ideologue. Scoffing at any suggestion of progress, Ann argued that "you are nearly popular *because* you have gone to the worldly men; they have *not* come to you . . . I see no change in them." Politicos ensconced in the capital were embracing abolitionists like Phillips because they were "going too much over to them [the politicians] unconsciously," not the other way around. "Let us abolitionists stick to antislavery," Ann admonished Wendell. "Leave worldly measures to worldly men." A Washington sojourn, she worried, would carry him too far down the path of politicization, blinding him with praise to the point that he strayed from his virtuous principles and discarded the far-reaching moral commitments of abolitionism.[1]

The story of abolitionists' political incursions proved more complex than Ann or Wendell Phillips anticipated, producing both concrete benefits and debilitating drawbacks for their cause. *The Abolitionist Civil War* examines the dramatic wartime transformation of the abolitionist movement: its origins, shifting contours, and drastic consequences for abolitionism and the nation. In founding their movement in the 1830s, immediate abolitionists, or immediatists, demanded racial justice for justice's sake. But they also grounded their mission in their own sense of nationalism. As this book asserts, their endgame was to construct a morally transformed Union: a land, purged through a moral revolution of its original sin of racial bondage and bigotry, that could fulfill its divine destiny as the lighthouse of democracy. Immediatists all premised this moral vision on two principled commitments: the immediate emancipation of all slaves and their inclusion in some form in the post-emancipation polity— a gamut of scenarios, ranging from rendering freed slaves as plantation wage laborers to making them equal citizens, subsumed under the wide-ranging concept of Black rights. Yet the exact dimensions of their delivered nation, and the path toward achieving it, were indefinite and unfixed, precipitating a civil war within abolitionism amid the strife of national conflict.

While abolitionists all originally aspired to achieve their perfect ends through equally perfect means, many grew frustrated in the dark decade before the Civil War. Leading figures from across the movement, including Phillips, the pioneering crusader William Lloyd Garrison, the famed editor and former slave Frederick Douglass, the young educator Charlotte Forten, the reformer-poet Lydia Maria Child, the radical minister George Cheever, and the renegade Virginian Moncure Conway, pivoted to form a new, majority school of thought, becoming what this book refers to as interventionists. In desperation, they fixated upon jump-starting their moral revolution through a sudden, apocalyptic crucible, or golden moment—and on working through the practical means available to them. These interventionists embraced the Union war at its outbreak in April 1861, hoping to ensure their golden moment by harnessing and reshaping an effort to preserve the Union into a regenerative war for emancipation. To do so, they embarked on a harrowing journey, plunging deeper and deeper into the Union political mainstream in response to military and political developments—and controlling their extreme moral ambivalence over such actions.

Early in the war, interventionists crafted and fleshed out a brilliant strategy, gradually remolding themselves into practitioners of pressure politics. They united in support of the government, promulgating arguments about the practical necessity of military emancipation in coordination with new political allies. All the while, they managed both their own inner turmoil and a dissenting minority of abolitionists who still held sacred reformers' emphases on perfect means, here known as moral purists. These figures, including the American hardliners Stephen and Abby Kelley Foster and Parker Pillsbury and most British immediatists, and whose points Ann Phillips echoed above, condemned the Union war as a siren that would lure reformers onto the rocks of moral decay, marring their mission to no material gain. They lashed out at their counterparts, as wartime abolitionism descended into its own internecine struggle between prowar interventionist and antiwar moral purist camps. By 1862, interventionists' expedient ideas nonetheless gained a foothold in a land scarred by war. As *The Abolitionist Civil War* contends, interventionists were essential in raising public and political approval for military emancipation, ultimately helping both pressure President Abraham Lincoln and provide him with the political wherewithal needed to revitalize a stalled war effort by issuing the Emancipation Proclamation.

Yet interventionists achieved such success through political submersion at the great cost of realizing purists' prophecies of a movement tarnished. Early in the war, the interventionist camp had begun dividing between narrow interventionists, like Garrison and Conway, with a vague but increasingly limited definition of Black rights, and broad interventionists, like Phillips, Douglass, and Forten, with an increasingly intense and deeper conception. After the Proclamation, this issue, and the government's indifference regarding it, took over the spotlight, further splitting the two groups. Despite Ann Phillips's worries, Garrison, not her husband, now enacted her greatest fears. Saturated in the mainstream, he adjusted toward his political partners by moderating his moral vision. He jettisoned his founding dedication to Black rights, adopting universal emancipation, Union victory, and Lincoln's continued leadership as the criteria of his truncated morally transformed Union. Phillips and Douglass instead joined moral purists to demand an egalitarian morally transformed Union far beyond what the administration planned.

By late 1863, the interventionist camp was in shambles, as wartime abolitionism reconfigured again into a messy proxy battle over Lincoln's reelection. Garrison and most narrow interventionists rallied to Lincoln alongside Child, while Phillips, Douglass, Pillsbury, the Fosters, and most broad interventionists and purists sought his defeat alongside Cheever and Conway. Though both sides engaged in an electoral arms race, the latter especially damaged their reputations through misguided forays into third-party politics. As the war ended and the Thirteenth Amendment passed in 1865, the abolitionist movement reoriented one final time into a naked ideological struggle over the continuation of antislavery reform. Over the cries of broad interventionists and moral purists that the movement had to secure Black equality, Garrison and the narrow interventionists moved to disband its most prominent organization, the American Anti-Slavery Society (AASS). Though Garrison failed, he retired to celebrate his attenuated but completed mission, abandoning the movement along with Conway. While Phillips, Douglass, Forten, the Fosters, Pillsbury, and the converted broad interventionists Child and Cheever fought on, theirs was a weakened remnant. Shorn of their significant wartime sway by Garrison, and by their own electoral compromises, they proved helpless to sustain postwar Reconstruction. As this book concludes, immediatists' fateful intervention in the Union war helps explain how that war achieved both so much and so little in terms of racial justice.

× × ×

The Abolitionist Civil War elucidates the history of the wartime abolitionist movement and its momentous impact on the nation by developing three themes. First, it extends the story of immediatism deep into the Civil War and beyond, fleshing out its true nature as a morally nationalistic, ideologically multifarious, and politically dynamic movement. Second, it demonstrates how interventionists during the first half of the war helped bring about a Union policy of military emancipation that had seemed far from inevitable. And third, it explores the unintended but disastrous repercussions of their intervention during the second half of the war, as abolitionism stunted its power to secure further, lasting change beyond formal emancipation. It tells the tale of a movement whose greatest victory came at the expense of its ultimate failure.

In recent years, a number of works have bored into the boundaries of immediatism. As historians from James M. McPherson to James Brewer Stewart have shown, antislavery views in the Civil War era existed on a wide spectrum, spanning from conservative supporters of Black colonization to the small but most radical bloc: immediate abolitionists. Immediatism emerged in the 1830s as a new wave of antislavery activism—an organized, transatlantic, and biracial movement that took inspiration from earlier movements for gradual abolition and more recent Black campaigns against colonization. A series of schisms soon convulsed the movement, most famously when a rebellion in 1840 against Garrison's leadership of the AASS rived abolitionists into Garrisonian and non-Garrisonian factions. Garrisonians such as Garrison, Phillips, Child, Conway, Forten, Pillsbury, and the Fosters endorsed women's rights, rejected the Constitution as proslavery, and sought as come-outers to pursue change from outside the political system. Non-Garrisonians such as Cheever and, eventually, Douglass instead portrayed the Constitution as antislavery and strove to form their own immediatist parties, including the Liberty Party.[2]

Despite such discordance, abolitionists shared certain key traits. McPherson and other scholars of immediatism have identified three main abolitionist attributes. Such figures all sought immediate and unconditional emancipation, demanded post-emancipation Black rights, and abjured membership in mainstream American political parties, which fell far short of their unwavering principles. Radical Republicans like Charles Sumner, who desired both emancipation and Black rights but hewed to a party that endorsed neither, were not abolitionists.

Yet this traditional definition only scratches the surface of abolitionism. It establishes immediatists' dedication to freedom and progress, but it omits their millennial motives. McPherson depicts the majority's support for the Union war as an almost cynical act, born of a resolve to achieve abolition at all costs rather than concern for an American nation-state in crisis. Abolitionists, however, were deeply invested in the fate of the United States—and had been from the start. In cofounding the AASS in 1833, Garrison penned a "Declaration of Sentiments": a manifesto that committed abolitionists to achieving immediate emancipation and "all rights" for African Americans, admitting them "forthwith to the enjoyment of . . . the same prerogatives, as others." By planting himself "upon the Declaration of Independence . . . as upon the Everlasting Rock," he aimed to "wipe out the foulest stain which rests upon our national escutcheon" and redeem his homeland. This book accordingly proposes a fourth defining characteristic of immediatists: their overall project of building a morally transformed Union that enshrined emancipation and Black rights, intertwining their concerns for racial justice and the nation into an inseparable whole.[3]

This animating ambition of immediatism emerged alongside the movement in the 1830s, an idiosyncratic twist on the heady intellectual brew of Protestant millennial and American exceptionalistic strains dominating northern culture. Even as the movement devolved into warring factions, Garrisonians and non-Garrisonians continued weaving together the far-flung realms of nationalism, religion, and antislavery into a common mission. As Cheever detailed in an 1857 tract, the Founders had engineered the Union as a "citadel of freedom for the world"—a divinely ordained beacon of global democracy. Its Declaration of Independence, grounded in assertions of universal equality, was the "hugest colossal maul, under God . . . that the angel of freedom [could] swing against the thrones of tyranny." American principles possessed the innate potential to stamp out despotism worldwide under their providential weight.[4]

In the decades since 1776, however, the Union had veered off course to become itself despotic and morally untethered—or, in abolitionists' parlance, demoralized. Slavery and prejudice had replaced freedom and equality as the watchwords of the land, forestalling its glorious destiny. Abolitionists took it as their divine duty to serve as the far-seeing prophets of America, laboring to elevate the fallen land from its depraved depths into its rightful, righteous place in history. "I love my country," Child affirmed in 1856, and "cannot resign myself to the thought that she must prove a warning, rather than an example to the other nations . . . [as] a heaven-light of freedom." As Cheever resolved in his tract, immediatists had to "resist *now*, more strongly [than] our revolutionary fathers"—to lead a second, moral revolution that would realize the promise of the first and beget a morally transformed Union.[5]

In illuminating immediatists' endgame of national redemption, *The Abolitionist Civil War* draws on a burgeoning scholarship teasing out their unique strain of patriotism. David W. Blight has portrayed Douglass as a "millennial nationalist" awaiting an antislavery epoch. W. Caleb McDaniel has delineated white Garrisonians as "cosmopolitan patriots" whose nationalistic dreams became transatlantic in scope, binding together transatlantic activists in a shared pursuit. And Peter Wirzbicki has illustrated how Transcendentalists adhered to a "higher law ethos."[6]

Yet the contours of national redemption, from the methods of moral transformation to the details of Blacks' post-emancipation inclusion, remained open to interpretation. As an ambiguous vision of a far-off future, the concept of a morally transformed Union was as divisive as it was unifying. In their exuberant early days, abolitionists cultivated a shared model of the path to salvation premised on their own saintliness. Garrisonians and non-Garrisonians alike envisioned themselves as aloof others guiding the nation from on high, employing high-minded moralistic appeals to achieve their high-minded ends. Garrison explained in 1843 that while mainstream parties sought the "advancement of men by any means," immediatists chose to perch above that dusty fray and "promulgat[e] righteous principles by righteous means." Their self-proclaimed "purity of purpose" enabled them to act as what Garrisonian Susan B. Anthony termed the "people's conscience," advocating what was best for the nation rather than what was expedient from their lofty "watch towers." Immoral measures, Garrison averred, were incompatible with "anti-slavery principle." Such flawed methods would inevitably result in failure while also debasing their practitioners, attenuating their moral grandeur. Because of their self-conceptions as unadulterated reformers, abolitionists could not countenance dalliances with the impure mainstream, even in the case of "half-way" antislavery men like the Whig Joshua Giddings. Searching for a "grain of wheat in two bushels of chaff," Garrison concluded, was a detour from the true path of pursuing racial justice for its own sake.[7]

As abolitionists witnessed southern slaveholders continue to dominate national affairs despite their own saintly agitations, their initial enthusiasm curdled by the late 1840s and 1850s into discouragement and fury. Historians have illustrated how the language, and actions, of antislavery militancy rose to the fore of abolitionist thought amid such events as Bleeding Kansas and the *Dred Scott* decision. But in despairing over the nation's demoralization, and their seeming inability to rectify it, immediatists also lent an increasingly dark and cataclysmic pall to their overarching project of a morally transformed Union. For decades, these activists had acted as Jeremiah-like prophets. Cognizant of the nation's rightful destiny, they had harangued the people to heed their warnings before it was too late, only to be ignored. Now, with slavery entrenched, many abolitionists concluded that only a millenarian trial of divine reckoning—a golden moment—could set in motion their moral revolution. From his Cincinnati pulpit, Conway declared in 1857 that he would "welcome the most hot-headed prophet . . . [to] let the axe be laid to the root of our tree." Only a fundamental upheaval could end the national downward spiral.[8]

Despite their factional differences, Douglass agreed with Conway's assessment. As Blight has discussed, he, too, anticipated a "jubilee"—a time when "God reigns, and Slavery *must* yet fall." This jubilee represented an American Armageddon. "If we ever get free from the oppressions and wrongs heaped upon us, we must pay for their removal," Douglass warned. "We must do this

... by suffering, by sacrifice, and if needs be, by our lives and the lives of others."
He was not predicting civil war: in the fog of proslavery dominance, he knew
not when this golden moment would arise. "You and I may not live to see" the
jubilee, Douglass admitted. Nor was the earthly form this apocalypse would
take clear. He awaited nonetheless an eventual providential judgement as his
last hope to bring about a morally transformed Union.[9]

Such ideas sparked discord by the late 1850s, splintering abolitionism into
competing schools of thought over how to fulfill their moral mission—a fracture that would transcend the older factional divide between Garrisonians and
non-Garrisonians. A transfactional majority of abolitionists, including Conway,
Douglass, Phillips, Garrison, Child, Cheever, and Forten, sought in desperation
to accelerate the apocalypse and shock the North out of its moral listlessness
however they could. These interventionists began sanctioning morally inferior
means to their grand ends, slipping off their own saintliness as they latched onto
any sign of progress. Increasingly, they fixed their gazes on an upstart party: the
Republicans. Historian Kate Masur has characterized Republicans as generally
supporting racial equality to some extent. Yet this moderately antislavery party
instead gained power by tapping into a white northern mindset that treated
slavery and race as distinct, if not unrelated, issues, disliking both bondage and
Blacks. Through a platform opposing the territorial extension of slavery, paired
with vague support for gradual emancipation and colonization, the mainstream
party aspired to build a free-labor Union premised on whiteness—a far less
inclusive cry from abolitionists' morally transformed Union.[10]

Whereas abolitionists would once have excoriated the Republicans as chaff,
many now shifted course. They still judged the party for falling short of their
own moralistic standards. Republicans, Garrison asserted in 1859, were "tem-
porizing" politicians who bore "awful guilt" for opposing slavery's expansion
rather than slavery itself. While imperfect, however, the Republicans were not
on the "same scale with the Democrat[s]." They were the lesser evil. Their popularity proved that antislavery was on the rise—that abolitionists' agitation had
enabled the ascent of a party that would chip at the proslavery consensus. "Was
it dangerous [to] admit that we had made progress?" Garrison asked. Douglass,
too, favored the Republicans in the upcoming election. While he would have
preferred a party "committed to the doctrine of 'All rights, to all men,' in the
absence" of that party Douglass "desire[d] the success of the Republican candidate," Abraham Lincoln. "There are gradations in all things," he concluded.
"A man need not be a William Lloyd Garrison" to be "an enemy of slavery."

Even Phillips, who lambasted Lincoln as the "slave-hound of Illinois" early in the campaign, later supported his candidacy. Realpolitik, not saintliness, was becoming the order of the day.[11]

Interventionists thus integrated Republicans into their plans as useful instruments at their disposal. Republican assaults on the Slave Power, they believed, could help inaugurate the golden moment. "I don't greatly admire the methods of politicians," Child told Massachusetts senator Charles Sumner. "But if you will enclose the monster, we will kill him." After the apocalypse, the party would fall by the wayside. "My hope is in the Republican Party not where it stands," Garrison argued, but in its "materials for growth." It was not what the James Oakes-led school of scholarship has portrayed as a matured antislavery force, ready and able to displace abolitionism as the standard-bearer of emancipation. Rather, it was a temporary stepping stone toward a future, genuine antislavery vehicle, uniting reformers and politicos like Sumner. In the meantime, Garrison, Douglass, and others tentatively dipped their toes in the political mainstream by toning down their criticisms of the upstart party. Casting about for light amid the proslavery darkness, they suffered the Republicans as imperfect means for imperfect times.[12]

While the vast majority of abolitionists moved away from the saintly model of national redemption, a hardline minority stood by the old ways and forswore involvement in the mainstream. The Fosters and Pillsbury had long served as Garrisonian foot soldiers—warriors for justice whom the leadership unleashed on its enemies. Now, they reluctantly turned their guns on their mentors. "I have never before differed with [you] on any material point," Abby Kelley Foster informed Phillips in 1856. Yet she maintained that righteous ends still required righteous means. With interventionists discarding that practice—or becoming "Republicanized"—she helped found a breakaway school of moral purists to keep the old banner aloft, challenging the pro-Republican consensus throughout the late 1850s. At one gathering, Pillsbury argued that lesser evils had no place in the pursuit of perfection. In "protecting slavery where it is," he asserted, Republicans were "as reprehensible as the Democrat[s]." Foster likewise lambasted Republicans as vampires "sucking the very blood from our veins" by siphoning support from abolitionists. Echoing Garrison's earlier words, Stephen Foster reminded another meeting that the "mission of true anti-slavery" was separating the "wheat from the chaff." By now "accept[ing] the chaff *as* wheat," interventionists like Garrison damaged the cause.[13]

Interventionists did not brook such affronts. Garrison tabled purists' anti-

Republican resolutions at meetings as "unduly desponding and lugubrious." Given the close-knit nature of abolitionism, professional disagreements quickly bled into personal tensions. Pillsbury and the Fosters became sources of ridicule among the majority. Referencing Stephen Foster, a Garrison ally sneered that the effort to "do one's duty as the wife of such a man would break down [a] Giantess." Matters escalated further in 1859, when Abby Kelley Foster, the AASS's fundraising agent, requested donations from all sources, including Republicans. Garrison subsequently alluded to her as a hypocrite. Foster then resigned her post, rebuking Garrison for intimating she was not a "woman of integrity." Garrison exploded in retort, declaring her course of branding Republicans as the "most dangerous obstacles in our path . . . utterly indefensible." In cruel, gendered terms, Garrison concluded that Foster needed to calm her "highly excited state of mind." Following this exchange, one observer informed Phillips, all "cordial feeling" between moral purists and their old colleagues disappeared. "It is *war* with them I think," or at least the prelude to one.[14]

× × ×

The onset of the Civil War fanned such flames, unleashing a full-fledged, abolitionist civil war. By expanding the temporal bounds of the movement past the antebellum years, on which most studies focus, this book situates the war as the center of, rather than a bookend to, its story—a trial by fire whose quandaries transfigured immediatists and exposed their incompatible plans for the antislavery millennium. While those works that discuss the war often dissect small slices of abolitionism, this study examines a cross-section of the movement. Within a large cast, it highlights immediatism's ideological diversity by focusing on ten figures spanning the movement's race, gender, and factional lines. Reflecting a movement where Blacks and women assumed key roles, it features the voices of Douglass, Forten, Child, and Abby Kelley Foster. Rather than limit itself by faction, moreover, it includes the non-Garrisonians Cheever and Douglass alongside the Garrisonians Phillips, Forten, Child, Conway, Pillsbury, the Fosters, and Garrison himself.[15]

Functioning as both update and corrective to the few large-scale studies of wartime abolitionism, chiefly that by McPherson, *The Abolitionist Civil War* explores how immediatists' millennial impulses shaped their war years. As interventionists argued, the national crisis represented their last hope for waking the benighted North from its moral hibernation. Through their dramatic intervention in the Union war, they aimed not just to attain emancipation and Black rights, but also thereby to redeem the nation. They were not cynics but idiosyncratic nationalists, working from within the war effort to forge the Union of their dreams—an initiative which moral purists deemed calamitous. Without grasping this fundamental motive, abolitionists' wartime actions— and the roots of their infighting and internal anguish—would defy logic. In line with such scholars as Melinda Lawson and Andrew Lang, this book positions immediatism as one of many northern blocs launching nation-building projects during the war.[16]

In entering the war, interventionists also revealed their political ingenuity, adapting to changed circumstances by altering the very fabric of their movement. As self-defined saints, immediatists had cultivated a sense of aloofness by hovering above the blighted mainstream and scorning its practices, from its language of expediency to its bargain-sealed political coalitions. Yet they were never the inflexible, hopelessly idealistic doctrinaires portrayed by scholars like Andrew Delbanco. As such scholars as Corey Brooks and R. J. M. Blackett have illustrated, abolitionists were political realists all along, testing the boundaries of their abstentions from mainstream politics across the antebellum years. Elaborating on that trend, this book unravels how interventionists ratcheted up such dynamism to an unprecedented height during the Civil War. They met the moment of chaos by shattering their senses of self, leaping beyond their cautious antebellum flirtations with the Republicans to obliterate their cherished aloofness once and for all. Moral reformers from Garrison to Douglass remade themselves into interest group political strategists over the first months of the war, holding their noses as they immersed themselves in the mainstream bilge and met white northerners on the once-taboo level of political utility and compromise.[17]

Through their tactical innovations, interventionists punched well above their weight, making a critical impact on the wartime quest for emancipation. As they made clear, they involved themselves in the Union war only because emancipation was not inevitable—because the conflict could just as easily conclude with slavery intact. In recent years, an emerging group of scholars has framed the war as a steady march to emancipation, led by Lincoln and supported by an antislavery public. James Oakes, in his newer works, has presented Lincoln as overseeing a concerted Republican agenda from April 1861 to end slavery through a careful series of incremental steps. Masur has described a united Republican push from the party's inception for emancipation and equality. And Chandra Manning has framed Union soldiers as antislavery bulwarks. These studies lend an aura of seeming inexorability to wartime emancipation, sidelining abolitionists while passing the baton of agency on to the Republicans.[18]

Yet abolitionists held no such illusions about the Union war—or its prosecutors. None trusted Lincoln in the least, dividing rather over his potential usefulness to the cause. Moral purists excoriated him as a proslavery villain. But interventionists grasped that he, the military, and the public initially went to war to save the Union—a motive they might channel for their own ends. This book therefore frames Lincoln not as we want him to have been, but as he was: a devoted Unionist and practical politician. As Paul D. Escott has argued, he was a middle-of-the-road Republican, subscribing over the long term to a model of gradual antislavery change—a free-labor Union. But Lincoln would never endorse emancipation unless doing so proved necessary to fulfill his constitutional duty of preserving the nation. Daniel W. Crofts, as well as Oakes in his older works, has also revealed Lincoln as a brilliant political tactician, attuned to the pulses of the public and his party. Lincoln would not deal slavery its death blow without a baseline of public and political support. But as Gary W. Gallagher and Adam I. P. Smith have shown, white northerners sought nothing approaching an abolition war. Joining such scholars, this book affirms the contingency of emancipation. More than any reformer, military developments (and politicians' reactions to them) would set the pace and extent of any antislavery progress.[19]

Though interventionists lacked power relative to these larger forces, they recognized that they still had parts to play in the events to come. As they now believed, the onset of an abolition war would be their golden moment, spurring a purifying revolution that culminated in a morally transformed Union. But this outcome faced overwhelming odds: a quick Union victory or drawn-out defeat would leave slavery untouched. Interventionists took it upon themselves to be the instruments of destiny, transfiguring a war for Union into an emancipation crusade before it was too late. To meet the wartime crisis and achieve their golden moment, these figures undertook daring gambles. They overhauled immediatism to its core, launching and then incrementally building upon a political intervention as they strained to pressure Lincoln into action.

Over the course of 1861 and 1862, Phillips, Garrison, Douglass, Forten, Child, Conway, and Cheever waded increasingly into the mainstream as they reacted to the developments of the war. At each step along the way, from the outbreak of the conflict in April to the emergence of Union general Benjamin Butler's contraband policy in May, and from the First Battle of Bull Run in July to Lincoln's revocation of General John C. Frémont's emancipation order in Missouri in September, these interventionists tore themselves further and further away from decades of precedent—and from their own moralistic beliefs—to hasten the golden moment. They descended ever lower into the mainstream, first endorsing the Union war and then reinventing themselves as interest group strategists to promote their newfound axioms about the expediency of military emancipation. In their desperation to reach enough northern hearts and minds before it was too late, these prowar abolitionists also began collaborating with an ever-growing group of politicos in an antislavery alliance, later formalizing such cooperation as the Emancipation League. Such pacts bore significant moral risk: old enemies turned allies such as Edward Everett paid little heed to abolitionists' coequal demand for Black rights even while taking up their call for expedient emancipation. But as interventionists bathed their words and actions deeper in the world of compromise, they found themselves in the unexpected role of national celebrities by the winter of 1861–1862, greeted not by the rowdy mobs of yore but by approving audiences. Seizing on their rising influence, they entered the national halls of power themselves, disseminating their utilitarian arguments in person from Congress to the White House.

Yet interventionists also agonized over their political journeys. As each stroke into the mainstream carried them further away from their moralistic roots, they struggled to stay afloat. They created internal moral contradictions, laboring to preserve their principles—and their identities as incorruptible reformers—while supporting a war not waged for such values. As their ambivalence over their transformations tore at their souls, interventionists diverged their private beliefs from their public actions. They hewed privately to their own standard of the ideal—of what was absolutely right—while publicly judging Lincoln by the standard of the possible—of what was politically feasible. But every contortion, each political bargain, compounded their suffering. By 1862, Phillips's and Cheever's tolerance of their own politicization especially neared its limits.

Simultaneously, moral purists sought to prevent interventionists from devastating the movement. Pillsbury and the Fosters, alongside most British activists, continued to avow that abolitionists' noble ends required noble means. By working through the immoral Union war, they argued, reformers would achieve neither emancipation nor post-emancipation Black rights. Expediency could never be the midwife of a morally transformed Union, especially the egalitarian version to which moral purists aspired. As purists stressed, moreover, abolitionists derived their moral strength and probity from their abilities to rise above the tumult. By pursuing this failed method, they prophesied, interventionists would lose their power—and themselves. They would grow complacent in the mainstream, sullying their identities and forsaking their missions. As such figures ramped up their interventions, moral purists attacked with increasing desperation. Put on the defensive, interventionists responded in kind. Abolitionism thereby realigned early in the conflict into a transatlantic civil war between pro- and antiwar immediatists.

The interventionist camp, moreover, strained at its own seams. While interventionists and purists grappled over the route to redemption, narrow and broad interventionists disagreed over what their promised land looked like—disparities that war magnified. Narrow interventionists like Garrison and Conway focused their attention on emancipation over post-emancipation Black rights. But as they examined the latter issue further in 1861 and 1862, they adopted increasingly restrictive visions of Black wage labor and, in Conway's case, Anglo-Saxon racial dominance. Broad interventionists like Phillips, Douglass, and Forten had instead long looked beyond emancipation, sharing purists' expansive conceptions of multiracial democracy. Even while fretting over their political transformations, they utilized them, refining such visions to become modern strategists of political change. They coalesced over time around the goal of legislative equality, advocating legislation to enshrine Black political, civil, and socioeconomic parity.

Overcoming their doubts and divides, and purists' resistance, interventionists ultimately gained their shared, immediate aim of military emancipation. They had leveraged their sway to advance public and political support for this measure, recruiting once-resolute foes of the cause to become advocates for freedom. By doing so, they both freed and prodded Lincoln to act. After military defeats reinforced the urgency of doing so, he made use of the tool interventionists had publicized. He accepted the war power, eventually issuing the Emancipation Proclamation. This book thus portrays abolitionists not as the passive observers of war George M. Fredrickson has described, but as its active movers. Without their involvement and influence, a Republican-led emancipation would have been much less likely. In conjunction with the march of events, and against all likelihood, they realized their golden moment and changed the nation.[20]

Though their interventions empowered abolitionists to help secure military emancipation, they also ruined the movement's long-term ability to advance equality. At first, interventionists met the aftermath of the Proclamation together, seeking the total emancipation of all slaves and some form of Black inclusion through their political alliance. But their golden moment had not spawned a bigger revolution. In contrast to Masur, this book argues that the white North, and the political mainstream reflecting it, had become antislavery but not proequality. They endorsed a war for—and only for—military emancipation, refusing to move past their self-interest to sanction further reform. In assessing this new reality, narrow and broad interventionists realized that their differences regarding Black rights now outweighed their commonalities. They had attained their unifying object, thrusting forward in its wake their divergent conceptions of a perfected nation.[21]

Over the course of 1863, narrow and broad interventionists' incompatible ideologies nourished a largely overlapping struggle over Lincoln. Garrison and most narrow interventionists developed a pro-Lincoln faction, expressing satisfaction with the changed war. They conflated the politically possible with the morally ideal as their public and private views of Lincoln converged into unfettered approval. As purists dreaded, these figures adapted to their positions within the mainstream by extinguishing their inner turmoil and retreating from their original commitments. They pruned Black rights from their missions, reducing their endgames to the goal of total emancipation. Even as she evolved toward a broad interventionist interest in expansive Black rights, Child also extolled Lincoln for sanctifying a bloody conflict with moral worth. But as their agonies grew unbearable, Phillips, Douglass, and most broad interventionists developed a contrasting, anti-Lincoln faction. They countered that the war had not changed nearly enough to foment their egalitarian endgame—and that Lincoln was fast becoming the chief impediment to such legislative equality. Cheever and Conway joined them, fueled by distrust of Lincoln. Pillsbury and the Fosters, too, flocked to this emergent faction, transferring their opposition from the Union war to the personage of Lincoln. The interventionist camp collapsed at year's end, rearranging the abolitionist civil war into a contest over Lincoln's reelection.

While immediatists aspired to higher purposes in wading into the 1864 election, their politicking only impaired the movement. Though Child also campaigned for Lincoln, Garrison especially reveled in his acceptance by the political establishment by defending the government at all costs. After months of auditioning candidates to usurp the Republican mantle, Phillips, Conway, Cheever, and, briefly, Douglass instead settled on Frémont. Pillsbury and the Fosters joined them, defying their longstanding convictions to embrace political tactics. Yet this faction's partisan gamesmanship proved far more baneful than beneficial. Frémont's movement quickly morphed into a third party, flirting with Copperhead Democrats and diluting its once-radical promises. But while Douglass abandoned ship, Phillips and other anti-Lincoln abolitionists redoubled their obsessive efforts to defeat the president. They pursued short-sighted means antithetical to their true ends, denting their reputations as objective reformers.

One bright spot emerged from the wreckage of 1864: the rise of a Black power politics organization. Tapping into a rich vein of scholarship, this book explores the wartime evolution of Black activism. At the war's commencement, Douglass had pressed for Black enlistment as the key to an egalitarian future. Yet most Black abolitionists, from William Wells Brown to Henry Highland Garnet, had refused to follow suit. The Union war, they argued, did not yet merit their military service. Nor did it deserve their political intervention. With some prominent exceptions like Douglass and Forten, the interventionist camp was mostly white. But after Lincoln welcomed Black troops into the military in 1863, African American abolitionists united to launch their own distinctive political experiment. Douglass, Brown, Garnet, and others intervened to become military recruiting agents, even as they soon chafed at the shortcomings of a system that denied Black recruits equal pay, protection, and advancement. Rather than abandon their agencies or campaign against Lincoln, these abolitionists siphoned their frustrations into politicized reform to carry the fight for equal treatment and legislative equality into the future.[22]

But the movement as a whole emerged from the election more divided than ever, lurching into the last stage of its civil war. Throughout early 1865, narrow interventionists jostled with broad interventionists and moral purists over the purpose of immediatism and the meaning of a morally transformed Union. As the passage of the Thirteenth Amendment and the looming defeat of the rebellion sealed slavery's doom, Garrison and the narrow interventionists declared victory. They averred that this formal freedom marked the conclusion of the abolitionist crusade—and that its foremost society, the AASS, should disband. Broad interventionists and moral purists, including Phillips, Douglass, Forten, Pillsbury, the Fosters, and, now, Child and Cheever, demanded it continue. Immediatists, they argued, had to persevere for a substantive freedom that stamped out slavery's political and socioeconomic legacies. Though the procontinuation forces eventually prevailed, theirs was a pyrrhic victory: Garrison resigned from organized reform in protest, while Conway dedicated his postwar years to his dream of white southern supremacy.

Over the next decade, the small, procontinuation remnant labored for its politicized vision of a radical Reconstruction. After the prosouthern policies of President Andrew Johnson made racial equality politically expedient, these immediatists helped write their values into the Constitution. Yet abolitionists' intervention in the war had set in motion their postwar doom. Garrison had forsaken his original mission, depriving the continuing cause of its former pull and resources. The remaining activists like Phillips had further diminished their own power through their partisan snafus. For decades, abolitionism had served as a bulwark in the fight for racial justice. But this movement became a shadow of its former self, lacking the wherewithal to keep Reconstruction afloat after it lost its political saliency. Building on existing scholarship, this book offers the crippling of immediatism as a secondary factor in the fall of Reconstruction.[23] It presents the story of wartime abolitionism not as an unalloyed arc of heroism, as Manisha Sinha depicts in her magisterial history, but as a tragedy. By intervening, immediatists helped win emancipation, but only at the price of losing the struggle for post-emancipation equality. They ensured their golden moment but sacrificed their chance to witness the antislavery millennium.[24]

x x x

In discussing the wartime trajectory of abolitionism, this book proceeds in chronological fashion. A prelude discusses the uneasy peace between warring abolitionists during the secession winter. Chapters 1 to 5 cover the period from January 1861 to March 1862, as prowar interventionists fought for military emancipation—and against antiwar moral purists in the first realignment of wartime abolitionism. Over each chapter, the former deepened their interventions—and exacerbated the abolitionist civil war. Chapter 6 then details the seemed stalling of antislavery progress from March to September 1862, during which time broad and narrow interventionists also fleshed out their disparate moral visions.

Chapter 7 represents a pivot point in the narrative. It delves into the period between September 1862 and January 1863, marking both the apogee of wartime abolitionism—the Emancipation Proclamation—and the beginning of its descent. Chapters 8 and 9 explore the disintegration of the interventionist camp between February and December 1863, as the new status quo of a war for military emancipation, but not Black rights, divided narrow and broad interventionists—and pushed purists toward the latter. Wartime abolitionism thus realigned a second time into pro- and anti-Lincoln factions. These chapters also examine how Black activists entered the war as recruiters, only to bristle at the constraints of their positions. Chapters 10 and 11 then discuss the fallout of abolitionist partisanship from January to December 1864. Finally, chapter 12 details the third and last realignment of wartime immediatism into pro- and anticontinuation sides from January to May 1865. It concludes by exploring abolitionists' significant achievements, yet overall failure, during Reconstruction.

To delineate these incremental changes over time, this book focuses on ten abolitionists from across the movement. William Lloyd Garrison was the elder statesman of immediatism. As a young man, the Massachusetts journalist had experienced a moral awakening, imbibing the demands of Black anticolonization advocates like James Forten. He inaugurated the organized abolitionist movement thereafter, establishing a newspaper, *The Liberator,* in 1831 and cofounding the AASS in 1833. After the antebellum movement fractured into factions, he helmed the AASS as the hub of the Garrisonians. His right-hand man was Wendell Phillips, a Boston Brahmin whom Garrison converted to the cause in 1836. Phillips became immediatism's preeminent orator—a staple on the lyceum circuit, known for his provocatively panoramic ideals. By 1837, Garrison also recruited Massachusetts teacher Abby Kelley, a Quaker by birth who rejected the religion for lacking antislavery fiber. Lecturing as a Garrisonian agent, she met and married Stephen Symonds Foster, a New Hampshirite who had fled a Congregationalist seminary for a higher calling. With Parker Pillsbury, another rogue Congregationalist from New Hampshire, the Fosters acquired reputations within abolitionism as confrontational firebrands.[25]

The prolific novelist and poet Lydia Maria Child, too, was an early Garrisonian convert. Like Abby Kelley Foster, she overcame resistance to her entrance as a woman into the public sphere, churning out immediatist tracts from the early 1830s. Though she ceased participating in the AASS in a formal capacity in the 1850s, she remained a vibrant player in the cause. By then, the movement had also attracted a new generation of reformers. Moncure D. Conway was the scion of a Virginia slaveholding dynasty. As a youth in the 1850s, he underwent a twisting journey from a proslavery secessionist to an antislavery Unitarian minister. Expelled from his Washington, D.C., pulpit for his radical views, he assumed a ministry in Cincinnati in 1855, becoming an out-and-out, pro-Garrisonian abolitionist. Charlotte Forten, James's granddaughter, had grown up in an elite Black Philadelphia family. As she trained as a teacher in Salem, Massachusetts, on the eve of the war, she, too, joined in the Garrisonian nexus.[26]

While the above activists had remained affiliated with the Garrisonians throughout the antebellum decades, Frederick Douglass had repudiated them. An accomplished author and orator, Douglass escaped slavery in Maryland in 1838 and ascended as a leading light in the abolitionist movement. Garrison quickly took him under his wing. But by the late 1840s, Douglass began to suffocate under Garrison's grasp, drifting away from Garrisonian doctrines—and anxious to chart his own path. He defected from the AASS to become its foremost non-Garrisonian competitor and a prominent newspaperman in his own right. Finally, the New York–based Congregationalist minister George B. Cheever left the AASS in 1840 to protest Garrison's attacks on organized religion as a proslavery force. With his brother, Henry, he founded the religious, non-Garrisonian Church Anti-Slavery Society (CASS) in 1859. Together, these figures exemplified the cacophonous currents and personalities that abolitionists carried into the Civil War—and the ensuing, clashing evolutions that would rend their movement by war's end.[27]

Prelude

The Dilemma of the Secession Winter

As she witnessed interventionists favor the Republicans during the 1860 election, Abby Kelley Foster also, counterintuitively, yearned for their success. She did not do so for the same reason, however: as her spouse, Stephen, noted, she "had no faith that anything good could be accomplished by political parties." Instead, she believed that the Republicans would reveal their true depravity once in power, forcing interventionists to realize the error of their ways. "We shall hardly need wait a year," she predicted, "to see Garrison . . . as condemnatory of the Republican as of the Democratic Party." Yet Foster could not foresee what upheavals that year would bring.[1]

Following Lincoln's victory, seven southern states seceded from the Union to protect slavery. Secession temporarily unified abolitionists in fear of sectional compromise. Immediatists had lived through decades of political brinksmanship, in which southern threats of disunion inevitably begat northern appeasement. Now, they expected the same outcome. Child fretted that the Republicans would "throw away the glorious vantage-ground they gained," while Conway labeled the politicians in Washington "Union-saver[s], which means there a compromiser of anything." Lincoln's March inaugural address, in which he swore to execute all slavery-related laws and endorsed a proposed Thirteenth Amendment guaranteeing the existence of slavery within its current borders, exacerbated their dread. Garrison called the speech a sign of Lincoln's "moral confusion," while Douglass labeled it "little better than our worst fears." Far from an antislavery waypoint, the Republicans seemed to be as morally bankrupt as their predecessors.[2]

Faced with the alternative, Garrisonian and non-Garrisonian abolitionists united in support, whether enthusiastic or grudging, for disunion—a rather remarkable development. Throughout the late antebellum years, Garrisonians had advocated disunion, envisioning northerners fed up with slaveholders instigating a sectional rupture. This separation, they had argued, would destroy slavery in three steps. Removing the southern slaveholding cancer would rejuvenate the North, awakening it from its demoralized lethargy. Southern slavery, deprived of the economic support of northern factories or the political protection of federal slave codes, would then wither. Finally, the North and South would somehow reunite on a free-labor basis. This idea of a temporary, salutary separation had vexed non-Garrisonians, who considered it tantamount to abandoning southern slaves to the unfettered whims of their masters.[3]

Now, separation was a fait accompli. This southern, proslavery secession bore little resemblance to Garrisonians' northern, antislavery disunion. Garrison stressed this contrast, labeling secessionists traitors of the "blackest perfidy." Yet the end result could be much the same. Southerners, an activist noted, were "too blind to see" that secession would "hasten instead of prevent [slavery's] overthrow." Disunion, Conway explained, would reconfigure a Union that had become the "hollow cloak of slavery"—an empty vessel of slaveholding ambition—"in the order of history of destiny." Especially given the alternative of compromise, Garrisonians embraced separation with gusto. The *Anti-Slavery Bugle*, a newspaper originally founded by Abby Kelley Foster, affirmed that "if the North, for the sake of freedom will not dissolve the Union, then let the South do it for the sake of slavery." Phillips agreed, putting aside his differences with Foster for the time being. The Union, he told a Brooklyn audience in January, was a "wall hastily built"—an artificial construction. Separation would "plant a Union whose life survives the ages"—a nation bound by moral values. "All hail, then, Disunion!" Phillips roared, to hisses from the hostile crowd.[4]

Garrisonians advocated peaceful separation over both a proslavery reunion and a third scenario: civil war. In part, they grounded their position in Garrison's doctrine of non-resistance. Garrison and many AASS members abjured the use of violence in principle. Yet Phillips, though not a non-resistant himself, asserted in an early April speech in New Bedford that abolitionists' concerns lay not with the idea of coercion against the Slave Power, but rather with the illusory chances of a sustained conflict to that effect. Upon hearing rumors of a Union attack on Charleston, Phillips warned that the public would not countenance prolonged strife. Demoralized northerners, he argued, would never choose bloodshed in an existential war over bloodless compromise. Instead of "conquering Charleston," the rumored attack would "create a Charleston in New England" by stirring up "sympathy for the South." Reconciliation on a disgraceful basis would then be inevitable. Disunion remained the only alternative to sectional compromise.[5]

Less enthusiastically, non-Garrisonians also came around on disunion. If the "price of the Union," Douglass sighed, was "compromises and national demoralization, then . . . let the Union perish." Cheever agreed, arguing that Republican plans for saving a nation dissolved by slavery through proslavery pacts were akin to a "madman brandishing an umbrella with a lightning rod . . . for security against a thunderstorm." Only separation could now bring about the "Union for liberty and justice to blacks as well as whites" he desired. As he witnessed Republican cowardice, he reluctantly endorsed separation as a last resort.[6]

Immediatists' unified disunionism provoked unprecedented public wrath. Mobs, blaming abolitionists for secession, threatened antislavery meetings. Pillsbury wrote that a "ferocious throng, composed of collegians, clerks, drunken Irish boys, lawyers, and plug-uglies of every hue," had pursued him across Ann Arbor, Michigan, after one lecture. Illuminating the breadth of opposition, one Boston intellectual sneered that Phillips's Brooklyn speech, which proslavery mobs had also attacked, was the "best [case] against free speech I ever read." The threat of disunion, it seemed, united northerners of all classes in an antiabolitionist front.[7]

Even Radical Republicans reproached immediatists, reinforcing their philosophical and tactical differences. Politicians like Charles Sumner and Governor John Andrew of Massachusetts let the political considerations of their mainstream party shape their actions, often placing them at odds with abolitionists despite their common moral interests in immediate emancipation and post-emancipation Black rights. Now, such figures again deferred to their party's moderate center of mass by toeing the line against disunion. In February, Andrew called Phillips into his office to plead for his friend's tactful silence, asking Phillips to curb his "exciting speeches" lest they destroy the Union—and derail the Republican agenda. Phillips answered that such destruction was "what he desired." Shocked, Andrew replied: "If this be [your] attitude . . . we need converse no longer. I differ from you entirely and the political paths we shall walk in will be wholly divergent." The gap between these blocs had never been wider.[8]

Andrew's rebuke illustrated the stark realities of the secession winter. As Lincoln seemingly prepared to dash antislavery hopes, abolitionists papered over their festering wounds to endorse disunion as their only option. But in doing so they alienated most northerners, rendering themselves passive observers in the ongoing national drama. To abolitionists standing on the sidelines, the nation's destiny seemed cloudier than ever, its chances for redemption slimmer. They had no idea that the Union would soon shift under their feet.

CHAPTER ONE

The Onset of Civil War, April–May 1861

I n mid-April 1861, Wendell Phillips approached journalist George W. Smalley, his friend and future son-in-law, in the throes of moral agony. Phillips, Smalley later recalled, faced the "most momentous decision in his life" following the unexpected eruption of civil war. Though he had dipped his toes in the political mainstream over the past decade, Phillips had stayed true to the Garrisonian tenets of disunion and opposition to the Constitution. Now, he was contemplating plunging wholesale into the muck and abandoning those stances by the wayside. Was such a torturous transformation, in which he had to "renounce my past, thirty years of it, belie my pledges ... and admit my life has been a mistake," necessary, he wondered? To steel his nerves, Smalley explained that theoretical ideals mattered little in a time of war. Abolitionists had to adapt to the new reality of a Union war buoyed by the masses to remain relevant. They could continue to stand apart, morally unchanged but "never listened to again," or they could seize the opportunity before them. After deliberation, Phillips assented. He would become a "soldier for the Union," painful as it was to do so.[1]

In the weeks after the start of the Civil War, Phillips and his fellow interventionists broke away from their antebellum moorings to become prowar abolitionists. They had watched, shocked, as a march toward sectional compromise transformed into a rush to battle. In part, practical considerations, such as the popularity of the Union war and the threat of Confederate victory, factored into their tortured calculus. Opposing the war seemed both unwise and unproductive. But above all, interventionists framed the war in millenarian terms. Divine will and popular progress, they believed, could help transmute the conflict into an antislavery crusade. The launching of an emancipatory Union war, they now argued, would be their golden moment. Yet fate alone could not seal this outcome. Lincoln prosecuted the war solely to save the Union, meaning that victory would bring the Slave Power back into the nation. Neither did a northern public also prioritizing the preservation of the Union inspire confidence. Emancipation, not to mention post-emancipation Black rights, were far from guaranteed. Amid the swirling chaos of war, interventionists thus came to see themselves as the instigators of moral revolution—cosmic agents who could nudge the nation onto higher ground from inside the war effort, ensuring an antislavery outcome during uncertain times.

In a decisive about-face, Phillips, Garrison, Child, Douglass, Cheever, Forten, and Conway rejected secession and embraced the Union war. While interventionists had inched toward political engagement with Republicans before the war, their wartime political intervention far exceeded such tentative prior interactions. They loudly praised the Lincoln-led war, even as they initially pursued individualistic and disjointed early efforts to perfect it. Douglass focused on promoting African American enlistment, clashing with other Black activists. Cheever fixated on uplifting British public opinion, while Conway sought to bolster the invasion of his home state of Virginia. Child, meanwhile, especially agonized over embracing the Union cause. These immediatists nonetheless all committed to their new course. Forced to accept the Republican Party as is rather than as a waypoint, interventionists began evaluating Republicans publicly according to the standard of the politically possible, even while still judging them privately by the morally absolutist standard of the ideal—a wrenching divergence, revealing their uneasiness over their transformations. They also tried, and failed, to unite around a temporary placeholder strategy of tactful silence, underscoring the difficulties of building a cohesive, interfactional coalition to achieve change before their window of opportunity closed.

Such behavior confirmed moral purists' fears. As they had done regarding the Republicans, this small band rejected the Union war as a false prophet. Pillsbury and the Fosters desired an egalitarian morally transformed Union, featuring expansive Black rights. But as they argued, nothing, not even emancipation, would arise from the war. It would, however, corrupt those who succumbed to its siren call. By pursuing false means to moral ends, interventionists would lose their souls. As purists attacked, interventionists pushed back, civilly but firmly. After a wintertime lull, tensions between the two schools of thought roared back into the open, crystallizing the realignment of wartime abolitionism into rival pro- and antiwar camps.

INTERVENTIONISTS AND THE NEW REALITY OF WAR

The rapid progression of events in April dumfounded abolitionists. Watching on as Lincoln determined the fate of the nation, immediatists had not expected a war, much less one that the masses endorsed. After Confederates opened fire on the federal garrison at Fort Sumter on April 12, however, Lincoln called for troops to suppress the insurrection, rallying northerners to the flag in defense of American exceptionalism. In shock, Garrison ally Edmund Quincy admitted that he had "no idea of the life that remained in the North. At the first gun fired . . . the whole people seemed to start to their feet as one man." Douglass similarly gasped that the "dead North [came] alive," pouring into the Union military. The sustained, popular war effort that Phillips had dismissed as impossible weeks earlier in New Bedford was now reality.[2]

Abolitionists subsequently took stock of their new environment. In past years, they had kept mainstream politics at arm's length, appealing to the public as their constituency. Yet a war unifying civilians, soldiers, and the Lincoln administration blurred the distinctions between politics and the public. Immediatists had to consider, as the AASS noted in a May circular, how the "means of influencing public opinion" had changed. Rejecting the Republican-led war would now also mean repudiating the northern people and destroying their own influence. As became apparent, jingoistic northerners saw little distinction between those who opposed the war on prosouthern or on antislavery grounds, brooking neither. The moral purist editor of the *Anti-Slavery Bugle* suspended his paper in May because "murderous feelings [were] entertained against him." Another antiwar abolitionist complained to Garrison that he had been labeled a traitor. An acquaintance who had once invited him to lecture about disunion now warned him that "they would lynch me" if he returned singing the same tune. Opposing the war seemed impracticable at best, and life-threatening at worst.[3]

Immediatists also had to adjust their calculations regarding the Union. While disunion had once seemed the only alternative to proslavery compromise, war had changed this equation. A Union locked in an epochal "death-grapple with the Southern slave oligarchy," Garrison informed his close associate Oliver Johnson, now appeared immune to the disease of sectional compromise. Abolitionists' choices no longer lay between disunion and proslavery reunion, but between the Union and Confederacy. The latter posed an existential threat to abolitionism. Cheever, who was engaged in an antislavery tour of Britain, noted that a rebel victory would render slavery "supreme and perpetual." It would, Douglass agreed in an April speech, entail the "decline and fall of American Liberty and Civilization." Douglass thus had to give every "persuasion of my heart [to the] American government, in its determination to suppress . . . this slaveholding rebellion." In this novel environment, the Union had become the only option.[4]

Garrison also appreciated the stakes of this zero-sum conflict. As the pioneer of non-resistance, he seemed the natural opponent of violence. In late April, however, he admitted to Phillips that war had become the "only thing that can preserve us from new and more disgraceful covenants." While the prospect of bloodshed was "indeed terrible," he continued, "such peace [as represented] its only alternative would be ten thousand-fold worse." Garrison, "Non-Resistant as I am," had to shove aside such beliefs. "Our sympathies and wishes must be with the government, as against the Southern desperadoes," he affirmed to Johnson. Other non-resistants followed suit. At a Quaker meeting, Susan B. Anthony prayed for the "triumph of the *less* guilty party." Her sentiments surprised Douglass, who had arrived "not knowing what he should speak upon," expecting the non-resistants to lead an antiwar chorus. He was instead gratified to hear that, non-resistance aside, the attendees realized that their mission now required Union victory.[5]

Beyond such practicalities, interventionists came to support the war because of its singular moral potential. The Union's adoption of emancipation as its war aim, they now argued, would mark their golden moment—their long-awaited catalyst for redeeming the nation. Though it was "strange to go in for the Union," Anthony informed Phillips, she did so in anticipation of the "glorious revolution" war would produce. Her close colleague Elizabeth Cady Stanton felt likewise, she averred. Douglass, too, expressed similar sentiments. "Now is the time. The opportunity has been given us by the slaveholders," he explained to a colleague. Abolitionists' chance to precipitate a morally transformed Union, delivered from its original sin, had arrived.[6]

Interventionists recognized that the Union cause as it stood was not a moral revolution, nor was its leader a revolutionary. While Lincoln embodied the Republican vision of a free-labor Union that cemented white liberty, his wartime goal was to make whole a cleaved nation. On a tactical level, the president also knew that it made little sense to bound beyond the rest of the political mainstream. He would not take up emancipation until it became a militarily necessary measure—or until the support of politicians and citizens granted him the political capital to act. Military and political developments hence remained the ultimate arbiters of abolition. As the war began, Lincoln stressed that his exclusive war aim was to preserve the Union. Rather than touch slavery, he allowed Union officers to return fugitive slaves. Lincoln, Garrison worried in the *Liberator,* appeared content to "restore the Union" of old, ending the rebellion with slavery intact. Neither were his officers inclined to attack the institution. In late April, Benjamin Butler, a Breckinridge Democrat turned general, offered his services in suppressing potential slave insurrections in Maryland. He seemed destined "not to be a hero, but a dastard," Garrison roared.[7]

Rather than the Union war as it was, interventionists believed in the war as it could be. Providence and popular progress, they asserted, could help bring about their golden moment. Invoking the trope of abolitionists as American Jeremiahs, they proclaimed that their long-prophesied divine reckoning was nigh. For years, Garrison informed his readers, "Abolitionists have been faithfully warning the nation that, unless the enslaved were set free, a just God would visit it with tribulation." Those "predictions [were] com[ing] to pass," he averred. Child sighed that the people had not heeded abolitionists' "warnings . . . and lo! The storm is upon us!" The conflict would take the form of providential punishment, "purging [by] a fiery process" the sin of slavery from the nation and wiping its moral slate clean, regardless of what Lincoln intended.[8]

Prowar abolitionists also took heart in the masses. Northerners seemed to be awakening from their demoralized slumber—a feat for which immediatists took credit in hindsight, erasing their past doubts about popular progress. Abolitionism bolstered the "moral sentiments of the North," Garrison wrote in May, spurring it to confront the Slave Power. Phillips, who had decried northern apathy weeks earlier, now crowed that the "North has come to this conviction, that the Union never shall be used to sustain slavery." While he gave the "administration generous sympathy," he placed his faith in an "unconscious, perhaps, but assured" popular sentiment that the Union "shall mean liberty in the end." Consciously, Phillips knew, white northerners rejected the Slave Power to preserve their own liberty, not to advance Black freedom. Yet interventionists could not help but feel sanguine witnessing the rush to war.[9]

These prowar abolitionists thus anticipated their new millennium. What Douglass termed the "inexorable logic of events," girded by divinity and popular progress, that could birth a morally transformed Union was clear. First, the conflict should, as Cheever argued, "prove the death blow of slavery." The Civil War, Garrison informed Phillips, "*must,* in effect, be a war of freedom against slavery. However crafty politicians may seek to cover this issue, it will assert itself." Slavery, he noted, powered the rebellion. No matter how much Lincoln tried to prosecute a war to "defend the 'stars and stripes,'" Garrison theorized, he would have to destroy slavery to win. Emancipation would be the "*forced* result [of the war], not the *chosen* one," Child added.[10]

By undertaking an abolition war, the Union would unleash a moral revolution toward perfection. Northerners, Phillips averred, prepared already to cross this antislavery Rubicon. "Abolitionists have doubted whether this Union really meant justice," he noted. But the "Northern conscience" was awaking, shaking off its enthrallment to the Slave Power. Achieving the golden moment would then propel the people on an irreversible course of progress, forging a "permanent union of the races that cover this continent from the pole down to the Gulf." A nation governed by the "Genius of Liberty," Phillips predicted, would emerge once the "smoke of this conflict clears away." Garrison likewise held that the nation would reach its watershed. The eventual abolition of slavery, he asserted, would open the way for a "glorious redemption. Complexional prejudice shall swiftly disappear, injurious distinctions cease," as a morally transformed Union worthy of global adulation replaced the shameful old one.[11]

While superficially similar, Phillip's and Garrison's statements illustrated their clashing interpretations of what the ambiguous endgame of a morally transformed Union, and the meanings of freedom and citizenship, entailed—a disagreement dividing the interventionist camp between broad interventionists like Phillips, Douglass, and Forten and narrow interventionists like Garrison and Conway. In his speech, Phillips outlined what James Brewer Stewart has described as his idea of a unified nationality. An emancipatory war against the aristocratic Slave Power, he argued, would reanimate northerners' democratic impulses, erasing odious distinctions of race, party, and class. Shorn of hierarchical restrictions, freed slaves and former proletarians could seek their own destinies. In this panoramic conception of national redemption, weighing heavily Blacks' post-emancipation futures, emancipation was the first step in a larger struggle for egalitarianism that required the lifelong attention of its reformer guides.[12]

Other broad interventionists framed emancipation similarly. Douglass, as David W. Blight has argued, portrayed the war as a transition from an old age of oppression into a new one of justice. In his millennial view, emancipation and Black military service would be the vanguards of regeneration, paving the way for a multiracial Union. Douglass, like Phillips, would refine this mission as the war progressed, developing an enduring conception of legislative egalitarianism. As historians including Stephen Kantrowitz and Martha S. Jones have demonstrated, many Black activists, from George T. Downing to Martin Delany, likewise cast abolition as the first step toward a righteous republic incorporating Blacks as equal citizens.[13]

Garrison and narrow interventionists instead discussed post-emancipation concerns in vague terms. To them, emancipation itself would be the climactic moment of redemption, after which other injustices would somehow fall away—a thin conception of a morally transformed Union that would grow increasingly thinner over time. As Stewart has shown, Garrison also viewed abolition in terms of liberating himself as much as slaves. He understood his struggle against slavery in personal terms, as a quest to be proven right in the eyes of history—to overcome decades of belittlement and become the vindicated prophet, a recumbent statue in the American pantheon. Emancipation would mark the apogee of his mission, signifying his own triumph.[14]

An April interaction between Garrison and Phillips underscored these differences. Visiting the *Liberator* offices, one reformer asked Garrison what the results of the war would be. "[Of] one thing only am I certain—the war will result in the death of slavery!" replied Garrison. Phillips then entered, declaring that "five years hence not a slave will be found on American soil!" Garrison framed events in terms of his own personality, presenting slavery as an impersonal institution to be conquered. Phillips, meanwhile, removed himself from the equation, portraying slaves as individuals whose rights would need to be secured following their freedom. The germ of the later troubles between the two were therefore already present.[15]

For the time being, with post-emancipation issues far on the horizon, prowar abolitionists put aside such disagreements in the face of a more immediate concern: ensuring an emancipatory conflict. Despite the war's potential, interventionists understood that emancipation was far from guaranteed. Their window of opportunity to achieve their golden moment was a small one, dependent upon the contingencies of conflict. While they believed that the exigencies of a prolonged war should eventually force the Union to take up emancipation in desperation, this conviction had an ominous corollary: a speedy Union victory would leave slavery intact. This outcome would be disastrous, as Conway declared after the surrender of Fort Sumter. It would extinguish the "torch of Liberty entrusted to America to bear in the van of nations," preventing the nation from assuming its rightful place atop the "throne of Eternal Justice." Through a swift victory without emancipation, he concluded, the Union "will have lost the day we seem to win." It would merely delay the divine reckoning with slavery, at the cost of future blood and treasure.[16]

Interventionists feared a rebel victory in a long war against, as much as a rapid rebel defeat by, a Union that had not yet endorsed emancipation. The Confederates, Douglass noted in May, had "not hesitated" to employ slaves in "erecting the fortifications which silenced the guns of Fort Sumter," and had "no scruples against employing the Negroes to exterminate freedom." Indeed, the rebels "often boast, and not without cause, that their Negroes will fight for them against the North." Douglass believed that, as the war dragged on, a desperate Confederacy would arm its slaves, coercing them into military service while making feigned gestures toward nominal emancipation. If the Union had not already embraced emancipation, European nations would then intervene on behalf of the supposedly emancipating Confederacy. By dallying too long, the Union would seal its own doom—an outcome that would again postpone the heaven-sent reckoning. The fight for the golden moment was thus time sensitive on both ends.[17]

Amid the fraught conflict, interventionists could not rely on divine will and popular progress alone to sanctify the nation. Any providential punishment could last for generations. From England, Cheever fretted that a "forty years' struggle under incessant judgments, until the carcasses" of the proslavery forces were "left bleaching in this wilderness, may be necessary, before the country will enter on the promised land." While he recognized the divine scheme in place, Cheever had no idea how much time, or suffering, it would require. Neither could interventionists rely on the people to enact a moral revolution by themselves. Despite their hopes about popular progress, prowar abolitionists recognized the limitations of that advancement. In May, Child lamented that her husband was "almost mobbed" at a war rally for mentioning emancipation. "Thus much for the motives" of the prowar crowd, she sighed. Douglass also worried that northerners had "but very imperfectly learned the lesson" that abolitionists had tried to teach them. Northern opposition to the Slave Power was based more on "irritation caused by the . . . pretensions of the slaveholders" than on "principle and a love of humanity." An anti-Confederate wave that had "come upon us with the suddenness of the whirlwind" could ebb in an instant, "leaving the slave still in his chains." Even if the people came to support emancipation, their embrace of Black citizenship was nowhere near assured. A populace animated by chauvinistic impulses, Child and Douglass observed, had a long way to go to attain perfection.[18]

By necessity, interventionists envisioned another primer to realize the golden moment: themselves. As Phillips told Smalley, his entering the Union war would mark a drastic break with decades of precedent. Far surpassing their lukewarm antebellum support of Republicans, interventionists would have to embrace the Lincoln administration, and the political system it now stood for, openly. Garrisonians would also have to renounce talk of a proslavery Constitution and disunion. This decision would be excruciating, requiring reformers to forsake their pasts. They would generate internal moral contradictions as they strained to preserve their founding dedications to emancipation and post-emancipation Black rights while simultaneously diving headlong into the political mainstream.

Yet interventionists believed that they had no other choice. They had to serve as the agents of divine will. Cheever's brother, Henry, argued that it was "only . . . the persistent declaration of the duty of a national emancipation, conjoined with the majestic march of events, that is to make the nation ripe for the inevitable result." Abolitionists needed to execute the heavenly plan, ensuring that the war regenerated the nation. They could guide the people down the path of moral progress only from within the war effort, as the popular hostility to antiwar abolitionists made clear. As the Cheever brothers' CASS asserted in May, the "patriotic few"—the interventionists—had to work until "masses of the people shall be so far abolitionized" as to take up the fight themselves. Prowar immediatists could thereby build up a baseline of public support for emancipation and pressure Lincoln into action. The president, Phillips later noted, was willing to become a "Liberator . . . [but] has not the courage to offer." Abolitionists had to "help him to that fame" before their window vanished. Only they could steer the national ship through dangerous shoals to the shores of salvation.[19]

Following the fall of Fort Sumter, interventionists shed their roles as scorned Jeremiahs and became Mosaic warrior prophets, leading the people from inside the war effort. As a correspondent told the *Liberator* in late April, abolitionists had to "with all our hearts sustain the flag, the war, the Government." By doing so, they could "seize the golden moment, and turn the rushing torrent into a perennial river of peace and freedom." Through their intervention, a war for Union could become a crusade for justice. The future was therefore "ours to mould [*sic*] it as we will." Abolitionists should not "stand back and say, 'I will wait until this is a noble war—a war for humanity,'" added Conway. "Let all enter and make it a noble war." Interventionists, he argued, needed to descend from their heights into the fray, harnessing the Union war effort to make real the golden moment as quickly as possible.[20]

A May article in the *Weekly Anglo-African,* a former—and future—Black newspaper temporarily edited by white reformer James Redpath, elucidated interventionists' rationale in embracing the Union war. The "climax" of the antislavery struggle, Redpath asserted, had arrived. Abolitionists, whatever their old means, or "justifiable instrumentalities," of pursuing justice had been, now had to embrace a different method as "one harmonious whole." They had to be "Realist[s], recognizing all values in their proper place and endeavoring to adjust them." Aloofness would no longer serve their moral ends. They could not influence the war from on high. The "day of sainthood has passed," Redpath affirmed, and "martyrdom has almost ceased to be a virtue." Only by wading into the grime of the political mainstream—by pursuing earthly, compromising tactics—could abolitionists shape the nation's path and ensure its divine destiny. They would have to get their hands dirty as never before.[21]

EMBRACING A WAR FOR UNION

Prowar abolitionists responded to Fort Sumter by embarking upon a remarkable tactical turnaround, pairing declarations against secession and for the Union war—and, with reluctance, for Lincoln—with attempts at public discretion. Yet they were still reeling from the national upheaval, individually clawing their ways out of the darkness toward solid ground. Reflecting their disorientation, and the complexity of constructing a coherent prowar caucus, their early efforts were muddled, haphazard, and divided. Garrisonian interventionists especially inveighed against secession, repudiating their former doctrine of disunion. Northerners, as they well knew, assailed proslavery secessionists and abolitionist disunionists alike. In the *Liberator,* Garrison took great pains to contrast the two groups. Southern secessionists, he asserted, had not the "shadow of an excuse" to justify their behavior. Disunionists, meanwhile, had drawn on the "patriotism of 1776" to espouse salutary separation. But Garrison now abandoned that tactic, supporting the subjugation of the "Southern traitors." Through a previously unthinkable disavowal of old dogma, he dissociated abolitionism from treason.[22]

Garrison feared that other abolitionists would not follow his lead. On April 19, he complained to Oliver Johnson about Phillips, whose disunionist speech in New Bedford, delivered weeks before Sumter's fall, had just reached his attention. While all Garrisonians had espoused disunion over the winter, this late-breaking speech would now prove most impolitic. Garrison confessed himself "taken aback" by how "not guardedly expressed" the oration was. The "pro-slavery press [would] seize upon it," he worried, reinforcing the public linkage between abolitionists and secessionists. The prosecession mayor of Baltimore, George William Brown, validated such fears by citing Phillips's speech to prove the legality of secession.[23]

Phillips had since converted to the pro-Union cause, renouncing disunionism. Reflecting the confusion reigning among prowar abolitionists, however, Johnson remained unaware of this change of heart. Throughout April and May, he declared himself "not a little astonished" that Phillips had "deliberately planted himself" against the war. It would be "most unfortunate for our movement," he warned, to "assume such an attitude." Another misinformed activist also wondered why Phillips remained an unrepentant disunionist, rejecting a government that had finally discovered "pluck and honor." Abolitionists were thus swept up in the fog of war following the loss of Fort Sumter, unsure as to who had changed their stripes.[24]

Amid such havoc, interventionists began embracing the war—and Lincoln—in disjointed fashion. For the time being, they acted independently of each other, rather than through any form of coordination. Leading the charge was the much-misunderstood Phillips. Following his anguished conversation with George W. Smalley, he revealed his transformed stance regarding the Union at the Boston Music Hall on April 21, on a "platform profusely decorated with the Stars and Stripes." Referencing his late positions, he noted that he had formerly urged "a peaceful separation of these States." Now, however, Phillips threw his weight to the Union as "all right" in its war. "Today Abolitionist is merged in citizen—in American," he affirmed, situating himself within the war effort. Garrison praised the speech, noting that Phillips had managed to stand "encircled by the drapery of stars and stripes without compromising your abolitionism," juggling the demands of the moment with his principles. Johnson, finally aware of Phillips's conversion, likewise praised the speech, entreating Phillips to distribute it to the troops.[25]

Reinforcing the paradigm shift within abolitionism, other interventionists followed Phillips's lead, even as each fixated on their own discrete issues. "Let the Administration . . . in its well-directed efforts to *humble the South,* receive the cordial sympathy and cooperation of every well-wisher of his country,"

Douglass averred. Within the prowar umbrella, Douglass focused on the topic of Black enlistment. Black men, he declared in May, should "be formed into a liberating army, to march into the South and raise the banner of emancipation among the slaves." Black soldiers would expedite a Confederate collapse while also proving their worth for citizenship through masculine glory. "Our men," he added, are "eager to play some honorable part in the great drama." Military service represented a gendered vehicle for Black rights.[26]

Most Black abolitionists approached the issue of enlistment differently. At an April meeting in Boston, and over the dissent of immediatist William Wells Brown, the restaurateur and activist George T. Downing and other attendees "expressed the patriotic feelings of the colored men" toward the Union. They stood "ready to defend the flag of the common country against the common foe." Downing, especially, declared himself prepared to "answer the call of duty." As he witnessed a state of affairs in which Union officials greeted Black volunteers with prejudice-filled rejections, however, Downing stressed that he would fight only "when the removal of disabilities allowed them to do so on terms of equality." While Douglass pressed for immediate enlistment to moralize the Union, Downing, not to mention Brown, strove first to help the Union war progress to the point that Black troops—and Black rights—became its clarion calls.[27]

A few Black elites, such as Cincinnati schoolteacher William Parham, forswore even the eventual possibility of enlistment. As he informed a friend who shared Downing's belief that the "time for black men to fight has not yet come," Parham could not "agree . . . in thinking that this war will bring it, if Negro equality is to be its precursor." Slavery, he believed, would soon receive its "fatal blow. . . . But prejudice against the Negro will not expire with slavery." Anti-Black racism seemed only to be increasing as slavery neared its end. Rather than help usher in the conditions that would make Black enlistment suitable, Parham disavowed the Union altogether, hoping instead to immigrate to the British West Indies.[28]

In Britain proper, George Cheever supported the Union war by focusing on another pressing matter: preventing British recognition of the rebels. The British ruling class, swayed by a pro-Confederate press and industrial demands for cotton, was largely sympathetic to the rebellion. "The impressions in regard to the conflict in America are . . . false and unfavorable," Cheever fretted in May. In Britain, "you would not suppose there was a slave in existence, much less that slavery was any cause of the present conflict between North and South."

Cheever thus advocated a petition against recognizing the Confederacy at an antislavery meeting in Glasgow.[29]

Conway, for his part, supported the Union's plans to invade his home state of Virginia, despite the presence of his brothers in the Confederate military. His revisionist autobiography, written decades after his split with Lincoln late in the war, omitted such details. Lincoln, he retroactively asserted, had deceived him in April 1861. Rather than an invasion of the Confederacy, Conway had supposedly believed that the Union military would "only occupy the border with camps . . . [as] asylums for slaves, so compelling slaveholders to return to their homes." Lincoln, however, had attacked Virginia—an action with which Conway "could not sympathize." Yet such recollections rewrote history. After Fort Sumter's fall, Conway wrote Lincoln himself to offer his services in the "solemn but ever-glorious emergency." He was "minutely acquainted with the topography" of the Richmond area, he volunteered, and wondered if the "War Department needed a question concerning such minutiae answered"—the language of someone advocating, not opposing, invasion. War, Conway had believed in reality, would redeem his home from the corruption of slavery, even if it entailed fighting his kin.[30]

Child, rather than Conway, was the interventionist most conflicted about the Union cause. While prowar abolitionists all embraced the war only with great difficulty, Child experienced especial distress, grounded in two concerns: racial justice and, as casualties later piled up, the human cost of the conflict. Writing a fellow abolitionist in May, Child abjured from the "universal enthusiasm for the US flag." When the government treated Blacks with "justice and humanity," she would "mount its flag in my great elm-tree." Until then, however, she would "as soon wear the rattlesnake upon my bosom as the eagle." Child soon wrote Johnson that she had chastised Phillips for "hurrah[ing] long before we could see our way out of the wood." Though Child "want[ed] to love and honor the flag . . . my love of country finds vent only in tears." Even as she recognized the potential of the Union war by expressing her hope that the government would do for the sake of "policy and revenge, what we ought to do [for] justice," Child refrained from displays of overt patriotism, tinging her own intervention with remorse.[31]

The most anguishing component of prowar abolitionists' new course concerned Lincoln and the Republicans. While they had toned down their criticisms of the Republicans in recent years, portraying the upstart organization as a stepping stone to a superior antislavery party, their support had been tepid and indirect. They had maintained their overall detachment from the political mainstream, at least in their own eyes. Now, interventionists needed to embrace the Republicans directly as the leaders of a united war effort. Moreover, they had to accept the party in its current form, working with the materials at hand in this brief window of opportunity.

Interventionists' ambivalence over their political transformation, and the moral contradiction at its core, manifested in the divergence of their private and public opinions of Lincoln. As Garrison revealed in praising Phillips's Music Hall speech, prowar abolitionists cherished still their self-conceived identities as righteous reformers. They fretted, one interventionist wrote in May, that their movement would "lose its identity in this absorption of parties"—that they would submerge themselves in "this din of war," blemishing their moral visions. Interventionists attempted to balance such concerns with their interventions. In private, they continued judging Lincoln by their personal, moralistic standard of the ideal, lambasting his disinterest in emancipation and Black rights. To Johnson, Child emphasized her low opinion of the government. "It is evident that the government *mean[s]* no good to the slave," she lamented, referencing its fugitive slave policy. Nor was she certain that it intended a prolonged war: she placed her "only trust in the blind madness of Jeff Davis," rather than in Lincoln, to avert compromise. According to her own standard, Lincoln had fallen short.[32]

Yet interventionists strained to avoid uttering such sentiments out loud. Antebellum immediatists had spoken harsh truths, valuing moral transparency. For the greater good, however, abolitionists now had to "let bygones be bygones" in public, as Edmund Quincy contended. "Minute criticism of Lincoln," as Garrison explained to Johnson, achieved nothing. It would only alienate the public, undermining efforts to perfect the Union from within. Interventionists thus began evaluating Lincoln publicly according to the standard of the possible—a metric of what was politically achievable in the present. The president became a leader doing his best in trying times, rather than one failing in his moral duty. Garrison, in a representative argument, noted in the *Liberator* in April 1861 that "on the issue raised by the secessionists, they are wholly and fearfully in the wrong, while Lincoln is indisputably in the right." In public, interventionists praised Lincoln for prosecuting the war, downplaying his shortcomings—and their own beliefs that he was a necessary evil at best. Through this dichotomy, they hoped to achieve change while keeping their heads above the current, preserving their innate dignity as upright reformers.[33]

Interventionists thereby adapted to their new normal after Fort Sumter. They hastened to join the war effort, even as they cast about for a true strategy that went beyond merely endorsing the Union war to actually changing it. Developing such a plan would require time and effort, as would uniting prowar abolitionists around it. Abolitionists, as Garrison's and Johnson's confusion over Phillips demonstrated, still had to sort out who was in the prowar camp. And, as seen below, lingering factional tensions between Garrisonians and non-Garrisonians presented a significant obstacle to the harmonious whole that Redpath envisioned.

Interventionists bided their time in the early weeks of the war by putting forward a placeholder plan. Their first attempt at a coordinated strategy was to do nothing. Over the winter, Radical Republicans like John Andrew had begged the abolitionists for tactful silence. Now, interventionists reluctantly adopted such a measure. Immediatists had accrued antebellum infamy as agitating provocateurs. Their conspicuous presence on the national stage, before northerners processed their prowar shift, could thereby prove problematic. Rocking the boat, they knew, endangered both their physical selves and their influence. "These unparalleled circumstances," Garrison told Johnson, called for "great circumspection," lest abolitionists unleash "popular violence upon ourselves, by any false step." A misstep could also imperil the fragile momentum against the Slave Power, forestalling the golden moment. The "Northern whale is bearing down, snout onward, upon the ship Slavery," declared Quincy. Abolitionists needed to tread lightly, lest they "divert it from its course" and close their window of opportunity.[34]

The annual May antislavery society meetings fit that impolitic bill. Prior to the surrender of Fort Sumter the *Liberator* had advertised the coming meeting of the AASS, proclaiming that, whether the Union "be dissolved or not . . . this Society will still have its work unfinished." Following the battle, however, Garrison announced the cancellation of the meeting as a "measure of sound expediency" to preserve the "mighty current of popular feeling sweeping southward." As he told a fellow immediatist, "there is a time to speak, and a time to keep silent." The latter moment had arrived. A member of the Cheever brothers-led CASS, Edward Gilbert, likewise warned Henry Cheever that a meeting of their society would give "occasion to those who seek occasion." Convocations would provide the proslavery press with the pretext to label the Union war an abolitionist crusade in disguise. Northerners fighting to preserve the Union would abandon the war before time had worked its moralizing magic. Gilbert therefore opposed holding "any anti-slavery meeting of any society" for the time being.[35]

Yet common worries did not translate into common policy. By late April, Garrison decided that "in this emergency" abolitionists should hold only one gathering: an abridged meeting of the AASS. Amid the general silence, Garrison wanted his society to take precedence in charting immediatists' future course. Gilbert hence asked Henry Cheever to cancel the CASS annual meeting. Cheever disagreed, desiring that his non-Garrisonian, religious antislavery society hold the one representative abolitionist gathering. He even asked Phillips to speak at the anniversary. Mimicking the language that Andrew had deployed against himself months earlier, Phillips demurred, warning Cheever to "let the popular mind turn its own way—and not have us risk any ripple." Both sides nevertheless refused to stand down, holding their own meetings. For now, old factional rivalries between Garrisonians and non-Garrisonians were bleeding into the emerging prowar camp, preventing even a unified stopgap strategy.[36]

THE FIRST REALIGNMENT OF WARTIME ABOLITIONISM

Despite such lingering wounds, antebellum factional lines were rapidly becoming irrelevant as more pressing divisions superseded them. Over the past decade, members of the interventionist and moral purist schools of thought had drifted apart. With the onset of war, Conway noted, the "antislavery fraternity was shattered" once and for all, realigning abolitionism into hardened camps of prowar interventionists and antiwar moral purists. Purists had previously chided interventionists for treating the Republicans as an ethical shortcut—a flawed, imperfect means that could never bring about their perfect end of a nation grounded in freedom and racial equality. Now, they trained their sights on the Union war and its abolitionist backers.[37]

These purists, led by Pillsbury and the Fosters, were a small but motley group. They included Quaker pacifists like Lucretia Mott, universal peace activists like Elihu Burritt, and doctrinaire non-resistants like Alfred Love, all of whom opposed war in general. As Mott confided to a friend, no "end justifies the means" of war. How wrong it was, Love agreed in April, to "seek to redress wrongs by the sword." Love, a friend of Garrison's, sought to persuade him to return to the non-resistant fold, later informing him that "carnal weapons" could not beget "devout ends." In Love's view, only nonviolent methods could redeem a fallen country.[38]

For the Fosters, Pillsbury, and their acolytes, however, the Union war specifically, rather than war generally, endangered their quest for a morally transformed Union. They portrayed this conflict as a moral dead end, bereft of any potential. In the weeks after Fort Sumter's capture, they refuted interventionists' arguments in favor of the conflict one by one. As they had done regarding the Republicans before the war, moral purists again rejected the notion of a lesser evil. The *Anti-Slavery Bugle* admitted in April that the Confederacy was more "avowedly proslavery than the government of the United States." That fact, however, did not "make us any more willing to support the latter than we have been for the last twenty years. . . . We have never recognized the rightfulness of choosing a moral evil, though a lesser one," the paper concluded.[39]

Moral purists, moreover, did not see the Union war as a lesser evil at all. Writing Phillips in May, Pillsbury drew a moral equivalency between the Union and the Confederacy. "At the South," he asserted, "we have desperadoes; at the North doughfaces; their only issue a bastard blood of compromises and corruptions." Both, he argued, were proslavery powers. The "most damnable slave-hunting ever known, is carried on by Republican marshals," he noted. The war, the *Bugle* added, was not "between Freedom and Slavery." Lincoln, it claimed, aimed to restore the proslavery Union as it was, rather than construct the antislavery Union as it should be.[40]

Interventionists also recognized that the Union war as it then stood was not an antislavery crusade. But while they believed in its potential to become a holy war, the *Bugle* derided this "strange infatuation." Like broad interventionists, moral purists sought a racially egalitarian nation. Given their conviction that just ends necessitated just means, however, they could not fathom how such an imperfect war could lead to emancipation, let alone Black rights in any form. The war, the *Bugle* averred, would not "result in the overthrow of slavery . . . the abolition of slavery was not the object of the Republican Party." Pillsbury agreed. "Would to Heaven I could agree with you in thinking slavery is to be damned, or even damaged seriously, by the present commotions," he lamented to Phillips in May. Though "God knows how I long and agonize to think otherwise," he could not perceive any emancipatory promise in the national strife.[41]

Moral purists thus refused to abandon abolitionism's antebellum doctrines for a worthless cause. Immediatists' work, Pillsbury insisted, was not "affected by any change whatever in the government, so long as it recognizes slavery."

Because he viewed the war as proslavery business as usual, rather than as a watershed moment, Pillsbury stood by the old Garrisonian arguments about the proslavery Constitution, disunion, and come-outerism. He denounced the war, asserting in a public letter that northerners should not "die and be buried like dogs . . . in behalf of slavery." These purists would, the *Bugle* declared, continue to "stand aloof" as saints above the fray.[42]

Antiwar abolitionists also dissented against their prowar counterparts. At times they kept their discontent private. Pillsbury complained to Phillips that the *National Anti-Slavery Standard,* the AASS organ, now featured the Stars and Stripes on its masthead. As Pillsbury decried, "I do not see how we as a Society, unfurl them at all, while slavery with all its horrible concomitants, is represented by them." He hence demanded that the AASS rectify its mistake.[43]

More often, purists criticized their colleagues in public. Interventionist attempts to moralize the Union war from within, they proclaimed, were a fool's errand. If abolitionists "are to support the war on the ground of its possible future antislavery character," one moral purist asserted, then let them "wait 'till it assumes that character." Abolitionists, he argued, should not intervene until the war had already become moralized—if it ever did. They could not mold a perfect sculpture out of flawed marble. They required pure materials—a public embracing emancipation and Black rights in the name of justice—to create an egalitarian nation. Most northerners, purists knew, remained far from such values. By intervening, prowar abolitionists would inevitably adulterate themselves and gain naught by it. As another purist pled, if "we might fight for the Union . . . let it be for an antislavery Union, and not for this cursed covenant with death." In the meantime, immediatists had to continue as dissentient gadflies, agitating for perfection from outside the mainstream.[44]

By instead following an earthly idol, purists contended, interventionists imperiled the entire immediatist movement. Writing to the *Liberator* in May, Love argued that the abolitionist "title has been the synonym of purity, love, and perfection." Immediatists had occupied a "stand-point high above" the polluted mainstream, their purity allowing them to guide the nation as its objective conscience. It was the source of their moral gravitas and unbending integrity. Should they become "drift-wood" submerged in the "rushing, swelling tide" of public opinion, however, that purity would be lost. The war, he added, was a "siren song"—a trial to test abolitionists' principles. By intervening, prowar immediatists would "surrender our strongholds of virtue." They would fail this trial, weakening their authority and sacrificing their deepest moral commitments as they lost themselves in the mainstream. It was appalling, a fellow purist lamented, to imagine immediatists who had "climbed to the serene heights of Peace and Love" lowering themselves into the "popular tide and be carried down, down into the whirlpool of strife." Interventionists had to turn back before it was too late—before they succumbed to temptation and "trail[ed] their beautiful garments thro' smoke and dust and blood," compromising both their cherished credentials as moral reformers and abolitionism itself while accomplishing nothing.[45]

Interventionists, wary of drawing attention and already anxious about their own moral integrity, were stunned by these attacks from their flank. They responded at first with a mix of appeasement and civil disagreement, defending their intervention without making a conspicuous row. In a May letter to Oliver Johnson, the *Standard*'s editor, Garrison noted that Pillsbury had felt "sensitive" about the American flag on the masthead. While Garrison disagreed with such sentiments, he asked Johnson to remove the flag to avoid a clash. At the same time, Phillips asked Pillsbury to "hold on awhile" before rendering judgment, at least in public. "Let us see what's coming" before dismissing the war as pointless, he urged.[46]

With reluctance, Garrison also took interventionists' case to the press. He loathed projecting disunity within the ranks, believing that infighting would attract undue publicity at the worst possible time. Yet he could not let such attacks go unanswered. He thus began publishing purists' criticisms and refuting them in levelheaded terms. After one immediatist wrote Garrison that "Order, Justice, and Humanity" had no stakes in "either side in the [war]," Garrison printed the missive in the *Liberator* alongside a reply affirming the distinction between the two sides. Later that month he issued a rebuke of those reformers who refused to perceive "any cheering significance" in the war. Such "morbid exclamations" as came from moral purists, he argued, were "blind to the progress of events." And when Love wrote to Garrison advocating non-resistance, the editor publicly replied that a celestial crusade, rather than the "moral paralysis" of a false, proslavery peace, would better serve the "sacred cause." Through calm discourse, Garrison hoped to prevent a conflict already simmering on the front burner from boiling over.[47]

In that endeavor Garrison would fail. After Lincoln's election, Abby Kelley Foster had anticipated a new era of unified abolitionist opposition to the Republicans. But as the nation descended into conflict, interventionists resolved to carry out their moral missions by joining the Union war. They began what would become an established pattern over the first months of the war, as prowar abolitionists reacted to military and political events by first initiating, and then escalating their political interventions. Shocked moral purists, meanwhile, clung steadfast to their saintliness of old—a model, they warned, that interventionists should not have deserted. In the coming weeks the divisions between these two emergent camps would worsen. Vitriolic attacks echoing across the Atlantic would replace civility as the stakes of the Union war, and the battle for the immediatist movement's very soul, soared. The abolitionist civil war had begun.

CHAPTER TWO

An Interventionist Strategy Emerges, June–Mid-July 1861

In June, Frederick Douglass penned an editorial extolling a previously inconceivable subject: Benjamin Butler. The general, recently the object of abolitionist wrath, had suddenly begun welcoming fugitive slaves into Fort Monroe in late May, appropriating them for the Union war as seized contraband. Douglass rejoiced at this surprising turn of events. "Better ideas are beginning to control the actions of our army officers," he declared. As Douglass recognized, the contraband policy was far from the abolitionist ideal, rendering fugitives into liminal laborers rather than free citizen-soldiers. In the fraught fight for the golden moment, however, Douglass also appreciated its importance. Interventionists, he understood, had to "radiate around our army and Government the light and heat of justice and humanity"—to somehow convince northerners to fight for freedom before it was too late. In Butler's policy, Douglass and other prowar abolitionists found their means of doing so, one that could motivate even a onetime proslavery politician into antislavery action: the utilitarian, expedient language of military necessity.[1]

Following the emergence of the contraband policy, prowar abolitionists coalesced around an innovative strategy for the new order, once again expanding upon their wartime intervention in response to military developments. Though they had entered the war effort in reaction to Fort Sumter, Butler's doctrine proved that they had to go further to save the nation. Even from within the Union war, the old rhetorical mainstays of abolitionism—morality and justice—would have little effect. Now that the day of sainthood had passed, immediatists needed to reshape themselves—to shed their long-worn skin of agitationist moral reform and become practitioners of political pressure, lobby-

44

ing northerners on their own decidedly nonmoralistic terms. With reluctance, interventionists like Douglass, Phillips, Garrison, Conway, Forten, Child, and Cheever began a wrenching transformation into interest group political tactics in June and July.[2] These figures solidified a new, animating interventionist consensus of conditional support for the government. In public, moreover, they began promulgating a collaborative set of axioms using the logical linchpin of military necessity. Slavery, they argued, both precipitated the war and powered the Confederacy. Military emancipation, enacted through the constitutional war powers clause, could thereby win the conflict at hand and prevent future strife. Through such arguments, prowar abolitionists integrated the formerly anathema rhetoric of utility and expediency into their lexicons, appealing to northern self-interest to attain their higher designs.[3]

To put their novel strategy into practice, interventionists needed to work together. In the first weeks of the war, this had proven easier said than done: antebellum tensions remained hard to overcome. But rather than let factional differences stand in the way of success, Garrisonian and non-Garrisonian interventionists strove to move past them. A tentative, informal antislavery alliance emerged in the early summer, bringing into unison prowar abolitionists of all stripes. Together, such figures promoted their shared, expediency-based axioms. Within this united front, interventionists still branched out, as Garrison veered into pro-Union chauvinism, Phillips into endorsing compensated emancipation, and Conway into the prospect of military chaplaincy.[4]

Moral purists watched, shocked, as their counterparts fell deeper under the sway of the Union siren. As members of an oppositionist fringe, Pillsbury and the Fosters had little influence on the interventionist majority's political evolution. Yet by constantly injecting the issue of racial equality into the discussion, purists reminded all of the large-scale concerns at stake in the Union war. Throughout the first years of the conflict, their increasingly alarmed opposition to interventionists also functioned as an oppositional yardstick, charting the growing politicization of their prowar colleagues. Now, in June, they began publicly deriding interventionists as traitors who were sacrificing the movement's long-term mission for the mirage of short-term gains.

In this endeavor, a new group of allies joined the American antiwar minority: immediatists in the British Isles. Most antislavery activists from across the Atlantic, including such figures as Thomas Guthrie and Richard Davis Webb, scorned the Union war alongside its abolitionist backers. As such assaults on their credentials as upright reformers forced them to justify their choices, interventionists like Garrison retorted at gatherings and in the transatlantic press. They reframed themselves as the pragmatic center of the abolitionist movement, often resorting to ad hominem vitriol and nationalistic chauvinism in the process. The abolitionist civil war thereby turned even hotter, evaporating all pretense of civility between the warring camps.[5]

THE CURIOUS CASE OF BENJAMIN BUTLER

As news of the contraband policy at Fort Monroe trickled north in the late spring, interventionists assessed what this unexpected development signified, in terms of both the national emancipation process and their own search for a wartime strategy. Prowar abolitionists sharply disagreed over the former. David Lee Child, Lydia's husband, refused to believe that a longtime foe like Benjamin Butler could open the door to abolition. Butler, he declared in a series of *Liberator* articles, was a "supremely selfish and totally depraved" man who intended "insidiousness and treachery." Child was not opposed to confiscation: as a legal theorist, he cited the international laws of war to argue that "victors in a just cause may seize" the property of their enemies. Since slaves were, by legal definition, property, the Union had the "right in war of stripping, weakening, and vanquishing the enemy" by confiscating them. Child advocated for a uniform governmental policy of confiscation, however, rather than a piecemeal effort initiated unilaterally by a seedy general with suspect motives. To him, Butler's policy was a "discreditable expedient" in the larger struggle for universal emancipation.[6]

Most interventionists instead put aside their distrust of Butler and welcomed his doctrine, albeit to varying degrees. Over the summer, Phillips called the policy a "convenient resource for the occasion." It "saved 350 slaves," he noted, and "I thank [Butler] for it." Nonetheless, Phillips dismissed its overall significance within the emancipation equation, labeling it a "benevolent dodge"—a "technicality, wholly unfit for a great people to rest thereon a national question." Charles Whipple, an editorial assistant at the *Liberator,* agreed that it was a temporary stopgap—an "ingenious trick for an existing emergency," but a mere trick nevertheless.[7]

Lydia Maria Child ascribed greater antislavery meaning to the contraband policy. Rather than the trifling dead end described by her husband, Child viewed it as a groundbreaking innovation—one both legally justifiable, given that military officers "had no shadow of right" to determine questions of slave ownership on their own, and conducive to a larger process of emancipation. "If the war continues," Douglass agreed, Butler's doctrine could catch on elsewhere. Soon enough, as thousands of former slaves labored in Union camps, pressure would build to free "all those slaves who have assisted the Government" in defeating the rebellion. Butler's policy could thereby serve as the building block of emancipation.[8]

Even as they disagreed over its emancipatory significance, interventionists recognized what the contraband policy meant for their own path forward. They had stood silent over the first weeks of the war, fearful about inflaming public opinion and unable to unite around a common strategy. Butler's doctrine addressed both of these issues. First, it demonstrated that antislavery actions, if couched correctly, were possible in the new wartime climate. Abolitionists, by implication, could safely exit the shadows and radiate light across the North. Edmund Quincy, who had formerly advocated a strategy of tactful silence, declared at a meeting in July that the "heart and mind of the North" was now open to immediatists' influence, enabling bolder tactics.[9]

Second, Butler demonstrated how abolitionists could exert such influence: through a strategy that contravened the spirit of their movement, which had been founded to achieve justice for justice's sake. Immediatists had long espoused the rhetoric of unqualified morality, scorning the idea of expediency. Before the war, Cheever had made his name attacking this concept. "You build upon the sand," he had declared in 1859, "if you build upon expediency, availability, anything but truth and righteousness." Even amid their intervention, prowar abolitionists strove to preserve their identities as unstained reformers, as Phillips had stressed to George W. Smalley in April.[10]

Now, interventionists recognized that they would have to descend further into the mainstream muck, refashioning their movement to realize their golden moment. As one Rochester antislavery society lamented, the "means used in former years for . . . disseminating antislavery doctrines, have been unsuited to the times." The path to northern hearts and minds, they now grasped, lay not through old, absolutist appeals, but through a concept that could turn a Breckinridge Democrat into an antislavery advocate: military necessity. While most northerners remained unwilling to move against slavery on their own, as a moral imperative, they might do so if convinced it would save the Union—and their own sons. In their fleeting window of opportunity, interventionists understood that their last, best chance for emancipation lay in persuading northerners to do justice not intentionally but incidentally, out of self-interest.[11]

In reaction to Butler's actions, interventionists decided to go beyond entering the war effort—an excruciating decision itself—to transforming the very nature of abolitionism. Such a drastic overhaul would be even more harrowing. It would exacerbate their internal moral contradictions, forcing them to try to uphold their moral identities and principles while employing explicitly nonmoral tactics. To justify such a decision, however, interventionists looked to their immediate objective. A war for emancipation was their crux—the achievement that would precipitate a moral tidal wave. Even if northerners embraced abolition for imperfect reasons, its salutary effects would consequently perfect them. Facing a constrained time frame, interventionists thereby resigned themselves to, as Garrison detailed, "merge ourselves, as far as we can without a compromise of principle, in the onward sweeping current of Northern sentiment." They would have to ensure emancipation as quickly as possible using the unsavory yet effective means at hand, without sacrificing their millennial endgames.[12]

Over the late spring and early summer, prowar abolitionists transformed immediatism from a moral agitation movement into a political pressure group that lobbied northerners in their own mainstream language. Such a transition was an astounding, if painful, adaptation to changing times. As an initial step, prowar abolitionists redefined the interventionist camp around a progovernment consensus—a common platform of conditional yet continued support for Lincoln as a wartime necessary evil. Interventionists also crafted a common rhetorical program through which to apply political pressure. While they cherished their long-used moralistic refrains, they purposefully crafted an innovative, interlocking series of five axioms packaging emancipation as a military necessity, giving once-taboo concepts like utility, expediency, and national self-interest pride of place in their articles, speeches, and tracts.[13]

First, interventionists, led by the newspapermen Garrison and Douglass, stressed that slavery—and, more specifically, southern slaveholders—had caused the war. This argument, Garrison informed Phillips, was one "which we can expose at the present time with great power and success." Decrying southern villainy was a natural starting point to winning over northerners. To that end, Garrison anonymously published a pamphlet, *The Spirit of the South towards Northern Freemen and Soldiers Defending the American Flag against Traitors of the Deepest Dye.* The tract drew in readers with its antisouthern title, which trumpeted the predominant northern motivation for war—preserving the Union. Inside, however, northerners would discover excerpts from southern newspapers, spitting venom at them for threatening slaveholding supremacy. Southerners, in their own words, had seceded to protect slavery.[14]

Prowar abolitionists also hastened to make this critical point themselves. In one editorial, Garrison illustrated how the "execrable system" of slavery had engendered the current conflict. Southerners had first seceded and then initiated a war to save slavery from the perceived Republican threat. Those northerners who insisted upon "ignoring the question of slavery as not involved in this deadly feud" were thereby "fools and blind." Try as such people might to portray the "preservation of the Union" as the sole issue at stake, Garrison emphasized that the true "*cause of all this*" was undeniable. In *Douglass' Monthly,* Douglass likewise lambasted the "self-deception" of those who denied that the source of the "bloodshed under which this country is now staggering is slavery." As much as northerners pretended otherwise, slavery was the real issue at play in the war.[15]

Second, interventionists argued that slavery fueled the Confederate war. In another pamphlet, *The War and Slavery; or, Victory Only Through Emancipation,* Garrison revealed that slavery "is not only the object of the rebellion, but it is the right arm of its strength." The "slaves, by their toil, furnish the sinews of the war the rebels are waging," he noted. Slaves "till their soil and produce their supplies," so that "no matter how many men they put into the field, they do not weaken their agricultural force." At the same time, the Confederate government impressed slaves to "build fortifications . . . perform the menial services of their camps," and in myriad other ways "contribute to their success." Slavery was thus the "vital point" in the Confederate war. It was the "center of this gigantic rebellion," Douglass agreed in his newspaper.[16]

To head off calls for a proslavery peace, interventionists developed a third axiom: permanent intersectional reunion was impossible with slavery intact. If the "slaveholding oligarchy" retained power after the war concluded, Garrison asserted, the "irrepressible conflict would continue." Political convulsions would begin anew, "until the flames of civil war become again enkindled" over the "same question." With slavery untouched, white southerners would remain formidable enemies in that renewed conflict. No "substantial victory or abiding peace," Garrison concluded, could emerge from a proslavery settlement.[17]

By demonstrating that slavery caused the war, propped up the rebellion, and prevented national harmony, interventionists built to the crescendo of the fourth axiom: emancipation was a military necessity. As Garrison noted in strikingly utilitarian terms, the "exigencies" of defeating the slaveholding rebellion, alongside the need to "save the lives of our brave men," required abolition. Slavery, he emphasized over the summer, rendered the Confederacy invincible. Emancipation was therefore a "wise stroke of policy in war"—a much-needed measure to defeat the recalcitrant rebels. Balancing the newfound rhetoric of national expediency with his own moralistic beliefs, he demanded emancipation "because it is a matter of necessity, [and] because it is right." With moral harangues alone not budging the people, Garrison bowed to circumstance and invoked their own self-interest to move the metaphoric needle.[18]

The language of utility also infiltrated interventionist paeans to a morally transformed Union. Emancipation, Douglass affirmed in July, would not only moralize the nation but also "place [it] on a firm foundation of peace and prosperity." Garrison made a similar point. "How instantaneously [after emancipation] would the flames of war be extinguished, the source of all our national troubles dried up, reconciliation everywhere effected, and a true and majestic Union organized," he argued. Garrison thereby couched his moral vision in terms of expediency, while also inadvertently revealing his relative lack of interest in post-emancipation concerns.[19]

Fifth and finally, interventionists stressed the legality of abolition. Garrison, who had theatrically burned the Constitution onstage seven years earlier, now invoked it ad nauseam to justify military emancipation. As he explained in a June editorial, the war powers clause of the Constitution allowed the government to protect the "general welfare by removing the source of danger and division." Taking up an argument introduced by John Quincy Adams in the 1830s, Garrison asserted that Lincoln could emancipate Confederate slaves under the war power by declaring this action a military necessity. He soon reprinted Adams's original arguments in another pamphlet. Douglass, Cheever, and other interventionists followed suit, aligning behind the war power as their chosen instrument in articles, speeches, and, in the case of interventionist Elizur Wright, a personal plea to Treasury Secretary Salmon P. Chase. Through such arguments, interventionists constructed the rhetorical foundations of their new political interest group.[20]

BUILDING AN ANTISLAVERY ALLIANCE

As interventionists quickly realized, their axioms meant little on their own. To be effective, a political pressure group had to employ concrete, concerted methods of influencing the structures of power. Isolated, individual efforts, like those which prowar abolitionists had pursued in April and May, would fail. Interventionists needed to give shape and form to their program—to create a vehicle through which they could work in tandem to popularize their shared arguments. Over the early summer, prowar abolitionists began the trying process of constructing such a vessel: the antislavery alliance. Though this coalition would evolve over time, it began as a tentative, awkward network of communication and coordination among interventionists. Creating such a cohesive grouping was no small feat: an inter-factional détente between Garrisonians and non-Garrisonians, not to mention an alliance, had seemed impossible in recent months.

These factional divisions lingered into the summer, fueled by personal resentments as much as doctrinal grudges. In June, Oliver Johnson complained to Henry Cheever that the non-Garrisonian CASS had maligned the Garrisonians. At its annual meeting, Lewis Tappan, who had helped inaugurate the 1840 split within abolitionism by revolting against Garrison's leadership, had praised George Cheever for representing the "Christian Anti-Slavery movement in this country." Tappan's tone in referring to Christian abolitionists was "invidious," Johnson claimed, sanctioning the "malignant slander upon our [Garrisonian] movement, that it is not Christian but infidel." Such behavior seemed "very shabby," Johnson fumed.[21]

Yet amid such venom appeared signs of hope. In the same letter, Johnson mentioned that Henry Cheever had invited Phillips to address his church. Johnson advised Phillips to accept, putting aside his anger in recognition of the benefits that cooperation would bring. This inter-factional thawing picked up speed as the summer continued. In July, a Garrisonian correspondent admitted to the *Liberator* that George Cheever, whom he had once considered to be "without a particle of radicalism in his nature," was now rising to "heaven on the wings of justice." As the correspondent recognized, he and the Cheever brothers were by necessity now in the same boat, employing similar tactics to meet the demands of the moment.[22]

Kind words soon kindled burgeoning ties of mutual support. The same month, Johnson asked another Garrisonian to solicit donors for the perpetually insolvent *National Anti-Slavery Standard*. In furnishing a list of names, he especially recommended George Cheever as a man of "perfect integrity" who might help sustain the paper. Another CASS member named Dexter Fairbank also seemed to be a worthwhile target. Owing to antebellum factionalism, Fairbank had once been "full of prejudice" toward the *Standard*. Lately, however, Johnson noted, Fairbank had "spoken highly of it." Johnson now wanted to reach out to show that "we can let bygones be bygones"—that prowar Garrisonians could overlook ancient enmities. "The effect on the whole would be good," Johnson concluded, fostering collaboration between the rival factions.[23]

The CASS proved helpful enough to have Johnson return the favor the following month, when Henry Cheever lost his ministerial position in Connecticut. In offering his sympathies, Johnson vowed to help find Cheever a "more agreeable field of usefulness." If funds allowed, Johnson noted, he could even "set you to work as a lecturing agent" for the AASS. Though this offer did not lead to a position, it was astonishing nonetheless: Cheever, after all, was an officer in a rival society. Amid the havoc of war, these organizations had come to recognize that they needed to pool their efforts for the common good. A nascent antislavery alliance was thus born.[24]

The demands of the hour, and the tangible benefits of cooperation, brought together even the bitterest competitors within immediatism: Garrison and Douglass. In the decade since the mentor-mentee relationship between the two collapsed into mutual recrimination, they had only further nourished their animosities. In mid-1860, Stephen Foster had planned a convention that would bring together Garrisonians like himself alongside non-Garrisonians like Douglass. Yet Douglass had refused the invitation, noting that the "difference between myself and Garrison might render me an unacceptable member to some from that side of the house." Around the same time, Garrison had declared that the presence of the "base and selfish" Douglass would "powerfully repel me from attending" an antislavery meeting in Syracuse.[25]

In the summer of 1861, however, these two rivals began a long process of reconciliation. In June, Douglass penned an article declaring their antebellum disagreements moot. His "old friends," he noted, had "shown themselves not above instruction" in embracing the Union. However patronizingly, Douglass stressed that war had brought Garrison and himself onto common ground. He later reiterated that every abolitionist, "Garrisonian or [not]," was both "clansman and kinsman of ours." Whatever differences once "distracted us, a common object and a common emergency makes us for the time at least, forget those differences, and strike at the common foe," he declared. Rising up to the wartime occasion, Douglass expressed his willingness to "form a common league against slavery." Garrison reciprocated this rapprochement. In contrast to his earlier feelings, Garrison in late 1861 praised the mayor of Syracuse for "having so nobly vindicated the freedom of speech" by letting Douglass speak there. As both men recognized, their personal qualms had to give way to their shared agenda.[26]

To be sure, old resentments died hard. Even as he extended the olive branch, Douglass remarked that he had been "in advance" of Garrison in adopting a pro-Union stance—a reference to his antebellum rejection of disunionism. Garrison resented such condescension. Though he later invited Douglass to a meeting of the AASS, he complained that Douglass's appearance "created some little friction." Given Douglass's "treacherous course towards our Society," his "assurance seemed to me excessive," Garrison grumbled. Nevertheless, he continued cooperating with his former protégé. Trust was a "plant of slow growth," he admitted, and "in his case will be particularly so with me." But the seeds had taken root. With Douglass and Garrison leading by example, interventionists superseded their old divisions, striving to put their fledgling political pressure strategy into practice—to reach as one into the halls of power.[27]

As first conceived, the antislavery alliance was a loose construction. Even as they united to succor Lincoln and espouse prowar axioms, interventionists could not entirely shake off their earlier, individualistic approaches toward the war. Phillips demonstrated both the push and pull of the coalition in the same speech. Speaking at the Garrisonians' annual Fourth of July picnic in Framingham, Massachusetts, he began by parroting alliance axioms. Emancipation, he declared, would enable national greatness, precipitating the "mightiest change of our age—the change of the Great Republic from hypocrisy to honor." Phillips also praised Lincoln, publicly retracting his labeling of the president as the "slave-hound of Illinois" during the 1860 election.[28]

In embracing interest group tactics, Phillips began refining his moral vision. For years, the broad interventionist had argued for a panoramic morally transformed Union, bereft of artificial barriers to multiracial unity. Now, politics began inflecting his thoughts about how to transmute a fractured land into a unified nationality, eventually guiding him toward a radically democratic conception of citizenship. In the service of his evolving mission, however, he occasionally ventured in surprising directions. At Framingham, Phillips, perhaps the most racially egalitarian white abolitionist, veered beyond the pack to endorse compensated emancipation. Immediatists had long recoiled from the idea of compensating slaveholders for the loss of their slaves. Slaveholding, they had maintained, was a sin. Slaves, not their masters, deserved recompense. Now, Phillips embraced that taboo. The government, he declared, should "say to the slaveholders, 'The Union shares the loss with you, if it takes your slaves from you by a military necessity.' No matter what it costs." Though Phillips recognized the strangeness of his position, he justified it by appealing to exigency. "Better pay the money to save the sinner from his sin," he argued, "than spend a million a day . . . in a cruel and brutal war." As throughout the war, anxiety lay at the root of his behavior. Phillips had embraced the Union war after much anguish, tying his hopes to a brief window of opportunity. If compensation could help ensure abolition before time expired, then it was a necessary compromise—a base expedient to soaring ends.[29]

Garrison, for his part, paired axiomatic pamphlets with an individualistic turn toward antisouthern chauvinism. As Corey Brooks has demonstrated, antebellum abolitionists had pioneered the concept of the Slave Power as a sectionalized, evil other. Yet they had consistently denounced northerners' moral failings alongside those of southerners. In 1855, for example, Douglass had reprimanded the "demoralized" North for appeasing the Slave Power and thereby heaping "shame and dishonor" upon the nation. Now, Garrison omitted any criticism of northerners from his public rhetoric. In one representative July editorial, he castigated rebel soldiers as "demonized spirits" terrorizing the heroic Union soldiers. By leaning into a prevailing tide of sectional sectarianism, Garrison hoped to garner support for the abolitionist cause.[30]

Garrison linked such sentiments to northern exceptionalism, envisioning at Framingham a victorious North reconstructing the South in its own likeness. A nation of "unparalleled glory, greatness, and renown," he declared, could arise from the war through the erasure of southern identity. By replicating the "free schools, and free presses, and free institutions . . . [of] the North" in the South, he continued in an appeal to northern pride, the nation could mold southerners into a "happy and prosperous people, as they never have been." Garrison was far from alone in exhorting the North to civilize the South: Phillips would later promulgate his own such civilizing vision. Reinforcing the emerging differences in their conceptions of a morally transformed Union, however, the broad interventionist Phillips would foreground Black southerners in imagining a postwar South. At Framingham, the narrow interventionist Garrison instead referred only to white southerners. He left the post-emancipation place of freed slaves in the nation ambiguous, opting to wax rhapsodic about white northern values supplanting those of white southerners. The seeds of dissent between Garrison and Phillips were sprouting already.[31]

Other interventionists also continued to meet the war's challenges in their own ways while working within the loose confines of the antislavery alliance. George Cheever carried on touring Britain to head off foreign support for the rebels. Yet he grew increasingly exasperated with the Confederate proclivities of the British aristocracy and press. In June, he lamented that his mission was "unlikely to succeed." Britain, he sighed, had proven itself cowardly in refusing to "stand against the Confederacy." He would return home, dejected, the following month.[32]

Conway, meanwhile, flirted with becoming a Union army chaplain. According to his revisionist autobiography, Conway had recoiled upon receiving the offer of a chaplaincy in July, "filled with horror at the thought of assisting a military invasion of people not for their rescue and that of their slaves." At the time, however, Conway informed his wife, Ellen, that a chaplaincy would offer "many opportunities for doing service . . . to the country." There was "scarcely any limit to the good a chaplain . . . could do." On her advice, Conway ultimately declined the offer. Yet his decision arose not from disgust over the Union invading his homeland, as he later claimed, but rather from his impatience over the "delay and timidity" of that invasion. Conway confessed that he would not be able to suppress his opinions on the need for a harder war, and would "get into trouble protesting" against the lack of abolitionist war aims within the ranks. He thus chose to remain in his Cincinnati pulpit. Like Phillips, Garrison, and other interventionists, Conway would find squaring the demands—and restraints—of a unified coalition with his own individualistic impulses to be challenging throughout the war.[33]

THE ESCALATION OF THE ABOLITIONIST CIVIL WAR

As interventionists forged their alliance, moral purists ramped up their unyielding attacks. After Fort Sumter, the Fosters and Pillsbury had chided prowar abolitionists to step back from the brink before the mainstream worked its corrupting influence, destroying the movement from within. Instead, they had witnessed interventionists deride their dire prophesies and commit further to a troubling course of action. At Framingham, Stephen Foster reiterated that the Union war remained a proslavery endeavor—an unrighteous means that could never produce abolition, much less racial equality. Butler's contraband policy was not progress: rather, it reaffirmed that fugitives were "goods and chattels." Not until slaves were "received and protected as men," Foster vowed, would he give "one drop of his blood for the support of the government." He thus offered a resolution that abolitionists should lend neither "support or countenance" to the war. The interventionists dominating the meeting, however, tabled it. One noted that, should Foster go "into any Southern State, and say a word in favor of the Constitution . . . he would receive the doom of a traitor to slavery." If a Unionist was considered an "Abolitionist in fifteen states"—those with slavery—then the Union war deserved Foster's support, he concluded dismissively.[34]

Such words confirmed purists' worst fears: that interventionists were already succumbing to the temptations of the political mainstream and surrendering their principles. Stephen Foster hence tore into the prowar coterie, bringing the two camps to open blows. Chief in his sights was Phillips, who had just endorsed compensated emancipation. Phillips, he declared, "seemed to have lost his confidence in the safety of impartial justice." Immediatists, he noted, should "never consent to pay the sinner to cease from his sin." Hewing to the rigors of moral purity, Foster affirmed that only means born of unadulterated justice could bring about moral ends. Half-measures girded in expediency and compromise like compensation were both useless and morally reprehensible—and their supporters were traitors. Soon, Foster proceeded to attack the prowar majority as a whole. In becoming "heart and soul in this war," he proclaimed, interventionists "had been seduced from their allegiance to principle." They had betrayed the cause, degrading their moral power, and their very identities, within the jingoistic frenzy. While the "honest friends of freedom" strove to keep the cause afloat, corrupted prowar abolitionists "stifled . . . [their] dissent," employing an old tactic of the proslavery forces—the gag rule—against the antiwar minority. Interventionists, he concluded, had become the enemy.[35]

Though she shared this hardline view of the war, Abby Kelley Foster followed her husband's fiery rhetoric with an olive branch, grasping for common ground with prowar colleagues that no longer existed. While there "appeared to be a confusion of tongues among the speakers," she began, there was "really more harmony than might be supposed." Interventionists still remained "on the platform of the old American Anti-Slavery Society" as aloof saints, she asserted, citing earlier statements from Garrison and Phillips that placed "more reliance upon the persistent diabolism of the South than upon the virtues of the North" for emancipation. Such words, she argued, proved that interventionists had "not much sympathy for those against whom Jefferson Davis is contending." They remained opposed to the government on principle, she claimed, their differences with moral purists a rhetorical illusion.[36]

Yet she could not bridge the deep-seated philosophical differences, and growing animosities, dividing the camps. While interventionists certainly distrusted Lincoln, they strove to perfect the Union war from within—a repudiation of the old come-outer values moral purists still espoused. They could credit Confederate intransigence for prolonging the conflict and giving them time to moralize the nation while still supporting the Union. Garrison made as much clear in rebuking the Fosters. "I cannot say that I do not sympathize with the government, as against Jefferson Davis," he proclaimed. Though he remained wary of projecting discord, he refused to tolerate accusations of betrayal. Garrison accordingly positioned interventionists as the commonsense center of abolitionism, defending the Union war against their impractical antiwar wing without losing sight of their higher principles. A Union that slaveholders "regarded with fierce malignity," he explained, was worth championing—and, by building a "great Northern sentiment" for expedient emancipation, perfecting. All the while, interventionists would keep their larger purposes in mind. Should the nation return to the "Constitution as of old," Garrison affirmed that he would "open all the guns that I can bring to bear upon it." But for now, he would continue supporting the Union war as a means to antislavery reform.[37]

While Garrison attempted to maintain some sense of decorum, other prowar abolitionists greeted their antagonists with personal insults. At the meeting, interventionist Samuel May Jr. noted that Stephen Foster had spoken three times that day. Because the audience "would not hear him four times," however, Foster "said he was gagged." As May concluded, Foster thus was a victim only in his own imagination. A week later, a *Liberator* correspondent mocked Foster again, arguing that he should "hold meetings of his own, and summon the tens of thousands" who shared his "peculiar views"—a sneering reference to the isolation of the few moral purists within the movement. The internecine feuding among abolitionists was going into full swing.[38]

The abolitionist civil war also expanded across the Atlantic, dragging Garrison into the fracas. While most American abolitionists embraced the Union war, the opposite proved true in Great Britain and Ireland—a situation that strained the decades-old networks linking transatlantic activists. Like Pillsbury and the Fosters, abolitionists throughout the British Isles could discern no moral promise in the Union cause. In May, Scottish minister Thomas Guthrie used his introduction of George Cheever at an antislavery meeting in Edinburgh as an opportunity to lambast the war. "There is no hope for the poor negro in this struggle," Guthrie declared. The South fought for slavery, while the North fought to extend its own territorial dominion. In their pursuit of empire at all costs, he averred, northerners "would cement their Union . . . with the tears of the negro." The Civil War, to Guthrie, seemed a pointless exercise bereft of greater meaning.[39]

In part, the pro-Confederate press influenced abolitionists across the British Isles. "When we read in the *Times* of . . . fugitive slaves being sent back by Northern men," Irish immediatist Richard Davis Webb queried Garrison, how "should [we] look upon this as an antislavery war?" Yet they were also taking the course of events at face value. Unlike Butler, most Union commanders returned fugitive slaves to their masters. Moreover, as Webb explained, neither the "government or the people" showed the slightest antislavery inclinations. Indeed, he heard "nothing except from abolitionists of this war . . . being likely to weaken slavery." Dismissing the "delicate distinctions" that interventionists made between the Union and Confederacy, Webb admitted that he had "no general interest" in the war. Rather than support the needless bloodshed, he aligned with American moral purists. He would hew still to the saintly abolitionist model of old and continue to oppose the "Union [as] one of the chief bulwarks of the slave system," at least until evidence demonstrated otherwise.[40]

Like American antiwar abolitionists, British moral purists could not understand why interventionists had abandoned such long-cherished practices. The "unqualified gratification" that prowar abolitionists showed toward the Union war shocked Webb, he admitted. "It looks odd that you should be so zealous for the Union," he told Samuel May Jr., "seeing that it is for the Union in its material sense." While Webb tried to chide his wayward American correspondents into changing course, others took a more pointed approach. Mirroring the Fosters, British purists began decrying interventionists as traitors. In a June letter to the *Liberator,* Irish reformer James Haughton accused interventionists of "surrender[ing] conviction to apparent expediency." Such treachery, he lamented, "weakens my hope that the principles enunciated by Jesus will yet rule in the hearts of civilized men." The *Herald of Peace,* a London antislavery organ, likewise lambasted interventionists for "plunging into the war spirit with a headlong violence which leaves almost all competitors behind." At a moment's notice, Garrison and allies had thrown away their decades-long "pacific moral agitation" in thrall to the "unchristian axiom that, in order to punish" one crime, "we are at liberty to justify another." The paper painted prowar abolitionists as misguided Machiavellians, chasing their ends through unjustifiable—and, ultimately, pointless—means that eroded their moral purposes as reformers.[41]

Interventionists could not suffer such transatlantic attacks on their integrity. At first, Garrison addressed his foreign critics in civil terms. Referencing Guthrie, he explained in a May editorial that his "transatlantic friends can see, at their distance, only the surface of things." While the Union war was superficially proslavery, American abolitionists on the ground perceived a "radical change in Northern feeling" toward the institution. With interventionists' help, he promised, the Union war would become a moral crusade. Garrison thus pleaded with his colleagues overseas to grasp the promise of the moment and cease their criticisms.[42]

As transatlantic critiques multiplied, Garrison discarded his evenhanded approach. Seizing on a wave of anti-British sentiment after Queen Victoria proclaimed her nation's neutrality, he employed the aggressive rhetoric of national chauvinism to rebut his foreign assailants throughout June and July, freed of the constraints of decorum that he strove still to preserve at home. In rebuking the *Herald of Peace,* Garrison sneered that the "American people cannot be guided by any transatlantic criticisms." The war "so involves everything sacred and precious to them, that they need no foreign opinions" on the subject. Turning to the paper's "unwarrantable and wholesale impeachment of the . . . antislavery consistency of American abolitionists," Garrison asserted that he had "inflexibly met every temptation to swerve a hair's breadth from the path of rectitude" for years. Prowar abolitionists "stand precisely where they have always stood": in the moral sun. Embracing the Union war was not a "repudiation of their principles," but rather a reaffirmation of the struggle for freedom. It was his opponents, wishing "for the sake of peace, to confound all moral distinctions," who endangered emancipation. The *Herald* staff, he declared, were doctrinaires out of touch with wartime reality, who would rather allow secessionists to "hold the country in abject thralldom" than acclimate to the evolving situation. In effect, they were the genuine traitors to the cause.[43]

Such outbursts took moral purists on both sides of the Atlantic aback. Garrison, an American purist wrote, "does not take up the article[s] like an honest man." The *Herald* offered its own rejoinder, deploring that Garrison had insulted them "just because we cannot run into the same excess of warlike riot" as himself. Garrison's articles, it maintained, had been "very angry, and, therefore, not very logical." What was clear, however, was that such articles demonstrated a "departure of principle on the part of those anti-slavery men, who, up to this time, disclaimed the use of any but moral means in their conflict with slavery." Garrison later responded in turn, decrying this "gross exaggeration and shameful caricature." Mocking the idea that interventionists would "stain our past career by compromising our principles, now," he stressed that a prowar strategy was the only method left to abolitionists for achieving a morally transformed Union. By the end of the summer, the transatlantic exchanges between these longtime allies thereby devolved into open hostility, as each side claimed the mantle of antislavery fidelity—and accused their opponents of forsaking it.[44]

In waging transatlantic war, Garrison championed those few British abolitionists who supported the Union, including the radical parliamentarians John Bright and Richard Cobden and the Garrisonian George Thompson. These abolitionists, as W. Caleb McDaniel has shown, championed American democracy as the catalyst for spreading liberty worldwide. As Bright explained, "[we] know what your great free Republic means on your continent—and also in Europe, and that the extension of freedom with you would do its extension here also." Accordingly, they stood against what Cobden termed the antidemocratic, "slave Confederacy" by refuting antiwar arguments. Over the summer, Bright asserted that the Union, rather than "those who wish to build up a great empire on the perpetual bondage of their fellow-men," deserved British sympathy. While Thompson admitted in a speech that the "abolition of slavery was not the declared object" of the Union war, the "prospects that the war would take an abolition turn [were] good." Thompson subsequently affirmed in a letter to Garrison that he and American interventionists shared "coincident" views of the Union war.[45]

While British abolitionist advocates for the Union were relatively few and far between, Garrison recognized their outsized symbolic value. They validated interventionists' decisions, confirming from abroad that the Union war and the antislavery fight for liberty worldwide were inextricably tied. Garrison hence hastened to publish Bright's and Thompson's words in the *Liberator*. In an editorial appended to Thompson's above letter, Garrison noted that he was "gratified to find that, while there seems to be a wide-spread misconception in England as to the real merits of the conflict now going on," his longtime friend Thompson remained as "clear-sighted as usual." Antiwar immediatists on both sides of the Atlantic, by implication, were not as discerning. Unlike such figures, Thompson understood that, "whatever paradoxical features are connected" with the Union cause, the Confederates would crush "popular liberty to dust." By praising Thompson, Garrison belittled moral purists as blind fools defying the logic of the times.[46]

In his response, Garrison did not acknowledge how strange his argument would have seemed months beforehand. He and Thompson had agitated from outside the political system for a generation, defying the Union—and Unionist mobs—to decry the debased language of political compromise. But as developments at Fort Monroe emboldened them, Garrison and other interventionists undertook a searing transformation. They reconfigured themselves into a political pressure group, promulgating change from within the Union war through ingenious arguments grounded in the rhetoric of expediency. They hammered out an inchoate antislavery alliance to begin publicizing their message. And, faced with increasingly harsh attacks from moral purists, they repositioned themselves as the prowar center of abolitionism, defending the Union—and themselves—against their movement's antiwar fringe. By mid-July, interventionists would have seemed scarcely recognizable to their former selves. To justify such an extreme overhaul, prowar immediatists anticipated the prospects of their success. As they would soon be reminded, however, they—and emancipation itself—remained at the mercy of military affairs.

CHAPTER THREE

The Impact of Bull Run, Late July–August 1861

In August, a large parcel arrived at Charles Sumner's doorstep. Its sender, Moncure Conway, had met the Radical Republican by chance months earlier. As Conway later recounted, Sumner had listened to and endorsed his interventionist arguments, entreating him to promote his ideas far and wide. Now, Conway enlisted Sumner to aid in such promotion. Enclosed in the package, Conway explained, was "The Rejected Stone," his manuscript about the "Nation's Emergency." He asked that Sumner "look it over and make amendations" in consultation with Phillips. Sumner did so, soon informing Phillips that he had "read all of Conway" and found it "far beyond my anticipation . . . [it is] among the best and noblest contributions which our cause has ever received." The senator subsequently submitted the manuscript to the publishing house Walker, Wise, and Company. Once the firm had published the tract, Sumner shepherded it even further by presenting it to Lincoln. Due to Sumner's "prompt attention to my little book," as an overjoyed Conway thanked the Bay State politician, his words would reach the White House.[1]

The eventually expansive collaboration between Conway, Phillips, and Sumner emerged from the ashes of Union defeat. The First Battle of Bull Run upended interventionists' calculus, pushing them simultaneously into two seemingly diametrical actions: excoriating Lincoln and deepening their political interventions. On the one hand, the July rout pushed their moral ambivalence to untenable heights. While interventionists had managed their internal contradictions by balancing private criticism of the president with public praise, they could not mask their fury over the loss. To assuage their qualms and head off antiwar critics, Garrison, Conway, Phillips, and Douglass briefly abandoned their restraint. From within interventionists' overall progovernment platform, they lambasted Lincoln for failing the Union, framing their critiques as strategic correctives to spur the administration in the right direction. On the other hand, Bull Run affirmed that military affairs would determine the fate of emancipation. Had the Union army triumphed and captured Richmond, the war would have concluded with slavery still intact, rendering abolitionists' efforts futile. While deploring the shocking number of Union casualties at Bull Run, interventionists recognized the debacle as a necessary tragedy that could chasten northerners into accepting their proffered solutions before it was too late—a moral quandary that especially tortured Child.[2]

As the potentially beneficial effects of Bull Run encouraged them, and the ticking wartime clock prodded them, interventionists redoubled their efforts. To disseminate their ideas, they considered turning to the closest mainstream politicians on the antislavery spectrum, Radical Republicans, spurring deep misgivings in the process. Prowar abolitionists had twisted themselves since April to achieve victory, repeatedly ratcheting up their intervention in response to military events—and ultimately stitching together a pan-abolitionist anti-slavery alliance. Yet at first, this coalition included only immediatists themselves. Uniting with Radical politicians pledged to the political dictates of their party had seemed one compromise too many.

To regenerate the nation, however, prowar abolitionists journeyed further down the path of intervention. In reaction to another military development, they now waded deeper into the political mainstream by incorporating Radical Republicans into their alliance—and heightened both their political transformations and inner turmoil. Conway, Cheever, Phillips, and other interventionists forged tentative networks of information and influence, relying on political partners like Sumner and James Ashley for news, patronage, and legitimacy. The two blocs began synchronizing their actions, as prowar abolitionists provided petitions and books like *The Rejected Stone* to their allies for circulation. Through such tracts, alongside their own newly emboldened speeches, Radical politicians lent themselves to interventionists' prowar strategy, introducing interventionist axioms into Congress and beyond.[3]

In the aftermath of Bull Run, interventionists also came to recognize that their struggle for the golden moment would be an incremental rather than an abrupt process. By the summer's end, they took heart in such developments as the First Confiscation Act as proof that their strategy was succeeding—that their sophisticated political techniques were accruing them unprecedented influence, hastening the onset of their millenarian crucible. Even as they pitched further into the mainstream mire, interventionists ended the summer full of hope.[4]

Such a spirit did not extend to moral purists. As the war's contours became clearer, the Fosters and Pillsbury began developing distinct perspectives regarding it. Stephen Foster warmed to the theoretical potential of the Union war. Abby Kelley Foster, meanwhile, held her ground as a hardliner by rejecting it categorically. And Pillsbury positioned himself between them. Yet all maintained an unwavering understanding of the true path to a morally transformed Union, meeting interventionists' intensifying political evolutions with proportionally alarmed resistance.

THE SOUND AND THE FURY OF INTERVENTIONISTS

After a green Union army seeking to capture Richmond and end the war almost as soon as it began collapsed at Bull Run on July 21, interventionists' doubts over their dramatic transformations spilled out into public view. Since April, their unease over entering the political mainstream had manifested in a rhetorical disconnect between publicly extolling and privately scorning Lincoln. But as the bloody rout raised their months-long suffering to a crescendo, they momentarily threw aside this dichotomy. Lincoln, they believed, had caused needless loss of life by spurning the war power and its promise of immediate victory. Prowar abolitionists also recognized the need to burnish their credentials as reformers, assuring both moral purists and themselves that they remained morally upright. Yet at the same time, they had to hold their newfound ground as the commonsense, reasonable center of abolitionism. Interventionists therefore struck a difficult balance by attacking Lincoln from within the war effort, portraying their words as constructive critiques for a languishing government.

Conway and Garrison, both enthusiastic supporters of the Union war, briefly turned to censure after the battle. Preaching in late July, Conway blamed Lincoln for Bull Run. No "drop of blood," he declared, "would be shed if the President proclaimed freedom for every slave." In a pamphlet, Garrison likewise thundered that "[for] all the blood and treasure that are expended, that emancipation would save, the government is responsible." The "loss of brave men" at Bull Run represented "divine chastisement" of Lincoln, who would "rather welcome disgraceful and ruinous defeats . . . than crush slavery." But even as

Conway and Garrison fell back on moralistic harangues, they employed ante-bellum tactics within a new, politicized framework. Their attacks were patriotic prods, pressuring Lincoln toward expedient emancipation. Through calculated criticism, they reasserted themselves as the moral consciences of the nation—prophets advocating its true interests at all costs, even as they continued backing the government.[5]

The loudest denunciations of Lincoln emanated from broad intervention-ists. At an abolitionist observance of the First of August, the anniversary of emancipation in the British West Indies, Phillips worried that the golden mo-ment was slipping out of reach. Every "moment of delay" regarding abolition, he argued, "renders more probable the interference of other nations." As the Confederacy persevered, and as the British and French grew more desperate for cotton, the odds of foreign intervention rose. Like Douglass, Phillips predicted that the Confederacy would soon "engage in a master-stroke of statesmanship" by "writing 'Emancipation' on her flag." This act would ensure European sup-port and force slaves, the "disappointed foes" of a Union that had procrasti-nated too long, into the rebels' ranks. The Confederates would thereby gain independence, dooming abolitionists' moral mission.[6]

Riddled with anxiety, Phillips now journeyed to new critical heights. While others might close their lips, he declared that month, "I shall not seal mine." He would "visit every man . . . with public rebuke, that fails on the great ques-tion of the hour." While Conway and Garrison limited their public critiques to policy, Phillips seemingly resurrected his antebellum attacks by unleashing a direct assault upon Lincoln. "How long it may be necessary to educate the President up to a level of efficient leadership, I do not know," he scathed. As Phillips averred, Lincoln seemed "no equal" to the task at hand, "either in cour-age, capacity, or statesmanship." The president, he feared, would never evolve regarding slavery, because he "was born in Kentucky, and no man gets over his birthplace." The hour of moral regeneration had arrived, but "not the man." By denigrating Lincoln as a bumbling buffoon, Phillips brandished his identity as an objective reformer, offering up tough truths that the nation needed to hear.[7]

Like Garrison, however, Phillips situated his absolutist harangues within a politicized context. While his attacks "may seem like disloyal criticism of the Administration," he stressed his patriotic motivations. The Union war, Phillips noted, was "your concern and mine as [much as] the Administration's. We are to be beggared, our neighbors are to be shot, our national honor is at stake." It lay "with the masses whether this war is to be made anything but the assertion of empire." Phillips thus distinguished his current condemnation of Lincoln from his antebellum assaults. Before the war he had assailed Republicans from the outside, moral high ground. Now, down in the mainstream, he deployed loyal criticism as a political instrument to pressure them into acting before it was too late. His critiques thereby signified his increasing political evolution.[8]

Douglass joined Phillips in lambasting Lincoln's shortcomings. In August, he observed that what he "feared would result from sudden success has come from defeat." Immediate victory, he explained, would have quashed any chance of emancipation. Yet the "Government defeated seems [just] as little disposed to carry the war to the abolition point." Lincoln, he lamented, appeared to be "resolved that no good shall come to the negro from this war." Douglass felt his "hope that the war would finally become an abolition war . . . dissipated." Only the "stern logic of events," rather than the administration, steadied his faith. The light that he had earlier wanted to radiate around the government, it seemed, had not traveled far enough.[9]

Douglass soon aired his disappointment in public. "Very little has been accomplished to justify [my] hopes and expectations," he declared in his newspaper. On the contrary, Lincoln "still seems very earnestly endeavoring to find out how *not* to put down and destroy" the Confederacy. It fought the rebels while protecting slavery—a policy that was a "mill-stone about the neck of our people." Lincoln, he concluded, had turned a potential war for progress into a "meaningless display of brute force." Douglass thus refused to repress his discontent any longer, even as he, too, stressed that his criticisms proceeded from within the Union war effort. His overriding point, he asserted in an editorial, was that the Union was "fighting rebels with only one hand." Through pointed critiques, he aimed to make the administration untie its other hand.[10]

Even as he labored from inside the prowar alliance, Douglass grew anxious over his own deepening political transformation. He had been undertaking anguishing changes to achieve concrete results. Yet the merits of such sacrifice now seemed debatable, especially given his isolation as a Black interventionist. The interventionist experiment was an overwhelmingly white endeavor. Most Black abolitionists supported the war from afar, remaining leery of both the most prominent interventionist, Garrison, and full-scale political intervention. Earlier in the year, in one of his last issues before selling the paper, Thomas Hamilton of the *Weekly Anglo-African* impugned Garrison's relatively thin moral vision. White interventionists, and especially narrow ones like Garrison, he noted, "directed their gaze so intently to the one phase of slavery, physical bondage," that they "lose sight of the fact" that the "removal of prejudice . . . [is of] equal, nay, paramount importance." Nominal freedom would be "comparatively worthless," Hamilton concluded, without post-emancipation rights. Garrison's crusade was thereby inadequate.[11]

Prowar abolitionists' political transformations also discomfited many Black leaders. In August, the physician-activist James McCune Smith told a white interventionist that he and the "Garrison party . . . [are] unequal to the exigency of the hour. After lives spent in signal devotion to the cause of the slave, you fairly abandon that cause in the hour of its trial." As Smith argued, intervention was tantamount to surrender. Rather than agitating from outside, interventionists "lent the sanction of your great name" to an administration "returning fugitive slaves." A "sort of Bull Run phrenzy [*sic*] seems to have seized on you, inasmuch as you flee from a half-won field," Smith averred. While he echoed moral purists' language, his was an antipoliticization stance, rather than an antiwar one. Smith advocated supporting and perfecting the Union war through moral agitation. By acting from afar, abolitionists could "cause the Administration . . . to move" without rushing recklessly into the mainstream, as interventionists had.[12]

The *Weekly Anglo-African,* which Thomas Hamilton's brother, Robert, relaunched in July following disputes with the buyer of the original paper, agreed. Under Robert Hamilton's leadership, the journal offered a forum for a variety of Black viewpoints, many echoing his prowar but antiintervention rhetoric. In August, minister James W. C. Pennington wrote the paper that the "duty of colored patriots [was] to go for the Union without slavery" while remaining detached from the war effort—and without endorsing the administration and its "present civil pro-slavery war." Hamilton concurred, editorializing the same month that the "nation will be saved in spite of its rulers," whose "efforts fall stillborn, for the simple reason that . . . it will not do right." The editor thus supported the war from the outside while avoiding a politicized intervention.[13]

Like Pennington and George T. Downing, Hamilton refrained from pressing for Black enlistment until the Union proved worthy of receiving Black soldiers. "Let no black hand lift a musket . . . unless it would be for immediate emancipation," he asserted in August. Doing otherwise would be "false to the white man," given that the "people can only be saved by doing away with the slave system." Proceeding from the "highest patriotism," Hamilton argued that African Americans should "go forth to battle, not to save the government as it was, but to uphold it as it ought to be." Until then, they had to remain aloof from the war. In adopting this cautious, antipoliticization stance, Hamilton contrasted himself with Douglass and his advocacy for immediate enlistment from inside the war effort.[14]

Douglass, for his part, refused to abandon his political push. In frustration with the stagnating course of events, however, he fell back from his original endorsement of enlistment. In August, he refused to back a proposed plan to arm Blacks in defense of the Union. Joining Downing, Hamilton, and Pennington, Douglass now declared he would support Black enlistment only when the Union gave "open recognition of the negro's manhood—his rights as such to have a country—to bear arms and to defend that country equally with others." The government, he lamented, offered nothing regarding emancipation, not to mention post-emancipation Black rights. He thus retreated for the time being from his outlier position regarding military service, even as he maintained his dedication to interventionists' political strategy.[15]

THE BENEFITS OF BULL RUN

In part, these interventionists continued their prowar advocacy after Bull Run because, though they expressed righteous indignation over the disastrous defeat, they also appreciated its value to their cause. The fiasco, they believed, increased the odds of the Union war becoming an abolitionist crusade. First of all, it eliminated any lingering chance of sectional reunion through proslavery compromise. "The die is cast," Conway declared. Any idea of "pacification by compromise [was] a pricked bubble now." Anti-Confederate anger would sustain the war, consigning the Union of old to the dustbin of history.[16]

Moreover, prowar abolitionists portrayed Bull Run as a salutary tragedy that could help precipitate military emancipation. The debacle, wrote Henry Cheever, was a divine act "for the purpose of convincing the nation" to accept emancipation "as a military necessity." The government, another activist elaborated, "cannot be led up to the duty of emancipation except through disaster." Bull Run was a teachable moment that would, as Edmund Quincy hoped, help sweep away "all nonsense" about waging a proslavery war. It would reaffirm abolitionists' arguments that victory was only attainable through harder, antislavery tactics.[17]

Anger aside, interventionists accordingly fixated on the silver linings of the rout. If Bull Run could "teach the Government this high wisdom" that war without emancipation was futile, Douglass argued, the "defeat, terrible as it is, will not have been entirely disastrous." As Douglass and his colleagues understood, one drubbing alone would not push the government into their arms. "It will take a few more defeats to whip the administration" into shape, Garrison's son Willie admitted. Over time, however, such setbacks would serve their purpose, eventually making Lincoln desperate enough to accept their drastic remedy.[18]

No matter how dire the military situation became, interventionists realized, Lincoln would move against slavery only with enough public and political backing. Here, too, Bull Run would prove useful by advancing support for expedient emancipation. The defeat, as Conway explained to his wife, would "prove the means of rousing this stupid country" to comprehend the "difficulty of the work it has to do." He would elaborate on this notion, albeit less acerbically, in *The Rejected Stone,* which featured an imagined conversation between Union generals and the populace. His generals blamed themselves for Bull Run, noting that the "malaria of slavery" had clouded their judgment. The people, however, responded that the blame was "much more their own." In Conway's idealized scenario, northerners came to understand that it was their duty to secure a war against "Slavery and Barbarism"—and to ensure that "whosoever shall put himself in the way of this purpose shall be swept off as by a flood." Bull Run would serve as a wakeup call, Conway hoped, spurring northerners to accept abolitionists' pleas for a more radical war.[19]

Interventionists hence found themselves in the strange position of both lamenting and welcoming the rout—a tortuous stance that spoke to the moral paradox inherent in their prowar endeavor. As the battle reminded them, military events shaped antislavery policy. A Union victory at Bull Run could have ended the war with slavery preserved. As Garrison had noted, they would have to hope for continued defeats to prolong the war. This predicament especially confounded Child, who became increasingly distressed about the war's human cost. The disaster, she informed a friend, made her "almost down sick. Night and day, I am thinking of those poor soldiers.... My heart bleeds for the mothers of those sons," including her own friends.[20]

Much to her own discomfiture, Child also recognized the necessity of such losses. "I have said all along that we needed defeats ... to teach us the lesson we needed," she acknowledged in the same letter. Echoing Conway, Child gloried over the avenues for abolitionist influence that the rout opened. The seeds of progress, she believed, were already taking root. "Only look at the sort of men who are now talking real fanatical abolitionism," she observed. People who were "pro-slavery demagogues" months ago—"men who were for killing Wendell Phillips"—now "curs[ed] the institution." And Bull Run let such seeds grow. A few more "salutary defeats," she confided, would only make "more extensive" the expanding national "Anti-Slavery Society." Child thus coped with her agony over the bloody war by taking heart in the antislavery future that such debacles could help ensure.[21]

EXPANDING THE ANTISLAVERY ALLIANCE

Emerging from Bull Run confident about its benefits yet chastened by contingency, prowar abolitionists again deepened their political intervention by extending their antislavery alliance beyond the abolitionist ranks. As with the first stages of their transformation, this was easier said than done. Even as they had dived into the mainstream earlier in the war, prowar abolitionists had sought to keep their heads above the current, refusing to intermingle with those they deemed beneath them. While most northerners rejected emancipation, George Cheever noted in May that a few bandwagon supporters were coming out of the woodwork, claiming that they were "always antislavery, but prudently so, waiting for the right time." Cheever labeled them opportunists—ersatz abolitionists "dumb in the cause of the enslaved" until it became "safe to speak." They had avoided the hardships endured by abolitionists for decades because they lacked the moral backbone of true reformers. By associating with such impure figures, interventionists risked drowning in the fray, abandoning their distinctiveness as reformers and disregarding their far-reaching agendas in favor of those of their more moderate partners.[22]

Alongside disdaining reaching beyond their own ranks, interventionists specifically distrusted their most logical allies: Radical Republicans. Sumner, John Andrew, and other Radical politicians were the nearest to immediatists on the antislavery spectrum, having long supported emancipation and an expansive form of Black inclusion. Yet they did so within the political constraints of their mainstream party. Unlike immediatist devotees of a morally transformed Union, Radical Republicans subsumed their moral convictions within the larger, less radical Republican project of a white, free-labor Union. Party politics made abolition expedient to them: it could create a southern power base against the Democracy. The quarrel between Phillips and Andrew the previous winter underscored the chasm separating the blocs.[23]

Tensions persisted into the war, grounded in festering personal resentments and, as James M. McPherson has illustrated, Radical Republicans' tamping down of antislavery rhetoric in deference to party demands over the spring. In June, Charles Frederick Winslow, a friend of Andrew, relayed rumors that the feud between the Massachusetts governor and Phillips had reignited. According to Winslow, Andrew had sought to move past their recent grievances ahead of Phillips's Music Hall speech in April, "encourag[ing] Phillips to utter what he chose." Phillips, however, had supposedly complained that the governor "grossly misled" him by endorsing the coming speech to his face and then suppressing it after the fact. As Winslow relayed, Phillips had fumed that only his heretofore "exalted sentiments of personal regard" for Andrew prevented his denouncing the governor "with as much severity as he had ever done to [Secretary of State] Seward." Phillips eventually did excoriate the governor to that effect. After he commissioned as an officer a federal marshal who had led a notorious antebellum fugitive slave capture, Phillips declared in August that Andrew had betrayed the "promise of his whole life." Amid such disagreements, an alliance between abolitionists and Radical politicians seemed far-fetched.[24]

As they faced pressing circumstances, however, interventionists once again contorted themselves. Just as they had earlier bridged their own differences, they now buried the hatchet with Radical Republicans, putting aside their lingering—and well-founded—fears over politicization to garner further influence. As both blocs recognized, war had brought their short-term goals, if not their long-term missions, into alignment. As Winslow recorded, Andrew had denied proscribing Phillips, noting that he had no reason to suppress a speech in which Phillips "chang[ed] his antiwar opinions" and endorsed the war. For now, the two blocs were on the same side. Interventionists also knew that they could not shift public opinion on their own. While they had embraced the unthreatening rhetoric of interest group politics, they knew that their decades-old public image as disunionist provocateurs was hard to shake. Radical Republicans could thereby prove valuable, lending their public faces and political prestige to the interventionist cause.[25]

As a result, several interventionists and Radical Republicans established tentative contacts even before Bull Run. Conway encountered Sumner and began an eventually fruitful correspondence. In May, Oliver Johnson asked the senator to distribute Phillips's Music Hall speech. By mid-July, Phillips requested that he condemn the return of fugitive slaves by the Union army, so that the "hope held out that this Government means freedom by this war" would not die. And around the same time, Henry Cheever asked Sumner to circulate his Congregationalist clerical petition to "implore Congress and the country for the governmental removal" of slavery through the war power, which he had also forwarded to Lincoln.[26]

Prowar abolitionists expanded on these connections after Bull Run, integrating Radical Republicans into their fledgling alliance. Such politicians proved willing partners, as the rout, and interventionists' innovative arguments, inspired them to resurrect their own antislavery rhetoric. Following the battle, Ohio congressman James Ashley wrote an abolitionist friend that he loathed "statesmen who with petty stratagems attempt to circumvent God, as Lydia Maria Child would say." Sumner told Phillips in August that the "defeat [has] done much for the slave." Phillips, he asserted, "read events as I do." Like the abolitionist, Sumner hoped for military emancipation, and was disappointed that Lincoln had not yet seen the light. The "government is not what it ought to be," he sighed. Rather than "openly denounce" the president, however, Sumner found it "better to try and lead" the administration toward abolition, endorsing Phillips and other interventionists' interest group strategy as the method of doing so.[27]

An enlarged antislavery alliance took shape over the late summer. These allied blocs pooled their resources and efforts into a common network, coordinating tactics and sharing intelligence. Though the dynamics of this partnership would later shift, interventionists initially depended on the sponsorship, publicity, and political authority and influence their allies provided to gain ground. Sumner, for example, offered inside political information to abolitionists. In August, he informed Phillips that Secretary of War Simon Cameron would issue an order "declaring every slave coming within our lines free." Such advance knowledge proved invaluable to interventionists as they grappled with the chaotic currents of wartime politics.[28]

Moreover, Radical Republicans funneled interventionist arguments into the halls of power. Sumner offered patronage to his abolitionist allies, providing their axioms with a far wider distribution than they could have attained alone. His budding relationship with Conway, by way of Phillips, illustrated how Radicals began circulating favors, money, and influence to aid interventionists. In early September, Conway inquired as to whether Sumner would help sponsor a lecturing tour through Ohio. The senator ran the request by Phillips, who spoke warmly in favor of the "grand plan." Sumner subsequently endorsed the tour as well, lending his name to the venture and covering its booking expenses. Conway thus leveraged Sumner's public power to give his arguments the light of day.[29]

Sumner also ushered Conway's book into print. *The Rejected Stone* was one among many abolitionist tracts written during the late summer, as interventionists churned out material for their allies to distribute. David Lee Child revised his *Liberator* articles on confiscation into a pamphlet, while Garrison released his tracts on the legality of abolition, the war power, and the evils of secession. Conway's work would prove the most influential of the bunch. Over the fall, Sumner took the manuscript under his wing. Walker, Wise, and Company, to whom he offered the project, informed him that they would publish it if "purged of a few needless ebullitions of bitterness." Sumner worked with Phillips to ensure its palatability. Conway deferred to the senator, declaring himself "willing to take out anything that you may deem advisable." By late 1861, the publishers printed the work under the byline of "A Native of Virginia," playing up Conway's southern roots—and playing down his role as a known abolitionist. In his book, comprising a series of dazzling if disparate, metaphor-laden essays, Conway framed an idealistic paean to a morally transformed Union in the commonsense language of expediency. He revealed his main argument in the prologue, expressing his "profound conviction" that military success depended "more upon the impregnability of principles than that of fortresses," and therefore "must be fought from a higher plane than any yet occupied by our forces ere it can be won." The following essays reiterated that the Union could achieve victory only through moral progress.[30]

Conway began by explaining the history of the old Union. Employing marine metaphors, Conway cast America as "fitted out in the order of God as the Life-Ship of Nations." The Founders had launched her, with a "continent for her deck," to save "voyagers that can struggle no longer"—to rescue the world from tyranny. Yet in the ensuing decades, the "true captain" of the national vessel had been "chained below, turned aside by mutineers" who flew the "black flag of the slaver." A once-proud nation thereby became the "hollow mask of slavery." A "Union-besotted" public, clinging to the Union as a material idol rather than as a moral ideal, had stood by as the mutineers steered the good ship America toward destruction. Secession, however, had abruptly altered the path of history. The wicked mutineers had abandoned ship.[31]

Switching to the language of masonry, Conway asserted in biblical overtones that the nation stood at a crossroads over the "stone which the builders rejected" in the Constitution: justice for the slaves. The Union, should it refuse abolition, would be "wrecked upon that stone." But should the nation-ship take up the rejected stone as its standard, it would prevail. By embracing emancipation, the nation would undergo a "second Revolution" and attain its providential destiny, showering the "rays of Freedom" upon a benighted globe. In concluding the section, Conway explained how disunionists could support the war. Unionism, he clarified, had formerly meant sustaining the "ulcer that was eating out the life of the real Union." Now, however, it meant laying the "foundation of a nation that shall be permanent, because founded on the rock of justice." Through an assemblage of mixed metaphors, Conway portrayed the nation's moralization as expedient: through it, the Union could triumph and ascend to greatness.[32]

Translating interventionist axioms into colorful imagery, Conway turned to the mechanism of moralization: the war power. Delving into Arthurian legend, Conway represented military emancipation as the sword Excalibur. Through "temporary obedience to military law and military necessity," he argued, Excal-ibur could "strike at the very root" of the war. Conway thus included a public letter to Lincoln pleading for "immediate and unconditional emancipation." The rebels, he noted from firsthand experience, would "destroy the Union, in the interest of Slavery. The Nation must destroy Slavery, in the interest of the Union." Abolition, he continued, was the "only path to a real success." Should the Union let slaves, its potential allies, continue "working most devotedly against us . . . we shall be defeated." Stressing a theme to which he would return throughout the war, Conway also maintained that emancipation would be an act of mercy for the South, removing the "evil spell" which kept his native region in perpetual torpor.[33]

Returning to the imagery of masonry, Conway then invoked the true source of progress: the Union populace. It was their providential calling to give the "Rejected Stone, whose name is Justice to Man . . . [to] the master-builder"—to make Lincoln lay that stone as the "Head of the Corner in the future fabric, the Republic of Man." With abolitionists' guidance, Conway asserted, the people could progress to the point that Lincoln could no longer resist the proemanci-pation chorus. As an impatient people thrust upon him the "torch of liberty," Lincoln would act to ensure his political survival. Slavery would end, and the nation would be saved. In vibrant yet practical terms, Conway laid bare inter-ventionists' righteous political strategy.[34]

Finally, Conway concluded the tract by outlining his imagined moral re-public, offering a resoundingly antiegalitarian socioeconomic vision. Like many immediatists, he cited the British West Indies as examples of successful post-emancipation societies. Yet while most abolitionists overlooked the racial inequities that persisted there, Conway celebrated them. Drawing upon his familiarity with slavery, he averred that the "one lesson that the Negro temperament easily learns . . . is obedience." Freed slaves would be "transformed into a controllable power and subject of the nation." As "far as their able-bodied workmen are concerned," Conway affirmed there was "plenty for them to do. Our broad lands north and south need their labor as much as ever." He delineated a racial caste system, relegating freed slaves into a permanent laboring underclass.[35]

Conway then pivoted to the subject of those former slaves unable to work. As for the "aged and the children," he noted, "Haiti sits at this moment waiting" for "every Negro who will go." By endorsing emigration in addition to Black agricultural labor, Conway sounded a resoundingly racist note—one that would become a constant refrain in his writing. The section added a sobering coda to a book that had deftly combined idealism and expediency to argue that right begat might. Conway, however, was not alone in this regard: the war would similarly tease out the restrictive, if less extreme, conceptions of post-emancipation Black rights of other narrow interventionists like Garrison. And Phillips, despite his sharply contrasting racial views, championed *The Rejected Stone,* recognizing its appeal to the racially conservative white North. In part because of its ending, the book would soon attain great success throughout the North.[36]

Over the late summer, the power dynamics of the expanded antislavery alliance thus became clear. Interventionists relied on their partners to exert influence on their behalf. Radical Republicans, in turn, gave their ideas public legitimacy. Politicians served as conduits for their axioms, whether by sponsoring interventionist tracts or by espousing interventionist rhetoric themselves. In August, Sumner wrote Phillips that he had "spoken to the President and a majority of the Cabinet on the new power to be the wheel" in the war effort: exigency, which would make the "extinction of slavery inevitable." Phillips, Sumner knew, would have made the same point.[37]

Likely influenced by *The Rejected Stone,* Sumner echoed abolitionist axioms point by point in a later speech to a Republican convention. Slavery, he noted, was the rebels' "be-all and end-all." Only the "overthrow of slavery will make an end of the war," securing perpetual "Peace and Union." And the mechanism for doing so, he elaborated, was the war power. Upon reading reports of the lecture, Conway vowed to "secure [it] a large circulation." Sumner, he recognized, was an effective surrogate, carrying interventionists' arguments further than they could at this point. Other abolitionist-allied Radical Republicans, including Congressmen Thaddeus Stevens and Owen Lovejoy, would also join Sumner in expounding such arguments before Congress. The expanding alliance, though fledging and informal, was already serving its purpose.[38]

THE PROGRESS OF THE LATE SUMMER

Events in the month following Bull Run offered interventionists further encouragement. In early August, their newly reenergized Radical partners in Congress passed the First Confiscation Act, authorizing the Union to seize slaves employed by the Confederate military. The act did not declare such slaves free, instead effectively nationalizing Benjamin Butler's contraband policy. By now, however, prowar abolitionists grasped that they could achieve their apocalyptic golden moment only through a slow and incremental struggle of gradual progress, rather than through one quick and painless fell swoop. They interpreted the legislation as an affirmation of their strategy, lobbying politicians like Sumner on its behalf and then celebrating its passage. The act, Garrison declared, was a "momentous stride" for abolitionism. An emancipation decree might even arrive "ere long," he predicted with growing sanguinity.[39]

That same month, Butler wrote Secretary Cameron to clarify the status of his contraband, declaring them "free . . . never to be reclaimed." In an ambiguous reply, Cameron upheld the sanctity of property rights, while noting that slaveholders' claims must be "subordinated [to] military exigencies." Going beyond Congress, Cameron authorized commanders to receive slaves fleeing from both loyal and disloyal masters, punting on the issue of compensation for loyal slaveholders. Immediatists rejoiced at this exchange. Garrison crowed that Cameron's letter "is almost tantamount to a proclamation of general emancipation." In his enthusiasm, however, Garrison overestimated the message's significance: most commanders ignored its convoluted provisions.[40]

As they lauded military decrees, prowar abolitionists warmed to the Union military as a potential engine of emancipation in practice. Later in the war, Phillips would identify soldiers as the linchpins of representative democracy. Other interventionists would also come to recognize soldiers as a key bloc of northerners susceptible to their influence. Throughout the fall, Lydia Maria Child would seek to provide pamphlets and antislavery songs to the troops in order to "educate them" into fighting for freedom. To the same end, Conway would try to distribute his own book to the troops. "We have only to let the cry run through the rank and file" to make them a "Holy Army of Crusaders," he informed Phillips.[41]

For now, interventionists largely embraced the military out of public relations practicality. With an eye to the white public, they portrayed the army, rather than escaping slaves, as the primary agent of emancipation. In the *Liberator,* David Lee Child proclaimed the "power of civilized and Christian warriors to unmake slaves." His argument that the Union military had the "right in war" to confiscate enemy property reinforced the idea that slaves themselves were inanimate objects. The Rochester Ladies' Anti-Slavery Society likewise hoped that the "spirit of the men who make our armies" would eradicate slavery across the land. Only a few Black activists, such as *Liberator* assistant William Cooper Nell, emphasized that fugitives had exhibited the "prowess and patriotism" to free themselves by fleeing to Union lines.[42]

As they gravitated to the military as a force for good, interventionists lavished attention upon Butler. Again, pragmatism was the motivating factor. Butler's letter, Phillips argued in August, was the "noblest document I have seen in the war"—and the most important, given its author. Coming from "you or me," he noted, such words "would have been called impracticable, fanatic." Emanating from a formerly proslavery "Democratic general," however, they "crystallize the sentiment of the North into one purpose." As Phillips knew, Butler resonated with the mainstream more than any immediatist, tarred with the brush of radicalism, could. To achieve abolition as soon as possible, he welcomed his old adversary as an ally of convenience.[43]

Interventionists also believed that Butler's evolution signaled a larger societal shift. That a man once devoid of "anti-slavery zeal" had taken up the "interests of the negro," the Black abolitionist *Christian Recorder* noted, indicated a "great revolution in public opinion." When the "times compel a Breckenridge Democrat to preach abolition," Willie Garrison added, "I think we need not despair of the Republic." For giddy interventionists, Butler's rapid wartime transformation further validated their political strategy, proving that their axioms were catching on. Butler, Charles Whipple elaborated, had seen that the "people are changing," and changed with them. He had aligned himself with a people moving from the old, "merely nominal union" toward one "priz[ing] freedom for all." As Whipple concluded, the "signs of the times, point to successful progress." Support for abolition, immediatists realized, was also permeating deeper into the mainstream. As one moderate Republican told an imme-diatist in August, "hitherto, I have been opposed to slave extension; hereafter, I shall be just as much of an abolitionist as I can be within the Constitution." Interventionists' spirits thus soared as the summer waned.[44]

THE DIFFERENTIATION OF MORAL PURITY

Antiwar abolitionists continued to reject the optimism of their prowar coun-terparts. Over time, however, the Fosters and Pillsbury each staked out their own idiosyncratic positions within their shared, moral purist worldview. Ste-phen Foster, for example, softened his antiwar stance. Early in the summer, he had rained fire on the Union war as irredeemably proslavery, joining his wife and Pillsbury as unyielding hardliners. But writing months later to Phillips, he tempered that position—and the bitterness he had previously displayed toward his friend. "Justice and national honor," he now explained, required the onset of "immediate emancipation as a war measure." Abolition, he declared, was the "only legitimate and effectual means of terminating" the conflict. In words that could have come from Phillips, Foster acknowledged that appeals to military necessity could foment progress—and that the war could produce emancipa-tion. By implication, it could someday become worthy of his support. Foster therefore emphasized the opportunity at hand. The "public ear is open to us as never before; its prejudices are fast dying out," he asserted. In contrast to his prior attacks, Foster now embraced interventionist positions on expediency, the war's promise, and public progress.[45]

Yet as Foster stressed, he still opposed intervention itself—and its adher-ents. He was open to supporting the Union war as it could be, not as it was. To realize its promise, Foster argued, abolitionists still had to remain detached from mainstream politics, evincing the "same policy . . . which characterized our movement in its early days." Phillips, he proposed, could be a "standard-bearer" to that effect, employing scorched-earth tactics to "compel a timid and reluctant Administration" to act in the name of both expediency and morality. After transforming the war into a moral crusade, abolitionists could transition from outside agitators into inside allies, having saved the nation without sacrificing their own personal integrity.[46]

Interventionists, however, had not followed any such plan consistent with the dictates of moral purity. Instead, Foster asserted, they had succumbed to the "petrifying influence of indolence." First, they had embraced an administration "more careful of the institution of slavery than of the lives of its loyal citizens." Then, they fashioned an alliance—a conservative mechanism that prevented them from making "our voices heard and our power felt." In a time when it fell upon them to "guide public sentiment" from on high, Foster sighed, interventionists chose to "sink away into utter obscurity"—to subsume themselves within the mainstream, wearing away their moral visions within the rushing cacophony. By forgoing their aloofness in the name of abolition, Foster reaffirmed, interventionists were destroying their ability to effect such change. He therefore begged them to stand back and let the war become deserving of their succor.[47]

Abby Kelley Foster, meanwhile, maintained her unbending stance toward the Union war. At an antislavery meeting, she averred that it could never receive her endorsement, dismantling one by one her husband's points regarding its potential. While Stephen praised popular progress, she labeled the nation "hopelessly lost, and its destruction sealed." Slaves, Foster noted, "may be freed, but only from a regard for our own safety." For the first time, she admitted that the war might, in fact, lead to emancipation. Yet expediency was a spurious source of progress. In a mere struggle for survival, she argued, "hate of the colored race will still continue, and the poison of this wickedness will destroy us." The clear-eyed Foster reaffirmed that northerners acting from necessity, rather than a commitment to justice, would not support post-emancipation Black rights in general, let alone the racial equality central to her moral vision. Even if abolition occurred, which she doubted, further changes would stall. She hence refused to believe that the war could ever become a noble enterprise. The golden moment, in her view, was nowhere near at hand.[48]

As interventionists accelerated their politicization, Abby Kelley Foster withdrew her earlier olive branch, reigniting her antebellum feud with Garrison over her fundraising activities. In August, Willie Garrison lamented that she "shunned" his father. The young Garrison mourned this "painful estrangement," implying that Foster's old grievances colored her opposition to the war. It "used to seem so grand that reformers could differ ... [while] retaining for each other affection," he signed. But Foster, he insinuated with gendered condescension, let emotion cloud her judgment. On that account, he concluded, the "pain of your and Father's separation was doubly poignant." Though Foster opposed the war on principle, she made clear in reply that she and Garrison "stand apart" on both policy and personal matters. Friendship, she argued, was impossible while the elder Garrison "continues [to place] on me the brand of criminality." Foster vowed to oppose him without quarter, seeking to save abolitionism from his misguided clutches while exonerating her own name.[49]

Pillsbury, meanwhile, triangulated between Stephen Foster's relative open-mindedness toward the war and Abby Kelley Foster's uncompromising fatalism. Like the former, Pillsbury came to believe that the Union war was not devoid of meaning. In an August public letter, he admitted that "one more compromise with Slavery, would to me be far worse" than the present war—a nod to the idea, decried by Abby Kelley Foster, of the Union war as a lesser evil. Pillsbury went further at an antislavery picnic by offering his hope that the conflict would beget "millennial peace, prosperity and honor to the whole of our vast country." The Union war, he argued, might eventually earn his endorsement. To that end, Pillsbury, like Stephen Foster, warmed to the idea of military necessity. He now declared that, "slavery being the cause of our present national calamity, a true statesmanship, a high patriotism" would demand its abolition. The "necessity for such a measure," Pillsbury resolved, was becoming "more apparent every hour." He thereby accepted expedient emancipation as a means to release the war's innate but untapped potential.[50]

Pillsbury, however, paired Stephen Fosters's openness toward expediency and the Union war with Abby Kelley Foster's doubts regarding public progress. Far from progressing, Pillsbury declared in August, northerners "had retrograded" over the summer, to the point that he found "no evidence . . . of hostility to slavery." Perfect ends, he reminded his audience, mandated perfect means. Expediency could complement appeals to justice, but it could not create a morally transformed Union by itself. Northerners had to act at least in part from moralistic motivations to eradicate slavery alongside its lingering effects. "Military necessity" alone, he told a friend, was "unable to save us from ourselves." Yet such pleas went unheeded. Abolitionists, he lamented, were never "so heartily hated as today." Over the fall, mobs attacked Pillsbury himself on a lecturing tour of Ohio. Northerners, he reported, were shirking their duty to "thunder in the ears of Lincoln" and uplift the war to a higher plane. Encountering this demoralized stupor, Pillsbury could only hope that "divine government" would save the nation.[51]

Even as he combined the respective optimism and pessimism of the two Fosters, Pillsbury shared their implacable opposition to both Lincoln and intervention. The government, he declared at the First of August celebration, had "no direction, no capability, and, what was far worse, no integrity." Lincoln had "no antislavery heart," to the point that he was the moral equivalent of Jefferson Davis. While providence might order events to ensure emancipation, Pillsbury was "far from expecting any sympathy, much less countenance, from the government" on that front. Like the Fosters, he sought to influence the Union war from the outside. Supporting Lincoln because of the war's hypothesized potential, Pillsbury proclaimed, would be akin to "fraternizing with Pilate" because Christ's crucifixion would redeem mankind. The "work of true abolitionists," he concluded, was still moral agitation, not political intervention.[52]

Pillsbury, moreover, continued the abolitionist civil war in public. At the First of August gathering, he dismissed Phillips's loyal critique of Lincoln as worthless. As an interventionist engaged in the horse races of the political mainstream, Pillsbury asserted, Phillips remained as complicit in upholding the president as any other prowar abolitionist. When "compromise came to be the order of the day again" as a result of that complicity, Pillsbury "wondered what Mr. Phillips' life would be worth." Intervention, he stressed, was dooming both the Union war and prowar abolitionists, endangering their principled reputations and their very lives. Appealing to antebellum ideals, Pillsbury declared that the "martyr age of the Abolitionists was [not] past." They had to remain aloof to foment a moral revolution. Reformers, he affirmed, should "consider ourselves rather the prophets of the anti-slavery millennium, than its heroes, to wear its laurels, or be the theme of its songs." They had to remain perched above the fray as the saints of old, rather than become warriors in the thick of battle, to achieve victory.[53]

Garrison, forced once again to justify his choices, took the lead in rebuking this attack. Even as he exchanged blows with British reformers, the *Liberator* editor continued to seek domestic decorum. In civil terms, he countered Pillsbury's "somber and depressing" position. Contrary to the equivalence that Pillsbury posited between Lincoln and Davis, Garrison illustrated the "broad difference" between them. Lincoln, he asserted, "would rather see slavery abolished than have it remain," while Davis "would rather see slavery established." Garrison then went further than most prowar abolitionists in publicly championing the standard of the possible—and in diverging from his harsh private opinion of the president as a necessary evil. As interventionists forged political partnerships, Garrison realized, their middling praise of the president might not suffice. Lincoln, he therefore argued, had not touched slavery only because "he was not yet convinced that he would be sustained by the popular feeling of the North, without which he could do nothing." By depicting Lincoln as a moral leader, more advanced in antislavery sentiment than his populace, Garrison bid for Republican support while warding off his antiwar wing.[54]

Civility aside, abolitionists ended the summer more divided than ever. As their anxiety over the golden moment overrode their moral agony, prowar abolitionists ramped up their political forays after Bull Run, expanding their antislavery alliance to include Radical Republicans. The progress of the late summer convinced them of the soundness of their strategy, as they veered further away from their old berths toward unfamiliar shores. They thereby exacerbated not only the fractures between warring abolitionists but also within themselves— the moral conflict at the heart of their mushrooming intervention. Yet even as they experienced further turmoil, interventionists deepened their access to power and advanced their cause, proving that purists had underestimated their ability to produce change through the mainstream. The war, as antiwar abolitionists now admitted at times, could lead to emancipation. In assailing interest group politics, however, purists also grasped that such compromises had consequences, such alliances limits, especially with respect to Black rights. The longer-term costs of this wrenching transformation, for interventionists and the nation, would reveal themselves only later.

CHAPTER FOUR

The Rise of the Emancipation League, September–December 1861

I n September, Lydia Maria Child wrote to a fellow reformer-poet, John Greenleaf Whittier, to elucidate the interventionist camp's evolving agenda. "The warmest of the Republicans, and the most unprejudiced of the abolitionists," she relayed, "are laying their heads together." After Bull Run, these unprejudiced abolitionists—the interventionists—had built an informal alliance with Radical Republicans. Faced with another watershed moment in the early fall, they would contort themselves once again—and suffer further moral anguish—to effect change. To that end, Child reported, interventionists were consulting with political allies to formalize their coalition—to create an organization to "influence popular opinion through the press." Whittier, she hoped, would aid them by penning articles on the war power for distribution to journals nationwide. But he would have to do so anonymously. Even as abolitionists transformed themselves from subversive agitators into political pressure lobbyists, Child understood that old prejudices died hard. Interventionists, she relayed, would have to act with "no more *publicity* than necessary," creating, setting the agenda for, and directing this organization from behind the curtain.[1]

The formal outgrowth of the antislavery alliance that would emerge, the Emancipation League, was the product of a new military crisis. Interventionists had ended the summer optimistic about their prospects of success. General John C. Frémont's emancipation edict in Missouri, issued in part thanks to their influence, further buoyed their spirits. But Lincoln's revocation of the act and removal of Frémont shattered their sense of ebullience. As after Bull Run, prowar abolitionists responded with outrage, mixing genuine anger with an awareness that Lincoln had provided ammunition to their antiwar fringe.

Now, however, they limited their public critiques in order to project moderation. Child, Phillips, and Garrison continued to hew publicly to the standard of the possible while privately lambasting Lincoln according to the standard of the ideal. Yet they could barely suppress their resurgent fears over the nation's fate—and over a prowar strategy that now seemed inadequate.

Perpetuating what was by now a well-worn pattern, prowar abolitionists again reacted to wartime developments by escalating their intervention, transforming their loose alliance into the cohesive Emancipation League. Garrison, George Cheever, and Phillips reinforced their advancing politicization by convening with Radical Republicans over the fall, working to unite prowar abolitionists and politicians in a public organization. The Boston-based League that emerged by November was a clearinghouse for expedient emancipation, coordinating a media campaign to influence public opinion through lectures, petitions, and articles for targeted markets. With public relations concerns in mind, prowar abolitionists led from behind. They authored the anonymous articles and, due to differences of opinion between Garrison and Conway, created rival petitions, while leaving it to their allies to espouse their axioms onstage and in Congress.[2]

At the same time, interventionists expanded their alliance. They reached another degree further away on the antislavery spectrum toward two groups: antislavery conservatives like Edward Everett and Daniel S. Dickinson, who had opposed immediatists' far-reaching demands—and immediatists—before the war, and antislavery businessmen like Edward Atkinson. While some in these interlinked groups refused to engage in open collaboration, Everett, Dickinson, and Atkinson joined the alliance. None were idealists, embracing military emancipation from political or business concerns while largely ignoring Black rights. To redeem the nation, however, interventionists accepted them into the fold, risking their moral visions by allying with figures whose racial views were nowhere near as inclusive as their own.

By the end of the year, this gambit began bearing fruit, as interventionist ideas—and interventionists themselves—steadily gained traction. Emancipation League affiliates sprung up across the Union. Sensing the shifting winds of public opinion, the Washington-based affiliate invited interventionists to headline its lecture series. As such success emboldened them, interventionists stepped out from backstage into the public eye, gaining increasing confidence in their burgeoning abilities to influence the centers of political power. Cheever and Garrison proceeded to sink themselves deeper into the mainstream, cleaving their public and private utterances—and aggravating their inner turmoil—as never before. They clung onto their original moral dedications to emancipation and some form of Black inclusion in private, even while increasingly appealing publicly to expediency and the standard of the possible. Phillips and Douglass resisted this trend to an extent by honing a radical idea of democratic citizenship. Yet they, too, ultimately bowed to exigency. As they welcomed new allies and embraced the spotlight, prowar abolitionists thus amplified their wrenching transformations from moral outsiders into interest group insiders.

REACTING TO AN UNCOOPERATIVE PRESIDENT

Interventionists entered the fall full of hope, convinced that the war's arc was bending toward justice. Their optimism peaked in late August, when John C. Frémont, Union commander of the Department of the West, sought to weaken secessionists in Missouri by confiscating the slaves of disloyal masters and declaring them free. That this military order echoed interventionist axioms about military necessity owed in part to Frémont's quartermaster, abolitionist Edward Morris Davis. As James M. McPherson has shown, Davis kept in touch with interventionists back home, delivering the scoop on the edict to the Garrisonian managing editor of the *New-York Daily Tribune,* Sydney Howard Gay. He also provided Garrison with an inside line. "Davis is expected home . . . and I hope to learn many particulars from him," Garrison wrote in October. Soon after, Garrison's son Wendell attended an abolitionist soiree where Davis held court, showing off "(most precious of all) the original draft" of Frémont's decree. In brandishing the document, Davis offered interventionists proof that officials were heeding their words.[3]

Naturally, prowar abolitionists were overjoyed. Frémont, crowed Douglass, followed the "highest dictates of justice" by attacking the "rebellion at its source." Child, who had long been loathe to engage in patriotic displays, declared that her uneasiness over "popular enthusiasm about the U.S. flag" had dissipated. "God [has] sent us the man" to bring the new millennium, she asserted. "We are at the pass of Thermopylae, and [Frémont] is our Leonidas." The edict, as Garrison argued, signaled not only the christening of a new antislavery champion but also the rapid progress of the cause, bringing within sight a morally transformed Union. Generals were now dispensing justice. Was the decree "not the beginning of the end, and is not the end near?" he mused.[4]

Yet Garrison's assessment proved overconfident. Though the Oakes school has portrayed Lincoln as a concerted emancipator early in the war, that astute tactician remained unwilling to move against slavery unless militarily necessary, and unless he had enough political leeway to act. While interventionists had made significant inroads, public support for military emancipation had not reached a level that could prompt the White House into action. The president, offended at Frémont's infringement upon his executive authority and intent on appeasing proslavery Border State Unionists, instead revoked the general's proclamation and removed him from command, continuing to prosecute a war without emancipation.[5]

As the president dashed their hopes, interventionists fell into despair. Lincoln had forestalled antislavery progress, reminding prowar abolitionists that military and political contingencies determined such a course—and that they had to achieve their aims before he subdued the rebellion with slavery preserved. He had also bolstered moral purists in their assaults on the Union war—and on their prowar counterparts. Lincoln, the British antiwar abolitionist Harriet Martineau crowed to Sumner, had substantiated her insistence "that the war is fully intended not to abolish [slavery]." Interventionists, she concluded, were in the wrong.[6]

Prowar abolitionists, both angered and under pressure, again rebuked Lincoln. Occasionally, they vented their outrage—and burnished their self-ascribed roles as the nation's conscience—in public. "Many blunders have been committed by the Government," Douglass excoriated in his paper, "but this is the biggest of them all." Frémont "loved his country better than negro slavery, and offered the latter as a sacrifice to save the former." Lincoln, by implication, was an unpatriotic, proslavery partisan. Even Garrison lashed out, noting in the *Liberator* that Lincoln was "guilty of a serious dereliction of duty." In relatively mild fashion, he depicted Lincoln as a neglectful leader, rather than Douglass's traitor. Garrison nevertheless feared the revocation would "depress the moral sentiment" that Frémont had inspired, stifling any momentum.[7]

Yet unlike after Bull Run, interventionists, fearful of alienating northerners and erasing their summertime gains, now curbed their public critiques. In adapting to meet this setback in a unified manner, they demonstrated how far they had come in political expertise since the spring. Child led the charge in this respect. "We ought to be very cautious about publicly censuring the government," she warned Whittier. Immediatists had to convey moderation during "this ticklish time." She thus vowed to muzzle her qualms. Her ambivalence over doing so, however—her need to manage the moral contradiction underlying her political intervention—manifested in private assaults upon Lincoln. "I will whisper in your *private* ear," she added, "that Lincoln . . . [has] a fool for a wife, and a knave for a counsellor." Together, the "secessionist" Mary Todd Lincoln and the "heartless" secretary of state, William Seward, rendered him a proslavery tool. As power corrupted him, Lincoln permitted such behavior. "No man could long act with any political organization and continue honest," Child concluded. "This imbecile, pro-slavery government does try me so," she confessed, "that it seems as if I *must* shoot somebody." Through such criticisms, Child vented her frustrations and held onto her principles amid increasingly difficult compromises, exposing an inner turmoil within interventionists that would only worsen.[8]

Other interventionists followed Child's lead. In contrast to his actions over the summer, Phillips refrained from public outbursts. But to Sumner he lamented that the revocation "destroy[ed] my last hope of anything from Lincoln." Garrison, too, revealed how much he had blunted his opinion of Lincoln in public. The president, he scathed privately, was "6 feet 4 inches high, [but] is only a dwarf in mind." Proslavery newspaper editors, he feared, conspired to control Lincoln, yet the president was too inept to quash the plot. As Garrison concluded, he had "neither pluck nor definite purpose." The editor hence masked from public view his personal conviction that Lincoln was the incompetent, unwitting puppet of proslavery forces.[9]

Privately, interventionists also panicked anew that their fight for the golden moment had stalled, rendering unlikely the eventual onset of an emancipatory war. "I bitterly fret oftentimes that our days as a nation are ended," with its inquest reading, "Died of Slavery," Henry Cheever admitted in October. Cheever later confessed that he could not understand why "we should be losing such precious opportunities of doing right." Every time there was "something to make us think the policy of freedom is to be inaugurated . . . we are put again all aback" by the president. With an intransigent Lincoln at its helm, Cheever worried that the nation was surrendering its only chance at salvation, both moral and material. Douglass, who was "bewildered by the . . . helpless imbecility" of the government, also despaired over the Union's fate. "Is there no hope?" he asked in a pessimistic foil to Garrison's earlier, optimistic query.[10]

Yet interventionists refused to abandon all hope. In a public call, Child argued that their prowar intervention had worked—to a point. Their alliance with Radical Republicans had achieved gradual progress, winning over circumspect northerners. It had been a "fire to warm the atmosphere of public opinion." Thanks to such efforts, she declared, the "moral thermometer can never again fall to the old freezing point" of demoralization. Northerners had become "full of generous enthusiasm," in need only of a leader—a "polar star"—to guide them to salvation. Such gains, however, paled in comparison to the remaining obstacle: Lincoln. The president, Child proclaimed, was a moral drag on a populace seeking guidance, spawning a "fog so dense that neither sun nor sunlight shall glimmer through it to guide the millions." Interventionists had yet to pierce that fog. To do so, she exhorted them to retool their strategy yet again and labor in "every way . . . consistent with our own conscientious convictions" to overcome Lincoln. To force change, Child and her fellow prowar abolitionists thereby resolved once more to dive even further into the mainstream muck—and bury even deeper their qualms.[11]

CREATING THE EMANCIPATION LEAGUE

Throughout the early fall, interventionists debated how best to recalibrate their strategy—what desperate measures they could employ to answer the equally desperate times. Henry Cheever proposed holding a national abolitionist convention to bring together prowar immediatists in a public show of strength. When Cheever pitched the idea to the AASS in September, however, Garrison dismissed it as inexpedient. Such a gathering, he speculated, would "excite popular prejudice at this crisis, and thus damage a movement for abolition under the war power." Like Child, Garrison believed that interventionists should "avoid conspicuity as radical abolitionists in convention assembled," yielding the spotlight for the time being.[12]

Garrison advocated an alternative method of achieving their shared "grand object" of expedient emancipation: working through the antislavery alliance. As he relayed, prowar abolitionists from across the movement, including himself, Phillips, and George Cheever, were huddling together in Boston with political allies like Francis Bird, a Boston power broker who led the Radical Republican clique known as the Bird Club. Through such consultations, they aimed to determine the "best method of influencing the powers that be." After a series of meetings, these abolitionists and politicians decided to solidify their ad hoc coalition into a formal organization. As interventionists envisioned, Radical Republicans would serve as the public faces of this group by chairing its meetings and lecture series, while they would function as its animating power behind the scenes. Through this tactical approach, prowar abolitionists could influence public opinion without inflaming it.[13]

Interventionists accordingly developed a centralized operation to sway public opinion, drawing on both innovative interest group techniques like media blitzes and time-honored tactics like petitions. As Garrison informed Henry Cheever, they planned a "wide use of the newspaper press" in a top-down effort to saturate mass media markets. Immediatist coordinators, including Child, industrialist George Luther Stearns, and Boston activist James Stone, would recruit authors to write "able articles, simultaneously," making uniform arguments about the war power. They would then distribute the articles "privately for insertion" in targeted newspapers, blanketing the Union with coverage of the interventionist axioms. By October, this media campaign was in full swing, as Stearns and Stone sent out form letters to "writers of known antislavery views" for articles on abolition as "a *necessity.*" Expediency would dictate both the content and bylines of the articles: like Child, Stearns and Stone asked that such articles be written "anonymously, so that the truths they present may have their due weights without prejudice." Writers like John Greenleaf Whittier assented, vowing to pepper the press.[14]

Interventionists also delegated to Garrison a more traditional approach: a petition. In crafting the memorial, Garrison drew on decades of precedent, adapting antebellum techniques to the demands of the times. He also stirred up resistance in the process, as a pan-abolitionist petition proved simpler in theory than in practice. Many interventionists wanted to address Congress instead of Lincoln, with whom they had become fed up. Douglass, for one, was tired of Lincoln's inability to implement a "straightforward policy." Yet abolitionists were also unsure of what congressional emancipation might entail. Robert Hamilton, of the *Weekly Anglo-African,* asked Garrison to jettison appeals to the war power, viewing it as an exclusively executive instrument. "Where is the war power now?" he scoffed. It was a "broken reed, dashed with one stroke of the President's pen." Garrison, Hamilton argued, needed to "forc[e] Congress to act" through other means.[15]

Along with such demands, Garrison grappled with the petition's substance. As he noted, a memorial with an "immense number of signatures ... will greatly aid and strengthen the government in the right direction." Lincoln could not easily ignore tens of thousands of voters. To garner such support, however, Garrison would have to dig deeper into the political well, appealing to the lowest common denominator of antislavery sentiment. As Stanley Harrold has demonstrated, immediatists had long designed broad-based petitions to secure maximum participation. In this wartime crisis, however, only memorials with such widespread appeal that "all but the inveterately pro-slavery [would] sign" would gain support. Moreover, only such petitions would provide political cover to allies in Congress, enabling them to champion the memorials as the will of the people—a fact that Garrison, who asked Sumner to track the number of signatures for petitions endorsing the war power that reached the Capitol, well appreciated.[16]

Garrison attempted to balance these fractious demands and political dictates in his petition, published in the *Liberator* in September. While he bowed to abolitionist frustrations by appealing to Congress over Lincoln, he disappointed Hamilton by championing the war power. Controversially, Garrison also championed compensated emancipation, echoing Phillips's earlier endorsement of such a measure. Compensation, his petition argued, would "facilitate an amicable adjustment of difficulties" and "bring the war to a speedy and beneficent termination." As he made clear to Henry Cheever, Garrison acceded to the formerly anathema concept to win over "loyal slaveholders" as signatories. To preserve his dignity as a reformer, Garrison clarified that he would offer such men the "pecuniary equivalent for their slaves as a conciliatory measure, without recognizing or implying the right of property in man," constructing a flimsy distinction between endorsing compensation and validating the concept of slave ownership. But such rationalizations aside, Garrison was crossing once-unthinkable tactical lines in deference to public relations.[17]

The Garrison petition, as a statement on behalf of the entire interventionist camp, provoked considerable dissent. Douglass adopted a strong—and, notably, singular—stance against compensation. As he made clear in his newspaper, "complete emancipation" was his unerring demand. Qualifications, such as compensation or gradualism, were "unnecessary, unjust, and wholly unwise," empowering the nation's enemies at the expense of its slave allies. For the sake of their newly collegial relations, however, Douglass refrained from attacking Garrison directly.[18]

Conway possessed no such qualms. He became intent on crafting his own petition, even consulting Sumner on the matter. In sending Phillips a draft in October, he also criticized Garrison's memorial, doubting whether its "form . . . is right." Conway agreed with much of that form: he, too, appealed to Congress in his own petition. Lincoln, as Conway told Phillips, "seems to be as obstinate as he is weak." He would not act "unless we send such thunderpeals down there as would change his chronic panic northward instead of southward," away from concerns over the Border States. Congress, Conway believed, could force Lincoln's attention toward emancipation. It could not, however, do so using the war power. Like Hamilton, Conway dismissed the measure as an executive action. He called instead for Congress to abolish the Fugitive Slave Act, thereby sending "every rebel to guard his own home" and effectively ending the war.[19]

Conway also attacked Garrison over compensation, though he, unlike Douglass, was not opposed to the concept in principle. As he informed Phillips, he was "perfectly willing" that the government "sanction such payment." Rather, his concerns were economic in nature. "When pay day comes," Conway predicted, "every scoundrel . . . will be loyal," bankrupting the government. He thus recommended instead that abolitionists continue to advocate emancipation as a military necessity. If Lincoln came to understand such a point, Conway argued, the "idea of payment thereafter would be as preposterous as for the bank repayment of the extraordinary taxes the rebellion costs." Even as he chastised compensation, Conway joined Garrison in veering further into the realm of expediency, portraying compensation as illogical rather than morally abhorrent.[20]

In response to this competing petition, most interventionists lined up behind Garrison, defending compensation—and illustrating the extent to which interest group politics had permeated their mindsets. In October, one Garrisonian labeled the *Liberator* memorial the "measure upon which to rally the people." Compensation, he declared, was a "good practical proposition—benevolent, not compromising." That same month, Phillips endorsed the "substance of Garrison's petition." In November, he reiterated his earlier call for compensation, regarding it "not only as just, but expedient, since a market would thus be secured to the manufacturers of the North." Though he attempted to apply a veneer of justice, Phillips presented compensation in substance as an act of free-labor profit—a notable departure for the moral ideologue. He and most interventionists nevertheless united behind the Garrison petition in the name of political utility, ingraining compensation into their wartime lexicon.[21]

As prowar abolitionists coalesced around the Garrison petition, their transformed coalition began to take definite shape. After further consultations, a hybrid abolitionist-politician executive committee, including Phillips, George Luther Stearns, James Stone, and Bird, formed in October to oversee the formalization of the antislavery alliance. By November, these efforts culminated in the creation of the Boston-based Emancipation League, featuring an interventionist-composed executive board as its controlling power but Massachusetts politicians like Sumner, Bird, and ex-governor George S. Boutwell as its public faces. Sumner offered a preview of the League's agenda later that month, when he spoke at Cooper Union about expedient emancipation. New York interventionists, such as George Cheever and Oliver Johnson, sat on the dais alongside Republicans in a rare display of the antislavery alliance in the open. Not all Radical Republicans, however, were comfortable with publicly associating with abolitionists. After a final round of consultations, Stone asked John Andrew to chair the League's inaugural meeting in December. Though he had enrolled in the League, Andrew demurred, fretting about a public backlash. Other Massachusetts Republicans like Bird and Boutwell nevertheless acceded to join such interventionists as Cheever and Phillips on the platform.[22]

At the inaugural meeting and beyond, interventionists sought to avoid any appearance of radicalism—and, at least early on, to avoid any appearances at all, putting Radical Republicans front and center. They selected Boutwell, an ex-Democratic governor turned Republican, to deliver the keynote address on "Emancipation: Its Justice, Expediency, and Necessity." The League constitution likewise blended utility and morality, presenting emancipation as a "measure of justice and a military necessity." The lecture series organized for the late fall, which showcased Republicans like Owen Lovejoy and Senator James Lane of Kansas, continued in the same vein, as did a series of forums offering "free discussion of the subject of Emancipation" to assuage public fears. Finally, the League subsumed the media blitz and petition drive, allowing interventionists to continue their work behind its politician front. They steered the League from backstage, accelerating in the process their wartime transition from loud agitation toward demure pressure politics.[23]

Within this codified alliance, interventionists publicly deferred to their Radical partners, including the members of the Joint Committee on the Conduct of the War. This congressional committee, which had been created to investigate the causes of Union military failure, quickly emerged as an antislavery wellspring. Its immediatist-allied Republican organizers and members, including Vice President Hannibal Hamlin, Indiana congressman George W. Julian, and Ohio senator Benjamin Wade, incorporated prowar abolitionist axioms about expedient emancipation into a formal congressional investigation, lending such arguments official sanction—and advancing interventionists' fight to control the levers of political power.[24]

At least at first, prowar abolitionists left the work of public speaking to these political allies. Interventionists recognized their own public notoriety, and the subsequent desires even of friendly Republicans like Andrew to keep their distance. In a December letter to Garrison, Oliver Johnson referred to the recent election of moderate Republican Richard Wallach as mayor of Washington, D.C. While campaigning, Wallach had explicitly denied possessing any abolitionist sympathies. Johnson surmised that the statement was "intended to secure the votes of some with whom" abolitionism is the "synonym of insurrection and fanaticism." Wallach "*is* a Republican, not an abolitionist," he shrugged. Johnson was willing to endure Republican disavowals, provided that those Republicans became cooperative allies once in positions of power.[25]

In private, however, interventionists sought control, striving to ensure that their political partners properly disseminated their axioms in public—an extraordinary display of their newfound political finesse. Phillips, for example, maintained a watchful eye over Sumner. After Sumner portrayed emancipation as the primary goal of the Union war in a fall speech, Phillips praised him for the "blow you've struck." Though the senator's advisors begged him to walk back the speech, Phillips exhorted Sumner to stay the course. "I don't ask you to trust me too much," he asserted, "but only consider what I urge." Through gentle reaffirmations, Phillips worked to keep his ally on message, lest the senator's political instincts lead him astray. Over the fall, prowar abolitionists like Phillips thereby established a coherent mechanism through which to spread their arguments—one that led them to avoid the overt appearance of political involvement while immersing themselves in interest group politics as never before.[26]

THE EXPANSION AND LIMITATIONS OF
THE EMANCIPATION LEAGUE

In constructing the League as a hub for expedient emancipation, prowar abolitionists also sought to extend their alliance beyond Radical Republicans. They began looking toward the right side of the antislavery spectrum, to antislavery conservatives—a wide-ranging group of moderate and conservative Republicans, War Democrats, and other political elites who had disliked slavery but opposed immediate emancipation and Black rights (and abolitionists) before the war. Once again chancing further compromise to accrue additional influence, interventionists uneasily embraced their former enemies. Phillips and the Massachusetts Whig Edward Everett, for example, had long been rival orators, vying to win over crowds across the North to their contrasting views. Everett was a vocal proponent of colonization, a concept antithetical to immediatism from its founding. He had also sought a proslavery reunion during the secession winter, condemning disunionists like Phillips as fanatical agitators.[27]

Everett, however, had since become a staunch defender of the war. His conservative Unionism now made him an attractive recruit to abolitionists—a means to broaden their mainstream appeal. In an astonishing, if excruciating, demonstration of how he was coming into his own as a political thinker, Phillips in October asked Edmund Quincy to recruit his longtime foe to advocate compensated emancipation. While he disdained Everett, whom he doubted had the "pluck" to take such a stand, Phillips again put aside his reservations about unholy alliances—and compensation—for the sake of utility. Everett's "endorsing emancipation as war policy would convert the neutrals," Phillips predicted, convincing skittish northerners to follow. Should he join the coalition, "all the fogies will come into it." Everett proved amenable to this overture, championing abolition as a military necessity. In an act once considered scarcely imaginable, he also publicly supported abolitionists by sitting onstage with Phillips at Daniel S. Dickinson's below-mentioned speech.[28]

Yet Everett's embrace of abolitionists and their agenda extended only so far. Antislavery conservatives were part and parcel of the mainstream, attuned to, and reflecting, a white North that still differentiated slavery from race. Even in accepting military emancipation as a wartime expediency, they glossed over or paid bare lip service to the unpalatable, less expedient issue of post-emancipation Black rights. Nonetheless, Phillips heaped praise upon Everett. Attending a Phillips speech in November, one immediatist noted how strange it was to hear him "applauding Everett." The exigencies of war were creating strange bedfellows within the antislavery alliance.[29]

Another target was Daniel S. Dickinson, an antiabolitionist doughface turned War Democrat from New York. To recruit him, immediatists turned to New York Republican John Jay. Jay, like Andrew, was leery of publicly banding with abolitionists despite their longstanding ties. But after interventionist Maria Weston Chapman asked Jay to help "move any conspicuous Whigs and Democrats" like Dickinson, he agreed to "do the work" behind the scenes. Such lobbying succeeded: in a December speech, Dickinson endorsed expedient emancipation. Repeating abolitionists' axioms, he demanded that the government "strike [the rebellion] hardest where it is weakest" by freeing its slaves "totally, absolutely, *immediately.*" As an overjoyed Garrison declared in the *Liberator*, "Dickinson has hitherto been a highly conservative Democratic politician . . . and, therefore, what he now so boldly declares is deserving of special consideration." Going beyond what Jay expected, moreover, Dickinson openly partnered with interventionists, bringing Phillips onstage alongside Everett in a remarkable display of the expanded alliance.[30]

Alongside conservative political elites, interventionists bit their tongues to recruit members of an interlinked bloc: antislavery business elites, such as the Boston textile magnate Edward Atkinson. Unlike Everett and Dickinson, Atkinson had cultivated antebellum ties with abolitionists by funding free-state forces during Bleeding Kansas. As Susan Schulten has shown, however, he and other such businessmen were not altruistic reformers but capitalist ideologues, advocating military emancipation to advance an economic vision of establishing profitable, free-labor cotton plantations across the South. "We claim emancipation for the white man," Atkinson explained in a wartime article. "It can only be secured by the freedom of the negro." George S. Boutwell endorsed this plan at the League's inaugural meeting, with Atkinson seated onstage.[31]

While abolitionists like Conway and, as seen below, George Cheever and Garrison also championed plantation wage labor, their new business allies hitched such visions to their personal economic interests. As the war continued, Atkinson and other antislavery businessmen would advocate a Union invasion of Texas as a thinly veiled form of cotton speculation, hoping to liberate shipments of cotton supposedly stranded on the banks of the Rio Grande. After several aborted attempts, they would embed New York trader John Austin Stevens Jr. on a late 1862 military expedition to Texas, with the "large amount of cotton in striking distance"—and the orders they had already placed with their envoy—foremost in their minds. Though this initiative would collapse, it illustrated the self-seeking motivations of abolitionists' new allies—figures who would deliberately serve as moderating influences on their immediatist partners during the war.[32]

While many New England business leaders joined the League at its inception, they faced criticism from the Boston Republican industrialist John Murray Forbes. Like Andrew and Jay, Forbes opposed slavery but was reluctant to mingle with "radicals and disorganizers" in public. To an extent, such caution was well-founded: the League, even as it attracted support through its relatively moderate program, also incurred a backlash in the local press. The *Boston Courier*, refusing to believe that abolitionists had abandoned their old doctrines, labeled the League a "scheme of Disunion." The *Boston Herald* likewise theorized that the "Abolition devils are at work to make Bedlam appear inviting." Even as they tried to mask their leading roles in the League, interventionists thus continued to receive blowback. Taking notice, the Republican state convention in Massachusetts rebuffed entreaties by Sumner to endorse military emancipation.[33]

This backlash colored the approach of New York political and business elites as well. Concurrent with organizing the Boston League, interventionists worked to create a sister coalition in Gotham. Chapman corresponded with "leading N.Y. merchants" about the venture, while Lewis Tappan held an organizational meeting for the affiliate, the Liberty and Union Committee. His proposed agenda echoed the League's, uniting abolitionists, Radical politicians, and antislavery conservatives and businessmen to endorse the war power. A wary Jay, however, asserted that Tappan's organization would "retard instead of hastening" abolition, its immediatist members alienating otherwise persuadable New Yorkers. A *New York Herald* editorial lambasting the meeting as a den of "Abolition heresy" buttressed his point. Jay subsequently stymied the Tappan affiliate, encouraging those who "have never been identified with the advocacy of abolition on moral ground" to rally for expedient emancipation on their own. Such rejections reinforced interventionists' commitment to caution—to attracting as many northerners as possible through noninflammatory rhetoric.[34]

THE INTERVENTIONISTS COME INTO THE OPEN

Such resistance aside, the League began to have a marked effect on public opinion in the weeks after its formation, as its respected surrogates offered succinct solutions to an endless war. Though they remained far from universally accepted, abolitionist ideas—and abolitionists—were attracting attention, much to their own surprise. Interventionists had designed the League so that they could remain as inconspicuous as possible. But by December they began to notice material signs of their growing influence. League affiliates popped up across the North, tying themselves to the Boston-based hub and its abolitionist engineers. That month, a colleague in Haverhill, Massachusetts, informed Garrison that the town was organizing its own auxiliary to advocate the "extinction of slavery" as a war measure, echoing the prudent tactics of the original League.[35]

Some affiliates espoused a conservative antislavery racial outlook, paying only brief and starchless lip service to post-emancipation Black rights. The Kansas Emancipation League proposed to deal with emancipation, rather than the "vexed question of 'What shall we do with the negro?'" As it declared in its mission statement, however, all Kansans, whether "colonizationist or anti-colonizationist," had to recognize that Blacks were in their midst and, "being here, cannot be removed." Given the practical obstacles to colonization, the logical alternative was to "elevate the class—to make them a useful element." The group studiously avoided moralistic language, even as it reluctantly alluded to Black inclusion—and as it successfully sought conspicuous cooperation with, and funding from, prowar abolitionists.[36]

By the end of the year, League affiliates also began seeking out interventionists as speakers. The group most illustrative of these changing political headwinds was the Washington Lecture Association, founded by antislavery clerk William Croffut. As Croffut later recalled, he had put out a call to the "young men in Washington" to organize an abolitionist lecture series. Among the respondents was the reformer and Treasury official—and septuagenarian—John Pierpont. When the antiabolitionist secretary of the Smithsonian, Joseph Henry, refused to host the series, Pierpont leaned on his political contacts, including Lovejoy and Hamlin, to browbeat Henry into submission. Henry eventually agreed, provided that a disclaimer that the Smithsonian "was in no way responsible for the sentiments avowed" be read before every lecture. In a sense, this political battle perpetuated the original power dynamics within the antislavery alliance: abolitionist supplicants had tapped into the influence of their politico partners. Perceiving the shifts in public opinion, however, Radical Republicans now flexed their political muscles to give interventionists a public forum. Soon enough, they themselves would become the supplicants.[37]

Their political allies having come to the rescue, Croffut and Pierpont sent out invitations for the Smithsonian series, which would take place early the next year. George Cheever received one such request, asking him to "poke up the sluggards of this slaveholding city." Conway, who had not received an invitation, nevertheless caught wind of the series. To Sumner, he stressed that he would love to "speak in the city from which I was exiled" for antislavery preaching before the war. After lobbying from the senator, who argued that Conway's triumphant return to Washington would be "poetic justice," Croffut complied. The speaking slate would end up running the antislavery spectrum, from abolitionists to conservatives, including Cheever, Conway, Douglass, Phillips, Republican George William Curtis, and Daniel S. Dickinson.[38]

This public opening to interventionists had its limits, however: the Washington Lecture Association deadlocked over whether to invite Garrison. Though some argued that he would be the ideal speaker, others maintained that a man who had burned the Constitution would "not be likely to strengthen the war for the Union." While, according to Croffut, Garrison sat in Boston "wondering why he did not hear from Washington," the Association decided against inviting him. Tarred as Garrison was with disunionism, they feared that he would pose a liability to their prowar message. Garrison took offense, especially since the organizers had invited his fellow erstwhile disunionist Phillips. "I am in the position of Benedick in the play," he sniffed, referring to the *Much Ado About Nothing* character who had foresworn love, believing that he would never become old enough to marry. "When I said I would not support the Constitution because it was a covenant with death and a league with hell, I had no idea that I should live to see death and hell secede from the Constitution," he explained. Beyond embittering Garrison, the affair underscored the fact that circumspection still ruled the day, to the point that the leading abolitionist proponent of expediency was himself deemed inexpedient.[39]

In Boston, the dynamics of the League also began shifting slowly toward abolitionist conspicuity. Its officers recruited Cheever, Conway, Douglass, and Phillips to deliver lectures in the new year, while also hiring Douglass and Conway as roving lecturing agents. Conway began speaking throughout the Northeast about emancipation as the "only true panacea for our national difficulties." Though the tour took a toll on his "nervous system and strength," Conway recognized its importance. He "found people everywhere with profound anxiety concerning the Republic," he told Sumner, and would continue his efforts until they were no longer required.[40]

Emboldened by the growing receptivity of many northerners to their axioms, interventionists stepped out into the spotlight in late 1861, ramping up their appeals to white self-interest and the standard of the possible—and exacerbating their internal contradictions. They understood that their agonizing evolution into sophisticated political actors was gaining them unprecedented influence. Their political partnerships, moreover, depended on their continued restraint, and on their toleration of their allies—a compounding cause of turmoil. In the public eye, interventionists had to cordon off their radical ideals from their public personas, further intensifying their productive, yet perilous, political transformations. "Unless we demonstrate our support in this war, we are lost," argued Garrisonian James Miller McKim. Though he loathed "mere expediency," he bowed nevertheless to its dictates by policing immediatist newspapers for impolitic sentiments. Any criticisms "at this juncture would be in effect evil," he warned.[41]

Chief among the newly confident, conspicuous interventionists was George Cheever. Over the fall, many northerners grew increasingly willing to listen to what the New York minister had to say—a fact his fellow abolitionists acknowledged. Garrison gaped at the "very large" audience assembled to hear an antislavery sermon from Cheever at his church, though, in a nod to antebellum factional tensions, he labeled Cheever's discussion of the antislavery Constitution "excessively tedious." Cheever's church was "crowded every Sunday with people eager" to hear him attack slavery, a less jaundiced abolitionist observed in November.[42]

Under the public gaze, Cheever painfully separated his private and public opinions. In private, he railed against the "suffocating gas of sophistry and expediency," maintaining his longstanding disdain for the concept. He likewise complained to Douglass that the "boasted love of freedom in this country is . . . only the pride of Anglo-Saxon superiority." To cultivate influence and sustain his political relationships, however, Cheever sang a divergent tune in public. In a November sermon, he detailed the "golden opportunity" awaiting the nation. Appealing to northern self-interest, he argued that abolition would save the Union and prove the "superiority of our republicanism." The concepts of "expediency, necessity, salvation, all . . . utter this one word—Emancipation," he asserted, invoking that hated concept.[43]

Lapsing further into expediency, Cheever allayed common concerns about the post-emancipation order. As his letter to Douglass revealed, he privately scorned racial antiegalitarianism. Publicly, however, he joined Conway and League allies in framing emancipation and Black rights in the harsh terms of white self-interest, envisioning freed slaves as powerless cogs in an economic caste system. While whites feared insurrections, Cheever argued that "no one proposes to release the slaves from" the "guardianship of law." Former slaves would work under an "orderly and benevolent government," rather than the "tyranny of the whip." The state would "organize a wise system of labor and law for them," keeping them working while paying them as "reasonable free agents." In free-labor terms, Cheever intimated that emancipation would allow northerners to replace southerners as the beneficiaries of cash-crop plantations. Though he rejected expediency in private, Cheever engirded himself in its armor in public.[44]

Garrison likewise exemplified interventionists' tortured disconnects between their private and public utterances. In his correspondence, the *Liberator* editor clung to his moral identity by disparaging Lincoln in even starker terms than he had done earlier that fall. Garrison took especial umbrage at the president's December message to Congress. Though the message included a few proposals to whet antislavery appetites, including recognizing the sovereignty of Haiti and Liberia and sanctioning state-initiated compensated emancipation, it offered no larger commitment to abolition. It also perpetuated the racially uninclusive idea of a free-labor Union, asking Congress to acquire foreign territory on which to colonize freed slaves. In outrage, Garrison wrote Sumner that Lincoln's message was "absurd and preposterous." To Oliver Johnson, he denigrated the president as a "man of very small caliber," who "has evidently not a drop of anti-slavery blood in his veins." Perhaps, Garrison speculated, the president was a willing collaborator with the proslavery press, rather than its spineless puppet.[45]

Garrison's uneasiness about suppressing his convictions, as well as his need to guard against his antiwar opponents, spurred a brief public outburst. In a December article he labeled the president "weak in his joints, and wholly disqualified to lead." Yet in general Garrison publicly lurched further toward expediency. At a meeting early the next year he again championed the standard of the possible. Abolitionists, he declared, should not "judge the present incumbent too harshly." While immediatists sought emancipation at all costs, he noted, "men in high office are not apt to be led by such lofty moral considerations." Interventionists, Garrison reiterated, had to assess politicians not by their own moralistic standard of the ideal but by what was achievable in the current climate. In an imagined conversation with Lincoln, Garrison judged the president acceptable in that regard. Lincoln, speaking through Garrison, explained that he favored abolition but wanted to be "assured of the Northern heart" before expending his political capital. In contrast to his private conclusion that Lincoln, though a weak-willed imbecile, was a necessary evil, Garrison continued publicly portraying him as a moral paragon—a leader morally ahead of the public, waiting for demoralized northerners to catch up before acting.[46]

Garrison went further that month in New York, where Johnson invited him to speak on "the War and Emancipation." In light of his earlier snub, Johnson explained, the lecture was a calculated effort to remake Garrison's image through a "careful speech for the New York press." It worked as intended, garnering Garrison widespread notice. Encouraged at his acceptance onto the stage—and equating his own vindication with the success of the larger movement—Garrison publicly downplayed cherished abolitionist tenets, from demanding justice for justice's sake to maintaining their moral distinctiveness. He began by portraying abolitionists as masculine, patriotic crusaders for white and Black liberty, working to prevent northern "manhood [from being] trampled in the dust" by despotic rebels. Deferring to the urgent moment, he addressed northern whites on their own self-interested terms rather than invoke his moral belief in racial righteousness.[47]

Garrison then blurred the lines between abolitionists and these other northerners. While immediatists had long valued their otherness as a badge of honor—a sign that they were saints, not carnal compromisers—he now publicly dismissed the concept. What, he asked, were such "paltry distinctions" between abolitionists and the rest of the North worth? The "South cares nothing for these distinctions," Garrison contended. "We are all heretics together." Though he admitted that Lincoln was not as radical as himself, Garrison minimized this contrast. "We are both so bad," he asserted to laughter, that "if we should go amicably together down South, we should never come back again." Paraphrasing Benjamin Franklin, Garrison concluded that he and Lincoln "should hang together." Through such rhetoric he tied himself to the president, loudly reaffirming himself as a prowar pragmatist in his wartime lecturing debut.[48]

After years spent largely skirting the topic, Garrison also echoed Conway and Cheever in introducing a relatively limited view of Black rights. Though Cheever publicly endorsed a racial caste system while privately deriding it, Garrison espoused the same perspective in public and private. He integrated expedient yet racially restrictive ideas into a vague, paternalistic plan that circumscribed freed slaves as menial wage laborers. "If [slaves'] labor was valuable" when extorted, Garrison asked in the *Liberator,* "will it be any less so when it is fairly compensated?" He sought merely to replace plantation slave labor with plantation free labor—a point he stressed by concluding that almost "nothing [was] wanted but emancipation." Blacks "are all needed where they are," he elaborated in private. Garrison thereby revealed his narrow vision of Black rights, fixated upon Blacks' labor potential over their political rights—a stark contrast with broad interventionists like Phillips and Douglass that would only widen over time.[49]

With qualifications, Phillips and Douglass also publicly embraced expediency further. In his own well-publicized lecture in New York in December, Phillips gestured to the political center. Rather than discuss Lincoln, he focused his attention on the northern populace. Like Garrison, Phillips moved to conflate immediatists and nonimmediatists, despite an initial protestation to the contrary. As he stressed, he "came onto this platform" of prowar Unionism "from sympathy with the negro," rather than from the "idolatrous regard for the Constitution" that motivated most northerners. With reluctance, however, he dismissed such distinctions as irrelevant. Everyone, Phillips declared, now stood "together on the same platform . . . our object to save the institutions which our fathers planted." Phillips spoke not "exclusively as an Abolitionist," but rather "as an American citizen" invested in saving the Union. By cloaking himself in the rhetoric of nationalism, he sought to persuade the loyal citizenry of his intentions.[50]

Unlike Cheever and Garrison, however, Phillips proceeded to draw a rhetorical line in the sand. Such defiance grew out of his own political transformation, which acted as a double-edged sword. Pressure politics had led him into publicly traversing once-unthinkable limits one by one, from endorsing compensation to playing down abolitionist distinctiveness. Yet it also inspired him to refine his conception of a morally transformed Union in an expansive direction. To manage his ambivalence over the compromises he was making, Phillips balanced interest group appeals with public declarations of his panoramic, evolving mission. The Union, he asserted, should be an "empire, the home of every race, every creed, every tongue, to whose citizens is committed . . . the grandest system of pure self-government." Even as he tried to win over northerners, Phillips pushed the envelope of public opinion by developing a nascent conception of a radical, truly democratic idea of citizenship. As he continued down the path of politicization, the push and pull raging within him between political restraint and moral righteousness would intensify.[51]

Douglass experienced a similar struggle. Speaking in early 1862, he invoked his preferred rhetorical mode, the harsh jeremiad, by mixing hope for war's potential with scorn for its shortcomings. "My purpose tonight is not to win applause," he began. "I have no high-sounding professions of patriotism to make." Rather, he sought to inform the nation that its crisis was divine retribution for its "defiance of the moral chemistry of the universe." Northerners, he thundered, had to abandon their "old Union, which has hobbled along" upon the "crutches of compromise," for a renewed nation founded on liberty and Black rights. Yet Douglass ended his exhortation against idolatry on a moderate note, declaring himself "for the war, for the Government, for the Union." After much qualification, he professed his own patriotism, tying a prowar bow onto his message of righteous fury.[52]

Addressing the League weeks later, Douglass further exposed his inner conflict. Like Phillips, he promulgated a soaring moral vision of egalitarian democracy, imagining a morally transformed Union in which Blacks received an equal opportunity. Douglass, too, put up an initial fight regarding abolitionist separateness, deploring that interventionists had "dropped their distinctive character." Doing so, he feared, "may have been more patriotic than wise." Yet Black abolitionists like Douglass could never truly merge with the mainstream. Moreover, he doubted whether such intermingling was productive: he confessed that he could not "rely very confidently" on political allies motivated by "national self-preservation" instead of empathy. The "little finger of him who denounced slavery from a high moral conviction . . . is more than the loins of him that merely denounces it for the peril into which it has brought the country," Douglass concluded, brandishing the jeremiad.[53]

Later in the speech, however, Douglass gave way to the demands of the moment. The differences between abolitionists and nonabolitionists aside, he admitted that the "result will be nearly the same to the slave, if from motives of necessity" or justice northerners ended slavery. Like Garrison and Phillips, Douglass weakened the reformer-citizen distinction, portraying himself not as a dissident abolitionist but, in "hopes, in aspirations, in responsibilities . . . an American citizen." As he concluded, "the circumstances of this eventful hour make the cause of the slaves and the cause of the country identical. They must fail or flourish together." Even while asserting his sweeping moral vision, Douglass joined Phillips in appealing to the political center, enrobing himself in the rhetoric of wartime nationalism.[54]

In the wake of the Frémont crisis, and with much agony, prowar abolitionists heightened their transition into pressure politics. To reinvigorate antislavery progress, they built the Emancipation League and recruited political and business elites into the fold. While they initially aimed to lead from behind, circumstances soon conspired to push them into the open. The interventionist strategy had begun yielding positive results, its ideas percolating into the public sphere and inspiring a growing demand for abolitionists themselves. Emboldened immediatists obliged, further embracing utilitarian means to achieve their high-minded aims.

By the end of 1861, Child, Conway, Cheever, Garrison, Phillips, and Douglass had endorsed once-taboo concepts like compensated emancipation and abolitionist indistinctiveness to appeal to white northerners. Such changes previewed those of the coming months. Soon, interventionists would become celebrities to whom politicians urgently appealed for aid. Taking advantage of their growing sway, they would transform themselves even further into practitioners of interest group politics. Over time, prowar immediatists were gaining the real power and influence to bring about emancipation. Yet as they steeped themselves in unsavory alliances and expedient rhetoric, many would lose sight of the post-emancipation components of their original agenda, stifling the fight for lasting equality—the tragedy of wartime abolitionism.

CHAPTER FIVE

On to Washington, January–March 1862

In March 1862, Charles Sumner received an angry missive from Walker, Wise, and Company. This small publishing house had printed Moncure Conway's *Rejected Stone* the previous fall at Sumner's urging, albeit with Conway's own name omitted—an attempt to mitigate the expected fallout from associating with an abolitionist. Contrary to their expectations, however, the book had achieved acclaim. Now flush with success, Conway had subsequently contracted with publishing giant Ticknor and Fields for a new book. In outrage, Walker, Wise, and Company complained that their rival "wouldn't have touched *The Rejected Stone* with a ten-foot pole at the time we were willing to risk it. But now that public opinion has so advanced as to make the venture reputable and safe, they seek it." Conway, they implied, had been catapulted from obscurity into becoming a household name, his works becoming profitable commodities as northern public opinion turned toward emancipation. Though Ticknor and Fields would print his new tome, Conway offered his aggrieved old firm a consolation prize: a second edition of *The Rejected Stone,* with his name now prominently featured.[1]

As this bidding war over Conway demonstrated, northern public opinion was rapidly evolving. Prowar abolitionists had amplified their political intervention over the first year of the war while still avoiding public scrutiny, laboring for their golden moment from behind the scenes. Yet as the carnage of war radicalized growing numbers of northerners, their arguments gained increasing currency. As distributed at first by their political surrogates, interventionists' arguments promoting military emancipation gave force to northern demands for retribution against the rebels. By late 1861, interventionists themselves had garnered a measure of acceptance.

In early 1862, these prowar abolitionists plunged deeper into the mainstream as full-fledged celebrities, welcomed into the public eye as vindicated prophets. Much to their own disbelief, luminaries like Garrison and Douglass now attracted attentive crowds who were drawn to their increasing roles as polished political actors promulgating sensible ideas. Young reformers like Conway and Anna Dickinson rocketed into rising stardom, at times surpassing the old guard in fame. At the same time, the equilibrium of power within the antislavery alliance shifted: whereas abolitionists had formerly beseeched political allies to popularize their ideas or patronize their books, their partners now did the beseeching. Congressmen like George W. Julian and James Ashley grasped that interventionists had become electoral assets, whom they could employ for their own benefit. These legislators began begging prowar abolitionists like Garrison, Child, and Cheever to edit and publicize their speeches, as well as to make appearances on their behalf.[2]

Cheever, Conway, and Phillips took advantage of this reversed power dynamic by journeying to Washington and entering the halls of power, proceeding to lecture at the Smithsonian, address Congress, and lobby Lincoln. By expounding on the war power to legislators and Lincoln, these interventionists swayed the national debate over military emancipation, thereby helping make such an initiative increasingly possible. But as they intensified their political transformations and took their turns in the limelight, Conway and Phillips especially upset the internal balances they had struck between their principles and their interventions. They thrust aside their moral ambivalence, lauding Lincoln both publicly and privately. Ann Phillips reproached her husband in response, fearing the allures of unbridled politicization. She worried that her husband and his fellow activists who were bogged down in the mire, bereft of their moral compasses and surrounded by allies maneuvering to manipulate them, would lose sight of their deepest commitments and attenuate their moral missions.

Nevertheless, interventionists strove to build on their success by once again expanding their political alliances. Formerly reticent New York antislavery conservatives and businessmen like George Bancroft and John Austin Stevens Jr. now hastened to partner with immediatists in organizing a proemancipation rally. Soon, interventionists reached out a degree even further on the antislavery spectrum to the emancipationists: a self-defined antislavery but anti-Black bloc. While abolitionists sought post-emancipation Black rights, and political

and business elites like Stevens glossed over them, emancipationists loudly disavowed them. Interventionists wrung their hands over this arch-conservative
bloc, a product of their own appeals to the lowest common denominator of antislavery sentiment. Yet they ultimately inducted this group into their coalition,
once again compromising, and heightening their internal moral contradictions,
to redeem the Union.[3]

The moral purists Stephen Foster and Pillsbury, meanwhile, began to retreat
toward Abby Kelley Foster's unyielding stance regarding the Union war as they
lost faith in the conflict's theoretical potential. All three purists also maintained
their roles as the oppositional yardsticks of wartime abolitionism, desperately
striving to curtail their prowar counterparts' deepening politicization. Throughout early 1862, they and their British supporters continued to decry prowar
abolitionists as unmitigated traitors to the cause. Interventionists returned
unsparing fire in response, as the abolitionist civil war roared on without an
end in sight.

INTERVENTIONISTS AS CELEBRITIES

As 1862 dawned, interventionists celebrated the growing popularity of military emancipation—and the fact that the public was coming to perceive the
interventionists more favorably. Of course, many northerners remained wary
of both. The vast majority fixated on achieving victory and reunion at all costs.
The northern public's deep-seated distrust of abolitionists as fanatics also died
hard. Such sentiments as those of one Union officer, who rejoiced in March that
there was not "one abolitionist in one thousand within the ranks," remained
far from uncommon.[4]

Yet in meeting prowar northerners on their own more conservative terms,
interventionists had helped reduce such hostility. Over the preceding months,
many of their arguments had caught on with a populace that was both tired of
war and desirous of vengeance against the Confederates. As they entered the
glow of the spotlight in early 1862, prowar abolitionists gloried in this evolution. "We see everywhere signs of a very remarkable change in the public
mind" toward slavery, noted Samuel May Jr. While northerners were "not yet
all converted," Phillips agreed, most seemed "ready to hear" interventionists'
axioms about the war power. As purists had warned, whites motivated only
by necessity were not nearly as interested in hearing the rest of immediatists'

agenda—in making emancipation the launching pad of an unstoppable moral revolution. Interventionists' desires for justice and post-emancipation Black rights fell on the deaf ears of a people increasingly prepared to move against slavery but not racial inequality.[5]

For now, interventionists focused instead on the palpable progress their pressure tactics had cultivated. As their more expedient ideas achieved purchase, and as they consciously toned down their formerly fiery public images, prowar abolitionists experienced an unexpected taste of celebrity. A shocked Phillips reflected on the opportunities now coming his way as he stepped out from behind his political surrogates. Venues "which could not formerly endure an abolitionist on any topic, now invite them" to discuss emancipation, he declared. A year ago, Garrison observed, "our anniversary was furiously assailed by the howling mob." Now, as he averred in astonishment, it instead featured a public "eager and ready to applaud."[6]

Garrison himself became sought after as a speaker, his omission from the Washington lecture series notwithstanding. In a February letter, Susan B. Anthony revealed how public opinion was migrating in his and interventionists' favor. Garrison, she noted, had traveled to Albany to address an antislavery convention. While there, locals invited him to address the congregation of the antiabolitionist minister Amory Mayo—a decision Mayo opposed by condemning "impractical visionaries" like Garrison. Yet Garrison's ensuing speech to a packed congregation, Anthony recounted, was a "glorious triumph." Mayo "may say what he can about one-deed reformers," she concluded, but "his people have seen the very chief, heard his own words.... *They know now.*" As Anthony relayed, once listeners lapped up Garrison's consciously practical ideas and witnessed that he was no longer a firebrand but a purveyor of pragmatism, they became proponents of expedient emancipation. Garrison was utilizing his notoriety to accomplish the work of political pressure on the ground, thereby winning citizens over one by one.[7]

Douglass, too, lectured to packed halls across the Northeast, advancing interventionists' prowar strategy as he continued to mix appeals to moderation with soaring paeans to equality. Over the past year, he expounded in Philadelphia in January, "everybody has changed—the North has changed— Republicans have changed." Ribbing his factional rivals turned wartime comrades, Douglass added that "even the Garrisonians" had transitioned from burning the Constitution to defending it. Such changes assured him that "slavery will be a conquered power." Speaking to the Emancipation League the following month, Douglass reaffirmed its purpose. By helping create a nation "guided by the principles which the Abolitionists know best to teach," he noted, the antislavery alliance was carrying out immediatists' providential duty.[8]

Yet Garrison's and Douglass's wattages paled to those of Conway and Anna Dickinson, whose unique backgrounds and youthful rhetorical prowess increasingly rendered them objects of fascination. Conway, the dissident southerner, became a fashionable personality—and his *Rejected Stone,* which Child labeled the "most powerful utterance the crisis has called forth," a hot commodity. Writing home between lectures in New York in January, Conway noted that "*Rejected Stones* are sold out here as fast as they come. It has made a deep mark." The AASS soon began distributing the tract, latching onto Conway's shooting star to amplify their efforts.[9]

Dickinson, the teenage daughter of Philadelphia abolitionists, rivaled Conway in newfound fame. Over the fall, she had gained local attention as a gifted orator for abolition and women's rights. Garrison, having heard her speak, had offered to support her lecturing career. In March, Dickinson sought to "trespass on that kindness" by requesting to address the Emancipation League in Boston and the AASS's annual meeting in New York. Oliver Johnson, Garrison's close ally, reacted with disdain. "We ought to bring into battle now," he asserted, "our proved guns and our heaviest"—leading abolitionists and allied politicians—rather than an "inexperienced, spasmodic" teenager. "There's no need of a woman now as a test, and I would not put one on who is not the peer of our best speakers," he concluded. In gentler but equally condescending terms, Garrison dissuaded Dickinson from addressing such events "under the great disadvantage of not being publicly known." Instead, he secured her a speaking slot at a less prominent venue in Boston alongside a tour across New England. This schedule, he noted, would offer an "excellent means of development," training her to lecture one day on the national stage.[10]

Dickinson, however, soon stole the spotlight, overtaking Garrison himself as a celebrity. After she was forced to postpone her Boston speech to make way for lectures by Conway and Phillips, she began her spring barnstorming tour. Across New England, she drew plaudits for packaging interventionist axioms in exuberant speeches laced with sarcastic wit—youthful bursts of fresh air that cut through the wartime doldrums. Despite disclaiming her politics, one Democrat praised Dickinson as a "new champion in petticoats of an antislavery war." The "sending forth of this modern Joan of Arc against slavery," the writer noted, was a "stroke of policy" by abolitionists. Recognizing her talent,

Phillips asked Dickinson to speak in his stead in Boston. Her speech proved a triumph, with Phillips confessing he had never been "so deeply moved." Garrison, meanwhile, took credit for her success, informing Dickinson that he had been "overturn[ed] with thanks for finding [her]." Now grasping the value of her prominence, he awarded her top billing as a speaker at the AASS anniversary alongside Cheever, Phillips, and himself. As Dickinson's meteoric ascent reinforced, abolitionists' popular image was rapidly improving.[11]

A REVERSAL OF POWER DYNAMICS

As their fame increased, prowar abolitionists began eclipsing their political partners. To this point, interventionists had relied on their allies to legitimize their ideas. Politicians, as public figures, had been the dominant partners in the antislavery alliance—patrons on whom abolitionists relied to sponsor their writings and distribute their doctrines. Now, in a humbling reversal, these politicians ceded center stage to interventionists and their rising prestige. Rather than avoid associating with prowar abolitionists, politicians began seeking out interventionists' stamps of approval to advance their legislative agendas and bolster their electoral fortunes.

This shifting relationship manifested itself throughout early 1862. Whereas Conway had entreated Sumner to usher *The Rejected Stone* into print, Radical Republicans now implored prowar abolitionists to sponsor their own antislavery speeches. Senator James Harlan of Iowa asked Cheever to examine a recent oration and "advise me if in your judgment it would be worth" circulating. Harlan thereby deferred to Cheever to lend his expertise and determine the best course forward. Politicians also asked interventionists to publicize their speeches in immediatist journals—once-shunned publications turned coveted forums for cultivating public opinion. Interventionists' endorsements, they recognized, now provided them political capital, lending their words popularity and legitimacy. Leading this growing chorus for abolitionist support was George W. Julian. After the Radical parroted abolitionists' axioms in a January congressional speech, he entreated Cheever, Child, Garrison, and Oliver Johnson to publish his oration. As Julian informed Cheever, he was "anxious to give it the widest circulation possible." He accordingly asked interventionists to "bring any influence to bear in my favor" in their journals.[12]

Interventionists agreed, validating Julian's role in the antislavery struggle.

Child affirmed that the speech would "help on the good work," vowing to "extend [its] circulation." Cheever requested copies to distribute, while Garrison penned an editorial endorsing Julian as a valued ally. Only Johnson dallied, hesitating to publish the speech in the *National Anti-Slavery Standard*. "I have printed lately so many speeches," he lamented, that Julian's might not make the cut. Though he eventually printed it, his demurral illustrated interventionists' ascendant confidence in their power, to the point that they dictated the terms of their coordination with Radical Republicans. Garrison soon rewarded Julian with a speaking role at the AASS annual meeting, lending him additional luster through conspicuous association with the interventionists.[13]

Republican officials also recruited interventionists to fortify beleaguered legislators across the North. In mid-January, Republican state legislators in Pennsylvania petitioned Cheever to provide them a "thorough understanding in the public mind of the course and cure of our national difficulties." Appreciating Cheever's "wisdom and patriotism," they invited him to lecture in Harrisburg. In an adjoining letter, legislature clerk Gordon Berry elucidated the request's political dimensions. The signees, Berry explained, faced pressure from Democratic "doughfaces" in the state. "A speech from your world," he hoped, would "save some weak but well-meaning men from disgracing" themselves, shoring up their electoral positions—and steeling their antislavery resolve. "I am very anxious to have you come here, let our people see a real antislavery man," Berry concluded. In contrast to many politicos' hands-off approach over the fall, Republicans now bade immediatists into the halls of power as welcome assets.[14]

Of course, abolitionists remained controversial speaking choices. After Cheever accepted the offer, word of his invitation caused an uproar. In late January, Berry informed Cheever that Peace Democrats, or Copperheads, had "scared many" of the petitioners to remove their names. Even so, these legislators confided to Berry that "they want to hear you [Cheever] and think you will do good." Cheever, they knew, remained politically useful in spite of the controversy—or, perhaps, even more because of it, since it would bolster his notoriety. Through their retrospective circumspection, they sought to accrue the political benefits of Cheever's visit while avoiding further blowback. Berry thus pleaded with Cheever to counter the "darkness reign[ing]" over Pennsylvania. Cheever complied by lecturing in Harrisburg in February—a development that a friend hailed as an "encouraging indication" of changing times.[15]

The following month, Cheever lent his services to Republicans in New York. There, local Garrisonians had petitioned the state legislature to compel

New York's congressional delegation into endorsing the war power, working in coordination with such Republicans as George T. Pierce, chairman of the State Assembly Military Committee. Their combined forces subsequently turned to Cheever, arranging for him to testify before the committee on the war power. Cheever, they hoped, could shore up embattled Republicans and secure support for the petition. His speech, which one onlooker labeled "very able," worked, emboldening Republicans to sponsor resolutions in line with the petition. Through his whirlwind campaign, Cheever revealed how interventionists were successfully harnessing their celebrity statuses to exert political influence.[16]

THE INTERVENTIONISTS GO TO WASHINGTON

Building on such successes, interventionists made their greatest impacts in Washington. In asking them into the capital, organizer William Croffut grasped the symbolic power of such trips. Immediatists, who had long been ostracized in the slaveholding city, would now enter as feted guests embodying the march of progress. More practically, they could lobby politicians in what one reformer labeled the "center of action for the continent." They could disseminate their message to officials, leveraging their influence to pressure national leaders in person. In doing so, they would also further bolster their politico allies. On hearing that Phillips was reluctant to leave the side of his invalid wife, Sumner begged him to come. "The way is now clear. Washington is now as free for you" as Boston, he entreated. Another Radical Republican likewise asked Phillips to "keep up the pressure upon Congress." Radicals, he noted, needed help in heading off plans to "give over the Union again to slavery. . . . Your voice in the Capitol will be felt in Congress and the Government." Phillips would accede, joining Cheever and Conway in opening up Washington. Through their allies' support, moreover, their visits would become massive spectacles extending far beyond the Smithsonian.[17]

Such trips would prove resounding successes. "It is not too much to say that these lectures helped change the moral atmosphere of Washington," Croffut later recalled. Julian similarly recounted that Smithsonian secretary Joseph Henry, per the agreement reached with Croffut's Washington Lecture Association, had read his disclaimer disavowing institutional support for abolitionists before every lecture. But as the "antislavery tide grew stronger," attracting "large and very enthusiastic crowds," this qualification "awakened the sense of the ludicrous." Before long, audiences met the disclaimer with "explosions of laughter," mocking Henry. By foraying into the capital, interventionists fomented progress in the nation's core.[18]

Cheever blazed the trail to Washington in early January. Before a packed crowd at the Smithsonian that included prominent politicians, he delivered a lecture on the "justice and necessity of slave emancipation" that integrated religious exhortations with expediency. An edict of military emancipation, he explained, would win the war and grant the Union "moral power"—the blessing of providence. Cheever's speech, which Julian labeled the "most terrific arraignment of slavery I ever listened to," inspired Republicans to invite him onto the House floor. His speech there so moved an army private in attendance that the soldier wrote Cheever. "Previous to this war, I hated the name of an abolitionist," he confessed. The exigencies of a prolonged conflict, however, were changing his mind. Cheever's appeals to military necessity cemented his commitment to fighting "on the side of Liberty." By holding forth in the capital, Cheever thereby accessed, and converted, audiences previously closed to abolitionist influence.[19]

Recognizing his value as a political pressure agent on the ground, Radical Republicans, including Sumner, Julian, Harlan, James Ashley, Owen Lovejoy, and Massachusetts senator Henry Wilson, petitioned Cheever to come back to Washington. In February, Cheever returned to the Smithsonian and preached on successive Sabbaths in the House. Again, as House Chaplain William Channing recalled, his words "completely magnetized" the "two thousand and upwards" in attendance. As listeners cheered Cheever's "trumpet calls to action," Channing gloried at the "utter transformation wrought by one year." Later, Croffut awarded Cheever pride of place in a printed volume of the Smithsonian lectures, underscoring the acclaim he had accrued in Washington.[20]

Conway became the next interventionist voyager. His own trip was almost canceled: as Henry lost control to the antislavery groundswell, he had "determined to fight" against Conway's speaking at the Smithsonian. Sumner and other congressmen spent a "tremendous time" securing his spot, Conway noted, prevailing only after Hannibal Hamlin again intervened. Conway accordingly arrived in mid-January. Political allies first organized a Senate lecture before a large crowd that included Salmon P. Chase. Conway then proceeded to the Smithsonian to lecture on "The Golden Hour," previewing his coming book of the same name from Ticknor and Fields. "Lost—Yesterday, sometime between sunrise and sunset, one golden hour," Conway declared in an imaginary notice for the golden moment. Action, he stressed, was necessary as soon as possible. Left unsaid was what the resulting morally transformed Union entailed—a means to mask the differences between abolitionists like the egalitarian Phillips, who fought for a soaring idea of democratic citizenship, and the antiegalitarian Conway, who desired a racial caste system.[21]

Sumner and Wilson then arranged for Conway to meet Lincoln. At the White House, Conway asked the president to be the "Deliverer of the Nation from its great evil." In response, Lincoln argued that the public was not ready to embrace emancipation. The masses, he pointed out, "care comparatively little about the negro." As the president reaffirmed, he would not budge until popular antislavery sentiment had risen sufficiently and imbued him with the political means to take the initiative. Lincoln, faced with Conway's pressure, nonetheless promised that "when the hour comes for dealing with slavery, I will do my duty." Their summit thus ended cordially.[22]

In lobbying Lincoln, Conway reinforced interventionists' growing sway. Allies had secured him the meeting because of his celebrity—a status that Lincoln, an avid reader of *The Rejected Stone*, recognized. Noncommittal as he was, Lincoln knew that interventionists were helping hasten his aforementioned hour for action. Alongside larger wartime developments, they were shifting the national discourse on slavery and facilitating public acceptance of expedient emancipation. At the same time, interventionists were gaining a foothold in the centers of political power and influencing politicians to spout their ideas. They wielded interest group tactics as carrot and stick, inducement and warning. By accruing public and political support, they offered Lincoln the wherewithal he required to act, while increasing pressure on him to do so. And in person, interventionists handed him a ready-made mechanism for when the hour came. While military emancipation remained far from inevitable, interventionists were helping make it a realistic, politically palatable possibility.[23]

As they basked in their influence, interventionists grew overconfident—and less uneasy over their immersions in the mainstream. These activists walked a difficult path. Pressure politics worked, enabling them to exercise power and effect change far beyond their antebellum abilities. Moreover, the pull of celebrity was strong after their decades of living as pariahs. Yet as they became enamored with their successes, interventionists began disregarding the downside of political mingling—the danger that complacent abolitionists would settle in the morally astigmatic world of Washington and adopt the more racially conservative visions of their allies, surrendering their commitments to racial inclusivity.

After months of struggling to keep their heads above water, they increasingly ignored these perils of intervention to themselves and the cause alike.

Conway experienced intervention's benefits but also exemplified its consequences. To this point in the war, interventionists' internal contradictions—their need to enter politics without forsaking their principles—had prompted them to scorn Lincoln privately but succor him publicly. Now, Conway discarded this dichotomy by expressing private and public faith in the president. After Lincoln endorsed gradual emancipation in the Border States in March, Conway told his wife that Lincoln had inserted a "wedge so neatly" into the proslavery camp as to "do credit to [his] knowledge of railsplitting." Buoyed by reports from Sumner, Conway confided that Lincoln was "convinced that this was a great movement of God to end slavery." Things "look hopeful for our cause," he asserted. In public, he likewise argued in his *Golden Hour* that Lincoln moved "steadily toward Emancipation." At least for now, Conway thrust aside his moral qualms.[24]

Demonstrating his emergent ease in the mainstream, Conway also cultivated his own political ambitions. In his postwar memoir, Conway recalled that Sumner had informed him in the spring of 1862 that Lincoln "would give me a foreign consulate if I desired it—which I did not." Again, Conway was rewriting history decades after his late-war break with Lincoln. At the time, he had requested the posting himself by asking Sumner if there would be "some little consulship . . . which the President would give an antislavery Virginian." Conway suggested a posting in Haiti. "My long acquaintance with blacks in Virginia might enable me to do that work properly," he wrote, obtusely. Phillips also lobbied Sumner on Conway's behalf. Though Conway did not receive the position, his query nevertheless reinforced how interventionists, as they grew flush with political prestige, were pushing their internal moral agonies to the wayside for the time being.[25]

Not all interventionists agreed with this course. Child was far less sanguine about national affairs than Conway. "Hope grows faint," she wrote a friend in January, wondering whether "God [will] allow us to be an example to nations . . . [or] use us as a warning." While interventionists were helping "people head in the right direction," she noted, "we are unfortunate in the men who we have placed in power." Lincoln, she sighed, was "narrow-minded, short-sighted, and obstinate." Because she was less convinced than Conway that their intervention would win the day, Child thus held firm in her private criticisms. Cheever also revealed his uncertainty over whether Lincoln could "be moved in the right direction, before it is too late." Though he was experiencing the boons of pressure politics, he yet remained wary of Lincoln and the mainstream.[26]

Phillips, however, now brushed past such qualms. Though he assented to politicos' pleas to travel early in the new year, resistance from Henry delayed his lecture until March. In the interim, Ann Phillips begged her husband to cancel his plans. She argued that his invitation was not a sign of popular progress, but rather of abolitionists' moral sliding as they enmeshed themselves deeper in the webs of their untrustworthy allies. Her husband was already endorsing the kind of compromising measures that such political tempters had always favored, such as compensated emancipation. Washington, she feared, posed an even greater risk to his self-conceived identity as an unassailable activist—and to the integrity of his moral program.

After Wendell nonetheless finalized his plans for the trip, Ann worked to limit any potential damage. "I want you to see the able men" in Washington, she told him—activists, not dissolute politicos. "I hate to have you mixed up with them [politicians]," she confessed. By getting swept up in his celebrity, her husband would "win yourself up too much with them" rather than show "you are not of them." Such a course, she warned, was counterproductive. Wendell should not "throw himself alone into the vortex of politicians." By "mingling yourself with them you lose all influence," she asserted in purist undertones. He could not influence politicians "unless you are outside"—a firebrand outsider instead of a congenial insider. Lobbying would win Republican support, but only at the cost of his own expansively minded soul.[27]

Such fears were warranted. As their sway swelled, interventionists assumed they could control their partners. Yet even as allies from Radical Republicans to antislavery conservatives and businessmen adopted interventionist axioms and ceded the spotlight, they pursued their own agendas. Disparate as these blocs were, many such politicos sought to moderate and redirect their immediatist partners behind the scenes, nudging them away from their more impolitic ideals. For example, J. K. Herbert, an allied army officer, was no moral crusader: he later joined antislavery businessmen in their scheme to seize Texas cotton. His 1862 letter to George W. Julian exposed how abolitionists' partners consciously sought to co-opt them. While interventionists had embraced prowar pragmatism within clear limits, Herbert demanded more, confiding that he would attend a Garrisonian meeting to "try and get some practical turn to their action." Activists, he accused, remained "very impractical in their manner of undertaking their work." As Herbert argued, "they should now join hands with us in some policy that will win, if not so radical as that they have heretofore cherished." Before meeting with Phillips and Garrison, Herbert asked Julian about the "most politic" way to steer them toward further expediency—and away from their dedication to racial inclusivity. The dangers of the mainstream, he revealed, were quite real.[28]

To head off such men in Washington, Ann Phillips asked Garrison to accompany, and check, Phillips. "Wendell needs you," she wrote. "Otherwise, you leave him alone with politicians." Garrison declined, claiming that an "artful and evil use would be made of my visit." In reality, he was saving face: Garrison had already asked allies like Julian to secure him an invitation to the Smithsonian. Even now, however, the "tender-footed" members of the Washington Lecture Association still opposed his presence, as Julian informed Garrison. Ann Phillips asked her husband to wrangle Garrison an invitation while "pretend[ing] it [his omission] was a mistake," but to no avail. Phillips journeyed to Washington alone.[29]

Phillips's resulting trip reinforced both his hopes about the effectiveness of political intervention and his wife's fears about its moral repercussions. A dyspeptic Garrison had predicted that a "ruffianly element" would ruin the visit. As Garrison's daughter soon admitted, however, "Father was certainly wrong." Washington feted Phillips so extensively that, on his deathbed decades later, he noted his "pleasantest recollections of that visit." Phillips had already achieved antebellum renown as a provocative orator. Yet his wartime celebrity now reached a different magnitude as he repeatedly expounded on his beliefs to Congress, before such luminaries as John C. Frémont, Hannibal Hamlin, and Lincoln. For Phillips's last speech, a remarkably bold paean to Toussaint Louverture and Black revolutionary freedom in the seat of American political power, Lincoln sat on the dais—a vivid illustration of how rapidly the Union was changing.[30]

Phillips raved to his wife about his immersion into the Washington elite, dismissing her concerns. After Sumner introduced him to leading Republicans, he dined with Hamlin and Frémont. Foreshadowing his later association with the latter, he noted that the general was "all I fancied him." Wendell, as Ann feared, seemed at home at such fetes. He also met Lincoln at the White House, where the president confided that he loathed slavery and "meant it should die." He stayed his hand only until resistance to such a measure abated. Phillips declared that he had left the meeting "rather encouraged." Lincoln was "better than his Congress fellows," he argued.[31]

Phillips left Washington aglow. He asked Ann to inform Garrison that "Washington is as safe to him as New York," echoing Sumner's earlier reassurance to himself as his own attitudes shifted. Garrison "ought to go on and lecture" there, Phillips blithely affirmed. "He knows not the enthusiasm with which he will be received—nor the good he will do." To his amazement, Phillips had accessed the upper crust of Washington society and exerted substantive influence across the capital. His trip demonstrated the dizzying power of pressure politics, advancing the cause alongside his own prestige. Phillips hence viewed his visit as an unmitigated success.[32]

Yet such success came with moral consequences. As Ann fretted, Phillips was now working within the constraints of the political system, rather than in his old moral framework. Like Conway, he began lauding Lincoln in private and public as he acclimated to his immersion in the mainstream. "Thank God for Old Abe! He hasn't got to Canaan yet but has set his face Zionward," he wrote Conway, later reiterating these sentiments onstage. Phillips cut through interventionists' Gordian knot—their moral contradictions—by jettisoning his moral apprehension and throwing off the inner turmoil that had accompanied his intervention. He had, Ann worried, strayed from the unerring path of righteousness and succumbed to political sirens.

Reflecting the complexity of prowar abolitionists' political paradox, Phillips understood his behavior differently. He would soon regret, and repudiate, both his flirtation with Lincoln and his brief stifling of his ambivalence. Rather than weaken his agenda, moreover, Phillips would increasingly utilize his inculcation in pressure politics to push the envelope of moral reform. He would reconcile his principles with the demands of the moment, harnessing politics not only to preserve but also to augment his panoramic moral vision. Ann's worries would prove misplaced, if only regarding her husband. As would become clear, many interventionists would not meet the moral challenges of politicization nearly as constructively.[33]

Regardless, prowar abolitionists at the time praised Phillips for lighting immediatists' ways to Washington. Edmund Quincy labeled Phillips's trip "one of the most striking incidents of our odd evolution," opening the capital to them en masse. Quincy soon journeyed to meet with legislators and Lincoln, after which Oliver Johnson led his own lobbying delegation. As times changed, moreover, antiabolitionist mobs became the salutary exception in the North rather than the perilous norm. Following his Washington trip, an exuberant Phillips began touring the Midwest in late March. On arriving in Cincinnati, he reported that the citizens "mobbed and pelted with eggs me whom Washington cheered." As journals nationwide publicized the incident, however, it only heightened Phillips's star power. "The interest excited in him," Garrison noted, enabled Phillips to schedule more lectures than planned. Phillips, as James Brewer Stewart explained, basked in this additional attention. Garrison, too, capitalized on the incident to garner support. The attack would "work well for our cause," he crowed. As they gained traction, interventionists now considered even the occasional angry mob a boon.[34]

EXPANDING THE ANTISLAVERY ALLIANCE:
NEW YORKERS AND THE EMANCIPATIONISTS

To sustain their momentum, interventionists also extended their coalition to include New York political and business elites—an interlinked, opportunistic mix of antislavery conservative politicians and antislavery businessmen who, after much resistance, now recognized the value of allying with immediatists. Among the politicians was the Democratic historian and former secretary of the Navy George Bancroft. Like his fellow antislavery conservatives Edward Everett and Daniel S. Dickinson, Bancroft was a onetime antiabolitionist who joined the antislavery alliance after military emancipation became politically agreeable. As one immediatist mocked, he was "the same affected sycophant he used to be, but now an abolitionist." The businessmen included Republican financier John Austin Stevens Jr., the leader of the plot to profit off a Union invasion of Texas. Like their predecessors who had entered the alliance over the fall, these elite New Yorkers stood far from abolitionists' own moral standards, expressing little interest in post-emancipation Black rights. In a tract advocating Black enlistment, Stevens discounted the idea of racial equality. "The attestation that the intelligence of persons of color is inferior to white men's," he noted, should not bar their service. A soldier was a "mere machine . . . whose mind has nothing or very little to do with the labor required from it." Invoking racist stereotypes of Black brutes, Stevens argued for Blacks' recruitment as mindless warriors—a far cry from Douglass's egalitarian idea of enlistment. Interventionists nonetheless welcomed such figures into the fold, wagering that the benefits of this association outweighed its moral risk.[35]

In February, these elites joined Gotham abolitionists like Cheever and Johnson in promoting an emancipation petition. "No harmony can be restored to the nation," they declared, "until slavery shall be wiped out of the land." Through this vague statement, which left unsaid the nature of such harmony, interventionists and their new allies revealed how far apart they were ideologically—and how perilous these figures' entrance into the coalition was. Yet the scorn of the Copperhead press for the petition now bound them closer together. "Some of the gentlemen named are accustomed to better company," sneered one journal. In a mocking rejoinder, Johnson reframed abolitionists, rather than the elites, as that better company. He had always known, as he averred in the *Standard,* that the "time would come, sooner or later, when those who derided our efforts in the holy cause of freedom would become our co-laborers." But now that "this day has arrived, we certainly have no disposition to quarrel with our present coadjutors" for "not coming over to our side sooner." A "common cause makes us equal," Johnson admitted. As he understood, interventionists needed all the help they could get.[36]

In March, this partnership debuted onstage. Whereas John Jay had previously sought to exclude abolitionists altogether from a planned proemancipation gathering, they would now take pride of place. Following a lecture by Conway at his church early in the year, Cheever organized the rally alongside gathered elites, including Bancroft, Columbia University president Charles King, and noted jurists William Curtis Noyes and David Dudley Field. The resulting call for the meeting relayed interventionist axioms, advocating military emancipation as the "only means of securing permanent peace." Its organizers invited Garrison to join Conway and Cheever on the platform, seeking to tap into their collective stardom. Though Garrison could not attend, Conway spoke. Recalling his trip to Washington, he averred that Lincoln had found the "people of the North not prepared for emancipation." Bringing figures from across the antislavery spectrum together in a show of unity, Conway recognized, would help raise public opinion and spur Lincoln to act.[37]

Interventionists celebrated the rally as advancing the fight for expedient emancipation. In the *Liberator,* Garrison labeled it a "great success . . . in view of its commanding intelligence, talent, and moral weight." In the name of their common objective, Garrison again conflated abolitionists and their allies, downplaying their differences. The only figure he singled out was the colonizationist postmaster general, Montgomery Blair, who had sent a letter in support of the rally. Blair's letter, Garrison scorned, "reek[ed] with the venom of malignant colorphobia." Interventionists yet continued working with antislavery conservatives and businessmen, tolerating their far less racially inclusive views for the sake of emancipation. On their end, these New Yorkers seized on interventionists' star power—and, like J. K. Herbert, influenced the interventionists behind the scenes, eventually helping remake Garrison into a vocal supporter of Blair.[38]

For now, interventionists remained conflicted about such partnerships. Recognizing the political utility of their alliances, prowar abolitionists dismissed naysayers like Ann Phillips and forged ahead. But their uneasiness over having to countenance morally unscrupulous figures to achieve political results was harder to ignore. Their hand-wringing reached new heights over a new group, even further to the right on the antislavery spectrum than antislavery conservatives and businessmen: the emancipationists. While the above elites bypassed Black rights, this self-styled bloc, formed in early 1862 by financier James Gilmore, poet Charles Leland, and Democrat Robert J. Walker, explicitly rejected them. In their magazine, *The Continental Monthly,* they asserted that they did "not care one straw for the Negro. . . . Let us regard him not as a man or brother, but as a miserable nigger." Through bigoted rhetoric, emancipationists presented themselves as the antislavery, anti-Black heirs of antebellum author Hinton Helper.[39]

As white supremacists, emancipationists took pains to distinguish themselves from abolitionists, even while appropriating their wartime arguments. In their magazine, Leland stressed that "the emancipationist sees [abolition] in a very different light" from immediatists. The "mere abolitionist of the old school," he asserted, "sees in the war only an opportunity . . . to free the black." But the "old abolition jargon" about justice for Blacks was obsolete. Rather than "fight for the Negro," emancipationists advocated abolition "for the sake of the Union and of the white man," disavowing talk of moralizing the nation. Yet interventionists had laid the ground on which they walked. In asserting that it was time to "try some other expedient" to shape public opinion, emancipationists echoed what interventionists had already understood—and acted on. Their argument that emancipation was an "inevitable necessity" because the "negro sustains the South" imitated that of prowar immediatists. Abolitionists both inspired and repulsed them.[40]

In striking this balance, emancipationists demonstrated both the extent and constraints of interventionists' influence. Their emergence further validated prowar abolitionists' strategy, as northerners who had possessed no antislavery inclinations before the war advocated abolition using immediatist axioms. Such figures elevated the level of public approval for the measure, increasing pressure on the government. Tellingly, however, Leland's journal singled out only one abolitionist for praise: Conway. Selectively citing *The Rejected Stone*'s antiegalitarian passages while ignoring its moralistic underpinnings, Leland praised Conway for exposing slavery as "an evil which threatens to vitiate the white race." Emancipationists supported interventionists only so far. They would now end slavery to save the Union. Yet their nation still had no place for immediatism's other aim of Black rights, as their advocacy for racial separation made clear. Their alliance with the interventionists had its limits—and its price.[41]

Interventionists quickly grasped this problem. "Nobody, except the old abolitionists, seem to have the faintest idea that [Blacks] have any rights," Child complained. In the *Liberator,* editorial assistant Charles Whipple noted that the "number of opponents of slavery in our nation is greatly increasing." Such growth, however, sprung "not from a recognition of slavery as a sin, but only as a nuisance." Whipple singled out the emancipationists and their focus on white self-interest. As he wondered, "What a prospect does it open for our future, when our efforts for the *body* of reform ... repudiat[e] its *spirit*?" In playing by emancipationists' rules, he knew, abolitionists might endanger their greater mission, which extended beyond the abolition of slavery. By choosing politics over principle, they would also further imperil their own moral equilibriums.[42]

To ensure their immediate task of abolition, however, prowar immediatists again escalated their intervention by welcoming emancipationists into the fold. Whipple aired his reservations in public to assuage his guilt. Yet by February he argued that "help toward the extermination" of slavery was "welcome ... from every quarter." War is "no time for the successful culture of moral principles, only for a choice of measures," affirmed a *Liberator* correspondent. Interventionists had to focus on short-term goals over longer-term repercussions. By May, the paper phased out its criticism, praising emancipationists for their "bold and trenchant" assaults upon slavery. As they did throughout the war, interventionists held their noses and compromised, scrambling to speed up their fight for progress while they still could.[43]

ABOLITIONISTS' CONTINUING CIVIL WAR

While interventionists pushed further into the mainstream to achieve their golden moment, moral purists fretted that their rivals had sacrificed the cause for illusory gains. As they grew increasingly alarmed, Stephen Foster and Pillsbury began migrating back to their original, hardline positions. Abby Kelley Foster had never stopped assailing the war as a false idol that would not beget emancipation and, even if it somehow did, would nevertheless forestall an egalitarian future. Though they had continued to echo her in rejecting the Union war as it was, her husband and Pillsbury had warmed in recent months to the potential of the war as it could be. To an extent, Stephen Foster still subscribed to this view. In a March letter to British interventionist George Thompson, he prayed that the government would "seize the present auspicious moment to proclaim emancipation." The war, he argued, could be a building block for a morally transformed Union.[44]

Over the summer, Foster had grounded his wartime hopes in the efficacy of expediency and the advancement of public opinion. Now, frustrated at the lack of antislavery progress, he lost faith in both. In January, he joined his wife in demanding that the nation "put away her great sin, *because* of its sin, without waiting for her dire necessities to compel the righteous act." Even if it occurred, emancipation proceeding from the "selfish issue of safety to the whites," not dedication to "justice to the slave," could never lead to any post-emancipation Black rights—and especially not to the expansive equality he demanded. Abolitionists, he reaffirmed, strove "not merely to destroy the *form* of slavery, but to destroy the *spirit of oppression*"—its penumbral effects, such as "relentless prejudice." While his words resembled Whipple's, Foster refused to abandon the spirit of reform for the sake of the body. He therefore rejected expediency, returning closer to his uncompromising spouse.[45]

Foster also soured on the notion of popular progress. At the meeting, he reiterated his opposition to Lincoln, avowing that "there never had been an Administration so thoroughly devoted to slavery." He now recognized, however, that Lincoln was only a "passive agent of the people." Northern citizens were the true obstacles to progress. "If the people wanted freedom, why did they not say so?," he wondered. The ear of the public, which Foster had previously believed open to abolitionist influence, had evidently been shut the entire time. While he still held out hope for the conflict, the foundations supporting such hope were slowly crumbling.[46]

Pillsbury also walked back many of his summertime stances. Like Stephen Foster, he clung still to the theoretical potential of the Union war. "The present moment is so important, that it should not be lost," he told George Cheever. Yet Pillsbury, too, retrenched. Unlike his friend, he had never put any stock in popular progress. He had, however, theorized over the summer that expedient emancipation could unleash the nation's moral potential. Now, at a February meeting in Albany, he demanded that the nation "do justice . . . as justice, not as a military necessity." A morally transformed Union that enshrined Black rights alongside freedom would not be otherwise possible. As with Foster, Pillsbury's earlier thawing toward the Union war was ending.[47]

Pillsbury, moreover, still rejected the Union war as it was, regardless of what it could be. "Hatred of the colored race" continued in the North, he asserted at Albany. At the same time, the administration was the "wickedest we have ever had": it had the power to end slavery, yet still did nothing. The people and government, he argued, made the war unworthy of his support. "I do not desire success to the Northern army," he reaffirmed. "I do not wish to see Lincoln triumph over the South in the way he himself has marked out." The North, he maintained, was unable "to improve any great success which may attend its arms." It remained unwilling to redeem itself. Further defeats, he warned, were necessary to foment "repentance, reform, atonement" among northerners. Until that point, he refused to endorse the war or mingle with its adherents.[48]

As interventionists flouted such warnings, antiwar immediatists grew exasperated. In private, Pillsbury tried to sort out with Garrison and Phillips "their different positions," but to no effect. "The growing difference between my old antislavery associates and myself," Stephen Foster confessed to Thompson, caused him "much anxiety and personal discomfort." Activists who had stood "on the rock of truth," he lamented, "abdicate their field of labor, [and] virtually make over our cause and themselves also to the government." Echoing Ann Phillips, Foster argued interventionists had gone over to the politicians, forfeiting their principles for ersatz gains. He vowed to rescue his colleagues "out of the murky vapors of a senseless and bewildering patriotism," reluctantly reprimanding them for the greater good.[49]

Purists soon intensified their public assaults. "A mighty work was entrusted to the hands of the abolitionists," Stephen Foster in January informed the Massachusetts Anti-Slavery Society (MASS), an AASS auxiliary group. It was their duty to uplift Americans to perfection. But to do so, "they must keep right themselves, or how could they set others right?" They could not save others if they had lost their own way. Any "fault in them was like poison cast into a fountain," Foster averred. Abolitionists, Pillsbury thundered, could not guide people out of the "murky darkness" if trapped themselves. Rather than "take counsel of flesh and blood" and defile themselves through politics, they had to agitate from on high as saintly others—aloof martyrs for justice, choosing to "die the death of the righteous." The day of sainthood, he stressed, had still not passed. In forsaking purity for celebrity, interventionists had failed the cause.[50]

British moral purists, too, ramped up their attacks. "Our abolition friends went with the current," scorned one activist, and impugned those "who still occupied the high ground." William Robson, another such activist, wrote Garrison's son Francis that he wanted the "abolitionists of America to take a broader" view. Robson had thought they were "universal men." Now, however, "they sink from this sublime height to the level of Americans." They had abandoned the mountaintop for the muck in a misguided intervention. Interventionists had "sunk their moral power, and gained nothing by the sacrifice," Robson concluded condescendingly.[51]

Interventionists, however, could not understand such logic. Have "we done wrong . . . in doing what we may to ensure the best result?" one asked. In meeting such attacks, interventionists nevertheless strove to preserve their places as the pragmatic center of abolitionism. Garrison again warded off his domestic antiwar fringe in civil terms. At the MASS meeting, he met Foster halfway by holding northerners accountable for the "fearful guilt they have incurred" over the decades. Yet he also rebuked Foster's "too despondent" tone. "I want you to feel hopeful in respect to the future, and the certain triumph of the Anti-Slavery cause," he told listeners. Immediatists, after all, were swaying the balance of power in Washington. "Is that not cheering?" he asked. Garrison asked purists to not "be too microscopic in endeavoring to find disagreeable things," countering them through optimism.[52]

Some interventionists also tried to restore transatlantic decorum. "The war has not turned us all crazy," Garrison associate Samuel May Jr. assured Irish moral purist Richard Davis Webb. May denied that he had abandoned the high ground, arguing that no government would initiate abolition "on the simple basis of right and justice." By taking the "ground of expediency," interventionists were ensuring that the "government will do a great and just act. Let them put it on what grounds they will." The ends justified the means. In a series of public letters to Thompson, Garrison likewise disregarded concerns about the dangers of fame, arguing that his camp had not "abdicated our high position . . . in order, for once, to be on the popular side." Far from being "carried headlong by a strong tide of popular feeling," they were shaping that tide. The war, he asserted, demonstrated their "growing power." While the North was not "up to the true Anti-Slavery Standard," its advancement in turning toward emancipation was obvious. "Is this not a hopeful state of things?" asked Garrison. "Are we . . . never to recognize that we have made any progress, because we have not yet effected all that we have been so long struggling to accomplish?" Interventionists, he affirmed, were gradually perfecting the war, block by block.[53]

Such civility, however, remained rare in the transatlantic theater of the abolitionist civil war. In his letters, Garrison again answered his British critics in trenchant terms by contrasting the prowar Thompson and his "mastery of American affairs" with purists and their "strange hallucination of mind." Garrison indignantly decried how Britons who "assume to understand matters three thousand miles off . . . better than those of us who are on the ground" dared question his integrity. Foreigners should mind their own business, he roared, again substituting national chauvinism for the transnational networks that had long undergirded abolitionism.[54]

More interventionists embraced chauvinism following the *Trent* affair, as the American seizure of Confederate envoys James Mason and John Slidell from a British ship became an international incident. The affair, Child confessed, gave her an "incurable dislike" of Britain. As national pride fueled her anger, she railed against abolitionist Harriet Martineau, who had written a slew of antiwar public letters. Her haughty "British conceit is so excessive, that it is comic. Has [she] lost her wits?" Child asked. Interventionists subsequently began responding to their critics in equally patronizing tones. "The only logical deduction" to be drawn from transatlantic disagreements was "that you are in the wrong," Edmund Quincy informed Webb, replacing May's civility with condescension.[55]

The abolitionist civil war heated up over early 1862 because the two sides were clashing over their fundamentally divergent values assumptions. Moral purists believed that interventionists had forsaken the cause. Interventionists, by contrast, grew comfortable in the mainstream, shrugging off their former wariness amid the limelight. Their intervention, they understood, enabled them to touch the levers of power in previously unimaginable ways. Prowar abolitionists were reaching, and recruiting, increasing swathes of northerners. Politicians now sought their help, rather than vice versa. As the new year dawned, interventionists were bringing the once-impossible scenario of military emancipation closer to reality. They entered the spring riding a wave of optimism, resembling that of the previous summer. Yet events would remind them once again that, despite their best efforts, military and political contingencies still ruled all.

CHAPTER SIX

Imagining Reconstructions,
March–September 1862

L
ydia Maria Child wrote to a friend in March 1862, brimming with confidence and hope. Over the winter, she had come to doubt the efficacy
of interventionists' wartime strategy. Now, as bills offering diplomatic
recognition to Haiti and Liberia and abolishing slavery in Washington wound
their ways through Congress, she changed her tune. "The progress of events
has impressed me with a deeper feeling of religious reverence than I ever had
before," she averred. Events, she argued, proved that God was directing the
Union. Interventionists had proven effective providential agents, whether they
"get the credit of it, or not." By foraying into pressure politics, they were helping to execute divine will. Though they remained at the mercy of political and
military actors, both seemed to be on their side. Politicians were doing work
"impossible for me to do," while Union soldiers were "instructing the whole
nation" about emancipation. Child therefore shed her reticence and looked to
the horizon, certain that slavery would die.[1]

In June, Child wrote to another confidante in markedly different tones.
A series of sobering developments had dashed her optimism over the interim
months. Lincoln had proven himself seemingly untamable by revoking an
emancipation edict issued by General David Hunter. This "timid, fluctuating
policy of the government" attracted Child's scorn. The army, meanwhile, had
reached the gates of Richmond, threatening to end the war without abolition.
If the vanquished "rebels continue [as] slaveholders, our terrible struggle will be
invested with no moral dignity," Child warned. Interventionists had not done
enough after all, she despaired, as her hope evaporated in favor of a fatalistic
sense of impending doom. "I cannot shake my despondency. . . . I cannot see

what right this nation has to expect to be saved," she sighed. Interventionists, it appeared, had failed.[2]

Over the spring and summer of 1862, Child and prowar abolitionists experienced a whiplash-inducing set of events. They entered the spring assured of their powers of persuasion. Interventionists celebrated long-awaited breakthroughs on the road to abolition, from the Union's recognition of Liberia and Haiti to emancipation in the capital, culminating in Hunter's May emancipation edict. Over the ensuing weeks, however, Lincoln revoked Hunter's order, while his military neared Richmond. Dispirited interventionists were reminded anew that larger contingencies, over which they had no control, still set the pace of federal emancipation.

Child, however, had been correct in her first letter. Interventionists' strategy of popularizing the war power had worked, building a public and political groundswell in favor of expedient emancipation that both enabled and compelled Lincoln to act. When he responded to the defeat of the Union offensive in July by seeking a harsher instrument of war, he seized on the constitutional mechanism abolitionists had proffered. Though he kept his decision private at first, he had cast the die against slavery. Prowar abolitionists had prevailed in their seemingly impossible quest to remake governmental policy. Alongside the exigencies of war, they had helped bring about the most remarkable transformation in American history to that point.[3]

Yet interventionists knew not of their triumph. Convinced that they had rather failed, they rekindled their flickering ambivalence over their interventions. In public and private, prowar abolitionists from Garrison to Child lambasted Lincoln and fretted over the war. An affronted Phillips especially resorted to censuring the president. Yet he, too, contained still his criticisms within interventionists' consensus of supporting Lincoln on a conditional basis. Conway also expressed renewed, but restrained, unease about his own politicization. Cheever, for his part, initiated a sharper break with the interventionist camp out of disgust with military affairs.[4]

While prowar abolitionists all fought for the same golden moment as their immediate priority, broad and narrow interventionists conceived of different endgames—clashing morally transformed Unions. Now, they began debating what freedom and post-emancipation Black rights meant more substantively, imagining starkly dissimilar Reconstructions. The broad interventionists Douglass and Phillips put their wartime political educations to good use by refining further their expansive moral missions, structuring them around the goal of legislative equality—the legislated achievement of Black civil, political, and socioeconomic rights—as the key to national redemption. Phillips deepened his conceptions of democratic citizenship and a unified nationality, envisioning enfranchised Black landowners and Union veterans knitting the war-torn nation back together. The young Black elite Charlotte Forten, meanwhile, joined the Port Royal Experiment—what Willie Lee Rose has described as the revolutionary program to plant northern civilization in the liberated Sea Islands through education and free-labor values.[5]

Narrow interventionists, meanwhile, developed further their restrictive conceptions of post-emancipation America. Garrison's ally James Miller McKim gravitated toward freedmen's aid—a movement to meet freed slaves' material needs, at the expense of agitating for their rights. In joining the Port Royal Experiment, he seized on its economic undertones, promoting a meager definition of Black rights premised on paternalistic wage work. And Conway fleshed out his own deeply unequal racial vision, cementing Black wage labor and Anglo-Saxon dominance—and centering on his native state of Virginia. These narrow interventionists imagined shallow Reconstructions based around Blacks' economic functionality rather than their political power.[6]

Even as broad and narrow interventionists drifted apart, they remained united against abolitionism's resilient moral purist wing. As national affairs seemingly grew dire, Stephen Foster and Pillsbury fully retrenched to a hardline antiwar stance. More certain than ever that the Union war was a dead end rather than a potential golden moment, these purists grew bolder in their opposition to prowar abolitionists. Like broad interventionists, Pillsbury and the Fosters aspired to construct an expansively egalitarian morally transformed Union. Yet they refused to believe that the war, or its immediatist supporters, would precipitate that future. As they burned with indignation and vitriol, interventionists returned fire once more in the scorching-hot abolitionist civil war.

Interventionists' own discontent regarding Lincoln worsened by the late summer, when the president restated that preserving the Union was his priority over emancipation and reiterated his support for colonization. As they panicked that their incremental struggle for the golden moment had again stalled out, Douglass and other prowar abolitionists lashed out at the government in desperation. But while most still clung to the interventionist camp's proadministration platform, Phillips began to contemplate joining Cheever in rejecting it.

THE PROGRESS AND REVERSALS OF THE SPRING:
MARCH–JUNE 1862

Interventionists' hopes, which were already soaring high amid their star turns, peaked amid a series of springtime antislavery measures. In March, Lincoln offered a proposal for gradual, compensated emancipation in the Border States. Immediatists had long denounced gradualism as a prejudiced policy. Yet Phillips now praised this program as "wonderfully suggestive," again acceding to an expedient policy he would have excoriated before the war. Child, meanwhile, republished her 1834 tract *The Right Way the Safe Way,* which portrayed the British West Indies as a model for compensation. Calling upon her decades of antislavery theorizing, she sought to disseminate her pamphlet in the Border States to win loyal slaveholders over to Lincoln's plan. "Surely the facts must impress all candid minds," she asserted, reflecting her faith in the march of progress.[7]

When Congress passed legislation recognizing Haiti and Liberia in April, Child again invoked her deep past to celebrate the passage of long-desired antislavery milestones into policy. She and other immediatists had long championed Haiti, the product of the Atlantic World's only successful slave revolt. Liberia, meanwhile, had emerged from the colonization movement and its conflicting impulses over race and slavery. Official recognition of these Black nations had long been unthinkable. That the Union now welcomed them into the "sisterhood of nations," Child declared, was "enough to make anybody religious." It also proved how war, and the interventionists, had wrought drastic transformations. Their course of "wise expediency"—of advancing "right *principles* by the best *means*"—had helped restore the nation to its proper bearing.[8]

Interventionists' confidence inflated further when Congress passed a bill initiating compensated emancipation in the District of Columbia. For decades, immediatists had petitioned Congress to end slavery in the federal district. Now, Garrison praised Republicans for enacting an "event of far-reaching importance." Abolishing slavery in an area only "ten miles square," Child admitted, was a "small beginning." As she and other immediatists had long posited, however, the act was an "entering-wedge, which will destroy the wicked system"—the first crack in its armor. It was, agreed the Black abolitionist *Christian Recorder,* a "great moral victory," restoring the nation to its "first principles of justice and freedom" after decades adrift. Interventionists thus rejoiced as the stuff of antislavery dreams became reality.[9]

As interventionists made clear, they had helped achieve these milestones. "All this is the reaping from our many years sowing," bragged one activist. They had laid the groundwork for change, facilitating public acceptance of anti-slavery measures while allying with legislators and bolstering their political fortunes. Prowar abolitionists had given such figures the political capital and incentive to act, rendering them able and willing to pass such legislation for the nation's, and their own, interests. At least in part, interventionists had ensured that their long-desired abolition policy was "now partially inaugurated," as Douglass affirmed.[10]

Interventionists' wave of optimism crested in May, when General David Hunter declared all slaves in Union-occupied South Carolina, Georgia, and Florida free. "[We] were rejoicing over the glorious proclamation," Garrison re-called. As he knew, prowar abolitionists had raised public opinion to the point of making the edict possible. As with John C. Frémont's emancipation decree the previous fall, moreover, interventionists also played a more direct role in Hunter's order. In March, Oliver Johnson informed Phillips that an officer under Hunter's command, having heard Phillips discuss the war power, agreed that the "policy should be pursued in the effort to put down the rebellion." The officer wanted Phillips to "propose just such a proclamation as you would yourself issue" in South Carolina. Should Phillips provide that draft, the officer vowed to "get Hunter up to the point of issuing it." Within weeks, Hunter issued his order—a tantalizing chain of events that was potentially more than coincidence. As Hunter later confirmed, immediatists had "no slight share in maturing" his antislavery views. His edict hence reinforced the growing affinity of interventionists like Phillips for the Union military.[11]

Yet within weeks prowar abolitionists' elation crumbled once more into de-spair. Soon after Hunter issued his military order, Lincoln revoked it, reserving to himself the right to initiate abolition only when vital "to the maintenance of the government." Throughout the war, military progress had shaped the extent of antislavery policy. Now, as James Oakes has detailed, the Union's setbacks had convinced Lincoln of this necessity. Abolitionists, moreover, had helped guarantee that he would have ample public and political succor in taking such action. Lincoln thus began contemplating issuing his own emancipation edict. Prior to doing so, however, the discerning tactician awaited the outcome of one further military initiative: the Peninsula Campaign. In June, Union general George B. McClellan moved to encircle Richmond, threatening to end the war and nullify interventionists' plans in one fell swoop.[12]

Facing as never before the fragility of their plans for emancipation, prowar abolitionists prayed for McClellan to fail. "Rapid success is our greatest danger," asserted Child. As another interventionist affirmed, the salvation of the nation depended on its "los[ing] the great battle now pending." The North, it appeared, needed one last "chastisement to bring us to the point" of emancipation. A Union collapse before Richmond could be that final straw.[13]

Such an assessment proved prophetic. In the Seven Days Battles in late June and early July, the Confederates under their new commander, Robert E. Lee, pushed back McClellan. The cowed McClellan soon withdrew, concluding the campaign. Faced with an embarrassing failure that prolonged the war, and apprised of how escaped slaves had aided Union forces as spies and guides, Lincoln settled upon enacting military emancipation. For now, he kept his decision to himself, waiting for a victory to act so as to avoid the appearance of desperation.[14]

In making his choice, Lincoln validated interventionists' wartime journeys. Together with the larger exigencies of the wartime emergency, they had fostered a baseline of public support for emancipation. Throughout the North, one Republican noted in June, "'Abolitionist' is fast becoming a noble word, baptized in martyrs' blood." In carrying out an increasingly deeper intervention over the past year, prowar abolitionists had offered northerners a path to victory—a way to save their own lives while punishing the traitors. Households sending their "cherished firstlings" into battle, the Republican averred, therefore came to support military emancipation. Simultaneously, interventionists had induced politicos to take up their call for abolition, accruing allies from Radical Republicans to antislavery conservatives to emancipationists. Prowar immediatists had helped make emancipation a realistic political choice, ultimately pressuring and convincing Lincoln into using their recommended instrument to reshape the nation. They had succeeded against all odds, thereby proving moral purists wrong—but only in part. They had won the battle for the golden moment, but not the war for a morally transformed Union.[15]

MORAL AMBIVALENCE, REAWAKENED

Interventionists, however, believed they had lost. After months of painstaking labor, an almost climactic battle and a seemingly uncontrollable president had reduced them to a feeling of utter helplessness. Emancipation, which they had believed to be in their grasp, now appeared out of reach. In the weeks after Lincoln rescinded Hunter's order, interventionists plunged from optimism back into their familiar state of anxiety and fear. Child especially gyrated into despair, predicting imminent doom. "I wonder how mothers, who have sons in the army, can keep from being crazy," she confessed in June. "What would make the matter worse," Child lamented, "is that I see so little of moral grandeur in the war." The war, she feared, would never be worthy of sacrifice. "I don't see how a just God *can* save a nation so morally corrupted as we are," she added. Lincoln had prostrated himself to slaveholders, acting from "fear of offending the Border States" in countermanding Hunter. To appease these "disguised lunatics," he was "dragging the whole nation into the gulf of ruin," Child scorned, abandoning her conciliatory tack toward loyal slaveholders. As she stressed, time was of the essence. Like other interventionists, she predicted that the rebels would gain European support through emancipation. Yet rather than prevent this eventuality, Lincoln moved backward. As her hope that the president would act before it was too late faded, Child resigned herself to failure.[16]

While prowar abolitionists had muffled their criticisms the previous fall, after Lincoln revoked Frémont's military emancipation order, their anguish over their wartime politicization now escaped to the surface. To release their outrage, they assailed the president in public—if only to an extent. Interventionists had achieved too much, and gone too far, to abandon their interventions. Having entered the wartime world of pressure politics and experienced its benefits therein, they could not easily disentangle themselves and return to their old, outsider agitations. They hence vented their controlled anger without abandoning their prowar program, maintaining their conditional support for Lincoln. In June, Garrison declared that Lincoln stood "ready to guard slavery." Yet he sought to spur the president onto higher ground rather than spurn him, entreating Lincoln to ensure a "permanent Union based upon universal freedom and equal rights." A fellow prowar abolitionist likewise concluded a critique of Lincoln by encouraging him to "abide by the principles he has hitherto avowed, on the strength of which he was elected." Interventionists toed a difficult line by setting public limits on their wrath.[17]

After months of dormancy, Phillips's own ambivalence roared back to life, as he pivoted from jubilation to frustration to anger toward Lincoln over the course of the spring. Though he had returned from Washington exhilarated, Phillips soon grew impatient. Throughout April and May, he reintroduced notes of uneasiness into his mostly upbeat assessments of Lincoln, reawakening his internal struggle between absolute principle and political action. The president was "an honest man, but a slow-moving machine," he grumbled. As he fretted over such dallying as an obstacle to his moral designs, Phillips invoked his longtime source of faith: the people. The "people [are] set on the abolition of slavery . . . if not through the Administration, then over it," he noted. This popular will, as nurtured by immediatists, would triumph. "A man halfway down Niagara . . . will go down," he affirmed, using his favored metaphor for moral revolution. As his skepticism crept back, Phillips thus questioned his reliance on politicians—and his own political turn.[18]

But Phillips, too, had so thoroughly inculcated himself in pressure politics that he could not see past its confines, protestations aside. After Hunter issued his military emancipation order, Phillips employed political backchannels in a fruitless effort to prevent its revocation, asking Charles Sumner to relay a message to Secretary of War Edwin Stanton—and thus Lincoln—about the "risk we run" if "Hunter be countermanded." Phillips, despite his impatience, continued to view Lincoln as well-intentioned, if slow-footed. Sumner did his part, reporting that Stanton "promised to read it carefully"—but that Phillips's note had arrived too late to have any effect.[19]

Phillips proceeded to lash out in private and public, his frustration—and his inner turmoil—boiling over. "Lincoln is doing thrice as much today to break this Union as [Jefferson] Davis," he fumed to Sumner in June. "We are paying thousands of lives . . . as penalty for having a timid and ignorant President." Carrying his criticism into the open, Phillips proclaimed at the AASS-affiliated New England Anti-Slavery Convention that Lincoln's decision had "diminished the chance of a Union," making European intervention on behalf of the rebels likelier. "We are dealing not with a great man," he observed. While Garrison had publicly portrayed Lincoln as ahead of northern opinion over the past year, Phillips countered that the president was a "second-rate man," lagging behind the true source of progress: the people.[20]

Yet even in reasserting his innate distrust of politicians, Phillips could not escape the pull of interest group politics. He, too, again adhered to interventionists' shared consensus by constraining his censures, issuing loyal criticism to prod Lincoln onto a higher plane. At the convention, Phillips distinguished himself from moral purists by declaring that he, unlike Pillsbury and the Fosters, "accepted his co-laborers, the President and Cabinet, though not Garrisonian Abolitionists." He tolerated Lincoln still, working from within the war effort to "take possession of the Government, and to spur it onto its duty." Phillips nonetheless reaffirmed before the convention his self-conceived identity as a moralistic reformer, clarifying that he "advises, not supports the Government ... to force it onto a better position." He was a moral adviser of the government rather than its unbridled supporter—a distinction that meant little in practice, yet which reflected his resurgent doubts regarding his own intervention.[21]

As Phillips elaborated in private, recent events had chastened him. The president had betrayed his trust, stymying progress despite his personal pleas. Phillips thus resorted to making Lincoln fear him rather than love him. The administration was "as likely to regard criticism as to value support," he informed Sumner. "Let them feel that we can criticize and demand as well as the Border State[s]." The antislavery alliance, he reiterated, had to "make the Government fear [us] or the Union is gone." With their axioms apparently falling short, interventionists had to offer firm, if tempered, criticism to budge the president. From within the coalition, Phillips deployed his ire as a targeted weapon to reform, rather than reject, Lincoln.[22]

Like Phillips, Conway again interrogated his own political evolution. He, too, had come to embrace Lincoln in public and private. As he witnessed the government's stagnation, however, Conway likewise snapped back to his former position of wariness. While Phillips vented aloud, Conway hid his rekindled outrage behind closed doors, disconnecting anew his public and private views. He expressed his anger most clearly in an unpublished essay, "The Southern Mote and Northern Beam," declaring that there was no one in "this Government who will not sacrifice the country to human bondage." Slaves fleeing to Union lines had "but changed masters," since slavery "reigns as much in our government" as in Richmond. Compensating for his late political flirtations with morally unsparing rhetoric, Conway painted a gloomy picture of affairs.[23]

Conway also resurrected his moral ambivalence from its recent slumber. His essay exposed the conflict raging within him over his intervention, and over his advocacy of emancipation in the name of expediency rather than justice and morality. Invoking abolitionists' roles as the nation's far-seeing and true-hearted conscience, he avowed his personal adherence to the moralistic standard of the ideal. "It must be something more than a question of mere power which justifies slaughter," he declared. Sounding like a moral purist, he explained that a just war required just motivations. The Union needed to fight for the "remission of the nation's sin" to be worthy of divine blessing. A war fought for flawed motives would fail.[24]

Conway nonetheless understood that such idealistic thoughts did not translate well into action. The tension between his thirst for justice and his recognition of political realities bled into his new book, *The Golden Hour*. Echoing his unpublished essay, Conway began with a paean to righteousness. Republicans, he chided, grew "red in the face with showing that they were maintaining freedom simply for strategy or expediency . . . [not] humanity or rectitude." Their speeches, he scathed, strove to avoid "any such little point as the moral ulceration of a whole nation." Conway thereby took a stand and reasserted his reformer's spirit. Yet even while decrying its undue influence, Conway saturated his book with the rhetoric of expediency—and the standard of the possible. *The Golden Hour* was a metaphor-laced argument for the necessity of emancipation, following the same logic as his caricatured Republicans. He contended that an emancipatory "golden hour" was the key to "peace and glory"—an act of need, not justice. Conway also deferred to the demands of the moment by praising Lincoln, deepening his separation of his private and public perspectives. "No one who has ever looked of late into your eye, as I have, can fail to see" your interest in ending slavery, Conway declared regarding Lincoln. He would "deal with the accursed thing *as wrong*." Unlike Phillips, Conway suppressed his qualms while reasserting his ties to Lincoln and the war.[25]

While Conway reaffirmed interventionists' progovernment consensus, and Phillips chafed at this platform but adhered to it still, George Cheever lurched toward repudiating it—and toward rejecting his own previous actions. Over the past year, he had quelled his private misgivings to deliver public endorsements of expedient concepts he despised, including a postwar order based on Black wage labor. Now, his agony over his compromises became intolerable. While he believed in the Union war, he had lost faith in its leader—and motivation to toe a futile line by continuing to support such a man.

Cheever's discontent sprung from military affairs in the West. After General Ulysses S. Grant's series of victories at Fort Henry, Fort Donelson, and Shiloh secured much of Tennessee, Lincoln established a military government there under the proslavery Tennessee Unionist Andrew Johnson. Cheever objected to this decision, writing Sumner that Lincoln's unilateral installation of Johnson was a "usurpation of the legislative power of our government." Lincoln, he seethed, had "taken into his hands the whole governmental authority of the subjugated province," overstepping his constitutional bounds. Such language could easily have emanated from the Copperheads, who were developing a line of attack against Lincoln as a consolidationist despot. Unlike the proslavery Copperheads, however, Cheever decried Lincoln's "military despotism" because it proceeded "in behalf of slavery." Lincoln, he feared, had become a puppet of the Slave Power, preventing legislators like Sumner from putting an antislavery footprint on military policy. More than his fellow interventionists, Cheever's support for the government thereby faltered.[26]

Moral purists, moreover, nurtured Cheever's rising discontent. Pillsbury, a Garrisonian and apostate Congregationalist, had long disdained the non-Garrisonian Congregationalist minister Cheever, deriding him before the war as "with the slaveholders." In a February lecture, however, Pillsbury moved beyond this past to praise Cheever as "almost alone" among ministers in following divine law. He carried his overtures into a March letter hailing Cheever's "qualities of mind and heart." In his grateful response, Cheever gravitated further toward his interlocutor. "I rejoice in your firmness," he affirmed. While most immediatists were "content with the least crumb of promise flung from an administration still pledged" to restore the old Union, Pillsbury stood steadfast in opposition. Cheever hence revealed his disillusionment not only with Lincoln but also with the interventionist camp and its progovernment consensus.[27]

Cheever also expressed guilt over his own intervention by renouncing the concept of expediency alongside the axioms it underpinned. "We do not wish to skulk into emancipation, but to come into it as an open right and duty," he declared in May, sounding like a purist—and, unlike Conway, doing so without qualification. The government, however, worshipped the "maxim of expediency." As Cheever noted in *The Principia,* a religious abolitionist newspaper in which he had taken an editorial role, Lincoln's revocation of Hunter's emancipation order was the "logical result" of expediency ruling the day instead of justice. Exceeding the bounds of loyal criticism, Cheever faulted interventionists for failing the nation alongside Lincoln.[28]

As the summer progressed, Cheever reached a clear, if temporary, breaking point with Lincoln and the interventionist camp. The president, he argued in June, schemed to "reconstruct the Union and slavery." Lincoln's war was "not going to end" bondage. The golden moment was already lost. Interventionists, Cheever accused, had caused this disaster as much as Lincoln. The "cringing time-servers" who warned, "we must not criticize . . . we must sustain the Government"—those abolitionists, such as himself, who had deluded themselves into aiding the administration—had led northerners down an errant path. The country was dying, his brother, Henry, added, and its epitaph would read, "died of expediency." Convinced that "trying any more to save the country from its impending fate . . . seems useless," Cheever withdrew from the spotlight in July. The interventionist star had become a dissident, unable to stomach such a life any longer.[29]

AN EVOLUTION OF MORAL VISIONS

For now, Cheever stood alone in his rebellion. Beneath its collective platform, however, the interventionist camp was far from unified. Broad and narrow interventionists began theorizing in detail about postwar Reconstruction, further developing, and diverging, their already disparate conceptions of what the anti-slavery millennium would actually look like. Broad interventionists had already begun to make productive use of their torturous politicization by conceiving visions of a radically democratic and revitalized nation. Now, they continued their wartime evolution into modern political operators. They honed this idealistic mission further in the forge of politics, centering it around the concrete goal of legislative equality. As he continued to press for African Americans' inclusion in the war effort, Douglass formulated an argument for legislative egalitarianism. He had abandoned his push for Blacks to volunteer for the military months earlier, demanding instead that the Union first invite them into its ranks. As he observed in July, Black scouts, spies, and camp laborers were aiding Union forces, serving the cause "with a pickaxe if [they] cannot with a pistol." It hence was past time to let Black men prove their civic value in battle.[30]

Over time, Douglass fleshed out his vision of the perfected nation that such military service would foster. Early in 1862, he began using the palatable language of white self-interest to advocate Black incorporation. Douglass hated doing so, going so far as to praise Cheever in May for forsaking the "spurious doctrines of expediency—which have cheated and deceived some of our [best] advocates of emancipation." In public, however, he bowed to political realities. "The destiny of the colored American," he emphasized in one speech, "is the destiny of America." Black inclusion, in the form of universal male suffrage and citizenship, would let the "American people learn lessons of wisdom, power, and goodness," benefiting white alongside Black Americans.[31]

This salutary solution, moreover, required no special concessions. All Blacks required, Douglass stressed, was an "equal chance to live." By permitting this right, the government would ensure "peace, joy, and permanent safety" to all. Summing up his formulation in a July speech, Douglass argued that the divisive issue of slavery had created a failed, flimsy Union, held together by a "rope of sand." Legislative equality, by contrast, would create a "union of ideas"—a multiracial nation bound through shared political ideals, working for country over section.[32]

Other Black abolitionists, including those who had opted against joining the interventionist camp, expanded upon this multifaceted goal. In his *Weekly Anglo-African,* Robert Hamilton contributed an economic plank to the agenda of legislative equality alongside suffrage and citizenship: the redistribution of former slaveholders' land to the formerly enslaved. Unlike Douglass, who advocated a laissez-faire economic approach to landholding, Hamilton called on the government to "immediately bestow" confiscated rebel land upon freed slaves, or at least offer them a "fair and equal chance to occupy confiscated lands." Nodding to the political landscape, Hamilton argued in the language of national self-interest that land redistribution was "conductive to the public weal and the national advancement." Blacks would regenerate the South as landholders and citizens, replacing a divided nation with a tight-knit Union.[33]

Phillips also prioritized national regeneration in his own developing mission. He had long espoused a panoramic vision of moral transformation, seeking to unite all the nation's disparate races and creeds into a single people. But he had begun to promulgate this vision in a more politicized fashion in recent months, as the problem of how to achieve postwar harmony increasingly dominated his thoughts. "Real peace is not to be expected for many years," he asserted in January. "In the Union or out of it, South Carolina will hate New England." Though no "speedy panacea for our disease of long standing" existed, Phillips nevertheless sought out solutions for this malady—"instrumentalities that will eventually wear out prejudice and hatred." He thus refined his vision of a reinvigorated "empire stretching from the Lakes to the Gulf," ready to redeem the world, by fleshing out the mechanisms through which it would function.[34]

The chief such mechanism would be freed slaves. Merging the language of wartime nationalism with his own political education, Phillips called for freedmen to rebuild the postwar South in the North's likeness, creating a representative democracy. The North, Phillips asserted in May, was the "better, purer, nobler" section. "Our civilization is ideas, rights, education," unlike the South's. The South, as he therefore concluded, had to be "annihilated, and the North spread over it." While such language recalled Garrison's rhetoric from the previous summer, Phillips, unlike Garrison, stressed that Blacks would be the "basis of the effort to regenerate the South." Like Hamilton, he pressed for former slaves to receive land and suffrage. Pragmatically, Phillips denied he was "asking for [their] rights." Rather, he was "asking for the use of [them]. . . . We have to make over the State of South Carolina, and we have not a white man in it." As Phillips explained, white southerners would never accept Yankee rule. "Black men alone to vote—to have representation," he thus urged. In practical terms, he cast legislative equality as the key to reunion. By giving Blacks political and economic power, the government would supplant the Slaveocracy, molding the nation through the mores of democratic citizenship into a common nationality.[35]

Freedmen would not be the only spearheads of the nation's redemption. Interventionists had long since latched onto the military as an engine of emancipation. Now, Phillips envisioned Union soldiers working alongside freed slaves as twin mechanisms of democratization and moralization. Should Lincoln invoke the war power, Phillips noted in May, the army would "accomplish in months the work of years" by ensuring emancipation on the ground. Its soldiers would become "500,000 pupils plastic to our hands," learning tolerance and accepting Blacks into their ranks. "It is a noble army that goes Southward," proclaimed Phillips, embracing "all colors but one. It is going to add that color, too, and realize the great idea of this people"—the egalitarianism of the Declaration of Independence. Once the military rendered the South a "tabula rasa . . . for us to write on at will," transplanted colonies of enlightened veterans would help freed slaves reform the region. Phillips thereby sketched out a radical political vision of the nation, which he would employ to expand and transform the fight for racial change.[36]

The youthful Black educator Charlotte Forten, meanwhile, labored to advance freedom on the ground by enlisting in the Port Royal Experiment—the Union program, instituted in early 1862, to educate and train freed slaves in the South Carolina Sea Islands. Teachers, missionaries, and reformers flocked to the region, sensing the opportunity emerging before their eyes. Thousands of freed slaves had entered their reach, allowing antislavery northerners to prove that freedom could proceed in an orderly fashion. Forten, the scion of a storied Philadelphia activist family, had little in common with these former slaves beyond their shared experience of race-based oppression. In her diary she chronicled the "many deprivations" she had suffered across the North, as whites rejected her as their equal. Frustration at her lack of opportunity inspired Forten to voyage southward. "The accomplishments . . . [I] longed for all my life, I am now convinced can never be mine," she wrote in August. "If I can go to Port Royal, I will try to forget all these desires." Over the fall she would escape her prison and seek to start anew.[37]

While broad interventionists enhanced their missions by deepening their explorations of democracy, narrow interventionists journeyed in the opposite direction. James Miller McKim, founder of the Garrisonian Pennsylvania Anti-Slavery Society and Garrison's close ally, initiated what would become a widespread trend by transitioning away from immediatism toward a more straitened field: freedmen's aid. As historians have shown, racial paternalism permeated this emerging movement to provide material support to freed slaves. It was far less ambitious than abolitionism, offering Blacks temporary aid rather than lasting empowerment. "The negro needs justice more than pity . . . rights more than training," Douglass later scolded McKim.[38]

Immediatism and freedmen's aid, moreover, eventually became incompatible causes—a development that McKim now foreshadowed. Over the spring he became involved in the Port Royal Experiment through his freedmen's aid work. After organizing a relief committee for the Sea Islands, McKim decided to survey the situation personally in June. The deprived condition of the former slaves shocked him upon his arrival. "I thought I knew something about slavery," McKim wrote, "but 'till I came here I was ignorant of it." As he witnessed the extensive suffering of the former slaves, he became convinced that freedmen's aid took priority over agitating for racial equality. Upon arriving home, he resigned the presidency of the Pennsylvania Anti-Slavery Society, causing an uproar across the immediatist movement. Abolitionism, he explained, sought the "pulling-down" of the oppressions that African Americans faced. With the end of slavery, however, such a mission would be obsolete—a reflection of the narrow interventionist view that emancipation would be the definitive blow of immediatists' entire struggle. McKim therefore abandoned his leadership role within abolitionism to focus on "building-up"—on the material program.[39]

McKim also revealed how narrow interventionists, as they thought about Reconstruction in greater detail, further embraced restrictive racial views. Like their broad counterparts, they sought Blacks' inclusion, in some form, within the post-emancipation nation. Yet theirs was a vague, thin commitment grounded in wage-labor economics rather than expansive empowerment—a stance Conway and Garrison had revealed the previous year alongside a now regretful Cheever. Elaborating on this idea, McKim latched onto the Port Royal Experiment not for its racial potential, as Forten did, but for its economic implications. The antislavery businessmen like Edward Atkinson who funded the project had begun developing free-labor plantations in the islands, prioritizing cotton productivity over justice. In July, McKim extolled the successes of this economic system. Because of their "susceptibility to control," he crowed, freed slaves had proven the "happiest peasantry in the world." The "blacks are very tractable," he reiterated. He thereby emphasized narrow interventionists' belief in the value of former slaves as workers, freed to toil on their old plantations according to northern precepts.[40]

Conway combined wage-labor economics and racial paternalism with Anglo-Saxon unity in a more extreme, and explicitly antiegalitarian, vision. Like other narrow interventionists, and as he had done previously, he asserted in *The Golden Hour* that integrating Blacks into the post-emancipation polity signified little more than ensuring their destiny as free laborers. Conway chided colonizationists, warning that whites needed a workforce lest they live "in the midst of wasted fields." In an appeal to white self-interest, he contended that Blacks belonged in the postwar nation as wage workers, not equal citizens—a far cry from Phillips's and Douglass's conceptions.[41]

Unlike Garrison and McKim, Conway also framed emancipation in terms of Anglo-Saxon supremacy—and white southern primacy. The "virus of slavery," he explained in his book, had infected southerners, rending them from their fellows up north. Once cured of this ailment, southerners could reunite with northerners and forge a common destiny for the white race. Abolition, Conway believed, would facilitate bisectional, Anglo-Saxon greatness. As he emphasized in an April article in *The Atlantic Monthly,* white southerners, and especially Virginians, would be first among equals in this reunited nation. His native state of Virginia, he argued, was a glorious land that slavery had corrupted. Yet it could return still to its former place at the forefront of the Union. Citing the examples of John Smith and Patrick Henry, he asserted that Virginia had been the "center of activity and rule upon the continent," whose inhabitants "lived as Anglo-Saxon blood should." Slavery, however, had doomed it to "splendid ruin." Ignoring Blacks, he portrayed slavery as a curse upon white Virginians. It had fostered a population of illiterate poor whites and a ruling class "trained to despise labor." Idleness, he explained, bequeathed sinfulness. "At the University of Virginia one may see the extent of demoralization," Conway elaborated. "There the spree, the riot, and . . . the duel are normal." Abolition would end such dissolution, restoring Virginian virtue. "Virginia is, still, a sleeping beauty awaiting the hero whose kiss shall recall her to life," he concluded, advocating a free Union in which white Virginians led northerners to racial glory.[42]

Conway also steeped his conception of a morally transformed Union in racial paternalism, as his attempt to liberate his family's slaves illustrated. As the Union military advanced near his family plantation in Falmouth, Virginia, Conway learned that "our negroes have taken to their heels." Upon hearing that the thirty-odd fugitives "were wandering helplessly within the lines of the army," Conway intervened. In July, he traveled to Washington and secured Lincoln's permission to spirit the escaped slaves from Virginia to the antislavery hotbed of Yellow Springs, Ohio, where friends would settle them. While still in the capital, however, he encountered the fugitives, who had already liberated themselves. A dumbfounded Conway then escorted them by rail to Ohio.[43]

Conway in later years often discussed the Yellow Springs group, whom he referred to, patronizingly, as "my little colony." In demarcating their place in free society, he reinforced his paternalistic postwar vision. Late in the war, Conway detailed how the group "faithfully . . . toiled under the new conditions of freedom." They "worked well enough," he reaffirmed, "to disprove the Southern slander, that their class will not work except under the lash." Conway drew on what George M. Fredrickson has termed the doctrine of romantic racialism, which theorized innate racial differences between intelligent but materialistic whites and child-like Blacks. As he relayed, the group's only problem was "their exceeding piety," which often carried them "suddenly away from the field to some prayer-meeting." Delineating the power dynamics between his colony and himself, Conway concluded that "I can pronounce them to be most fit for freedom." His socioeconomically antiegalitarian imagined Reconstruction was worlds apart from that of broad interventionists, if only a harsher, southern-friendly version of Garrison and McKim's visions.[44]

THE HARDENING OF THE ABOLITIONIST CIVIL WAR

Despite their diverging worldviews, broad and narrow interventionists continued banding together to achieve military emancipation, and to confront their antiwar rivals. Amid the reversals of the spring, Pillsbury and Stephen Foster fully retreated to their original stances of unequivocal opposition to the Union war, rejoining Abby Kelley Foster. Pillsbury lost hope in the conflict's potential, resolving before the AASS in May that "we should never see slavery abolished by the war power." A flawed measure could never produce any flawless ends, he reaffirmed, jettisoning talk of the war's promise. Stephen Foster likewise offered a resolution denouncing a government acting from "selfish motives," rather than interest in Blacks' "rights as citizens." Abolitionists had to "abstain from giving it their support under the mistaken belief that they are thereby aiding the cause," he pleaded. Interventionists nonetheless swatted away this reunited opposition by tabling the resolutions.[45]

Moral purists grew more aggressive at the New England convention later that month. Stephen Foster led off the first day of the gathering by reiterating his opposition to the war, averring that Lincoln was "as truly a slaveholder as Jefferson Davis. He cannot even contemplate emancipation without colonization." Northerners, who "don't want liberty, except for themselves," were no better. They stomached abolition only as a "derrier [sic] resort"—a last-ditch war measure, lacking any moral value. Foster therefore assailed the war from outside, waiting still for the "principles of impartial justice" to foment equality through a pure, nonpolitical moral revolution.[46]

The next day, purists excoriated prowar abolitionists and their seeming failure. "Those abolitionists who gave the Administration any degree of support," Abby Kelley Foster asserted, had surrendered the high ground. "When we are ready to accept the less of two sinners," she chided, "the serpent of compromise has crept into our midst." As she concluded, interventionists should have returned to their "old ground of total abstinence" from mainstream politics. Stephen Foster then paired a resolution that he would "rather take his chances with Davis at the last judgment" than Lincoln with an assault upon his colleagues. A "marked change had come over [interventionists] in their dealing with slavery," he contended, again intimating their betrayal. Interrupting this attack, Pillsbury proclaimed that immediatists had to be moral agitators rather than political hangers-on to force change. As a longtime Garrisonian, Pillsbury admitted that he "disliked to differ with the antislavery leaders—his teachers." Purists, however, had "learned more than they." They, not interventionists, had become the keepers of the antislavery flame.[47]

Interventionists, unable still to abide such accusations, put aside their own dissatisfaction over the war to repel their assailants. Any "logic which put Jeff Davis above Lincoln" was nonsensical, asserted one interventionist. Should Davis win, the "platform from which Foster speaks would be taken from under him." Later, Garrison stated that he "had no pulse that did not beat for Lincoln against Davis." Though he criticized the government "when deserved," Garrison stood by the war, through which the "gains of freedom have been so rapid and magnificent." Amid cries of "Shame!" from Stephen Foster, Garrison tabled his resolution once again.[48]

Other interventionists resorted anew to ad hominem vitriol. Following the convention, Samuel May Jr. argued that Pillsbury was "characterized by fanaticism." Sarcastically, May prayed "not to part with our common sense" in equating Davis and Lincoln, as Foster had. And McKim mockingly coined the term "Parker Pillsbury-ist," connoting "too free a use of sepia." Beset by their own insecurities, prowar abolitionists lashed out in defense of their actions.[49]

The abolitionist civil war carried into the annual Fourth of July picnic at Framingham. In a letter to the gathering, Pillsbury declared that the government, with interventionists' support, was "murdering its young men in behalf of slavery." In response, interventionist Andrew Foss condescendingly explained interventionists' self-defined positions as the pragmatic center of abolitionism. "There are people so stupid that they cannot understand how you and I can be in sympathy" with the war, "yet not fully and entirely endorse all the . . . actions of the government," he asserted. Interventionists had to cling to the Union war as their only hope for the nation's salvation. Foss derided his opponents for overlooking this bigger picture. Yet purists felt that interventionists were doing much the same. "What have we to hope?" Pillsbury asked a friend. As both sides made clear, their worldviews had become incompatible.[50]

SUMMER DOLDRUMS, JULY–SEPTEMBER 1862

Despite their defiance against moral purists, interventionists began to doubt the Union war's continuing potential themselves as the summer wore on. "Enthusiasm has nearly become extinguished," Garrison confessed in July. Even the "hitherto most hopeful" had sunk into a "state of despondency." Not all news was bleak: that month, Congress passed the Second Confiscation Act, freeing all slaves entering Union lines. An unmoored Garrison, however, railed against both the legislation and expediency in general, labeling the act a "frightful exhibition of pride and folly" motivated by necessity over morality.[51]

Interventionists' despair worsened in August. Early that month, Lincoln invited Black leaders to the White House to extol the benefits of colonization. Days later, he wrote a public letter to newspaperman Horace Greeley vowing to preserve the Union at all costs, irrespective of slavery. Such were the actions of a consummate politician, appeasing conservatives in advance of his emancipation edict. Yet interventionists were appalled. As David W. Blight has shown, Douglass argued that appeals to racial separatism rallied whites in favor of further oppression—a view he maintained even as his sons Lewis and Charles expressed their disgust with the war by joining a governmental colonization scheme to resettle African Americans in Panama. In his journal, Douglass labeled Lincoln a "representative of American prejudice and Negro hatred." The president, he affirmed, sought "to shield and protect slavery." As his hopes dissipated, Douglass confessed he had "less ground" than ever to suppose that Lincoln would use the war power.[52]

Interventionists, yet unaware that the gears of emancipation were turning, assailed Lincoln's character. Conway turned on the president in an August speech, portraying him as "worse than worthless." Like Phillips, Conway contested Garrison's public assertion that Lincoln was more morally advanced than the northern public, declaring that the president, far from leading, was "simply staying [still]." Garrison, for his part, fumed privately that Lincoln was a "wet rag" under Copperhead control. "I am growing more and more skeptical as to [his] honesty," he sighed. Douglass, meanwhile, lamented to a friend that the "nation was never more completely in the hands of the slave power." The Union, he concluded, ought to sue for peace. Interventionists were struggling to see how their fight for the golden moment could succeed.[53]

Even amid their sinking hopes, prowar abolitionists would not—or, perhaps, could not—pull away from their own interventions. They had made clear early in the war that they would stand by Lincoln for the time being, yet would abandon him if necessary. But such a point had not yet arrived. In June, Garrison reported a "concurrence of judgment" among interventionists to persevere. That accordance still held at summer's end. Interventionists, Garrison noted, would continue to "condemn where we must, and approve where we can." Their sole path forward was to hold the progovernment line, tolerating Lincoln as a wartime necessary evil. They thus continued to work through the antislavery alliance over the summer, organizing another proemancipation rally alongside antislavery conservatives and businessmen in New York.[54]

Conway affirmed his dedication to interventionists' strategy by vacating his Cincinnati pulpit for Massachusetts to edit the new Emancipation League organ, *The Commonwealth.* In his journal, he again brandished his credentials as a moralistic reformer while simultaneously espousing expediency. In his September inaugural issue, he declared he was "in favor of the Union as it *wasn't,* as it was meant to be"—a righteous one. Later, he lamented that justice had to "be urged as a nauseous dose." The nation had to enact justice for "justice's sake," he averred. Yet in the same issue he urged readers to "stand by the government." Conway spilled interventionists' inner moral conflict onto his journal's pages, invoking principle in theory but pragmatism in practice.[55]

Despite her own despondency, Child also opted not to change course. "Long-conflicting hopes and fears, which have agitated my soul, have subsided at last into resignation," she sighed in August. Part of the problem was "how dreadfully slow Lincoln is." As she informed Sumner, however, "I do not blame the President." He merely followed public opinion. As Carolyn L. Karcher has argued, Child also suspected that William Seward was dissuading Lincoln from action. A demoralized public and cabinet were thereby causing his stagnation. Child subsequently wrote a public letter to Lincoln, lauding his virtues while begging him to "look upward instead of downward. Place your reliance on *principles* rather than men." Lincoln, she pled, had to lurch ahead of the public and his advisers and take charge.[56]

Though Child continued to support the war, its human cost remained etched in her mind. "The war is an unmitigated horror to me," she asserted in July. In corresponding with Sarah Blake Shaw, a fellow immediatist and her boon companion, Child confronted still what Karcher has labeled the "excruciating" moral quandary of desiring for the Union to suffer further defeats until it embraced emancipation. Upon hearing the "cannon booming from the navy-yard for victories gained, I cannot feel exultant, as others do," she confessed. When faced with the carnage of the war, her hope for its prolongation yet gave her a "pang, as if it were something wicked and monstrous." In the throes of anguish, Child continued to grapple with her "inward struggle" by simultaneously mourning Union losses and demanding that such bloodshed continue.[57]

Phillips, by contrast, joined Cheever in drifting away from interventionists' progovernment consensus. While he had remained loyal to the government over the spring, the course of events now impelled him to reconsider his support of the president. Phillips still backed the war, affirming in an August public letter that "I believe in the Union." The Union, however, was "one thing. This *administration* is quite another." Like Cheever, Phillips began to distinguish the Union war, which he endorsed, from its chief prosecutor, Lincoln, whom he did not. "The Union belongs to me as much as to Lincoln," he continued. The president, however, was "dragging the Union to ruin." Phillips thus concluded that he had to forswear Lincoln and oppose the government in order to rescue the nation. His provocative letter incited controversy among both abolitionists and the wider public, as antiabolitionist politicians called upon Lincoln to arrest Phillips.[58]

The logical tenuousness of his stance aside, Phillips believed that he had no other option—that Lincoln was irredeemably proslavery. The president, he elaborated the same month, was fighting for the "Union as it was, [not] the Union as it ought to be"—a nation grounded in the "equality of every man before the law." Loyal criticism would not suffice. In reply to the claim of abolitionist Sydney Howard Gay that Lincoln remained persuadable, Phillips gave voice to his disenchantment. "He won't be flattered," Phillips offered from experience. "He can only be frightened or bullied into the right policy." Others "agree with you and your method," Phillips continued. "I did awhile. I don't now." Phillips therefore vowed "not to support such an Administration of imbeciles." By repudiating Gay's approach of loyal persuasion, he also renounced the interventionist platform. Phillips was "no longer exclusively a Garrisonian—I'm a citizen," he told a friend, breaking away from the interventionist camp to save the Union on his own terms.[59]

Over the spring and summer, a cascading series of developments set prowar abolitionists like Phillips back on their heels. While interventionists largely denounced Lincoln within set limits, Cheever and, later, Phillips soured on doing so. The cracks within the interventionist camp also began to widen, as broad and narrow interventionists clarified their divergent post-emancipation visions. Only their shared focus on the golden moment, and on countering purists, still bound them. Yet interventionists would soon learn that their pressure campaign had worked. As their strategy achieved its long-desired results, Cheever and Phillips would halt their defiance of the interventionist consensus to join in celebration of emancipation. Theirs was not a linear tactical evolution: only after further disappointments would they adopt a full-fledged program of opposition to Lincoln, anchored in their new realm of political change.

CHAPTER SEVEN

The Afterglow of Emancipation, September 1862–January 1863

On January 1, 1863, William Lloyd Garrison gathered with other prominent Bostonians at the Boston Music Hall as they nervously awaited news about whether Lincoln had kept his word and issued a final version of the Emancipation Proclamation. When the crowd learned that Lincoln had done so, an observer reported that a "storm of enthusiasm followed. . . . Shouts arose, hats and handkerchiefs were waved, men and women sprang to their feet to give more energetic utterance to their joy." As the *Liberator* relayed, all those assembled recognized that the "first of January, 1863 has now taken rank with the fourth of July, 1776, in the history of this country." As musicians played Handel's *Messiah* onstage, the ecstatic attendees cheered first for Lincoln and then for Garrison himself. Interventionists, they understood, had helped usher the momentous proclamation into existence.[1]

Garrison, who had delayed the printing of his next issue, soon dashed to the *Liberator* office. In relaying the news of Lincoln's edict, he added: "It will be hailed with joy and thanksgiving by the friends of freedom. . . . It is a great historic event, sublime in its magnitude." The moment, Garrison knew, was the most significant of his lifetime—an unprecedented restructuring of the nation, launching the largest appropriation of private property in Western history to that date. At last, the Union had awoken from its demoralized slumber to align with the forces of freedom and purge its original sin. Thanks in part to the antislavery alliance, the nation finally warranted abolitionists' decades-long project of national moral redemption. In this consummate victory of the interventionist camp, however, lay the seeds of its unraveling during the war's second half.[2]

Between September 1862 and January 1863, abolitionists took in the historic changes sweeping over the country. As they staggered into September full of despair, they were caught off guard when Lincoln issued his preliminary Emancipation Proclamation. This edict created a crisis of meaning for interventionists, exposing the challenges inherent in conceptualizing a morally transformed Union. By endorsing military emancipation, Lincoln had validated their interest group strategy. Yet the form of his decree, from its delaying of emancipation until the new year to its calls for colonization and gradualism, disconcerted them. Perplexed activists like Douglass and Garrison responded disjointedly, reeling between hope and anxiety. As they, too, grasped for a sense of coherence, Phillips and Cheever halted their breaks with Lincoln and the interventionist camp. Moral purists, meanwhile, rejected Lincoln's edict as a proslavery trick.

Once Lincoln issued his binding final proclamation, replacing talk of colonization with that of moral duty, interventionists coalesced in celebration—and in taking credit for military emancipation. In the wake of achieving their golden moment they also pivoted to the future, vowing to perfect Lincoln's limited edict by making abolition unconditional and permanent. Yet behind their unified facade hid two related divides: the older struggle between narrow and broad interventionists and a new one over Lincoln's deepest intentions. While narrow interventionists like Garrison began framing the formal abolition of slavery, or total emancipation, as their endpoint, broad interventionists like Douglass, Forten, and Phillips portrayed it as the opening salvo in a larger struggle for legislative equality. Along mostly congruous lines, narrow interventionists, joined by Child, extolled Lincoln for his edict, while broad interventionists, joined by Cheever and Conway, downplayed his agency in issuing it. Purists, meanwhile, realized they had misjudged the chances of emancipation and, accordingly, jettisoned their antiwar positions.[3]

Interventionists tried to sidestep these disagreements and return to their proven tactics, pursuing change through their alliance on a number of fronts. On select issues, such methods still worked. After New England Republicans solicited abolitionists' aid in a series of spring gubernatorial contests against a resurgent Democratic Party, Anna Dickinson helped turn the tide. Black activists from Douglass to William Wells Brown, meanwhile, united to advocate military enlistment with support from antislavery businessmen like John Murray Forbes. As such elites stressed, however, they would gladly let Blacks fight, but they wanted nothing approaching racial equality.

Yet now that the coalition had fulfilled its animating purpose of achieving military emancipation, mainstream politicos began to shunt aside immediatists when they no longer proved politically useful. The public appetite on reform extended only to expedient emancipation as a war measure, rather than to further advances born of racial justice. On employing the usual channels for less palatable issues like unconditional emancipation, let alone Black rights, interventionists encountered insurmountable difficulties. In December, Cheever entreated the president to make emancipation both permanent and motivated solely by justice. He failed, reigniting his opposition to Lincoln and the interventionist camp. In January, Phillips and Conway met with Lincoln to similarly dismal results, while also lobbying Radical leaders to create an Emancipation Bureau to render abolition complete and meaningful—a vague idea that masked their differences regarding Black rights. Yet their allies, too, declined to act. In a rude awakening that inflamed their tensions, interventionists realized that their influence, and the benefits of their once-effective alliance, reached only so far.

ASSESSING THE PRELIMINARY PROCLAMATION

Interventionists limped into the fall of 1862 bent but not broken, hoping against hope that their pressure strategy had not failed. After the Union victory at Antietam in late September, however, Lincoln decided to issue his long-gestating preliminary proclamation, declaring that any slaves in areas still under rebellion on January 1 would be "forever free." By embracing the war power, Lincoln proved interventionists correct. They had channeled the political mainstream to help transform military emancipation from a far-fetched dream into a politically acceptable reality. In significant part thanks to their efforts, the Union was on the cusp of a truly earth-shattering act.[4]

Yet the preliminary proclamation also threw interventionists off stride, impelling them to shake off their fatalism and adjust to a rapidly changing war. Accentuating their disorientation, the edict combined the promise of emancipation with a series of dispiriting provisions. First, Lincoln delayed emancipation, enabling rebel states to return to the Union before the new year to save slavery. Douglass fretted that abolition was "put off—it was made future and conditional—not present and absolute." January 1, he declared, would be "the great day which is to determine [the nation's] destiny." Whether that day would bring freedom or slavery remained unclear. Child likewise worried over the "contingencies that may occur," such as the rebels preempting Lincoln by declaring emancipation. "I think the peril of the country was never so great as now," she confessed. As these reformers agreed, Lincoln had blundered by putting slavery's fate in rebel hands.[5]

Second, should Lincoln's proclamation go into effect, it would apply only to those states engaged in rebellion. Even as it labeled Lincoln's decree a "staggering blow," the AASS lamented that the four "so-called loyal slave states" would continue as such, leaving emancipation incomplete. In proposing this qualified abolition, Lincoln also employed dry, legalistic language, grounding his arguments entirely in the rhetoric of military necessity. "An expedient can never proceed as an act of justice," scorned Conway, taking the high ground to call for right, not might. Douglass likewise charged that the edict "touched neither justice nor mercy," containing "[not] one expression of sound moral feeling against slavery." Interventionists, unlike moral purists, believed that emancipation proceeding from any motive could foment a perfecting moral revolution. Yet they regretted that Lincoln was depriving the moment of any moral gravitas. "I should have been glad if it [was] put on principle of justice and right, not of mere war necessity. . . . Nevertheless the deed is done," one interventionist sighed in resignation.[6]

Finally, Lincoln's preliminary proclamation reiterated his support for compensation and colonization. While interventionists from Garrison to Phillips had endorsed compensation over the past year, they had long made repudiating colonization the beating heart of their agendas. Garrison therefore assailed the preliminary edict's "mean, absurd, and proscriptive device to expatriate the colored people from this, their native land," emphasizing abolitionists' shared commitment to incorporating Blacks into the polity—and downplaying the wildly divergent models of broad and narrow interventionists of Black rights.[7]

In processing the preliminary proclamation, interventionists experienced a crisis of coherence, revealing the difficulties of translating their distinctive visions into material realities during an evolving crisis. As they cast about for a consistent response to the edict's bewildering mix of uplifting and alarming aspects, they lurched between optimism and dismay. Douglass registered relief in October that his wartime lobbying may have worked—that the "Star Spangled Banner is now the harbinger of liberty." Soon, "America will, higher than ever, sit as a queen among the nations," he imagined. "We shout for joy that we live to record this righteous decree," Douglass enthused. Yet he lamented the preliminary proclamation's shortcomings in anxious tones later that fall, averring that no "thrill of joy [ran] round the world" because of the edict.[8]

Other interventionists also responded in disconnected fashion. Garrison, who was usually publicly supportive of Lincoln, declared in the *Liberator* that the "proclamation is not all that the exigency of the times and the consequent duty of the government require—and therefore [we] are not so jubilant over it as many others." At the same time, he noted tepidly that "it is an important step in the right direction." Distilling her own uncertainty, Child confessed that she "was thankful for the President's Proclamation, but by no means jubilant." Interventionists, unsure about the future they were transitioning to, met the complex times with perplexed ambivalence.[9]

As they evaluated whether the president had enacted abolitionists' will, Phillips and Cheever reconsidered their recent ruptures with Lincoln and the interventionist fold. In November, Phillips announced that he was "not going to criticize the President." He did not hold Lincoln in especially high regard, deeming him the "only instrument we have got." Phillips nonetheless believed he had "turned the corner, and recognizes the fact, not simply that the slaves of rebels, but that *slaves* must be freed." In reentering the progovernment fold, however, Phillips offered Lincoln a short leash, implying that anything less than total emancipation and Black rights would reignite his wrath.[10]

George Cheever especially exemplified abolitionists' autumn incoherence. In late September, he opted against reconciling with either Lincoln or the interventionist camp as he protested the "oppression of such moral degradation forced upon us by the President." Reiterating his argument from the previous spring, Cheever asserted that Lincoln served the "proslavery democratic despotism." The preliminary proclamation, he argued, was a "bribe to win back the slaveholding states." Should the rebels refuse, Lincoln would "adjourn indefinitely" the order. Even if it went into effect, it was a debased "measure of mere political expediency." Rather than evince "humanity towards the poor black race," Lincoln endorsed colonization. Cheever thereby vowed in purist tones to oppose the "frightful demoralization" of the edict.[11]

But as the proclamation's deadline approached, Cheever reversed this purist turn. In November, he penned a conciliatory letter to Lincoln. "Will you kindly permit an individual, who daily implores for you the protection and guidance of Heaven, to plead with you in behalf of the enslaved?" he began. Dissembling through flattery, Cheever asked the president to offer unconditional emancipation on a moralistic basis. Lincoln, he argued, should allow "God and justice" to animate the final edict alongside the "plea of expediency" and the "necessity of our own existence." By allowing the "moral to inspire the martial," Lincoln could ensure divine backing of the Union army and "guarantee success to our arms." Cheever thereby retracted his recent assertions to argue that morality and necessity together could regenerate the nation.[12]

Turning to the topic of total emancipation, Cheever further embraced expediency. Lincoln, he argued, should make the "emancipating clause universal and unconditional." Out of concern that the Confederates would return to the Union with slavery intact, Cheever proposed that returning rebels "be guaranteed, instead of the exception from emancipation as at first proposed, an equitable compensation for the freedom of their slaves." Such a measure would employ morally questionable means for the greater good. "In absolute justice, compensation is due not to the masters, but to the slaves," Cheever admitted. "Yet if you deem compensation of the masters a necessity, better that, than the offer of the slaves as chattels," he concluded, choosing the path of least resistance—and repudiating moral purity. Cheever thus returned to the progovernment fold, veering from absolutism to pragmatism as he made sense of the preliminary proclamation.[13]

Moral purists, by contrast, firmly rejected the preliminary proclamation as unlikely to go into effect—and insufficient even if it did. "Many rejoiced," Pillsbury observed in December. "I, too, tried hard to be glad." The decree, however, was a "pledge to the South of full forgiveness." Pillsbury assumed that the rebels would forestall its onset by rejoining the Union. But even if it were enacted, the decree would be a failed, imperfect instrument. "Until somebody calls for justice, until we talk of something besides compensation and colonization and act from higher considerations than military necessity . . . [I have] little over which to be cheering," Pillsbury informed a friend. The preliminary edict lacked any moral underpinning. It refused to "recognize the slave as a man, with equal and inalienable rights," Pillsbury and Stephen Foster argued before an antislavery meeting. An order proceeding from white self-interest over racial justice, they reaffirmed, would never create their egalitarian morally transformed Union. It was "as unworthy of respect as [it was] devoid of the means and assurances of national salvation." Pillsbury therefore swore to "maintain our old position" by holding fast against the war.[14]

A series of concerning developments soon bolstered moral purists' arguments—and interventionists' confusion. Ahead of the November midterm elections in New York, the Democratic gubernatorial candidate, Horatio Seymour, campaigned against the preliminary proclamation. His victory, Douglass warned, would be disastrous. "If the state goes for Seymour a shout will arise for peace at *any* price," he feared, eroding Lincoln's antislavery resolve. Reinforcing the endemic racism and antipathy to racial equality of the white North, however, Seymour rode a backlash against the edict into power as part of a Democratic wave nationwide. As interventionists realized, this result endangered both Lincoln's decree and their own cause. New York abolitionist Theodore Tilton wondered to Phillips if there would be "a recall of the Proclamation." Lincoln, he reported, was "lamenting the issue of his Proclamation, and calling it the great mistake of his life. That looks ominous!" The administration, it seemed, was faltering.[15]

In December, Lincoln compounded such anxieties by reaffirming the predominant Republican vision of a white, free-labor Union in his annual Message to Congress. He again endorsed colonization, while appealing to the Border States by outlining a gradual program to phase out slavery by 1900. Naturally, immediatists were outraged. Straying from his standard praise of the government, Conway denounced Lincoln in the *Commonwealth* as a "man of inadequate caliber." The preliminary edict, he observed, attacked slavery "directly and immediately" through the war power by making the army into an emancipatory instrument. Yet Lincoln "impaired that action by a Message, running counter to it," supplanting the immediate war power with a gradual scheme. While some reformers advocated compensation to expedite the onset of emancipation and Black rights, Lincoln dangled it to delay emancipation and enable colonization. The "vacillations of President Lincoln will greatly perplex the future historian" and contemporary abolitionists alike, Conway sighed. Immediate emancipation, he added, would bring "vastly less trouble" than Lincoln's plan. It would restore order, keeping freed slaves "where they have hitherto lived, if good treatment is given and fair wages for labor offered, by their former masters." Even in assaulting Lincoln, Conway thereby reiterated his paternalistic postwar vision.[16]

As Lincoln ran roughshod over the core beliefs of immediatism, Garrison also shed his typical moderation, scathing in the *Liberator* that the message bore "marks of crudeness, incongruity, [and] feebleness." Though he had endorsed compensation months earlier, Garrison now rejected it in a fit of moral conflict, arguing that the proclamation preempted the need for such an unsavory expedient. Why, he asked, would the Union retreat from the war power to "bribe the traitors?" Garrison scorned that Lincoln's retrogressive proposal "borders on hopeless lunacy . . . it would, in our judgment, warrant the impeachment of the President by Congress as mentally incapable." Regarding colonization, he stressed that former slaves "have as good a right to remain here as the President." Blacks, he added, are "of immense value, and indispensable to the South in the cultivation of cotton . . . as free laborers." Garrison thus joined Conway in censuring Lincoln—and in affirming a narrow postwar vision predicated on Black menial labor.[17]

Cheever, meanwhile, responded to the message by pivoting yet again, rethinking his overture to Lincoln and regretting his relapse into expediency. "I begin to think there is no actual intention of doing anything more, except by compromise," he lamented. If Lincoln could endorse such vulgar proposals so near January 1, Cheever had little faith that military emancipation would actually occur. In a state of panic, he contacted Radical Republican allies in Washington to gain further insight into Lincoln's plans, inquiring "whether there is hope." James Harlan assuaged Cheever that Lincoln would not "recede from the proclamation," while James Ashley comforted that "in heart—he was far in advance of the message." A conflicted and unconvinced Cheever, however, would soon decide to seek assurances from Lincoln himself.[18]

Douglass also worried about Lincoln's true intent. In his journal, he feared the message "cast a doubt on the promised and hoped for proclamation." He soon turned his gaze to Britain. Acting like what David W. Blight has called a "one-man political action committee for emancipation," he began lobbying his friends for aid. Many offered support while assuring him that "things seem leading in a more antislavery direction." Further bolstering Douglass's spirits during this trying time was the collapse of the colonization scheme in which his sons had enrolled. He, too, thus ended the year awaiting a potential new epoch with equal parts anticipation and trepidation.[19]

ABOLITIONISTS IN THE AGE OF EMANCIPATION

Abolitionists' anxieties evaporated when Lincoln issued the final Emancipation Proclamation on January 1, declaring slaves in rebel-held areas forever free. While it exempted the Border States and most Union-held areas of the Confederacy from its purview, the final edict improved upon the original version—and upon his recent message. As James Oakes has argued, Lincoln was demonstrating moral growth by evolving from a leader fixated on preserving the Union into a committed, idealistic emancipator. His edict expunged mentions of colonization and gradualism, injecting moral purpose into the war by declaring emancipation an "act of justice" as well as a military necessity. He also endorsed Black enlistment in the Union military.[20]

Unlike after the preliminary version, interventionists recognized that the final proclamation signified their clear-cut victory. They had realized their millenarian golden moment, remaking the war into a fight for emancipation and a crucible for moral revolution. They accordingly began exulting in the afterglow of emancipation. Days after Garrison's celebration at the Boston Music Hall, Phillips ascended its flag-festooned platform. As he noted, he had first "spoken under the United States banner" in 1861, when he had outlined the war's antislavery potential. On the same stage, Phillips now declared that potential realized. The Union, he proclaimed, "finally unsheathes its sword, and announces its determined purpose to be a nation"—a singular unit bound by principle. Now, "Nationality means Justice; the Union is synonymous with liberty." As Phillips marveled, "Are these not glorious times?" In his diary, Conway labeled the president's edict "as awkward as [Lincoln] himself—but still it liberates nearly 3,200,000 slaves!" As he gloried, the "object of the war [is] the abolition of slavery." Speaking in New York, Douglass likewise labeled military emancipation the "greatest event in our nation's history." At last, the "wings of the American Eagle afford shelter and protection to men of all colors." As interventionists agreed, the Emancipation Proclamation was an epochal milestone which returned a nation that had lost its way onto its providential path.[21]

Awash in jubilation, prowar abolitionists trumpeted their roles in precipitating the edict. "Thirty-two years ago this day Garrison unfurled the banner of immediate emancipation," one abolitionist wrote on January 1, connecting the two moments in history. After decades of frustration, interventionists had taken a chance by latching onto the war and gradually building a powerful lobbying machine. Without the carrot and stick they waved at the White House in equal measure, Edmund Quincy asserted, the proclamation "would never have been issued." Prowar abolitionists had helped render the once-impossible possible. At the January meeting of the MASS, Garrison labeled them the "commanding power of the nation"—the shaper of its destiny. Interventionists thus basked in their influence—and overestimated its extent going forward.[22]

Even amid their revelry, interventionists craned their necks ahead to the future. While the Union had adopted emancipation as a war aim, putting the nation on the path to moral sublimity, it had not destroyed slavery. "I value the proclamation," Phillips informed the MASS, "[but] not as a finality . . . [it]

covers only half the ground." Even now, it remained an imperfect and incomplete mechanism in three respects. First, it was temporary—an impermanent and revocable executive order. Garrison hence emphasized that Lincoln was "solemnly bound to finish what he has so largely performed" by executing his order and ensuring freedom's triumph.[23]

Second, Lincoln's edict was dependent, relying on the progress and compliance of the military for its implementation. Slavery "can only be extinguished under the Proclamation by actual conquest of the country," Quincy observed. On the ground, emancipation extended only as far as Union forces penetrated into the Confederacy. Officers, another immediatist added, had to "push forward ... with a sincere determination to carry it into effect." Interventionists like Phillips had gravitated during the war to the army as an emancipatory instrument. Yet Conway fretted that Lincoln had installed a cadre of proslavery generals who would ensure that "emancipation shall not too soon become actual." And finally, the decree's version of emancipation was partial and riddled with exemptions. "It seems a blunder that slavery was not everywhere abolished," Douglass lamented. Lincoln, Garrison agreed, "may rightfully decree the emancipation of all the slaves." Despite their exuberance, interventionists recognized the continued uncertainties of the emancipation process. The total emancipation they sought remained far from inevitable.[24]

In the ensuing weeks, interventionists dedicated themselves to the task of perfecting the Emancipation Proclamation and securing the formal end of enslavement. Their unity in doing so, however, was specious. As became clear, two fissures divided them: the long-simmering struggle between narrow and broad interventionists and a new, largely overlapping one over Lincoln. Regarding the former, narrow interventionists like Garrison now reframed their longstanding conceptions of total emancipation as not just the climactic, but also the concluding battle of organized antislavery reform. "Let no one suppose that the Abolitionists wish to continue in the field a moment longer than their labors are needed," he asserted before the MASS. As he stressed, their mission was emancipation. Immediatists, he argued, could not "dream of disbanding our organization ... [until] every human being shall rejoice in his freedom. Then, and not until then, will our work as Abolitionists be acceptably ended." Lincoln's decree thereby marked the beginning of their end. They had only to build on their established success and complete the process of military emancipation to fulfill their lifelong work.[25]

Yet Garrison's argument contradicted his original view. In launching the immediatist movement, he had established its dedication to emancipation and post-emancipation Black rights. While he had imagined a limited Reconstruction thus far, with a fairly restrictive conception of Black inclusion, he now began cutting post-emancipation concerns from his agenda entirely. In his speech he referred to freedmen's aid by noting that activists had to "succor and elevate the liberated bondmen." Yet as "Abolitionists distinctively," their work concluded with the "overthrow of slavery." As he settled into a mainstream that granted him success yet prodded him away from his founding aims, Garrison was reorienting toward a white North that treated slavery and race, and now emancipation and equality, as disconnected issues. He began distinguishing formal freedom from Black rights, the first as his all-consuming goal and the second as a separate matter that was perhaps beyond his purview. Fulfilling purists' prophecy, Garrison and his clique of fellow narrow interventionists like Quincy, James Miller McKim, Oliver Johnson, and Samuel May Jr. were losing sight of their deepest moral commitments amid their productive political forays.[26]

Broad interventionists, meanwhile, depicted emancipation as the starting point of a more extensive crusade. After a "period of darkness," Douglass declared, the "dawn of light" had emerged. At a January celebration, Phillips labeled Lincoln's edict a "step in the progress of a people rich, prosperous, independent." These broad interventionists portrayed the decree as a clarion call to inspire sweeping change—an initial victory in a lifelong war for legislative equality, rather than Garrison's beginning of the end. Total emancipation would complete this catalytic first step, not culminate their campaign. As Phillips explained, the "proclamation is not a thing that annihilates the system. You do not annihilate a thing by abolishing it. You have got to supply the vacancy." To eradicate slavery, immediatists had to push beyond formally abolishing it to stamping out its lingering effects in an expansive Reconstruction. Invoking his idea of a unified nationality, Phillips asked northerners to "take the system of the Gulf States to pieces" by offering land to former slaves and Union veterans. A "United States uniform" would further empower freed slaves to regenerate the South, he added in a call for Black enlistment.[27]

Forten, meanwhile, undertook moral regeneration on the ground after arriving in the Sea Islands over the fall. Initially, her northern classist attitudes shaped her approach toward educating former slaves there. She treated her wards as alien others, chronicling their behavior in a detached and ethnographic manner. Soon after her arrival, she described a ring shout in her diary as "very wild and strange," adding in a report to the *Liberator* that the "people [sing] with a peculiar swaying motion of the body." Forten also promoted the elitist theory of racial uplift in striving to elevate freed slaves to a respectable social status. "I am *truly* glad that the poor creatures are trying to live right and virtuous lives," she confided condescendingly in her diary.[28]

But as she grew more familiar with her students, Forten softened her attitudes and moved toward a more mature perspective on race and reform. As a victim of prejudice herself, she came to recognize that racial oppression had no regional or class bounds. "I wish [northerners], who say the race is hopelessly and naturally inferior, could see the readiness with which these children, so long oppressed . . . learn and understand," she wrote the *Liberator*, making an all-encompassing case for Black equality. To inspire her pupils "with high purpose" about what "one of their own color could do for his race," Forten lectured them on Toussaint Louverture. She also evinced a broad interventionist's understanding of emancipation and Black rights. In her diary, she reacted to Lincoln's proclamation by noting that "Freedom was surely born in our land." At the same time, she cautioned that the "dawn of freedom which it heralds may not break upon us all at once." The edict had dawned a new day, but noon remained distant. Forten, like other broad interventionists, would further rarefy an expansive vision of what such daylight entailed.[29]

Over time, the disagreements between narrow and broad interventionists would roil abolitionism, permanently splintering the movement at war's end. More immediately, they would bleed into a burgeoning battle over Lincoln's leadership, fought along similar, but not identical, lines. Despite their attempts at unity, interventionists presaged this looming division in discussing the Emancipation Proclamation. Those narrow interventionists like Garrison who would soon become pro-Lincoln partisans credited him for the decree. At the January MASS meeting, Garrison lauded the "language of the President" in framing military emancipation as an act of righteousness as well as practicality. "I take it for granted," he affirmed, that Lincoln would be "consistent in carrying that proclamation into effect." In addition to publicly praising Lincoln as a great emancipator, Garrison also trusted him to execute his edict.[30]

Though Child, as discussed in later chapters, was not a narrow interventionist, she also acclaimed Lincoln for issuing his edict. As Carolyn L. Karcher has argued, Child's earlier doubts about the president melted away in the new epoch. By following through on his decree, Child asserted, Lincoln proved that he "has got his back up." Now, she averred, the nation "shall at last rely upon principle." Child thereby began to gravitate closer toward the president.[31]

Broad interventionists like Phillips led the other side of this growing divide over Lincoln. Though they shied away from breaking anew with the president in the aftermath of the proclamation, they revealed their seething discontentment in assessing his decree, jumping through rhetorical hoops to minimize Lincoln's role in issuing it. Throughout early 1863, Phillips depicted it as a popular mandate forced upon a reluctant president. "The people are fighting this battle," he argued in January. As in the past, he maintained that the public had morally leapfrogged over Lincoln, asserting that they had embraced emancipation over the "prejudices of the President." The edict, he averred, was "wrung by the determined heart of the masses from the reluctance of leaders." Lincoln deserved little, if any, credit for its issuance.[32]

In light of the previous spring's reversals, Phillips also refused to trust Lincoln, or suppress his moral ambivalence, again. While he hoped that the "mighty current is too strong for any reluctance of individuals," immediatists still had to hold the president accountable. As Phillips noted at a January gathering, they had three months to make Lincoln enact total emancipation before a more Democratic Congress came into session and stymied progress. Until then, Phillips would maintain his détente with the administration, albeit with chagrin. "It is not to be expected of [Lincoln], that he shall be a ripened statesman, with . . . an entire appreciation of events," he sighed. Still, Lincoln was the "best we can get; and we can have nobody else for two years." Abolitionists had "no choice, [but] to stand by him" for now, Phillips concluded. As his half-hearted endorsement implied, however, he would oppose Lincoln again if necessary.[33]

Cheever, though he was not a broad interventionist, followed Phillips's example because of his distrust of Lincoln as a despot. In January, he, too, deemed the proclamation a "reluctant step" by the president. While Phillips credited the people for forcing his hand, Cheever thanked God. When the Senate invited him back to Washington in February, Cheever framed the decree as "gone forth from the throne of the Most High, and not from any mortal Administration." Lincoln, who had "proclaimed to the world the sacredness of property in man," was "under God's compulsion." As Cheever argued, the president could "do nothing but stand now in the bell tower where God has shut him up, and pull the rope at God's bidding." The minister thereby reduced Lincoln into the unwilling yet powerless puppet of divine will.[34]

Conway, who was a resoundingly narrow interventionist, also refused to laud Lincoln. Though he, unlike Phillips and Cheever, remained mostly supportive of the president in public, he decried the proclamation's dry language.

"It must have required considerable ingenuity" to offer the "priceless boon of Liberty in such a cold and ungraceful way," he wrote in the *Commonwealth*. Conway also critiqued Lincoln's "almost contradictory" approach toward freed slaves. "In one breath he intimates a desire that the negroes should stay where they are and work . . . in the next, he invites them to become our soldiers," Conway exclaimed with evident bemusement.[35]

Through their responses, Phillips, Cheever, and Conway sowed the seeds for a split with Garrison that would realign wartime immediatism a second time. In this reconfigured abolitionist civil war, they would find common ground with moral purists. Pillsbury and the Fosters had rejected the war from its inception, as they simultaneously doubted its—and interventionists'—ability to foment abolition and emphasized the inadequacy of any potential expedient emancipation. Now that their former assumption had proven erroneous, purists reappraised their antiwar positions. They could not deny that freedom was at least taking hold, if only imperfectly. These figures still clung in theory to their saintly model of activism, in which virtuous ends mandated virtuous means. Yet in practice, they began moving haltingly past their doctrine of unassailable aloofness and their vow to wait until the conflict had already attained perfection before getting involved. As purists now argued, the Union war had become worthy of their support, especially against proslavery Confederates and Copperheads. In a February public letter, Pillsbury assailed the "machinations of traitors and tyrants South and North" who sought a peace "more dreadful than war." In a startling about-face, he also endorsed the prowar Republicans in upcoming state elections.[36]

As they shed their antiwar stances, moral purists began transferring their animus from the Union war generally to Lincoln specifically. Forced to acknowledge that expedient emancipation was better than nothing, they reframed the war as not proslavery but imperfectly antislavery—an insufficient vehicle for racial egalitarianism. They accordingly refocused their fire on the Emancipation Proclamation and its author. One purist labeled the edict a "snaking, impotently wicked thing." In gentler terms, Stephen Foster pled for Lincoln to enact "unconditional emancipation in every portion of the country" rather than settle for half-measures.[37]

As they witnessed this seismic shift, interventionists declared victory over the antiwar camp. In the *Liberator*, Garrison crowed how the Emancipation Proclamation had rallied antislavery Britons, including formerly antiwar moral purists, to the Union cause. "There is a unanimity of feeling as surprising as it is unexpected," he boasted in February about a pro-Union rally in Bristol. Erstwhile opponents like Richard Davis Webb now supported the Union with gusto, justifying Garrison's triumphalism—but not his resulting expectations of restored abolitionist unity.[38]

POLITICOS AND THE GROWING LIMITATIONS OF THE ANTISLAVERY ALLIANCE

In attempting to tackle this new age, interventionists fell back on their tried-and-true methods. Over the past two years, they had papered over their internal differences to advance change in concert. Now, they attempted much the same, pursuing a variety of additional reforms through their antislavery alliance. In certain respects, the bonds of this coalition strengthened in the new year. Antislavery conservatives and businessmen such as Edward Everett, George Bancroft, Charles King, John Austin Stevens Jr., and John Murray Forbes formed a plethora of Unionist organizations, including the Union League, the Loyal National League, the Loyal League of Union Citizens, and the Loyal Publication Society. All such groups embraced Lincoln's proclamation. At a meeting of the Loyal League of Union Citizens, a member gloried that "by the progress of our arms, slavery is overthrown." And in May, the Loyal National League outlined how the "material forces of liberty and slavery [were] arrayed in deadly strife," thereby normalizing military emancipation as a Union war aim.[39]

These Unionist organizations quickly became fundamental cogs in the antislavery alliance. Sydney Howard Gay sat on the Loyal National League's executive committee, while another activist noted that Anna Dickinson was the "only woman who belongs to the Union League." Male immediatists, including McKim, joined as well. Organizations such as the Loyal Publication Society, which endeavored to combat treason using pro-Union literature, also collaborated with interventionists. The Society's New England branch chairman, Forbes, had formerly been skittish about associating with immediatists. Now, he distributed speeches by Phillips and coordinated with John Bright to promote Unionist sentiments in Britain.[40]

To avoid repeating their autumn losses in critical spring elections, Republican officials also sought to tap the political capital of their interventionist allies. Ahead of the March gubernatorial contest in New Hampshire, state party leader Benjamin Prescott asked the abolitionist celebrity Anna Dickinson to campaign across the state. "Many of our people are anxious to hear you," he affirmed. To neutralize the Copperhead threat, Dickinson answered the call. With the assistance of Garrison, who supplied pamphlets to help her "sav[e] New Hampshire from the traitors," she toured the state to acclaim. "They tell me of man after man who was supposed lost who is brought round" by Dickinson, one official reported. "We must have Miss Dickinson in our town if possible, for it may be the means of saving us," pled another. Conway, too, joined this fray. "He makes up horrid faces but his speeches are good," Prescott noted. Stephen Foster also stumped in his native state, portraying Democrats as the greater evil in a stunning turnaround. The Democrats subsequently harassed him, including by throwing pepper on a stove to disperse the crowd at one meeting. Ultimately, the Republicans triumphed—a victory Prescott attributed to Dickinson, who "did more good than any other." After Dickinson similarly turned the electoral tide in Connecticut, New York, and Pennsylvania, Prescott gloried that she had "a national reputation, and one our best minds might well envy." As they had done in 1862, immediatists hence exerted their influence to shore up progovernment forces.[41]

Abolitionists, and especially African American activists, also coordinated with politicos on the matter of military service. Since 1861, this topic had divided Black abolitionists. Douglass had initially advocated immediate enlistment before backtracking to join William Wells Brown, Robert Hamilton, George T. Downing, James W. C. Pennington, and other Black leaders, such as New York minister Henry Highland Garnet, in demanding that the Union first welcome Blacks on equal terms as a prerequisite to any such advocacy. Now, Lincoln permitted Black enlistment. John Andrew, meanwhile, moved to create the 54th and 55th Massachusetts Volunteer Infantry Regiments as Black units, promising enlistees equal treatment. Douglass rejoiced that the nation had met his preconditions by recognizing Black soldiers as men and Americans. "The colored men were as ready to give their services to the country now as they were at the commencement of the war," Douglass averred, again exhorting Blacks to enter the military.[42]

This time, other Black leaders joined Douglass in adopting such a position. At a January gathering, Brown abandoned his opposition to enlistment by declaring that "in the strong arms of 600,000 colored men, the country would find added strength and added safety." In the *Weekly Anglo-African,* Hamilton concurred. "It is now, or never," he asserted. "Freedom is ours, and its fruit, equality, hangs temptingly on the tree, beckoning our own brave arms to rise and clutch it." Martial valor, he averred, would lead to equal rights. Embodying this newfound enthusiasm, Garnet roared that "We must fight! Fight! Fight!" Soon, these activists would translate their words in favor of enlistment into politicized action.[43]

In this endeavor, they and supportive white interventionists like Phillips found willing partners in antislavery conservatives and businessmen like Everett and Forbes. The Loyal Publication Society coordinated with immediatists to advocate Black enlistment through mass pamphlets. Yet such allies viewed Black service as a convenient method to spare white lives, not as an egalitarian crucible. To Lincoln, Forbes advised the recruitment of "acclimated blacks, who are by many considered more valuable at the South than white soldiers," and could be offered a "much lower bounty." While "it may be necessary to force the blacks into the ranks," he added, "their greater ignorance [would] make it much more difficult." In a letter published by the Society's New York branch, southern Unionist Andrew Jackson Hamilton stressed that he "shall not dispute" the idea of Black inferiority, emphasizing instead their fitness as soldiers. Even in collaborating with abolitionists, these elites again revealed themselves to be morally suspect allies, working—and trying to enmesh immediatists—within a much less racially inclusive worldview.[44]

Following the onset of military emancipation, interventionists' political partners of all stripes—from antislavery conservatives and businessmen, who were largely uninterested in Black rights, to Radical Republicans, who supported such advances, but only when politically feasible—also began circumscribing their collaborative efforts. As they recognized, northerners' desires for antislavery change, and immediatists' influence, were limited. In feeling this popular pulse and deferring to political considerations, these politicos aimed to channel abolitionists toward the expedient issues suited to them, such as electoral politics and Black enlistment, while otherwise easing them out of the spotlight. "I have endeavored to keep our old anti-slavery men quiet," John Austin Stevens Jr. averred, "by telling them that . . . they should be satisfied to watch the full fruition of their hopes of Freedom without seeking further prominence." Prescott, too, informed Dickinson that immediatists, despite their recent electoral aid, remained too radical for his comfort. "The methods they would want adopted would have been impeachable," he told his star speaker.[45]

As they applied their tactics to achieve more impolitic objectives like unconditional emancipation, interventionists experienced unprecedented, and unexpected, resistance. Their battle-tested approach of utilizing their coalition to pressure the government would function no longer. Politicos asserted themselves as allies of convenience. Northerners who had welcomed interventionists' appeals to their own self-interest proved unreceptive to additional measures, belying hopes that an abolition war would catalyze a larger revolution to purify northern souls. And Lincoln, ever the perceptive political tactician, shrank from going further in response. Interventionists thus ran up against the walls of the new world they had helped create.[46]

Cheever first experienced these constraints in December 1862, when he entered the White House as part of a "fanatical abolition committee" of ministers. Anxious as he was to discern Lincoln's emancipatory intentions, he was equally keen to wash his hands of the grime of expediency. Cheever hence petitioned the president to implement an emancipation policy that was both "unconditional . . . [with] no exception" and "adopted [not] as a mere military necessity," but as a "policy of justice." In lobbying Lincoln for an emancipation that was not only total but also animated solely by morality, rather than practicality, he was rechanneling interventionists' political pressure methods to combat the disease of expediency. Yet the president instead issued a partial order partly in the name of military necessity. Cheever thus failed, eroding his brief rapprochement with both Lincoln and the interventionist experiment.[47]

Exacerbating Cheever's frustrations, interventionists disavowed his petition as counterproductive. In January, newspapers reported that he had asked Lincoln to act "on high moral instead of simply military grounds." This report, Conway observed, implied that Lincoln was "in a state of fierce antagonism to the abolitionists in giving this Edict." To immediatists' embarrassment, Cheever had inadvertently resurrected their antebellum image as wild-eyed idealists, undermining their current advocacy for total emancipation—and denying them due credit for the Emancipation Proclamation. Though Cheever's *Principia* had already printed the petition, Conway issued a denial in the Emancipation League organ, *The Commonwealth*. "No abolitionist . . . has ever held that the President had any right to declare the slaves free except on pure military grounds," he claimed. While this spurious statement quelled public relations concerns, it also alienated Cheever, reigniting his determination to break away from the pack.[48]

That same month, Conway joined Phillips to advocate a two-pronged agenda for total emancipation as part of an Emancipation League delegation to Washington. These delegates aimed to ensure the Proclamation's proper execution by pressing for the removal of proslavery military governors. They also sought to bolster its assault against slavery by lobbying for the establishment of a Bureau of Emancipation. Through such a bureau, moreover, interventionists hoped to gloss over their disagreements and address the looming issue of post-emancipation Black rights as a united movement. In a petition to Congress shepherded by Henry Wilson, the delegation sketched the bureau's mission in purposefully vague strokes. It would, they argued, make emancipation meaning-ful and secure by safeguarding former slaves' freedom, ensuring their "right to fair play" through education and the "speedy organization of the emancipated labor." To buttress this request, a committee that included Conway surveyed Union officers about the skills of freed slaves and publicized the results.[49]

Far from resolving their differences, this plan buried them beneath the sur-face. Their advocacy of the hazily sketched agency allowed interventionists to display superficial unity while blurring their clashing conceptions of Recon-struction. In a letter to Lincoln, the MASS envisioned the bureau as "providing land and labor" to freed slaves and helping them attain self-sufficiency—a broad socioeconomic vision akin to that of Phillips and Douglass. In the *Common-wealth*, Conway instead detailed its mission in far narrower terms. It would not "be safe to leave the negroes entirely to their own control," he averred. Nor were ex-slaveholders trustworthy. The agency, he asserted, had to create a "code of laws to regulate labor of the freedmen, and the contracts they form with their employers." By again relegating former slaves to socioeconomic inequality as a plantation underclass, Conway underscored how little his proposal had in common with that of the MASS.[50]

The Emancipation League committee presented a common front nonethe-less in Washington. But as they again approached the levers of power, Phillips and Conway, like Cheever before them, found that their tactics now held less weight. After preaching to the Senate, Conway joined Phillips and Wilson to meet with Lincoln. Phillips lobbied the president to replace military gover-nors like Edward Stanly, the ex-slaveholding administrator of eastern North Carolina, with officials who were "heart and soul for freedom to carry out the new policy," such as John C. Frémont. Lincoln, however, demurred. Phillips, stunned by this setback, responded by flexing his political muscles. "If we see this administration earnestly working to free the country from slavery," he in-timated, "we can run it into another four years of power." Abolitionists, he implied, could make or break Lincoln's reelection. Conway added that unless Lincoln acted, his "moral and intellectual support . . . would be honeycombed." Though Phillips and Conway hewed to interventionists' progovernment consensus, they stressed that their tolerance of Lincoln had its limits. In a reflection of their reduced sway, however, the president ignored their ultimatums.[51]

In frustration, the delegation shifted its attention to Capitol Hill, where Conway and Phillips mingled with a number of Radical Republican allies, including Wilson, James Ashley, and Ohio congressman John Bingham. At dinner afterward, Phillips demanded that "these men should not whisper in the ear of the President but speak boldly" on the floor about the military governors. Over the past year, interventionists and their allies had whispered in Lincoln's ear to great success. After faltering in their latest attempt, Phillips and Conway now looked to their Radical partners to effect change. Yet these politicos refused to act. They also tabled the bureau idea, endorsing in its place a proposed executive commission to investigate the condition of freed slaves—a milquetoast compromise to which the League agreed. As Phillips and Conway learned, their influence with Lincoln and their own partners had weakened. Their alliance was producing diminishing returns, rendering the interventionist camp and its approach to reform ineffective.[52]

As their failures compounded their senses of turmoil, Phillips and Conway would soon pull away from Lincoln and the interventionist consensus. Once again, Cheever led the charge on this front. In a letter to his new confidante Pillsbury, he assailed the antislavery alliance. The League, he informed the purist, was "afraid to make a bold, vigorous movement" to fortify the "proclamation on the highest, safest ground possible," settling instead for a weak commission. Its cautious tactics, he believed, were not up to the challenge of securing and expanding upon emancipation. "Of what use is such a league?" agreed Pillsbury. These once-adversarial activists were thereby moving onto the same territory: that of supporting the war but doubting abolitionists' chances of advancing further change through a compromised coalition—or with Lincoln in power.[53]

Reinforcing their point, the commission's political proponents sidelined its abolitionist creator, James Miller McKim. On returning from South Carolina, McKim had proposed an inquiry into slavery's horrors that would interview freed slaves in Union-occupied areas. By late 1862, he was attracting support across Washington by pitching his commission as a wartime tool. Its reports "will do more to justify the war ... [than a] half-dozen victories in the field," he declared. Sumner soon signed on to become its public face. "We must give Sumner all the credit," McKim told a friend. "What matters it who has the credit so that the thing can be done." Behind the scenes, McKim planned the project. After Sumner asked him to recommend potential commissioners, he sought out "respectable outsiders—persons not known as partisan abolitionists," to avoid controversy. He accordingly rejected Sumner's suggestion of immediatist Franklin B. Sanborn, who had been one of the financiers of John Brown's raid on Harpers Ferry, as politically toxic. McKim also reserved the position of secretary for himself, which Sumner affirmed in January.[54]

Sumner then cut off communication. Assuming the project had died, McKim lamented its failure in March to social reformer Robert Dale Owen. Yet Owen replied that Edwin Stanton had created the American Freedmen's Inquiry Commission that month, appointing him as a commissioner and William Croffut, of the Washington Lecture Association, as secretary. An incredulous McKim proceeded to ask why Sumner had spurned him, the plan's "first mover." "I desired to be secretary," he fumed. Rather than reply, Sumner intimated to intermediaries that McKim had played no part in his enterprise. He had coordinated in parallel with Sanborn, Andrew, and Secretaries Stanton and Chase on their own plans, bypassing McKim. In a fit of fury, McKim decried Sumner for stealing his project. "Can it be that I played my part so well" in crediting Sumner as to make him "actually believe that the measure was . . . his own?" he mused. Sumner, McKim argued, had cultivated an "inordinate vanity . . . [having been] pampered by his friends" since his 1856 caning on the Senate floor. "But these debts have all been paid now," McKim seethed. While he later asked friends to burn these letters for propriety's sake, McKim never forgave Sumner for demonstrating his, and interventionists', waning influence.[55]

As Cheever and Pillsbury anticipated, moreover, the commission proved ineffective. Croffut complained that the commissioners engaged in "high-toned conversation not relevant to the purposes of the meetings." They waxed philosophic about Confucius, "which seemed superfluous in dealing with runaway Negroes." Perhaps underplaying its influence upon the eventual creation of the Freedmen's Bureau, Croffut concluded that the commission was not "fruitful of results," beyond producing a few reports. Interventionists, their plans for a bureau already dashed, thus saw their fallback commission itself sputter.[56]

That such defeats came on the heels of interventionists' signature victory was no coincidence. As the new year began, prowar abolitionists celebrated their triumph. They set themselves to improving upon Lincoln's edict, expecting that their antislavery alliance would help attain further, albeit less militarily necessary, change. Yet their political partners largely resisted additional reforms, sidelining interventionists and dismissing their proposals. As the afterglow of the Proclamation subsided, interventionists would realize that their common, binding fight for expedient emancipation was over. In the wake of their victory, they would suddenly have to grapple with the newly pressing issue of what emancipation entailed for freed slaves—and what rights Blacks deserved. In doing so, they would heat up their divisions to the boiling point. The interventionist camp would collapse, a victim of its own astounding success.

CHAPTER EIGHT

The Stirrings of Realignment, February–June 1863

In April 1863, a succession of African American abolitionists exhorted a packed audience at Henry Highland Garnet's New York church to dedicate themselves to a new sacred purpose: joining the 54th Massachusetts. At the start of the year, these immediatists, including Frederick Douglass, Garnet, Robert Hamilton, and William Wells Brown, had come together to support Black enlistment. In the ensuing months, the latter three and myriad other former opponents of wartime intervention joined Douglass inside the world of power politics, refashioning themselves as military recruiters to render emancipation irreversible through blood and toil. Now, they assembled in New York to make their collective case. Though he had once "hesitated in recommending this measure," Garnet called on Black men to "come forward and enlist, as they might never have such another opportunity." Their service, he stressed, could vanquish slavery and racial bigotry. Elaborating on this point, Douglass added that Blacks could enact the "retribution which, as a race, they owe to the slaveholders." Finally, they had the sanction to "shoulder muskets, and go down and kill white rebels"—to gain righteous vengeance.[1]

To these leaders' surprise, only one man volunteered. As one attendee declared to applause, "if the government wanted their services, let it guarantee to them all the rights of citizens and soldiers." Instead, Black enlistees received lower pay than white recruits, were not eligible for commission, and, as Jefferson Davis had decreed, would be sent into slavery if captured. In a follow-up meeting days later, Douglass "confessed that his blood boiled at [these] discriminations." As a government recruiter, however, he had to look past such short-term imperfections toward the greater good. The Union war, Douglass reiterated, offered Blacks a route to permanent freedom and equality. They had to stomach its flaws and fight, James W. C. Pennington added, or else "permit the anarchical Copperhead party to prevail." In making such arguments through gritted teeth, Douglass reached a deeper understanding of, and his formerly anti-intervention colleagues discovered for the first time, what interventionists had learned back in 1861: power politics bestowed substantial benefits, but only at the anguishing cost of compromise.[2]

Entering wartime politics simultaneously empowered and hemmed in Black abolitionists. Such leading activists as Garnet, Hamilton, Brown, Pennington, George T. Downing, James McCune Smith, Charles Lenox Remond, John Mercer Langston, and Mary Ann Shadd Cary aligned with Douglass to advocate Black military service, remaking what had largely been a white, Garrisonian foray into politics into a biracial, ideologically diverse one. Yet their breathtaking political blossoming was divorced from that of their white coadjutors. They directed their efforts to expand on the Emancipation Proclamation less toward Washington high politics than toward the battlefield as recruiters. In unison, they portrayed enlistment as an egalitarian touchstone, a vehicle for masculine patriotism, and a means for revenge against slaveholders. In the process, such figures publicly brushed off their private qualms about the inequities of the enrollment process.

As Black leaders embraced mainstream politics, their predominantly white interventionist forerunners chipped away at their own harmony. Throughout the war, prowar abolitionists had balanced their moral principles with the demands of pressure politics. They had tried to preserve their identities as righteous reformers while uniting behind a platform of continued yet conditional backing of Lincoln, tolerating him as a necessary evil. And they had masked their disagreements behind their urgent fight for the golden moment. But now that they had achieved that unifying priority, they had to adapt to the new status quo of Lincoln's war: a fight for a partial emancipation, without consideration for post-emancipation Black rights. Interventionists had to evaluate whether Lincoln would facilitate or hinder their own visions of a morally transformed Union—and, in the process, had to deal head on with the thorny issue of Black rights. Yet they could not do so united. Broad and narrow interventionists met the brave new world they had helped birth, and exposed their incompatible designs for that world, with nothing left to hold them together. As a consequence of its success, the interventionist camp began rupturing from inside.

Between February and May, interventionists' differences floated to the fore, fueling a fight over Lincoln that unraveled their platform at both ends. In taking charge of a fledgling pro-Lincoln faction, narrow interventionists like Garrison and McKim began to praise the president both publicly and privately, thereby silencing their ambivalence over their wartime actions. They embraced Lincoln's limited new status quo, personally accepting the standard of the politically possible over their former standard of the morally absolute ideal. As purists had warned, prowar reformers had achieved their stunning gains only at a terrible cost: after years of submersion in the mainstream and partnerships with morally astigmatic allies, narrow interventionists now tempered their moral programs by implicitly separating Black rights from their overriding goal of total emancipation. Preceding the rest, McKim endorsed Lincoln unequivocally, renouncing the notion of conditionality. Child, though she was not a narrow interventionist, also warmed to Lincoln as she sought to make moral sense of the war's terrible toll.[3]

Broad interventionists like Douglass and Phillips, by contrast, inaugurated an incipient anti-Lincoln faction. As they fleshed out their missions for a radical Reconstruction, they cited the flaws of the emancipation process and of Union general Nathaniel P. Banks's regime in Louisiana to lambast the new status quo. These figures avoided criticizing Lincoln directly. Yet they grew reluctant to support either him or a platform that seemed incapable of securing total emancipation and Black rights, thereby endangering that consensus from its other end. The less expansively minded but equally frustrated George Cheever and Conway joined these dissidents, with the former embracing electoral alternatives to the interventionist camp and its now-stultifying methods. Moral purists like Pillsbury and the Fosters, meanwhile, entered into further alignment with these disgruntled interventionists by fully shifting their opposition from the Union war to Lincoln. Over the first half of 1863, abolitionism thereby hurtled toward another wartime realignment.

BLACK ABOLITIONISTS AND RECRUITMENT POLITICS

Over the spring of 1863, a chorus of Black abolitionists translated their newly concordant words in favor of enlistment into action by creating a recruiting machine, shaking off their former apprehensions over military service and engaging in a political intervention. While Black immediatists had long recognized the war's promise, most had avoided entering the political fray for a government that refused to accept them as soldiers. Now that Lincoln had done so, Black activists launched into power politics to secure African Americans lasting freedom and rights through military service. This experiment took inspiration from the white-dominated interventionist camp yet was distinct from it, reflecting how many white abolitionists failed to devote serious attention to the enlistment issue.

Beginning in March, Black abolitionists took charge of the enlistment drive as government recruiting agents. Initially, they focused on the 54th and 55th Massachusetts, John Andrew's Black volunteer outfits. Activists including Douglass, Brown, Garnet, Remond, and Langston crisscrossed the North recruiting for the units, coordinating with Andrew's point person, white immediatist George Luther Stearns. Douglass mostly toured across upstate New York, garnering over a hundred recruits. "The first to put his name down" for the 54th, he beamed, was his son Charles. Lewis Douglass soon followed, quickly rising to the rank of sergeant. Whereas the siblings had joined a colonization effort the previous fall, they now signed on to secure their rights at home as Union soldiers.[4]

Unlike the elder Douglass, many recruiters, including Garnet, Brown, Smith, Hamilton, Downing, and Pennington, had held off from advocating enrollment, and intervention, at the war's start. Ohio activist William Parham had foreclosed the possibility of the prejudiced Union's ever warranting such volunteers. And Cary had long since fled to Canada, washing her hands of America's sins as an emigrationist. Now, all entered the field, conceptualizing military service as their chance to dash slavery and racism into dust. Alongside the Massachusetts agents, Downing and a repatriated Cary recruited for the newly inaugurated federal United States Colored Troops (USCT) regiments, brandishing letters of support from George W. Julian and other Radical Republican allies. Parham, for his part, established a committee to "see what could be done" to enlist troops in Cincinnati. He also abandoned his long-cherished emigration plans, vowing, like the Douglass siblings, to ensure a "brighter and a better" future at home. Douglass, Langston, Smith, and Downing also organized the American Freedmen's Friend Society to press further their cases for Black enrollment.[5]

Charlotte Forten, meanwhile, labored to nourish the minds of emancipated men turned troops in the Sea Islands, a fertile recruiting ground and transit stop for Black units. She requested permission from Union commanders to educate such soldiers, arguing that it was "very important that [they] should be taught." As she affirmed in her diary, "so much depends on these men" in the struggle for emancipation. In witnessing a Black regiment "doing itself honor" on military parade by proving its prowess to the assembled white officers, she proclaimed that it was "typical of what the race, so long downtrodden . . . will yet achieve." Putting aside their past differences, Black activists worked in tandem to seize the opportunity before them.[6]

Like their interventionist predecessors, Black recruiters inaugurated an unprecedented coordination of tactics. In articles and at meetings they promulgated a unified series of arguments, framing enlistment as a gendered crucible for total emancipation and racial egalitarianism. As he toured the Northeast throughout the spring, Douglass argued that the "best possible way open to us to manhood, equal rights and elevation, is that we enter this service." The "opportunity is given us to be men," he asserted, remodeling Black men from the brutish, sexualized predators depicted by white supremacists into martial heroes. Let a Black man "get an eagle on his button, and a musket on his shoulder," he claimed, and none could deny him eternal freedom and the "right of citizenship." In a broadside, "Men of Color, to Arms!," Douglass reiterated that, through martial valor, Blacks could "rise in one bound from social degradation to the plane of common equality." Their destiny, he concluded, was "in our own hands. We may lay here low in the dust . . . or we may, like brave men, rise and unlock to ourselves the golden gates of a glorious future." Douglass hence asked Black men to be men and win glory for their race.[7]

Other recruiters echoed Douglass's point. In the *Weekly Anglo-African,* Robert Hamilton asserted that the "first battle in which a Negro brigade does it share . . . will do more to drive away the murky clouds of prejudice than a century of argument." At the April meeting at Garnet's church, Downing predicted that through "valor in the field, will rewards, acknowledgment and promotion be awarded us." These activists also tapped into the rhetoric of masculinity to promote male patriotism—and to shame shirkers. Black men, Downing argued, had to "stand by the Government in every way we may," defending liberty. Only emasculated recreants would avoid doing so. Chiding those who refused to enlist at Garnet's meeting, Hamilton derided that "[I] detected far more cowardice than logic." Garnet, too, hoped that future generations would "remember with pride that their fathers were not cowards when their country called them to its defense." The fates of Black manhood and the nation, he asserted, were deeply intertwined.[8]

Like Douglass, these figures also incorporated masculine rhetoric into calls for vengeance against the white South. At the April meeting, Garnet reminded attendees that they could, "in the language of old John Brown . . . march through and through the heart of this rebellion." Back in 1843, he had urged slaves to rise up in armed revolt. Now, he enjoined Black soldiers to succeed where Brown had failed by liberating slaves and cutting down their masters. As Hamilton asked, "can you ask any more than a chance to drive bayonet or bullet into the slaveholder's heart?" Blacks, he affirmed, now had the ability and authority to avenge centuries of oppression.[9]

Yet as they traversed the North and evolved into political power players, Black abolitionists also learned that their political interventions ran up a moral cost. While Union officials like Andrew had initially promised to welcome Black recruits on equal terms, Black enlistees instead faced unequal pay, a lack of advancement, and an unanswered threat of Confederate enslavement. In private, Black abolitionists loathed these inequities. "It is a little cruel to say to the black soldier that he shall not rise to be an officer . . . whatever may be his merits," Douglass sighed in March. But rather than abandon their interventions amid such imperfect conditions, Black activists stayed the course and refrained from speaking out. As David W. Blight has argued, they feared that their public protest or criticism would curtail enlistments and forestall their glorious future. As they continued recruiting, Stearns also warned that they had to mind the constraints of their positions by avoiding "criticizing the Administration." Black activists accordingly muffled their qualms for the moment.[10]

Throughout the spring, these politicized abolitionists compromised for their greater ends. When forced by dissenters to acknowledge the unequal terms of service, they often changed the subject. Compared to such inequities, they stressed, standing pat caused greater harm. At his April meeting, Garnet warned the opponents of enlistment that "there are men watching all your words to find some means of slandering you." Blacks, he emphasized, needed to prove to skeptical northerners that they were patriots, not cowards. Instead, antienlistment advocates gave off a negative impression, harming the fight for equality. The "reluctance of colored men to enlist," Douglass added, aided proslavery forces. As he reiterated, Black troops would vanquish slavery and prejudice. But the "hateful political reptiles," the Copperheads, railed against their enlistment for that very reason, as a fellow Black activist detailed to the *Weekly Anglo-African*. Black men had to outsmart their enemies rather than play into their hands.[11]

At other times, recruiters played down the shortcomings of enrollment.

Discussing Black soldiers' lack of upward mobility in the *Weekly Anglo-African,* Hamilton asked bluntly, "Are you most anxious to be captains and colonels, or to extirpate these vipers from the face of the earth?" At a February meeting in New Bedford, Brown elaborated that prejudice "must be overcome by degrees." Blacks had to exploit their opportunity and build on it, using military service as a means to eventual equality. If they chose instead to hold out for perfection, "they would forever be left out in the cold." Douglass agreed in his newspaper in March that "half a loaf is better than no bread—and to go into the army is the speediest and best way" to win that full portion. At a later meeting, Douglass added that he was "not in favor of having the first black regiments commanded by colored men." In part, his declaration stemmed from a practical concern: Black soldiers had not received training and experience in leadership roles. But in concluding that "white officers are necessary" to command such troops for the time being, he was also accepting another compromise. These activists thus consciously stifled their internal doubts to encourage enlistment at all costs.[12]

In June, after USCT troops successfully defended the Union supply depot at Milliken's Bend, Louisiana, in a pitched battle, Black activists rejoiced that their soldiers were achieving justice on the battlefield. The government, they expected, would soon reciprocate such bravery by rectifying its policies. In reviewing the battle, Hamilton conceded that "it is asking too much at *this time* to request the promotion of those brave fellows who actually led on that memorable occasion." Nonetheless, he declared that "the day is rapidly approaching when full justice will be done them by the government." Douglass likewise predicted that "we shall see black officers" before long. As these immediatists made clear, they suppressed their misgivings only because they believed that justice was nigh—an assumption they would soon be forced to reconsider.[13]

ADAPTING TO THE NEW STATUS QUO

In both practicing power politics and struggling to handle their frustrations, Black abolitionists echoed the wartime trajectory of the mostly white interventionist camp. Prowar immediatists had soared to dizzying heights, putting aside their differences to help achieve their golden moment. Now, as their euphoria faded, they realized that their victory had destabilized their movement. Interventionists' unifying campaign had passed. In its wake emerged a divisive, new status quo: a Union war for a qualified emancipation, without regard for any Black rights. Interventionists had sought military emancipation as part of a larger moral revolution. Yet as they had discovered, this agenda represented the upper limit of the public's appetite for change, bounding Lincoln's further moral evolution even as he grew into a resolute emancipator.[14]

Interventionists had to measure this new normal against their own visions, especially regarding Black rights. For decades, most had played down the issue of how to incorporate Blacks into the post-emancipation polity in favor of more proximate priorities. Antebellum abolitionists had not expected to see slavery end, much less prepared for its aftermath. During the national crisis, broad and narrow interventionists had fleshed out diverging understandings of Reconstruction: the former had deepened their conceptions of Black rights, while the latter had grown more racially restrictive. Yet both had still subordinated the issue to the struggle for expedient emancipation. In the wake of the Emancipation Proclamation they had moved together to address this suddenly pressing, and profoundly more complicated, issue by proposing an Emancipation Bureau, only for this initiative to fail. Now, as the question of what would happen to Blacks beyond freedom soared into the foreground, interventionists could no longer bury their disagreements.[15]

Over the spring, Black rights quickly became the divisive topic of the day within immediatism. At one meeting in May, Aaron Macy Powell, a broad interventionist and associate of Phillips, discussed the composition of the postwar Union. Powell invoked Charles Sumner's theory of state suicide, which postulated that Congress could treat conquered Confederate states as "unorganized territory." Applying this principle to freed slaves, Powell demanded the "immediate confiscation" of rebel land to redistribute to "all freedmen"—and to reinvigorate a stalled moral revolution. Narrow interventionists like Garrison, however, unceremoniously tabled his demands. Black rights thereby ascended into conspicuity as an unavoidable, snowballing point of contention and controversy that would ultimately tear apart the movement.[16]

THE PRO-LINCOLN FACTION

In the shorter term, the ideological tensions between narrow and broad interventionists fueled a largely overlapping fight over the Lincoln administration and its new status quo. A civil war between prowar interventionists and antiwar moral purists would reconfigure by year's end into a struggle between a pro-Lincoln faction, mostly consisting of narrow interventionists, and an anti-Lincoln faction, mostly consisting of broad interventionists and moral purists. Narrow interventionists like Garrison, James Miller McKim, and Oliver Johnson helmed the developing pro-Lincoln faction, moderating their visions as they gravitated to the president. Interventionists had taken an extreme risk by diving into politics, threading an impossible needle by trying to reconcile the practical pitfalls of interest group politics with the moral absolutes of unvarnished immediatism. To an extent, they had succeeded: through expedient words and pacts, they had helped to bring about military emancipation. Yet for narrow interventionists especially, the moral consequences of this politicization now materialized. Continuing down the path they had staked out earlier that year, Garrison and his cadre discarded entirely their original commitments to Black rights, thereby abridging their missions for a morally transformed Union.[17]

Garrison pioneered the way in warming to Lincoln, as his public and private opinions of the president converged. To manage their moral unease in supporting the government, wartime abolitionists had separated their tactful public praise of the president according to the standard of the possible from their private criticisms according to their internal standard of the ideal. Garrison had constructed an especially sharp rhetorical disconnect, publicly portraying Lincoln as a moral leader who was ahead of the people while privately mocking his leadership abilities. Now, he abandoned this approach, resolving the internal moral contradiction it signified by endorsing Lincoln both publicly and privately. In public, he continued to exalt the president as a moral paragon. Rebuking immediatist critics like Phillips, he observed sarcastically in May that "Lincoln has shown his hostility to Abolitionism by proclaiming emancipation to 3,000,000 slaves." For this offense, "I thank him . . . with all my heart," Garrison concluded.[18]

For the first time, Garrison also privately embraced Lincoln as an antislavery hero. Upon learning in April that the Massachusetts state legislature had not endorsed the Emancipation Proclamation, he proceeded to berate John Andrew. Whereas he had once emphasized the edict's shortcomings, Garrison now hailed it as in "accordance with the claims of justice." Massachusetts legislators, he stressed, should offer their "most emphatic approval of [Lincoln's] course." Should they fail in "sustaining the President to the extent he has gone in this matter," Garrison warned that the "enemies of the Administration" would pounce. If the legislators would not back Lincoln out of altruism, he concluded, then they should at least do so to thwart the "copperhead opposition." This fear of a Copperhead-led backslide into slavery in part motivated Garrison to rally to the president's side. But he was also evolving from a position of tactfully tolerating Lincoln into one of championing the president as a true admirer. In his view, his stance was morally consistent and uncompromising: he believed that he had redeemed the mainstream, bringing such politicos in line with his vision of perfection. Yet in reality, Garrison's own views were changing as much as, if not more than, those of his political counterparts. He was cutting his tethers to the moralistic standard of the ideal, throwing his moral balance out of whack.[19]

Garrison heightened this moral departure by embracing Lincoln's new status quo. While he had publicly defended the government earlier in the war, he had also called out its many faults. Now, he fixated solely on protecting Lincoln from his abolitionist detractors. At the May New England Anti-Slavery Convention, Garrison referenced the recent march of the 54th Massachusetts through Boston to assert that Lincoln had recognized Blacks' "manhood and citizenship." When one attendee objected to the lack of Black officers in the regiment, Garrison rebuked him. While Black activists defended the government's policies for a greater good, Garrison did so in genuine acceptance of Lincoln's policies. As he explained, "much indulgence was due the government, in its very difficult position." Despite facing Copperhead opposition, it had "taken immense steps already" by arming Blacks. While he hoped that the government would commission Black officers, he argued that Lincoln had "done well, and made progress in the right direction." Immediatists, he concluded, should celebrate the war's victories, and its leader, instead of harping on its deficiencies. They should settle, rather than keep aiming high.[20]

Privately, Garrison practiced what he preached by internalizing the standard of the possible as his own personal standard. He not only accepted the political realities of Lincoln's racially circumscribed new status quo but also thereby lowered his moral aims, claiming that interventionists, and the president, had nearly secured the Union's new millennium. Audiences, he informed his wife, now greeted him with applause. "What a change from the old mobocratic times!" Garrison marveled. Equating his personal recognition with political triumph, he averred that "our distinctive movement is nearly swallowed up in the great revolution in Northern sentiment"—one now supposedly not stalled but succeeding. Ignoring rampant racial prejudices, he affirmed that northerners were progressing closer to his tempered version of perfection. As a result, abolitionists soon would no longer need to guide the nation as its wise prophets.

After decades of alienation from the benighted citizenry, they could dissolve fully into a body politic that finally matched their enlightened moral values. "[I am] glad that we are apparently so near the end of our great conflict," Garrison noted to Johnson, in anticipation of ending his lifelong quest.[21]

Cementing his turn away from post-emancipation concerns after the Emancipation Proclamation, Garrison proclaimed that his endpoint would be the victory of an emancipatory Union. His goals did not yet align perfectly with his politico partners, who remained reluctant to push for total emancipation. But Garrison now adjusted to the mainstream and its racial values by fully decoupling the issues of emancipation and Black rights. In addressing the New York Sixteenth Ward Republican Association in May, he referenced the upcoming anniversary of his AASS, offering his wish that "there will be no need of celebrating another." He explained that he was "for the abolition of the rebellion, for the abolition of Slavery, and for the abolition of this Anti-Slavery Society." To his audience, Garrison asserted that "those who want that Society abolished must do all in their power, at once and forever, to put down Slavery." Affirming his disinterest in the aim of Black inclusion, he merged the success of the Lincoln-led Union with the formal abolition of slavery as his narrowed criteria for the end of immediatism—and for his morally transformed Union. McKim likewise expressed his desire to witness the AASS's "final anniversary," marking the "extinction of slavery" as its denouement.[22]

By the late spring, narrow interventionists interwove support for Lincoln, the new status quo, and their own moral aims into a unified whole. They embraced the president as the embodiment of their watered-down purposes, advocating a Republican-led, emancipatory future—and shed Black rights from their agendas. Leaping ahead of Garrison, McKim hastened this trend to its natural conclusion by endorsing Lincoln unconditionally, thereby challenging the interventionist consensus. In joining the Union League of Philadelphia early in the year, he explained that he acted "from a deep conviction that it is the duty of everyone . . . to stand by the Government and be publicly recognized as among its unconditional supporters." McKim reiterated this rationale at the AASS's annual meeting. Garrison instead shied away from torpedoing the interventionist platform, warning his fellow immediatists against "identifying ourselves with the government." But he could not help but admit that he "felt . . . he could consistently give [the administration] his support," if not yet on an unconditional basis. Though his reluctance to forego decades of self-avowed political objectivity stayed his hand, Garrison hinted that his resolve

THE ABOLITIONIST CIVIL WAR

was weakening—that he was inching toward joining McKim and embracing Lincoln unequivocally.[23]

Garrison's evolution also colored his personal relationships. Back in 1835, the British immediatist George Thompson had cut short a tour of America to flee for his life. Now, Garrison harnessed his celebrity to recompense his friend by coordinating a public testimonial in Thompson's honor. Wary of exciting "old or new prejudices," Garrison sought a "committee of Republicans rather than of Abolitionists" as the campaign's face. While Garrison had acted from such conscious public relations concerns throughout the war, he now leaned further into such a course. "I would make the appeal not an Abolition one, but an American one," he urged. The drive should "avoid abolition issues," highlighting the "service disinterestedly rendered the American Government ... by Mr. Thompson" in opposing the rebels. As he lay adrift in the political mainstream, Garrison organized an abolitionist testimonial stripped of abolitionism.[24]

While narrow interventionists formed the core of the emerging pro-Lincoln faction, Child also embraced the president as she worked through the war's human cost. She had long writhed in moral agony, mourning the war's casualties yet advocating its continuation to force Lincoln's hand. At times, she had doubted whether the conflict would merit such bloodshed. Following the Emancipation Proclamation, however, Child concluded that the war was gaining moral value. "We are coming out right, *at last,*" she proclaimed in April. "Our army stand before God the champions of human freedom." Gratified that she could now desire the success of Union soldiers, Child prayed that "their long-deferred hopes be crowned with victory." Alongside God, and interventionists, she credited Lincoln for infusing the conflict with moral meaning and relieving her burden, thereby enabling her to cheer the Union without reservation. "I must confess, President Lincoln has grown very much upon me!" she admitted. He had evolved from an obstacle to antislavery progress, who refused to act even as interventionists "loosen[ed] the ice-berg of popular feeling," into its facilitator. She still criticized him on occasion, averring in May that, "if the Lord wanted slow work to be done, He could not have employed a better hand." Yet she, too, would inch toward pro-Lincoln partisanship over time.[25]

Though narrow interventionists endorsed Lincoln as they moderated their missions, Child did so while developing a sweeping vision of a morally transformed Union akin to broad interventionists'. Though she approved of Lincoln's policies, she also began seeking to expand upon the war's achievements. In May, Child signed onto the efforts of Elizabeth Cady Stanton and Susan B.

Anthony to advocate total emancipation through a new organization, the Women's Loyal National League. She endorsed its use of petitions to employ political pressure, vowing to fight "till the last vestige of slavery has *certainly* disappeared"—a resolve which would impel her in an egalitarian direction. Acting from conviction, Child would migrate toward the pro-Lincoln faction while expanding her own moral vision, illustrating the complexity of the abolitionist civil war.[26]

THE ANTI-LINCOLN FACTION

In contrast to narrow interventionists, broad interventionists like Douglass and Phillips powered a rising anti-Lincoln faction, protesting the president's policies as they refined their moral visions. More tentatively, they interrogated their continued support for Lincoln and the interventionist experiment, threatening the prowar platform from its other side. Throughout the spring, Douglass pressed the administration to advance beyond its new status quo to end bondage and implement racial equality. "Our country is not safe," he warned in April, "while a single vestige of Slavery remains in any corner of it." Yet Lincoln refused to wipe out the peculiar institution, settling instead for an incomplete, and woefully inadequate, emancipation process.[27]

Douglass also contrasted Lincoln's Union with the egalitarian nation he desired. Military emancipation, he asserted in the same piece, would fail to "root out wicked prejudices"—the penumbral effects of slavery that would persist past its formal expiration. Unenlightened white northerners might tolerate slavery by another name, with former masters maintaining control over nominally freed slaves. To his horror, Lincoln sanctioned such a labor experiment in Louisiana. Upon assuming local command in December 1862, Nathaniel P. Banks had outlawed Black vagrancy, inducing freed slaves to sign wage-labor contracts on white-run plantations. In May, Douglass thundered that this government-sanctioned regime "emancipate[s] the slaves in form yet retain[s] them as slaves in fact." As he critiqued the government's failures on abolition and Black rights, Douglass nevertheless abided by his official constraints by avoiding attacking Lincoln directly. His simmering discontent, however, would soon render this position untenable.[28]

Even as Douglass grew increasingly tormented over his wartime intervention, he continued to make use of his politicization to hone his moral vision.

Over the past year, he had developed a lucid conception of a morally transformed Union in which enlistment paved the way for legislative equality. Yet as he postulated, politicos sought to "put this Negro question out of the pale of popular thought." Officials like Banks desired the bare minimum of nominal freedom, "abolishing slavery, without conferring equal rights." Discarding "all the hay, wood, and stubble of expediency," Douglass demanded the "most perfect civil and political equality" through Black citizenship and male suffrage. In May, he reiterated this argument at the New England Anti-Slavery Convention. In one of his first appearances at a Garrisonian meeting in years, Douglass warned against narrowing the abolitionist mission. He called for an expansive Reconstruction, asserting that "emancipation is coming, and another question appears. What shall be done with the slaves?" The answer was clear: they should be "wholly free, [and] equal at the ballot-box." Pushing back against narrow interventionists, Douglass stressed that immediatists needed to secure Blacks not only their unconditional freedom but also their full rights before declaring victory.[29]

Phillips, too, chafed against the new status quo while further augmenting his moral vision. In January, his attempts to advance total emancipation and Black rights had run into mainstream opposition. As he realized, the interventionist camp's approach of pursuing change through the antislavery alliance, and within the boundaries of its progovernment platform, had become insufficient and inhibitory. At first, Phillips stifled his concerns to focus instead on promoting Black enlistment through lectures and financial support for Black recruiters. In one February speech, he dismissed the inequities of the enlistment process by calling on Blacks to "secure the advantages now offered." White officers, he rationalized, would be "better for them at present," facilitating public acceptance of the units.[30]

Over the next few months, as James Brewer Stewart has illustrated, Phillips's moral ambivalence soared as Lincoln languished. In January, he had warned that the government had three months to ensure total emancipation before a less sympathetic Congress came into session. That deadline passed unheeded. As he bristled at another reminder that his coalition was unable to push beyond the new status quo, Phillips renewed his drift away from Lincoln and the interventionist fold. At the Sixteenth Ward Republican Association meeting in May, Phillips followed Garrison's moderated arguments with an assault upon Lincoln's war aims. "Never, until we welcome the Negro, the foreigner, all races as equals . . . melted together in a common nationality," he argued, "will the

North deserve triumph." Yet he questioned whether Lincoln would even allow this outcome. Publicly rekindling his doubts about the president, Phillips advised his audience to "cease to lean on the government at Washington. It is a broken reed, if not worse." Lincoln, he condescended, was "Kentucky honest." He had accepted "partial emancipation," but stopped there. Phillips hoped that a progressing public would overcome such governmental intransigence. But he bristled at his camp's constraints nonetheless, anxious to advance radical policies beyond its limiting consensus—and beyond what Lincoln permitted.[31]

Phillips again took aim at the new status quo in early July. The administration, he scorned at a meeting, promoted "wicked prejudice . . . in order to make base use of it" for the coming election. Though he railed against the president's policies, Phillips strained still to avoid breaking with Lincoln and his fellow interventionists. He offered another in a long line of half-hearted public statements supporting the president, clarifying that "I, for one, have no objection to the Presidency of Abraham Lincoln for four or eight years longer." His frustrations, however, were multiplying beyond repair. "What is the creed of Abraham Lincoln, I cannot tell," he pondered, voicing aloud his inner uncertainty. Beneath his weak approval of the president he was wavering, his commitment to the interventionist consensus more tenuous than ever.[32]

Like Douglass, Phillips also sharpened his vision of moral transformation. He, too, had evolved in a political direction to make legislative equality his goal. Now, he stressed another aspect of this agenda: racial amalgamation. Flouting the government, Phillips proclaimed himself an "amalgamationist to the utmost extent." He had "no hope for the future," he declared, "but in that sublime mingling of races." For decades, antiabolitionists had used the specter of race mixing to attack immediatists. In promoting just such a radical policy, Phillips further fleshed out his panoramic dream of remaking a people blighted by prejudice into a unified and redeemed nationality. In the process, he also defied the interventionist camp and its stultifying consensus.[33]

Phillips also became further at odds with Garrison. Following the Republican ward meeting, one narrow interventionist delineated the "contrast in Garrison's state of mind" with Phillips's. While Garrison engaged in a "constitutional march," seeking some progress, "Wendell's course is towards bloody negotiation"—toward demanding more, even at the cost of burning political bridges. Foreshadowing later events, the writer noted that Phillips now pinpointed his hopes on one figure: John C. Frémont. Phillips's confidante George W. Smalley, a journalist embedded in Frémont's command, likely influenced his views by lauding the general's antislavery bona fides at length in his letters back home. Soon, Phillips would drift further away from Lincoln's political orbit and into that of Frémont.[34]

Though broad interventionists led the charge against Lincoln's policies, less egalitarian-minded, but equally disgruntled, abolitionists like Cheever and Conway also joined their faction. Cheever had long distrusted the president for mismanaging military affairs, bowing to slaveholding interests, and otherwise consigning the Union to moral ruin. Months earlier, moreover, Lincoln had rebuffed his lobbying efforts for total emancipation. Cheever had subsequently questioned his brief détente with Lincoln—and with the interventionist camp and its increasingly ineffective approach to reform. Over the spring, he began lambasting the new status quo, refusing at the May meeting of his CASS to espouse a "rose-colored view" of affairs. As he had done the previous year, Cheever distinguished the Union war, to which he remained dedicated, from its chief prosecutor, about whom he had resurgent doubts. He excoriated Lincoln's emancipation process as flawed, "regretting as a serious error that any rebel [areas] should have been exempted." He also proclaimed that the government had failed to make military emancipation a "reality, not a sham," by installing "anti-slavery men in office to execute it," such as Frémont. Lincoln, he implied, prevented the war from fulfilling its moral potential.[35]

Like Douglass and Phillips, Cheever avoided breaking with Lincoln—at least in public. Ahead of them, however, he privately abandoned the president and the interventionist consensus, fleeing its stifling confines to advance further reforms. Cheever yearned to assuage his surging ambivalence over his own intervention, which had carried him too far down the road of expediency. Yet he had been drawn so deeply into the world of pressure tactics that he now could pursue change only through such political methods. He thus put his political skills to better use by spurning the interventionist camp, pivoting from working with the administration to plotting against it. With his brother, Henry, he channeled his inner turmoil into replacing Lincoln with a stronger antislavery candidate in the coming election, seeking to defeat the president and his immediatist enablers in one fell swoop. They soon began plotting their strategy. In April, George informed Henry of the "importance of the circulation of right sentiments in the Army, constituting as they will, so vast a body of votes." As he concluded, "Whoever governs the Army will govern the nation; so we must look out." The brothers nonetheless refrained from public action for now, biding their time as they honed their plans and scouted the ideal candidate.[36]

More gingerly, Conway also rethought whether he should remain by Lincoln's side. He, too, had run into a wall using the antislavery alliance to seek further change, shaking his faith in such mainstream political tactics. He soon began critiquing Lincoln's policies, especially the president's enabling of the "miscreant (such as we know him all to be) Banks." By supporting him, Conway lamented, Lincoln proved his aversion to reform. The president "should dismiss from his service . . . all who do not openly avow their hostility to slavery," he averred in the *Commonwealth*. Instead, Banks's "proslavery policy [is] negatively sustained by the Administration." For now, Conway held back from further criticism. As his frustrations waxed, however, so would his patience with Lincoln and the interventionist experiment wane.[37]

In assailing Banks, Conway mischaracterized him as proslavery rather than antislavery yet antiegalitarian, thereby downplaying the similarities between the general's wage-labor scheme and his own paternalistic vision of a racial caste system. To create distance between himself and Banks, he constructed a thin, dissembling patina of support for sweeping Black rights over his true definition of Black incorporation. In *The Atlantic Monthly,* Conway argued that, since slaves would soon gain freedom, it was worth considering "what are we to expect from the unsealed Afreet." While slaveholders pretended that "degradation [was] his normal condition," Conway offered a counterexample: Black intellectual Benjamin Banneker. Banneker was "scarcely known," he claimed, ignoring decades of Black commemoration of the esteemed polymath. Conway lauded him as the "most original scientific intellect which the South has yet produced," chiding Thomas Jefferson for famously dismissing his mental capacity. In the *Commonwealth,* he also advocated Black citizenship, noting that, "if the negro is not a chattel, he is a man, and must certainly be allowed all the rights of a man." Conway thus postured in favor of Black intellectual and civil parity, while steering clear of such ideas as socioeconomic equality.[38]

Conway also prepared himself to undertake an abolitionist diplomatic mission to Great Britain. Early in 1863, Garrison solicited Phillips and other abolitionists to tour Britain "in favor of our Government and the cause of Emancipation." Through this foray, American abolitionists could bolster the "antislavery demonstrations bursting out in every part of the kingdom" in the wake of the Emancipation Proclamation, solidifying "public sentiment in opposition to any official recognition of the Southern Confederacy, and in hearty support of President Lincoln." Garrison soon learned that Conway was also "endeavoring to raise the means to go to England" to defend the Union war.

After his other candidates declined to go, Garrison grafted his plan onto Conway's. "As a Virginian, in addition to the brilliancy of his talents, [Conway] would be a potent witness" against the Confederacy and its envoy, James Mason, he asserted, fatefully.[39]

In March, Garrison and Phillips arranged Conway's voyage in coordination with abolitionists on both sides of the Atlantic and political allies. Phillips raised funds and convinced Sydney Howard Gay to publish in the *New-York Daily Tribune* an "introductory sketch" by Conway trumpeting his "character, history, and ability" as a reformed southerner. Gay then reached out to antislavery businessman John Austin Stevens Jr., confiding that leading abolitionists "think it very important that Mr. Conway should go to England." Stevens agreed, securing Conway's passage overseas. Garrison and Phillips also organized Conway's lecturing itinerary in conjunction with coadjutors in the British Isles like George Thompson and Richard Davis Webb, stressing to them the importance of his "anti-slavery mission." They even supervised Conway's grooming habits, recoiling at his "general state of unwashedness" when he visited the *Liberator* office prior to his departure. To prevent an international incident, Edmund Quincy educated Conway about the "particularity of the English as to diets and appearances." The abolitionist community thus orchestrated and promoted Conway's mission down to the smallest detail.[40]

Upon arriving in Britain in April, Conway began touring on behalf of the war. In his London opening lecture, he averred to those Britons skeptical of the Union war's antislavery nature that he would not "adhere to the Union or any other cause except as far as I believe it to be that of the right." Interventionists, he declared, "support the Union . . . because it is identified with all for which they have been these many years striving." For "whatever object Mr. Lincoln's army goes forward into the South . . . the seeds of liberty, justice, and Christianity are being sown," he added in June in Manchester. Even as he promoted the Union, Conway nevertheless exposed his wavering support of Lincoln by vowing that he would oppose the government without hesitation should "slavery show any gains" in the future.[41]

Conway also cultivated his image as an authoritative southerner. In London, he confessed that he had "for many years sympathized with slavery." As an officer of his local Disunion Society as a youth, he had invited Mason as a guest and heaped praise upon the Virginia senator's dream of a "magnificent slave empire." Speaking from experience, Conway affirmed that Confederates like Mason fought solely for slavery. For decades, he continued in Manchester, these men had "sowed our country with every wrong and corruption. We are all the slaves of slavery." Harking back to his 1862 *Atlantic Monthly* article, he asserted that abolition would free the benighted South, granting it the "blessings of education and civilization." By backing the Union war, he would redeem his native land alongside the entire nation. Throughout his inaugural circuit, Conway fulfilled Garrison's expectations by upholding the government and playing up his southern roots. Within weeks, however, he would veer perilously off course.[42]

While broad interventionists and other dissatisfied prowar abolitionists moved away from Lincoln at varying speeds, moral purists continued to redirect their hostility from the war to the president. These figures had formerly spurned the conflict, positing a moral equivalency between the warring parties. After the Emancipation Proclamation, however, Stephen Foster and Pillsbury had campaigned for the Republicans as lesser evils compared to rebel-sympathizing Democrats. Foster again attacked the Copperheads at a May antislavery meeting, warning that they loathed the "very discussion of anti-slavery ideas." When a pacifist assailed the government for arresting and trying under military tribunal the Copperhead Clement Vallandigham, Foster objected. "So long as the government confined its violations of law to the sons of Satan, [I] would not find fault," he declared, overruling his previous stance and siding with the Union.[43]

Like George Cheever, moral purists distinguished the Union war from its leader. Lincoln, they argued, obstructed their plans for an egalitarian morally transformed Union. They hence refused to hold back in scathing the new, imperfectly antislavery status quo. At the same meeting, Foster demanded total emancipation. "A million of men yet remain in slavery, the Administration keep them there," he asserted. The government also fell short regarding Black rights. Though Garrison marked the march of the 54th Massachusetts through Boston as a sign of progress, Foster disagreed. "The very people who cheered" the regiment, he averred, "would refuse to take the hand of a negro." As purists had predicted, whites who embraced emancipation and Black enlistment in the name of utility, not righteousness, failed to support racial equality. "Not one inch of progress has been made" in that area, Foster confirmed. After narrow interventionists hastened to rebut him, he retorted that, "on the score of principle, our Government stands just where it always stood": bereft of morality. "We have controversy with Lincoln as well as with Jefferson Davis," he reiterated. Foster had spoken similarly in previous years, lambasting Lincoln to stand in for the general war. But he now took issue with the president alone. He aligned with disquieted interventionists, migrating from diametric positions onto a common ground of supporting the war but resisting Lincoln—and the limitations of the interventionist camp.[44]

Over the spring, interventionists confronted the complications of their crowning victory as they grappled over the new status quo and its post-emancipation implications—and as they careened toward another realignment. Black activists became military recruiters, biting their tongues regarding Lincoln to forge a path to equality. Garrison and narrow interventionists diminished their moral missions and, alongside Child, flocked to the president. Phillips, Douglass, and broad interventionists instead sharpened their visions and, alongside George Cheever and Conway, attacked the president's policies. They also drew closer to moral purists. As these burgeoning factions evolved in divergent directions, interventionists' unity grew tenuous. Their camp had begun to fracture, its platform threatened from both ends. A scandal centered on Conway would soon exacerbate these divisions beyond repair, fundamentally reshaping the abolitionist civil war.

CHAPTER NINE

The Collapse of the Interventionists, June–December 1863

A
s the summer of 1863 began, interventionists awaited news of Moncure Conway's British mission with bated breath. As reports trickled back across the Atlantic, however, their anticipation curdled into dread. In late June, Conway had written to James Mason, claiming his "authority to make the following proposition on behalf of the leading Anti-slavery men of America, who have sent me to this country." This statement was misleading: while leading immediatists had sponsored his trip, they had not granted him negotiating power. Nonetheless, Conway proposed unilaterally that, should the rebels "agree to emancipate the Negro slaves," American abolitionists would "immediately oppose the prosecution of the war" by the Union and endorse peace. A wary Mason solicited his ambassadorial credentials, forwarding the letters to the British press when Conway failed to furnish them. This affair quickly provoked controversy on both sides of the Atlantic, shredding Conway's reputation at home—and upending wartime abolitionism.[1]

Over the first half of 1863, interventionists had started to divide over Lincoln and their own consensus of conditionally supporting the government. Narrow interventionists like Garrison had germinated a fledgling pro-Lincoln faction alongside Child. Broad interventionists like Phillips and Douglass, meanwhile, had developed an anti-Lincoln faction alongside George Cheever, Conway, and moral purists. The Mason affair became one of several summer catalysts that crystallized these emergent fractures within the interventionist camp, hastening its downfall. In July, abolitionists fixated their attention on the anti-Black draft riots breaking out in New York. In blaming Lincoln for the racial violence, Cheever and his brother, Henry, escalated their pursuit of antislavery reform through electoral change. Garrison, perceiving the riots as a Copperhead plot against Lincoln, instead tied himself more closely to the president in their wake. And Child, too, further embraced Lincoln's leadership after the death of family friend Robert Gould Shaw in the assault on Fort Wagner, comforted in the belief that he had given his life for a just war.

Above all, the Mason affair was a turning point for the interventionist camp. To head off British recognition of the Confederacy, Conway made Mason a disingenuous offer, hoping to bait him into admitting that the rebels would never end slavery. Mason, however, saw through his ploy. Though American immediatists universally rebuked Conway, their diametric reasons for doing so clarified and exacerbated their rift. Garrison and the pro-Lincoln faction disowned Conway and swore unconditional support for Lincoln, abandoning the camp's consensus as insufficiently patriotic. The narrow interventionists like Garrison helming this faction also affirmed their diluted visions of technical freedom, cementing an emancipatory Union as their endgame. Phillips and the anti-Lincoln faction instead scorned Conway's offer not as disloyal but as dishonest, while nevertheless hailing the implication of his words: that reformers need not tie themselves at the hips to the government. Phillips grew increasingly unwilling to succor Lincoln over the fall, while a bitter Conway disavowed the interventionist experiment altogether.[2]

As he recruited troops in the face of unfair enlistment policies and a stagnating emancipation process, Douglass reached his own breaking point by July. He unleashed his pent-up frustrations, halting his enlistment efforts and publicly assailing Lincoln. Douglass sought to return to the recruiting field after the president partially redressed his concerns in a private meeting, only to run up anew against official prejudices. Most other Black activists, by contrast, still kept their private qualms in check. Robert Hamilton especially heaped praise upon Lincoln in public, lashing out instead at the largely white interventionist camp for ignoring Black rights.

By late 1863, that interventionist experiment was crumbling. Garrison and Child had already pledged allegiance to Lincoln, while Cheever, moral purists, and, more gradually, Phillips, Conway, and Douglass were moving against him. In December, these divisions marred the thirtieth anniversary of the AASS. Garrison envisioned a unifying celebration of the Society as it neared its emancipatory end. Yet the Fosters upended the meeting by scalding that Lincoln impeded an egalitarian morally transformed Union. As the proceedings devolved into a fractious referendum on the White House, Garrison and his followers hastened to defend Lincoln and their own moderated missions. Douglass, by contrast, questioned their compromises and decried the government's catering to prejudice, espousing a refined vision of expansive Black rights.

The final blow came days later, when Lincoln issued a proclamation offering the rebels lenient terms for reentry should they accept the end of slavery. Garrison and his associates endorsed the plan as aligning with their abridged missions. Phillips, by contrast, proposed an alternate agenda that secured Blacks legislative equality. As he now concluded, Lincoln would not allow such advances, nor could the interventionist camp achieve them. Phillips thus funneled his moral turmoil into defeating the president as an intolerable evil, forswearing him—and abandoning the pro-government consensus as insufficiently antislavery. The interventionist experiment disintegrated from within, realigning wartime abolitionism a second time.

THE TRANSFORMATIVE EVENTS OF JULY

Over the summer of 1863, pro- and anti-Lincoln abolitionists filtered a dramatic series of military and political developments through their diametric worldviews, further amplifying their differences. George Cheever, for example, excoriated Lincoln over the New York draft riots. Soon after the Union victories at Vicksburg and Gettysburg in early July, mobs of largely working-class Irish immigrants rioted in New York at the instigation of leading Copperheads, rising against the onset of mass conscription. As Iver Bernstein has shown, they targeted elites, who could pay a commutation fee instead of serving, while lynching Blacks with abandon. Cheever, who fled the city, denounced the "blood of the Irish" in nativist tones. But he reserved the brunt of his anger for Lincoln, whose failure to suppress the "democratic muttering[s]" had enabled such violence. Moreover, as Cheever's brother, Henry, averred, "the draft would have been entirely unnecessary, had [Lincoln] done his duty" by organizing mass Black enlistment early in the year. By instead constructing a tinderbox, he bore responsibility for the anti-Black race riot.[3]

The Cheever brothers had repudiated both the president and the interventionist camp in recent months, channeling their outrage over Lincoln's antislavery failings into lowkey partisan opposition. Now, they settled on a candidate to replace the president: Treasury Secretary Salmon P. Chase, an old Liberty Party man with impeccable antislavery credentials. In August, Chase contacted

George Cheever, vowing to persuade Lincoln to bring occupied regions of the Confederacy under the Emancipation Proclamation's purview. Cheever, convinced that Chase was dedicated to "delivering the colored race," quickly reciprocated. Lincoln, he agreed, should "denounce the possibility of withdrawing from the proclamation . . . pronouncing the whole slave population free." Instead, he "brought all this mischief upon us," letting opposition thrive within the lacunae of his inconsistent emancipation process. To create a "just policy of emancipation," Cheever asserted, immediatists required "friends in authority" who, unlike Lincoln, refused to "measure justice by expediency." Chase, he believed, fit that bill. "I am thankful to God that there is one member of the Cabinet" who advocated universal emancipation, Cheever exclaimed to his man of electoral destiny. "Men who believe in the Cause will need to put forward all their efforts, or miss the only opportunity . . . of having their principles represented in the government," Chase subsequently urged, alluding rather unsubtly to the election. With Chase's blessing, the siblings thus worked on his behalf. But though they had rejected Lincoln to climb out of the compromising mainstream, they would soon learn that oppositional politics required further moral contortions.[4]

Unlike the Cheever brothers, Garrison drew closer to the president in the aftermath of the riots. As he understood, the national backlash against the Emancipation Proclamation had hamstrung Lincoln from pursuing additional reforms. Rather than assail the president for enabling the riots, he blamed the draft's opponents as racist traitors—stark contrasts to his own son George, who had volunteered as an officer in the 55th Massachusetts. The Copperheads, he asserted, preferred to burn the North rather than let Lincoln "succeed in putting down the rebellion at the cost of slavery." Garrison thereby argued in defense of the president that the riots occurred not because Lincoln was failing to fight slavery, but because he was succeeding.[5]

Weeks later, abolitionists were sent reeling when Robert Gould Shaw, commander of the 54th Massachusetts, died leading his unit in an assault against Fort Wagner, in Charleston Harbor. "His death is a very sad loss for us," lamented Forten, who had encountered him in the Sea Islands. She tended to the returning wounded, seeking "to do the slightest service" for men who "fought bravely" to uplift the race. Child especially grieved Shaw, the son of her confidante Sarah Blake Shaw. "Would to God my old life could have been sacrificed instead!" she proclaimed. "Every inch of freedom . . . [is] bought at the price of so much blood," she mourned.[6]

Shaw's death also pulled Child nearer to the president. It sealed her conviction that the Union war had become sacred—and that such bloodshed further sanctified it. As she consoled his mother, Shaw had blessed the Union cause by dying "nobly in the defense of great principles." As she drew affirmation from his sacrifice, Child reiterated her satisfaction with Lincoln's war. At interventionists' urging, she believed, the president had imbued the conflict with the moral substance to render the young Shaw a martyr for freedom. The war was "full of signs to inspire faith in God," she confirmed in August. Ex-slaveholders now "talk like Garrison," further demonstrating the war's moralizing effects. In squaring her long-running suffering over the conflict's human cost with its moral necessity, Child rallied behind Lincoln as its north star.[7]

THE FALLOUT OF THE MASON AFFAIR

Above all else, Conway's actions cemented the divisions among interventionists and pushed them past the breaking point. In May, the stakes of his pro-Union mission rose when the rebel envoy in London, James Mason, convinced the parliamentarian John Roebuck to put forth a proposal for British recognition of the Confederacy. Conway initially leaned on the familiar methods of the interventionist camp to counter them, delivering a staid speech laced with expedient rhetoric in London. In refuting Roebuck's claims that the Union mistreated Blacks, he defended Lincoln's racial policies—and hid his own displeasure with the president. Blacks were "in some free states on an equality with whites," he added, playing down the rife racial inequities there. Yet Roebuck gained momentum nonetheless, scheduling a parliamentary vote for his resolution for late June.[8]

After failing to halt Roebuck's resolution through respectable lobbying, Conway pivoted to a more drastic measure: tricking Mason into defeating it himself. He had again fallen short in employing interventionist tactics, exacerbating his dissatisfaction over their inefficacy—and pushing him toward bolder methods. As a wartime celebrity, he was also assured of his powers of persuasion. Prior to the vote, Conway therefore contacted Mason to offer American abolitionists' support for a slaveless Confederacy. His proposal, as he would later inform British associates, was a stratagem "undertaken only in the interest of my country." His "intent was to make Mason say that the South had no policy of emancipation in view, even for . . . independence." Conway would then publicize this admission to sink the resolution. He remained a "faithful supporter of Lincoln, and the war, as things are now going on," he averred, affirming his conditional adherence to the administration—and his determination to bolster it on his own terms.[9]

Yet the overconfident Conway flew too close to the sun. Mason answered him by brusquely demanding proof of his nonexistent representative authority. Caught in a lie, Conway blustered that, while he could "easily give you the evidence that I represent the views of the leading abolitionists in America," he would write home for further proof. Sensing that Conway had overstepped his bounds, Mason vowed to embarrass him and his sponsors by going public. "It will, perhaps, interest the Government . . . that abolitionists want to negotiate," he sneered. Mason condescendingly extended "some reward" to his outsmarted foe, deflecting the emancipation question by concluding vaguely that the Confederates would never "be in a position requiring them to answer [it]." He then leaked the correspondence to the British press.[10]

As the exchange attracted widespread attention, Conway agonized over its potential fallout. "It is bad enough, I fear," he despaired to his wife. In the British Isles themselves, abolitionists' responses to the incident varied. Though Conway clarified his true intentions to local abolitionists, his offer still baffled many reformers. One denounced "his treason," misconstruing his act. George Thompson fretted that American abolitionists supported a "withdrawal of their support from their own government," while an outraged John Bright demanded that Conway be "promptly disavowed." Other immediatists understood, and appreciated, Conway's ploy. A London antislavery newspaper proclaimed that the scheming Mason had not anticipated that Conway would "bait a trap for *him*." The affair made it "impossible to pretend that the South cares for independence, except as a means for perpetuating slavery," the journal gloried, asserting Conway's success.[11]

As he cherry-picked the positive reports, Conway regained confidence in late June. To the *Commonwealth*, he admitted that his offer was "made in some strange mood and moment, which will perhaps always seem inexplicable . . . to myself." He nevertheless gloated that he had "startled [Mason] into dropping his mask" by refusing to endorse emancipation, taking credit for the eventual defeat of the Roebuck resolution. "I obtained a confession from Mason which all think damages him," Conway claimed. He asserted selectively that the "friends of America are in high glee," concluding that American abolitionists would afford him a hero's welcome home.[12]

Conway's initial pessimism, however, had been warranted. When word of his actions reached American shores in early July, interventionists there universally condemned him. Yet pro- and anti-Lincoln immediatists did so for contrasting reasons, exposing and aggravating their differences in a transformative moment of clarity. Unlike their British counterparts, American abolitionists generally discerned the nature of the ploy. Phillips affirmed to Ellen Conway that her husband made his proposal "as a means of cornering Mason." Garrison noted likewise, informing Oliver Johnson that Conway "certainly meant well, but he acted upon the vicious maxim . . . that the end sanctifies the means." Despite the fact that he had used that same maxim to endorse the war in 1861, he faulted Conway for making a well-intentioned but misguided error.[13]

Yet rather than forgive Conway, Garrison and the pro-Lincoln faction forswore him, simultaneously exposing and completing their shift into unfettered partisanship—and torpedoing the interventionist consensus. In a July editorial, Garrison castigated Conway for "assuming to speak . . . in the name of the Abolitionists." He sought to discredit Conway, and obscure his own patronage of Conway's mission, by labeling the Virginian an unsanctioned renegade "in England on his own responsibility." Garrison impelled the AASS to issue another misleading disavowal, which claimed that Conway had journeyed "entirely of his own motion . . . he was neither sent by the Abolitionists, nor is in any sense their agent." Though they acknowledged Conway's noble intentions, the AASS executive board nevertheless censured him for his "ill-judged and unwarranted" offer.[14]

Even though he recognized the offer's disingenuous nature, Garrison excoriated Conway for forsaking the government for the promise of Confederate emancipation. Unlike rebels "black with perfidy," he asserted, Lincoln had earned immediatists' trust. Garrison roundly dismissed concerns about the president's emancipation process, affirming at the annual Fourth of July gathering at Framingham that he "*will* abolish slavery, and is slowly but steadily moving in that direction." Lincoln "has advanced as fast as public sentiment . . . sustain[ed] him," he declared. In past years, Garrison had publicly argued that Lincoln was ahead of the people, while privately believing otherwise. Now, he took this argument to heart, hailing Lincoln with true conviction as an antislavery hero.[15]

Picking up steam, Garrison swore unequivocal fealty to the administration. Even as he quenched his inner moral conflict to embrace Lincoln's new status quo over the spring, he had chastened James Miller McKim for pledging boundless support to the government. Now, he revealed how profound his own support had become—and how far he had strayed from the interventionist platform. In the unlikely event of a rebel emancipation, Garrison clarified he would remain "for the Government, because [it] is in the right." Abolitionists, he asserted, "are incapable of doing a dishonorable act, even to forward the anti-slavery cause." They would not support the "wrong side, even for so good a purpose as that of abolishing slavery." Garrison thereby endorsed Lincoln no longer on a contingent basis as a necessary evil, but on an unconditional one as a moral paragon. He left the interventionist consensus and its insufficient patriotism by the wayside, becoming a full-fledged presidential partisan.[16]

Other pro-Lincoln abolitionists followed suit. In the *Liberator,* editorial assistant Charles Whipple refused to "purchase even the abolition of slavery . . . [in] alliance with the wrong side." A like-minded abolitionist scathed at Framingham that Conway had committed an "unpardonable offense alike against loyalty and Anti-Slavery principle." These immediatists offered the same arguments in private. To a friend, Samuel May Jr. averred that any "loyal American or true Abolitionist" would avoid such "transparent stupidity." Garrison and his followers, having silenced their moral ambivalence over their wartime politicization, conflated commitment to the cause with partisan loyalty to the Lincoln-led Union. In rebuking Conway, the narrow interventionists like Garrison spearheading this pro-Lincoln faction also exposed their weakened moral visions. Drenched in the political mainstream, they had reframed as their moral endpoints the victory of a totally emancipatory Union—a significant, yet limited goal relative to their original missions. Garrison implored Lincoln at Framingham to "put down the rebellion" and "put an end to slavery," ignoring Black rights to reiterate that Union emancipation was his singular priority.[17]

The Mason affair also clarified and heightened the positions of anti-Lincoln abolitionists, imperiling the interventionist platform from its other end. Like Garrison, such figures affirmed their dedication to the Union. Franklin B. Sanborn, who was editing the *Commonwealth* in Conway's absence, noted that immediatists advocated a "vigorous prosecution of the war . . . [none] more than Mr. Phillips." Yet Phillips found the theoretical logic underlying Conway's words, of spurning the Union war on antislavery grounds, revelatory. Rather than reject the Union itself, he applied this calculus to scorn Lincoln. "After two years' war," he wrote in July, "we should have a right to object . . . and claim a Government strong and wise to watch over the slave's path to happiness, not merely secure him a formal freedom." Phillips had long contorted himself to defend Lincoln, only to see the president ignore Black rights. His frustration with Lincoln, and with a coalition unable to advance his desired policies, had festered over the spring. The Mason affair distilled such discontent, intensifying his drift away from the interventionist consensus.[18]

While Phillips joined Garrison in lambasting Conway, he did so for opposing reasons. Rather than impugn Conway's disloyalty, Phillips lamented that he had deployed his brilliant logic for a "mean device"—a ploy—rather than a genuine, principled protest against the administration. Phillips accordingly decided to give form to such protest himself at Framingham. While he condemned Conway, he nonetheless asserted that "I entirely agree with the essence which underlies that offer . . . Union without liberty I spit upon." Refusing to bind himself to Lincoln, Phillips stressed that abolitionists should remain loyal to their moral mission, not to a political leader. The president and his inadequate goals, he implied, were especially unworthy of their unquestioning fealty—a line of attack that Phillips would soon develop further.[19]

The broad interventionists like Phillips at the heart of the anti-Lincoln faction also objected to Conway's incomplete depiction of the immediatist mission. Sanborn argued in the *Commonwealth* that emancipation, the Conway proposal's singular demand, was not a "fair and just end" to their crusade. Abolitionists needed to "wipe off from the soil not only slavery . . . but [also] the curse of a landed aristocracy which is all ready to take its place," eradicating slavery in its penumbral guises. But the rebels would never sanction land redistribution, thereby rendering any talks with them pointless. Sanborn hence chided Conway for ignoring such realities.[20]

In the months following the Mason affair, Phillips inched toward a break with Lincoln as the president continued to avoid further antislavery action. In September, the anti-Lincoln abolitionist Elizabeth Cady Stanton spurred him on. "Verily this is your hour of temptation!" she warned. "Our strongest, best men have one by one all been swept down with the current—all bought by Cunning Abe." Garrison had "forgotten the divine heights" for the mire of political corruption. Stanton begged Phillips to pursue radical reform by coming out against both Lincoln and the stifling interventionist consensus. "I believe in you, Wendell Phillips," she pled, imploring him to embrace the only effective mode of resistance left within the realm of pressure politics: electioneering.[21]

As his colleagues disparaged him, meanwhile, an embittered Conway cut ties with the interventionist camp. Initially, his friends downplayed the extent of the blowback against him. In late July, Sanborn assured him that the "Mason episode is blown over, and does you little harm." But as the controversy lingered, Sanborn advised Conway to remain in England six months longer before "retriev[ing] all you have lost in the way of reputation." Conway, however, would not return to the wartime Union at all. The "shrill blast" from America dashed his hopes of a triumphant homecoming, convincing him that "my public life there will now end by an utter loss of influence." Rather than return home a persona non grata, he chose self-exile in England.[22]

From Britain, Conway rebelled against the interventionist consensus. He had long upheld its dictates, despite his increasing ambivalence over doing so. Now, the outcry against him crystallized his disillusionment. "I am disappointed in the best of the antislavery men," Conway informed his wife. Garrison's unveiled partisanship especially repulsed him. Like Phillips, Conway believed in the innate logic of his ploy, maintaining that immediatists should redeem the nation using any means, or leaders, available. "It had never entered into my mind that any leading antislavery man would question [this] principle," he averred, or "support the war simply for conquest or Union, whether Liberty were or were not involved." Yet Garrison chose chauvinism over the "holiest cause" by endorsing Lincoln without limits—or heed for more moral alternatives. When Sanborn relayed to Garrison Conway's wish that "we had been more ready to see the war ended on a guarantee of freedom," moreover, Garrison again disregarded his logic. As Garrison succumbed to the "dirty rut of politics," Conway vowed to "wash my hands of it forever"—to disavow the interventionist camp and its constraining political program.[23]

Conway also professed weariness with politics generally. As he explained to his wife in July, his impatience with the interventionist camp had prompted his offer to Mason. But he now regarded that proposal as a "blunder." In seeking to shed the strictures of the interventionist fold, he had created his own bargain of a "political kind," unleashing his inner political animal. To avoid further compromising entanglements and preserve his integrity, Conway vowed not to "enter into the political arena again." As pro- and anti-Lincoln abolitionists were discovering, however, war had intertwined reform and politics. Immediatists had no recourse left outside the world of interest group politics—or on the sidelines of the coming clash over Lincoln.[24]

Conway strained against this pull. Even in renouncing the interventionist experiment he shied away from rejecting the president, both out of fear of his own political turn and gratitude that Lincoln had declined to prosecute him for treason. Yet his antipolitical stance would be short-lived, as a fall feud with Black activist J. Sella Martin foreshadowed. The past spring, Conway had claimed that Martin had publicly labeled Lincoln a "negro-hater." In September, Martin countered in the *Liberator* that he avoided "any such expression[s]" that the Copperhead press might seize on—a tact unknown to Conway, whose offer had "shamefully failed" the cause. In reply, Conway affirmed that he had rebutted Martin months earlier in deference to the interventionist platform, "defending Mr. Lincoln . . . [though] no easy task did I find it." Now, that mandate to tolerate Lincoln no longer constrained him. He refused to brook compromise any longer, repudiating the *Commonwealth* upon hearing that Sanborn would not "criticiz[e] the Administration." As his frustrations with Lincoln mounted, Conway would soon find oppositional politics unavoidable.[25]

BLACK ABOLITIONISTS AND THE INEQUITIES OF MILITARY SERVICE

Black activists, meanwhile, agonized over their own distinctive political intervention. For months, Black recruiters had played down the shortcomings of enlistment for the greater good of freedom and equality—and in the belief that Lincoln would address their concerns. As Douglass explained, he had waited with "patience and forbearance" for the government to uplift Black enlistees. Yet it still declined to pay them fairly, commission them, or defend them from rebel barbarities. Douglass had grown increasingly disenchanted, perceiving the government's enlistment failures and disinterest in total emancipation as threats to his expansive mission.[26]

By July he had had enough. In a public letter to George Luther Stearns, head recruiter for the 54th Massachusetts, he lashed out at the administration. "Colored men have much overrated" Lincoln, Douglass proclaimed. They "had been betrayed into bloody hands by the very Government in whose defenses" they fought. In reflecting on the assault against Fort Wagner, which his son Lewis had luckily survived, Douglass wondered "how many 54th must be cut to pieces, its mutilated prisoners killed and its living sold into slavery," before Lincoln protected Black soldiers in the field. While Douglass sought to "expose [such] wrongs," his official position prevented him from doing so. As his turmoil over his own wartime compromises boiled over, he therefore resigned his agency. "When I plead for recruits, I want to do it with all my heart, without qualification. I cannot do that now," he declared, vowing to hold Lincoln to account.[27]

Yet Douglass's repudiation of the government was brief. In late July, Lincoln authorized Union forces to answer Confederate violations of the laws of war by executing rebel prisoners. At Stearns's urging, Douglass then traveled to meet with administration officials in August. At the White House, as James Oakes has detailed, Douglass reaffirmed his demands for fair enlistment policies and total emancipation. Lincoln demurred about the former, but vowed to press forward on emancipation. Douglass opined afterward that, while Lincoln "will not go down to posterity as Abraham the Great," his word seemed his bond. Their interview reassured Douglass that "slavery would not survive the war." The appeased activist therefore reentered the fold, accepting an offer of a commissioned recruiting position in the Mississippi Valley. In preparation for his new role he shuttered his newspaper, informing readers that he was joining the "physical as well as the moral struggle against slavery." The government, however, ultimately reneged upon his commission, forcing Douglass to cancel his plans—and again shaking his trust in the president. Douglass thus entered the fall wary anew of both Lincoln and his own intervention.[28]

Other recruiters diverged from Douglass in continuing to stand by Lincoln, bowing to the dictates of power politics. Robert Hamilton, editor of the *Weekly Anglo-African,* proclaimed in a September editorial that Lincoln had "done much more than we ever dreamed he would." The president, he averred, knew "that the destiny of the colored man . . . is intimately connected with the life of the nation." As Hamilton traveled as a reporter through Union-occupied Virginia over the fall to chronicle the conditions of Black soldiers, he accordingly praised Lincoln's enlistment policies. For the time being, at least, he remained unwilling to unleash his inner turmoil.[29]

In his journal, Hamilton stressed that Black activists also aspired beyond formal freedom. Abolition without suffrage, he argued, was a "partial emancipation unworthy of the name." As he observed, "It would naturally be supposed that the Abolitionists" would take up the cause of post-emancipation Black rights. Yet many white interventionists, namely narrow ones, were not doing so. Echoing the point his brother, Thomas, had made back in 1861, Hamilton asserted that abolitionists' "mission was . . . destructive"—to tear down slavery. By fixating even further on emancipation, and by deferring to the political mainstream, they were now atrophying beyond repair their "gift of construction"—of building an egalitarian system in slavery's stead. These white interventionists, rather than Lincoln, were failing African Americans.[30]

Hamilton especially singled out one such derelict activist: Theodore Tilton.

In August, Tilton derided the *Anglo-African* in his own journal, *The Independent,* as a "specially African" paper that discouraged racial assimilation. In retort, Hamilton advocated for Black separatism, setting himself apart from avowed assimilationists like Douglass. Merging the "individuality of our people into that of the nation," he argued, would blunt racial progress. "In this country we are colored people," Hamilton explained. Blacks were "determined to be something else" and become citizens. But they had to elevate themselves to such heights, preserving their distinct identities in order to remain united. They could not "rely upon white men for our enfranchisement," he added. Men like Tilton professed to fight for Blacks' freedom "without giving us a compensating lift in the way of practically helping us along." Aside from exceptions like Phillips, white interventionists thus fell short in the struggle for liberty and rights.[31]

THE FALL OF THE INTERVENTIONISTS

By autumn, interventionists were also failing to preserve their own unity. They had drawn battle lines around their solidifying factions over the previous months, squeezing their wartime platform from both ends. Garrison and Child had endorsed Lincoln, forsaking one half of that platform. George Cheever had long since repudiated him, alongside the other half. More cautiously, Phillips, Conway, and Douglass had moved toward a break with the president. Mirroring the mindsets of these dissident interventionists, meanwhile, moral purists strove to perfect the Union war by opposing its leader. Over the fall, Pillsbury argued that Lincoln had enacted an emancipation process that was both imperfect, as a "political expedient," and incomplete, as it allowed "for the longer continuance of slavery." He and the Fosters threw themselves into the petition drive of fellow Lincoln opponents Elizabeth Cady Stanton and Susan B. Anthony's Women's Loyal National League, lobbying for total emancipation in defiance of the president. Radical Republicans like Charles Sumner and James Ashley shed their recent reluctance to collaborate with abolitionists by endorsing the campaign, moving concurrently to draft a constitutional amendment to abolish slavery. While Garrison initially demurred, the Fosters soon pressured him into backing the drive—and into putting aside factional enmities for the moment.[32]

In December, however, such factionalism reared its head again at the thirtieth anniversary of the AASS. In planning the ceremony alongside McKim, Garrison envisioned a celebration of what he perceived as the AASS's, and his own, approaching victory in the "long thirty years' war" with slavery. "The Society will have the sublime privilege," he informed invitees, to salute military emancipation "as the result, primarily of its disinterested labors." Slavery would soon end. The anniversary would therefore serve not as a call to additional activism but as a retrospective, honoring the AASS as its mission, in his moderated view, neared completion. McKim likewise looked to the past by advising Garrison to update his 1833 "Declaration of Sentiments." While the original document announced "what we would do," McKim desired a new version trumpeting "what we *have* done." He and Garrison affirmed their self-conceived roles as vindicated prophets who awaited the emancipatory end to their careers—and who thereby overlooked that Garrison had sought Black inclusion alongside emancipation in his 1833 manifesto.[33]

Garrison and McKim sought not only to commemorate but also to control the past by foraying into the realm of antislavery memory. In curating a guest list for the affair, McKim made a point of inviting estranged former AASS members. For the "fact of history," he argued, "bygones should be bygones." By reaching out to old rivals like Douglass and Lewis Tappan, the organizers would prove their magnanimity in triumph. They would also shape the historical narrative by judging who had "maintained their anti-slavery integrity" enough to attend the marquee event—and who future generations would remember as the true heroes. For posterity's sake, the organizers also invited a number of Radical Republican allies, including Sumner, George W. Julian, and Henry Wilson. But only Wilson would attend, demonstrating once again immediatists' reduced sway in the wake of the Emancipation Proclamation.[34]

As the anniversary approached, Garrison and his pro-Lincoln associates worried that anti-Lincoln abolitionists would ruin the proceedings. Voicing his public relations concerns, McKim stressed that "we must put our best foot forward . . . to sustain the high opinion that begins to be entertained of us." The planners desired a unifying, nonpolitical celebration rather than a contentious row over Lincoln that aired abolitionists' "dirty linen" in public. Yet they had to invite potentially disruptive AASS members like Phillips and the Fosters onstage for the sake of unity. "Phillips must go on," Garrison agreed. He fretted nonetheless that purists like the Fosters were in a "morbid state . . . relative to the Administration and the Rebellion, and would be more inclined to criminate the former than to denounce the latter." McKim vowed to have speakers ready with "words of cheer" to set the meeting back on track.[35]

The anniversary commenced in Philadelphia in December, with a banner trumpeting "Liberty and Union" flying above the stage in summation of Garrison's narrowed mission. In his addresses, Garrison reflected on the history of abolitionism, awaiting the "judgment of posterity" to celebrate its triumphant trajectory. Observing that "all signs of the times . . . are cheering," he proclaimed that "we are very near the jubilee." Soon, he could "dissolve the American Anti-Slavery Society." It "organized to abolish slavery," Garrison argued. "When slavery is abolished, of course our mission ends, in that particular." For its aftermath, he referenced the "new field of philanthropy opened to us": freedmen's aid. Yet this movement circumscribed racial reform, replacing abolitionism's struggle for long-term Black empowerment with short-term material assistance. In the city where he had penned the "Declaration of Sentiments" years earlier, Garrison laid bare the dissonance between that uncompromising manifesto and his current agenda.[36]

While Garrison had hoped to inspire unified revelry, his premature victory declaration outraged the Fosters. Stephen Foster subsequently rocked the staid proceedings the following day by asserting that "we have become over-confident in regard to the success of the movement." Garrison anticipated the imminent end of slavery, and with it the completion of his moral mandate. But Foster rejected this fait accompli. He portrayed Lincoln as a villainous obstacle to a truly morally transformed Union, predicated on complete emancipation and racial equality. Like Pillsbury, he blamed Lincoln for not using his "constitutional power to abolish slavery," emphasizing that total emancipation was far from nigh. The president also fought for the "white man," refusing Blacks their deserved rights. "I would not trust anybody's liberty in the hands of such a Government," Foster proclaimed, lambasting Garrison by proxy for standing by Lincoln.[37]

Later, Abby Kelley Foster rose to dispute the extent of antislavery progress. Invoking the moral purist argument that emancipation had to proceed from perfect means to unlock an egalitarian morally transformed Union, she lamented that northerners and their officials endorsed military emancipation "not from the highest but from the lowest motives." Such were not rationales "upon which we can rely, and which should make us jubilant," Foster warned, cautioning those "who think the mission of the Anti-Slavery Society is finished," or nearly so. "Nothing is done while anything remains to be done, so far as the death of American slavery is concerned," she averred. With Lincoln in power, their end was nowhere in sight. To overcome the president and unleash the war's egalitarian potential, the Fosters and Pillsbury would soon enter the electoral fray, journeying far from their purist moorings—and trafficking in the same impure compromises against which they had warned interventionists.[38]

The anniversary soon devolved into the embarrassing row Garrison had dreaded. He and the other narrow interventionists leading the pro-Lincoln faction shed their nonpolitical pretensions to refute the Fosters, defending the president and their own diminished missions. Samuel May Jr. accused Stephen Foster of doing Lincoln "great injustice" by maligning his motives. The president, he declared, "has made great progress." From a "low plane . . . he has risen faster than the people," May averred, echoing Garrison. Lincoln, he concluded, would "rise as far as righteousness shall demand." On the emancipation issue, Garrison added, "We have passed the Rubicon." In their confidence that Lincoln would end slavery, May and Garrison reaffirmed their rejection of an interventionist consensus that was insufficiently faithful to the president.[39]

Garrison and his like-minded associates also justified their abridged visions. In rebutting Abby Kelley Foster, Oliver Johnson called it a "sign of progress when men who have long resisted our movement" found that its mission now coincided "with their worldly interest." While the Fosters deigned to act only from justice, Johnson countered that, if slavery could not end before the "people are brought up to [that] standard," it would continue "for centuries." Self-interest would accomplish what morality could not, he concluded, celebrating the results regardless. "It is not at all our province" to determine why people have "come into sympathy and cooperation with us for the abolition of slavery," Garrison agreed. "Whoever will come up now, and speak a word for freedom, I will hail as . . . a brother, and will leave his motives to God." Having internalized the standard of the possible, Johnson and Garrison abolished any distinction between reformers and politicos, identifying fully with their political partners and their less inclusive agendas.[40]

As Garrison reveled in the mainstream, Phillips, Douglass, and the broad interventionists animating the anti-Lincoln faction castigated his compromises. Phillips, long the AASS's most prominent member after Garrison, shunned the anniversary in a protest louder than words. Douglass, meanwhile, voiced his concerns in person. In a speech that no doubt infuriated Garrison, his old protégé refreshed his memory about the AASS's founding aims. "This Society was organized," Douglass attested, "for two distinct objects: one was the emancipation of the slave, and the other the elevation of the colored people." Like moral purists, he argued that immediatism should end not with formal emancipation but with a substantive "abolition peace." He laid forth an evolved image of Reconstruction centered around the achievement of Black legislative equality, contending that the AASS's work "will not have been completed" until Blacks were freed and "admitted, fully and completely, into the body politic." More than material aid, they required citizenship, property, and "immediate enfranchisement"—advances which would empower them to help themselves. Black voters would also be the Union's "best protector against the traitors" in "reestablish[ing] republican institutions in the South." Ensuring Black rights was both right and necessary, he maintained, reminding Garrison in vain of his onetime commitments.[41]

Douglass also stressed the tenuousness of his tolerance for Lincoln. "While the Government lays down as a rule ... of pay a complexional one," he warned, "we are in danger of a compromise" to the "element of prejudice." Dashing interventionists' expectations that a war for emancipation would precipitate a moral revolution, racism remained endemic. Many northerners "accept the term abolitionist with qualifications," acceding to military emancipation but nothing further. Others did not even go that far, forcing politicos to "spin out elaborate explanations and denials" about fighting an "Abolition war." Lincoln bowed to such forces by permitting discriminatory policies, Douglass asserted, as he chafed at supporting a leader whose political interests did not align with his own agenda. The meeting adjourned thereafter, its fete turned debacle having exposed an interventionist camp verging on collapse.[42]

Days later, Lincoln dealt this camp its death blow by issuing a Proclamation of Amnesty and Reconstruction. As his criteria for readmitting a rebel state, he envisioned that 10 percent of its extant voters would swear fealty to the Union, and then appoint delegates to a convention that recognized the abolition of slavery. Lincoln also proposed an amnesty for most rebels. In the *Liberator,* Garrison objected that such leniency would "give over the sheep"— freed slaves—"to the guardianship of wolves"—the rebels. Yet he and his narrow interventionist followers welcomed the plan's larger import. Lincoln now incorporated total emancipation into his party's agenda—a significant leap in his moral evolution. But he remained in step with the public, and with the prepotent Republican dedication to a free-labor Union of white liberty. He therefore continued to separate out the issues of slavery and race by opposing bondage but ignoring post-emancipation Black rights—a distinction Johnson accepted by equating his own morally transformed Union with Lincoln's model. "God bless A.L.," he declared, rejoicing that his reduced mission for an emancipatory Union now aligned fully with that of the political mainstream.[43]

Phillips, by contrast, revealed a developed version of his alternative Reconstruction at Cooper Union in late December. Even as he struggled over his own politicization, he, like Douglass, had harnessed that political instruction to push the bounds of his activism. Now, he promulgated a rarefied argument for a morally transformed Union premised on the goal of legislative equality, furthering his wartime transformation into a modern agent of political change—an activist fusing his old moral and new political frameworks into an indelible whole. In his soaring speech, Phillips elucidated a tripartite legislative agenda to ensure that the "South will be secured," binding the reunited nation through a radically democratic idea of citizenship. First, he asserted that the "nation owes to the negro not merely freedom—it owes him land." Invoking his notion of a unified nationality, he advocated "plant[ing] a hundred thousand negro farmers" to remake the South alongside soldier colonies. "Land dictates government," Phillips explained. Land redistribution would transform the South from a closed oligarchy into an open, representative democracy. Second, federally mandated public education would give freed slaves the intellectual wherewithal to thrive as citizens. Finally, constitutional amendments ensuring total emancipation and outlawing racial discrimination would secure Blacks "not technical freedom, but substantial protection in all rights." Phillips proposed using the power of the government for good, enshrining racial egalitarianism to moralize a still-sluggish nation.[44]

Phillips then contrasted his plan with Lincoln's, as his agony reached a fever pitch. While Garrison had forsaken the conditionality of the interventionist consensus, Phillips had been reluctant to shatter this platform from its other end by repudiating Lincoln. Yet his discontent over his intervention, and his compromises in upholding the government, had grown untenable. Now, Phillips framed Lincoln not as a necessary evil but as an intolerable one who prevented total emancipation and Black rights. The president sought a piecemeal abolition, not an amendment. He would also restore voting and land rights for slaveholders, "giv[ing] the negro back into his master's legislative control." A "Union so reconstructed ... would be a machine not to work," Phillips scorned. Concluding that he could no longer advance his mission by working with Lincoln, and within interventionists' ineffective consensus, Phillips heeded Stanton. He forswore Lincoln and threw off the constraints of the interventionist camp, rejecting its platform as insufficiently antislavery. "Next year we launch into President making," he announced, following the Cheever brothers into electoral opposition as he hammered the final nail into the camp's coffin.[45]

A year earlier, interventionists had attained their signal triumph. Yet in helping achieve military emancipation, they had also caused their camp's collapse. Bereft of a common animus, they had drifted apart. Garrison, caught up in political success, abated his quest, embracing Lincoln alongside Child. After they failed to advance further reforms through their antislavery alliance, Phillips, Douglass, Conway, and George Cheever soured on the president and banded together with purists. The Mason affair hardened this divide over the summer, before the AASS anniversary and Lincoln's decree rendered it irreparable. Interventionists splintered at year's end, realigning wartime abolitionism a second time—and commencing a new stage of its civil war, as a struggle over the Union war fully transformed into one over Lincoln. Garrison and Child would channel their moral acceptance of Lincoln into electoral aid. Phillips, the Cheever brothers, Conway, the Fosters, Pillsbury, and, at times, Douglass would instead reroute their moral ambivalence over their interventions into oppositional politicking, making electoral hay of their political inculcations. As all these figures recognized, politics was as alluring as it was inescapable—a proven avenue to unparalleled power. These pro- and anti-Lincoln abolitionists would hence clash as warring partisans in the months ahead.

CHAPTER TEN

The Competing Conventions, January–June 1864

In June 1864, William Lloyd Garrison traveled to the city that had launched his career as a reformer: Baltimore. A young Garrison had come into his immediatist views while working there for the gradual abolitionist editor Benjamin Lundy, culminating in his jailing on libel charges in 1830. After his release, he had decamped to the North. As he returned for the first time since then, he observed that the jail "I once had the honor and happiness to occupy ...has been torn down." Garrison found deep symbolic meaning in its destruction. Once, he had been an outcast, persecuted in the slaveholding city for his antislavery beliefs. Now, in that same city, he witnessed Lincoln's renomination for president on a platform calling for military victory, a constitutional amendment to abolish slavery as an act of "justice and national safety"—the Thirteenth Amendment, which had passed the Senate but would fail in the House that summer—and protections for soldiers "without distinction of color." As the Republicans matched his mission of a Lincoln-led, emancipatory Union, without mention of post-emancipation Black rights, Garrison gloried that the proceedings "gladden my heart, and almost make me fear that I am at home dreaming." As he awaited the imminent completion of his life's work, a giddy Garrison claimed that "even my friend Phillips would have been highly gratified" by the convention.[1]

Yet Garrison's assertion proved to be wishful thinking: following the interventionist camp's collapse, he and Phillips had become rival partisans in a new phase of the abolitionist civil war. In early 1864, pro- and anti-Lincoln abolitionists began dipping their toes into electoral politics, morally contorting themselves for what each saw as their greater good. The latter redirected their turmoil over their wartime politicization by seeking to advance mostly expansive agendas through candidates such as Salmon P. Chase, Benjamin Butler, and John C. Frémont. Phillips, the broad interventionist leader of the anti-Lincoln faction, vowed to vanquish the president as an intolerable evil who prevented an egalitarian morally transformed Union. He soon prevailed upon Conway to come off the sidelines and oppose Lincoln from England. Moral purists like the Fosters and Pillsbury, meanwhile, finally descended into the muck by politicizing their opposition to Lincoln alongside their moral missions. George Cheever, for his part, championed Chase's doomed candidacy while embracing a broad interventionist conception of legislative equality. Douglass, by contrast, avoided partisanship, even while he and other Black activists scathed the government's Reconstruction and enlistment policies. And Forten completed her maturation into a champion of equality for freed slaves as she left the Sea Islands.

Garrison instead reaffirmed his unconditional support for the president as an antislavery hero whose goals paralleled his reduced vision of a morally transformed Union. Even as he feigned political impartiality, he campaigned for Lincoln as an unalloyed partisan. In elucidating her own agenda, meanwhile, Child envisioned a socioeconomically and politically egalitarian Reconstruction, aligning her more with purists and broad interventionists like Phillips, Douglass, Forten, and, now, Cheever than with the narrow Garrison. Yet she joined Garrison in pro-Lincoln partisanship, touting the president as a force for good. As they pursued irreconcilable objectives, the two factions turned their pressure tactics against each other. Each side accused the other of trafficking in moral compromise as partisans, while engaging in such behavior themselves.[2]

Both sides soon escalated their partisanship by taking part in rival political conventions in the late spring. Phillips, Cheever, Pillsbury, and the Fosters joined the incipient Cleveland movement, which looked to Frémont to wrest the Republican nomination from Lincoln. These abolitionists overcame their moral hesitation to delineate an expansive agenda for the political group. Douglass, who now opted to translate his moral outrage into partisanship, and Conway soon endorsed the fledgling movement as well. Yet even after Frémont repositioned his campaign as a third party by recruiting a group of ambitious War Democrats whose ideals were incompatible to abolitionists' own, his immediatist supporters remained by his side. At the party's May convention in Cleveland, they settled for a Democrat-dominated and muddled platform which was far from what they had desired, mixing watered-down antislavery and overtly pro-Copperhead planks. Soon after, Garrison journeyed to attend the Republican convention. In Baltimore, and at an audience at the White House afterward, he reiterated that his endgame was an emancipatory Union—and that Lincoln represented the sole means to achieving it. Abolitionists thus pitched into defeating or reelecting Lincoln with single-minded determination, leading many into once-unthinkable positions that increasingly impaired their larger missions.[3]

SEARCHING FOR AN ALTERNATIVE TO LINCOLN

Anti-Lincoln abolitionists remade themselves in early 1864 into the president's political opponents, pursuing electoral alternatives to realize their politicized visions of perfection. In the weeks following his Cooper Union speech, Phillips led the way in articulating a moral argument against Lincoln. At the January meeting of the MASS, he reiterated that giving Blacks "land, education, rights" would enable the North to "cover the South" and supplant the Slaveocracy with true democracy. Yet Lincoln blocked this outcome. As Phillips admitted, the president intended that "the negro shall in the end be free." He had become an ardent emancipator—one who would soon move beyond advocating a state-based abolition process toward championing the Thirteenth Amendment. "But there he unfortunately stops," Phillips decried, short of demanding "those rights which this Society was established to secure." His Reconstruction plan returned the "slave into the hands of his master with technical liberty"—a status "no better than apprenticeship"—rather than the rights necessary to protect himself and secure northern civilization. Conjuring the metaphor of a drowning man, Phillips expounded that Lincoln would "bring him to the low-water mark, at high tide," and strand him there. The president thus stood in the way of a panoramic morally transformed Union.[4]

Phillips subsequently threw himself into electioneering by casting about for candidates to overtake Lincoln as the Republican nominee. As a long-time champion of the military as an engine of moralization, he particularly touted the candidacies of Generals Benjamin Butler and John C. Frémont. In his January speech, he proclaimed that Butler would set the drowning man "on Plymouth Rock, high and dry." He "recognizes that everything that fights votes," Phillips averred the next month, contrasting this idea to Lincoln's plan to "make the Union one on the simple platform of the abolition of slavery—the negro a tool . . . [not] a man. That policy is Louisiana in the hand of Banks," who administered a free-labor plantation regime—and who oversaw a spring constitutional convention that rejected Black suffrage. "That is the freedom ... under Lincoln," Phillips concluded: one which was both nominal and insufficient. "Why employ a president ... who cannot see justice for the negro?" he asked. Peering across time to the year 1964, Phillips wondered how the war would "read in history." To prevent it from becoming a chronicle of shame, he would "leave no stone unturned to put Butler or Fremont [*sic*] in the presidential chair," thereby replacing Lincoln with a "man who means to put the white men of the South on a level with the negro ... and reconstruct the Union on that basis." He would get "in the trenches," he informed a friend, by "turning things upside down in hopes to bring them right side up"—by engaging in deeply compromising politicking to ensure his egalitarian ends.[5]

Phillips's electoral efforts soon inspired Conway to reengage with political affairs. From his self-exile in London, the Virginian learned of his fellow anti-Lincoln abolitionists' flirtations with Republican challengers. "Old Abe is more cunning and slow than ever," Phillips informed him in March. Lincoln was "no believer in the negro—as a citizen—is indeed a colonizationist yet." Abolitionists needed a "man who sees that to save the nation (white and black) you must recognize the blacks' rights." Phillips hoped that Conway would weigh in "while we choose our pilot for the next four years." The "Mason matter ... is dead," he avowed, freeing Conway to lend his voice to the campaign to trounce Lincoln and facilitate antislavery change.[6]

Conway responded by repudiating Lincoln. Unlike broad interventionists like Phillips, he sought a narrow morally transformed Union premised on Black plantation labor and Anglo-Saxon supremacy. Yet he also detested Nathaniel P. Banks's wage-labor system. He continued to distinguish Banks's regime from his own post-emancipation vision by mischaracterizing it as proslavery rather than comparably antislavery but antiegalitarian. In March, he decried anew its "meanness and infernalism" in the *Commonwealth*, to which he returned as a correspondent. Conway subsequently targeted Banks's presidential patron by declaring that the general's rule "bears marks of having been framed at Washington." In addition to "re-enslaving the negroes," Banks was overseeing the creation of a "sham government ... to aid by their electoral vote the re-election of Mr. Lincoln." As Phillips's "utter [loss of] faith" in the president emboldened him, Conway proceeded to rebuke Lincoln's campaign as "most discreditable." Abolitionists "have much to fear from the Kentucky in him," he proclaimed, shedding his antipolitical stance to join Phillips in oppositional politicking. "It is not by adhering to men simply because they have done some good things, or moved with the average mass . . . that the abolitionists can do work in this emergency," Conway averred, rejecting Garrison's resolve to judge Lincoln by the standard of the politically possible. "Suppose Mr. Garrison had only gone as far as the people sustained him, what would he have accomplished?" Conway asked. Rather than settle for the "downward tendencies of the present administration," he, too, started to seek out potential Republican replacements.[7]

Phillips also galvanized the Fosters and Pillsbury to transmute their moral opposition to Lincoln into political electioneering. Even as purists refocused their antagonism on the president in recent months, they had continued to cling to their aspirations of saintly aloofness from the impure mainstream. As Phillips now demonstrated, however, entering the mainstream grime had become the most effective medium for removing Lincoln and ensuring an egalitarian morally transformed Union. Stephen Foster thereby declared after Phillips's speech to the MASS that "your chart of the channel through which we are sailing corresponds so entirely with our own that we do not fear to trust the ship to your hands." Abby Kelley Foster added that her "joy exceeds all expectation" over the "crystal clearness of your vision." Pillsbury likewise averred that "all earnest eyes are turned to you." Phillips had "the most anointed vision of any in our prophetic school," Pillsbury proclaimed, engirding him in the holy imagery of moral purity.[8]

But while they aimed still for purity in theory, the Fosters and Pillsbury now fully abjured it in reality. They entangled themselves as political actors, abandoning their lifelong emphasis on perfect means to attain their expansive ends. Lincoln, as they still maintained, obstructed their goals of total emancipation and Black rights. Stephen Foster went beyond Phillips at the MASS meeting by labeling the president the "embodiment of the Dred Scott decision," fighting to "save slavery" as well as to oppress Blacks. Since "Lincoln has awful advantages; and it seems impossible to circumvent him" to achieve change through their old methods, as Pillsbury told Phillips in March, moral purists embraced politics to dethrone him. As Foster averred at a May gathering, he now sought to have Lincoln "succeeded by a better." Pillsbury likewise explained that he "had never voted for President; but rejoiced in the prospect of a platform whereon, without compromise, a man could stand"—and in the prospect of a candidate who embodied such values.[9]

Though purists aspired to uncompromised activism on behalf of a perfect alternative, they began undertaking the same political accommodations against which they had long warned interventionists. Stephen Foster and Pillsbury had supported Republican candidates the previous year, recognizing Copperheads as the larger threat. Now, they dismissed such a sense of perspective by fixating on Lincoln instead as the overarching evil. In April, Pillsbury informed Phillips that he was "not the champion . . . of any party, or any party's candidate." Indeed, his and Foster's anti-Lincoln crusade had led to the "Republicans rejecting us and Democrats taking us in," increasing the appeal of a pioneering—and morally hazardous—partnership with the latter.[10]

As they overcame their moral unease, these purists also followed Phillips into politicizing their egalitarian visions of a morally transformed Union. They had heretofore envisioned their moral revolution in antebellum terms as a pure, nonpolitical process. But now, Pillsbury reframed his ideal nation "regenerated . . . to begin the world's millennium" in terms of legislative equality. At times, he hesitated over transforming his perspective. "I cannot yet speak on Reconstruction . . . it is not yet my calling," he admitted to Phillips in April. At a meeting that month, Pillsbury nonetheless vowed to "support no Presidential candidate" who did not endorse the "equal, inalienable rights of all men before the law," the "duty of Congress" to end slavery, and "Constitutional amendments as shall forever . . . prohibit its reestablishment." Stephen Foster likewise overhauled his moral mission to imagine a politically expansive Reconstruction, asserting at a May antislavery gathering that Blacks should be "political equal[s] of the white."[11]

After months of politicking behind the scenes, George Cheever exposed his own anti-Lincoln campaigning to the light of day. Like Phillips, he ceased his criticisms of Lincoln's abolition policy as the president inched toward embracing total emancipation. Instead, Cheever focused his attention on arraigning Lincoln's "principle of ultimate necessity"—of expediency, a concept he had dramatically renounced. He also attacked the president at length from his New York pulpit, leading one Lincoln ally to denounce the "lunatic Cheever" to the White House.[12]

In their quest to replace Lincoln as the Republican leader, Cheever and his brother, Henry, still favored Salmon P. Chase. In recent months, the Treasury secretary's tentative candidacy had also attracted abolitionists like Franklin B. Sanborn and Theodore Tilton, antislavery business elites like John Austin Stevens Jr., and Radical Republicans like John Andrew. In particular, Gotham businessmen like Stevens mobilized their Unionist organizations, such as the Loyal National League, for Chase. In part, they strove to replace the "inefficient and

inglorious administration" with one that would "finish the war" and build a racially restrictive but profitable free-labor order in the South. But these elites also
had business interests in elevating Chase, whom they lobbied to support their
banking concerns and cotton speculations in Texas. Radical Republicans, meanwhile, desired a stronger antislavery war, seeking to push beyond their party ideal
of a free-labor Union to address their longstanding moral interest in expansive
Black rights. But while Kate Masur has portrayed the entire party as champions
of equality in some form, even Radicals still subordinated this goal to political
considerations. In drafting both the Thirteenth Amendment and a harsher alternative to Lincoln's Reconstruction plan, the Wade-Davis bill, they contemplated but ultimately omitted Black rights measures as inexpedient. Congress
"is not going to do as much for the elevation of the race . . . as we expected," one
activist fumed. Radical leaders again ignored the issue when they publicized
their support for Chase in a February manifesto, which lamented how Lincoln had allowed the war "to languish" and squandered party fortunes. These
self-interested politicos thus conditioned their post-emancipation policies on
their own economic and political concerns—a tenuous commitment at best.[13]

Cheever repudiated such equivocation as he evolved toward a broad interventionist understanding of Black rights. After Radical leaders asked him to
sermonize on the "cowardice of our statesmen," namely Lincoln, and prepare
public opinion for "our next President," he addressed Congress in May. Belying
such expectations, Cheever instead castigated his allies over the Wade-Davis
bill. "I did not spare them," he later reported. The bill, he declared, held Blacks
"down forever as an inferior, oppressed race" by withholding the "rights be-
longing to them." That policy was both unwise and immoral, since it restored
political power to their "old masters" and presented a "compound of hypocrisy
and oppression before God, unexampled in history." In its place, he demanded
a "uniform suffrage law," irrespective of "race or color." Cheever, fueled by his
guilt over bowing to the dictates of expediency early in the war, thereby pivoted
to an expansive vision of a morally transformed Union.[14]

Cheever also met in Washington with Chase, whom Lincoln had outma-
neuvered in the weeks following the manifesto's release. "It is hardly likely" that
Chase would attain the presidency, Cheever acknowledged afterward. "I am
greatly afraid that Mr. Lincoln is to be there another four years," he confessed.
To forestall that future and accomplish his newfound goal of Black legislative
equality, Cheever would soon turn to another political challenger.[15]

Unlike his fellow anti-Lincoln abolitionists, Douglass refused still to escalate his distrust of the president into political opposition. Yet even as he steered clear of partisanship, he, too, expressed outrage over the government's policies on Reconstruction and enlistment. As he lectured across the North, he demanded a postwar Union far exceeding Lincoln's bounds. The government, he argued, had not "understood . . . the true mission of the war." In order to ensure "national unity," it needed not only to end slavery, but also to create a "new order of social and political relations" grounded in "fidelity to justice and liberty." Unless Blacks gained "civil and political equality," the Slaveocracy would still "command . . . the whole South." But the administration hampered this goal of legislative equality. At an April dinner honoring Louisiana Unionists, Douglass decried Banks for "taking the elective franchise from our friends and placing it in the hands of our enemies." He also lambasted the government's policies depriving Black soldiers of equal pay and advancement as the insidious "dark shadow[s]" of slavery.[16]

A growing number of Black abolitionists joined Douglass in criticizing the government, refusing to hold back their discontent any longer. Robert Hamilton had defended Lincoln over the fall. But after the military executed William Walker, a Black sergeant who had protested for fair pay, he began to tear into the government. In his newspaper, he scalded that its unequal enlistment policies dispossessed Blacks "of all the attributes of soldiers and free American citizens." Rather than rush into partisanship, he and other activists hit upon the idea of channeling their frustrations into the first national "convention of colored people" since 1855. They could thereby push for total emancipation, fair enlistment, and equal rights without forsaking their recruiting agencies, which they still valued for promoting a pathway to freedom. These leaders shared the expansive ends of most white anti-Lincoln abolitionists, but not their means.[17]

As she, too, steered clear of the partisan tumult, Forten refined a mature, broad interventionist perspective on race. Upon returning to the North in May, she chronicled her experiences educating freed slaves in the Sea Islands for *The Atlantic Monthly*. In her articles, Forten fully shed her classist views to laud the capabilities of her former wards. "The haughty Anglo-Saxon race, after centuries of such an experience as these people have had, would [not] be very much superior to them," she declared. Whites had denied them "every right," she fumed, in entire recognition that she shared their plight—and their need for expansive equality. In its fight for freedom, the "Government had left much undone," she lamented. "The sky is dark; but through the darkness we can discern a brighter future"—a "day of final and entire deliverance," in which Blacks become free and equal citizens. Forten therefore committed herself to realizing that day.[18]

RALLYING AROUND THE PRESIDENT

While anti-Lincoln abolitionists mostly lurched into oppositional politics over the spring, their pro-Lincoln counterparts rallied to the president's candidacy. Garrison, the narrow interventionist leading this faction, had long since silenced his inner turmoil to champion the president unequivocally and pursue the goal of an emancipatory Union. Now, at the April dinner for Louisiana Unionists, Garrison stressed that "our government stands solemnly pledged" to destroy slavery alongside the rebellion. Seated onstage with Douglass, he felt compelled to allude to Black rights by noting that "we mean, as far as possible, to leave nothing undone until in this country the distinction of color is abolished." Yet his qualification was significant. The standard of the possible shaped his moral mission. Black inclusion had become an afterthought—an issue distinct from the abolitionist crusade as he now saw it. As Garrison clarified in May, his AASS "was not organized specifically" to deal with subjects like the "political status of the freedmen in Louisiana." Reconstruction was beyond the purview of his abridged agenda.[19]

As the campaign began, Garrison attempted to conceal the extent of his adherence to Lincoln. Sensing that his rivals had vacated the high ground of moral objectivity, he staked a claim to political impartiality by framing his support of the president as practical rather than partisan. In part, it was: Garrison was desperate to prevent a Copperhead victory that would doom emancipation. Since the Copperheads aimed to "divide the Republican Party," Garrison wrote in March, the "best thing that can be done politically, is to stand by Lincoln, with all his shortcomings." Yet he believed that the president had shed any such flaws over his term. While he professed in the *Liberator* that he was "independent of all party ties," Garrison could not help but portray the president as a genuine paragon who strove to abolish "the whole slave system" in the name of justice. Despite his pretensions of dispassionateness, he engaged in partisan partiality by inveighing against the other candidates to clear the field for Lincoln—and for his own mission. Lincoln's Republican loyalists, in return, greeted Garrison as a useful ally once again. New Hampshire party official Benjamin Prescott had previously shrugged off abolitionists as impractical. Now, he hailed Garrison for saying the "strongest things why Mr. Lincoln should be re-nominated," while reserving scorn for the "always impracticable" Phillips. "It is a peculiar pleasure to me that we agree upon the Presidential question," a New York Republican likewise wrote Garrison, grasping that he had shunned Phillips's inexpedient demands to align with the political mainstream.[20]

After laboring for months to garner recognition for George Thompson's service to the Union, Garrison now seized on these political connections to arrange a series of receptions in his honor. In contrast to Thompson's disastrous tour of the nation decades earlier, members of the antislavery alliance from across the antislavery spectrum celebrated his triumphant return to American shores. John Andrew and other Radical Republicans welcomed him to Boston, while New York antislavery businessmen feted him in Gotham. Congressmen and the Lincoln administration then invited Thompson to a grandiose reception at the Capitol in March.[21]

Garrison lauded the tour as a validation of his course, demonstrating how pro-Lincoln abolitionists and the mainstream had come into antislavery convergence. "The Washington overture," he crowed, offered "another glorious indication that we are entering upon a new era" and nearing moral perfection. One attendee at Thompson's Capitol fete recalled that the "deafening thunders of applause ... sound[ed] like the crack of doom to the infernal Slave Oligarchy." As Thompson later reflected, in 1834 "I was reviled, mobbed, persecuted." But in 1864, "I was invited to the capital ... as the guest of the people" and its leaders. "In both years ... I was, and still am, a Garrisonian abolitionist," he concluded, implying that the nation had moralized around unswerving immediatists. Yet as Ann Phillips had once warned, abolitionists had also gone over to the politicians. Narrow interventionists like Garrison now shared a common, near-complete mission with the political mainstream—one that had advanced racial justice far beyond its antebellum bounds, but well short of their founding purposes.[22]

Unlike Garrison, Child expanded her moral vision by adopting a broad interventionist view of legislative equality. "We need the labor of all" to create a harmonious nation, she now asserted. Through "schools, the protections of equal laws, and the stimulus of just wages," Blacks could become equal and productive citizens and help build this new order. To secure their civil and political rights, Child moved to support expansive socioeconomic measures like land redistribution. In March, she lauded George W. Julian's homestead bill, which would provide confiscated rebel land to freed slaves, soldiers, and loyal southern whites. "Land monopoly," she wrote him, was "another form of slavery." Drawing on her oft-cited example of the British West Indies, she approved the "cutting up of large plantations into little lots" to keep southern planters and "Northern capitalists" at bay. While she disliked Julian's "outright *gift* of lands," arguing that sales at cheap prices would better invest the new owners in their upkeep, she nonetheless demanded land reform as an integral component of an egalitarian Reconstruction.[23]

Yet unlike other broad interventionists, Child looked to secure that future through the president. "I am sorry Wendell Phillips feels it his duty to attack Lincoln," she confessed. "I know of no man, except Charles Sumner, who would be so reliable for a President." In February, Child acknowledged that she had once "been out of patience" with Lincoln. But he had since "continually done better than he promised," growing into a wise leader who imparted purpose to the conflict. She thus endorsed him as a moral paragon, seeking the "equality of races" under his aegis—and taking solace in his leadership as Union forces ground on toward Richmond in the grueling Overland Campaign. "I rejoice over our victories, because I see in them the approaching of the end; but the amount of suffering is terrible!" she wrote, lamenting the campaign's human cost while nonetheless crediting Lincoln for imbuing such sacrifice with moral value. Child labored to ensure that Lincoln could guide the nation through carnage to perfect shores, aligning in the short term with Garrison despite their long-term ideological differences.[24]

THE ABOLITIONIST CIVIL WAR, TRANSFORMED

Even as broad and narrow interventionists' differing denouements loomed in the background, abolitionists became consumed with the means to those ends: electoral politics. In a new phase of the abolitionist civil war, the pro- and anti-Lincoln factions began accusing each other of betraying immediatism through foul partisanship, overlooking in the process their own unrestrained politicking. This gamesmanship began at the January MASS gathering. After Phillips offered a resolution condemning Lincoln for pursuing a "sham peace" that would leave freed slaves "under the control of the late slaveholders," Garrison pushed back. Though Phillips meant that Lincoln pursued only a technical freedom,

Garrison accused him of labeling the president as proslavery. Lincoln would never restore the "slave oligarchy," Garrison declared indignantly.[25]

Building on his pretension of impartiality, Garrison presented himself as a dispassionate reformer opposing the machinations of anti-Lincoln political animals. Phillips, he derided, openly endorsed candidates like Frémont, who had not "expressed any satisfaction in regard to the President's emancipation proclamation." Garrison claimed to abjure politics by contrast, preferring Lincoln as a practical alternative to the Copperheads. He also reintroduced his well-tread argument that the "President must be judged by his possibilities, rather than by our wishes, or by the highest abstract moral standard." Yet Garrison was masking that he had merged these standards to make Lincoln's politically possible mission his own. In defending Lincoln, he soon shed his claimed objectivity. "There was a time when I had little confidence" in the president, he noted. But Lincoln's support for Black enlistment and "everlasting emancipation . . . changed my opinion," convincing Garrison that his reelection "would be the safest and wisest course." He thus countered Phillips's resolution with one endorsing Lincoln, exposing his true partisanship.[26]

Anti-Lincoln abolitionists responded by employing the same approach. In successfully shooting down Garrison's resolution, Stephen Foster expressed "surprise that [Garrison] should nominate for President" Lincoln. Phillips then staked his own faction's claim to the high ground by clarifying that he was "not here to oppose [Lincoln's] renomination." Far from a partisan, he claimed to be an unprejudiced reformer who criticized the president's "capacity to carry us into port" only as a moral imperative. Following this debate, the public relations-conscious Garrison downplayed its significance. In the *Liberator*, he asserted that he and Phillips "have always seen eye to eye," differing on minor points rather than principle. Yet as the two factional leaders had made clear, their goals, and their conceptions of each other, had become irreconcilable.[27]

The factions clashed again at the May anniversary of the AASS. Pillsbury proclaimed that immediatists should not "be led into the service of an Administration careless of freedom and justice for the oppressed." He then turned Garrison's professed impartiality on its head. Those immediatists who "stand by the Administration," he declared, were the real partisans impairing their "moral earnestness and integrity." As he leapt to the president's defense, Garrison again shed his purported objectivity. Lincoln would ensure the "speedy consummation of our work, the entire abolition of slavery," he argued, restating their shared goal of a total, formal emancipation without mention of Black rights. Phillips, unable to stand this abridgment of the abolitionist mission, replied that, "if with [Lincoln] the negro may have freedom, he may not be admitted to citizenship." Phillips then reclaimed the high ground by excoriating his old friend's partiality, declaring that "a million dollars would have been a cheap purchase for the Administration" of the *Liberator*'s support. In the name of public relations, Garrison let Phillips's slight pass. "I did not wish to seem to be in antagonism to him—for I know that our enemies would like to see us . . . at personal variance," he noted, minimizing how apparent that variance already was.[28]

Relations between the two sides deteriorated further at the New England Anti-Slavery Convention later that month. After Garrison again appealed to the standard of the possible to excuse Lincoln's, and his own, disinterest in Black rights, Abby Kelley Foster castigated him for "judging men by their position" rather than by principle, portraying her own faction as the righteous one. Phillips joined in this rebuke of his erstwhile comrade by vowing to be "bolder than Mr. Garrison." He then proceeded to explain why he "want[ed] a Butler and a Fremont [*sic*]" to replace the president. Lincoln had "touched slavery only when it was indispensably necessary," and opposed still the "only sound basis" for Reconstruction, Black legislative equality. As he cast about to overcome the president however he could, Phillips also began to echo Copperhead arguments accusing the president of despotism. "He crushes habeas corpus. He imprisons individuals," Phillips thundered, overlooking that such policies targeted Confederate sympathizers rather than abolitionists.[29]

Garrison could no longer explain away the rifts within immediatism after this convention. One attendee recalled how he "shook with emotion and disgust" at Phillips's attacks on Lincoln and himself, containing his anger only by treating Phillips "as impartially as if he had never seen him." Garrison "grieved [over] Wendell's condition," arguing afterward that Phillips's "recent political contact has upset him . . . his ambition is touched." He believed that Phillips had fallen under the sway of political demons, mirroring what his opponents believed about himself. Tensions increased when the *National Anti-Slavery Standard* omitted a series of resolutions which Pillsbury had delivered at the convention from its printed account, declaring the transcript lost. Garrison hoped "it was not the work of an enemy, making it appear as though I intentionally suppressed" them. But Pillsbury assumed that Garrison had conspired to keep him "as much as possible from the public." When one writer accused Garrison of malicious intent "for partisan purposes," Garrison replied in the *Liberator* that his rivals possessed "state[s] of mind far worse than ordinary partisanship," putting the ugliness of abolitionists' civil war on full display.[30]

ABOLITIONISTS AND THE COMPETING
POLITICAL CONVENTIONS

The opposing factions soon ramped up their brutal gamesmanship by joining competing political campaigns. Over the spring, Phillips, the Cheever brothers, Conway, Pillsbury, and the Fosters became involved in a political project centered on Frémont, known as the Cleveland or, later, the Radical Democracy movement. Karl Heinzen and a group of German-American radicals, all veterans of the 1848 democratic revolutions and antislavery stalwarts, had admired Frémont's administration of Missouri. In late 1863, they began plotting to draft the general for a presidential run. As A. J. Aiséirithe has discussed, they quickly won over Frémont. His military aide and political strategist, Gustave Cluseret, subsequently launched a party organ, *The New Nation*. Elizabeth Cady Stanton and Susan B. Anthony, the anti-Lincoln leaders of the Women's Loyal National League, and Edward Gilbert, of the Cheever brothers' CASS, signed on in early 1864. By February, these activists were reaching out to Phillips, Pillsbury, and George Cheever. In lobbying the "sword of Goliath," Phillips, to join, Gilbert argued somewhat obtusely that he supported Frémont, the 1856 Republican nominee, "because he never was a politician and therefore never learned the art." Frémont, he claimed, was the moral alternative to the politician Lincoln.[31]

Initially, the Cleveland organizers aimed to replace Lincoln with Frémont as the Republican nominee. They would, as Frémont aide and abolitionist Edward Morris Davis informed Phillips, independently nominate the general at a May convention in Cleveland, hoping to "create such a sentiment that Baltimore in June must also ratify our candidate." Davis looked to Phillips to build that groundswell. "There is no man in the land [who] can do what you can in this crisis," he averred. By ensuring their success, Gilbert added, Phillips could persuade Garrison to "unite with us in electing a President who will not squander a God-given opportunity" like Lincoln did, thereby securing a morally transformed Union and healing abolitionism.[32]

By March, Phillips, Pillsbury, the Cheever brothers, and the Fosters slotted this campaign into their quixotic plan to pry the Republican Party from Lincoln, helping to establish "Frémont Clubs" across the North. Pillsbury and

George Cheever's New York club promoted Frémont by delineating an expansive campaign platform at its rallies, calling for a harsh Reconstruction, the "immediate and entire extinction of slavery," the "absolute equality of all men before the law," and the banning of plantation "serfdom." As Pillsbury affirmed to Phillips, the "Fremont [*sic*] folk are doing more than everybody else, and it is a pleasure to cooperate with them." The German-American radicals, who espoused similar goals, subsequently organized a pro-Frémont convention in St. Louis in late March. At Davis's suggestion, Frémont selected Stephen Foster to represent him there. Foster then proceeded to St. Louis to voice his dedication to Frémont "for President, Butler for Secretary of War, and Chase where he is," cementing his political turn.[33]

At times, these abolitionists expressed trepidation over their course. Over the past year they had decided to stop settling for Lincoln, rerouting their agonies over their wartime interventions into oppositional politics. Yet they debated whether they were compromising themselves further by doing so. "You sacrifice your position, the moment you pronounce decisively for any man as President," Phillips's confidante George W. Smalley cautioned. "The weight which your opinions now have," owing to "[your] independence of politics," would "not be the same when . . . made in the interest" of a candidate. In order to avoid the appearance of partisanship, Phillips informed Stanton that he would not "take part in nominating our Fremont [*sic*]" at Cleveland. He also advised her not to make the Women's Loyal National League a "partisan machine." Anti-Lincoln immediatists, he detailed, should support Frémont without sullying themselves.[34]

Anti-Lincoln abolitionists were wary not only of sacrificing their integrity but also of working with a political organization. In April, a Frémont aide reassured Pillsbury that the Cleveland organizers shared his goals, affirming that the "platform will be radical enough." Pillsbury nonetheless queried Phillips if it would be "too late to . . . backtrack, when the platform is made, if it is too weak?" He worried that politicians would dilute the Frémont Club's planks, and begged Phillips to "be at hand to give them lessons." Though Phillips declined, Pillsbury would attend the convention in order to cement an egalitarian agenda—and to avoid committing himself to a flawed platform.[35]

In the weeks before the late May convention, its abolitionist supporters reiterated their expansive expectations. Phillips echoed the New York Frémont Club by advocating a platform of total emancipation, Black citizenship and suffrage, and land redistribution. Invoking Frémont's moniker, he affirmed to the

THE COMPETING CONVENTIONS, JANUARY–JUNE 1864

abolitionist Worcester Freedom Club that Frémont would be the "Pathfinder for the great Republic," using such policies to secure its permanent unity. The Cheever brothers and the New York club, as well as another German-American assembly attended by Stephen Foster, issued convention calls for Cleveland along similar lines.[36]

Conway and Douglass now joined Frémont's party as well. Conway endorsed the general from abroad, informing a friend in May that "I have given up Abe long ago: he is fearfully weak. Am hurrahing for Fremont [*sic*]." Douglass, meanwhile, broke with Lincoln anew, confessing to an associate that the government's unamended enlistment practices had "worn my patience quite threadbare." He also assailed its Reconstruction policies, decrying the "swindle by which our Government claims the respect of mankind for abolishing slavery" while "practically re-establishing the hateful system in Louisiana." Nor did he see "any purpose on the part of Lincoln . . . to extend the elective franchise" to Blacks. Unlike Hamilton and other Black activists, Douglass turned to a political outlet for his frustrations by seeking Lincoln's defeat. He penned a letter endorsing Cleveland, assuming that his aims, including total emancipation and Black equality "at the ballot-box and on the battlefield," would match those of the convention.[37]

By May, however, Frémont and his aides were no longer depicting the Cleveland movement as a vessel for high-minded reform. As it became clear that Lincoln would win out at Baltimore, they abandoned efforts to unite the two conventions and shifted their sights from the Republicans to the Democrats. Cluseret soon recruited into the fold a small bloc of War Democrats, led by New York's Attorney General John Cochrane. Cochrane, an opportunistic antislavery conservative, had heretofore supported the administration and its push for emancipation. Now, sensing a political opening, he pivoted. In his own call endorsing the upcoming Cleveland convention, he nodded cursorily to its immediatist backers by labeling emancipation "as among the practicable effects of the war." But he appealed primarily to the Copperheads, declaring that the "Rebellion can be suppressed without infringing the rights of individuals or of States"—a reference to Lincoln's violation of civil liberties. This statement should have given egalitarians like Phillips pause: a states' rights platform was antithetical to their desire for a federal-run, radical Reconstruction. It also refashioned Cleveland, with Cluseret's blessing, into a Copperhead-friendly movement.[38]

By this point, most of Lincoln's antislavery opponents had resigned themselves to support him. The Republicans' electoral rebranding as the National

Union Party won over most antislavery conservatives, including Daniel S. Dickinson and Edward Everett. After a last-ditch attempt to delay the Baltimore convention, many of the Radical Republicans, antislavery businessmen, and abolitionists who had previously favored Chase also fell in line, accepting Lincoln as the only loyal option. "Do not commit yourself too far in the anti-Lincoln matter, for it may be necessary to support him after all," Franklin B. Sanborn advised Conway. Sanborn had been willing to resist Lincoln to a certain extent, alongside Republican allies. He would not do so alongside capricious War Democrats who were making naked overtures to Copperheads—a far more morally questionable alliance.[39]

Phillips, Pillsbury, the Fosters, the Cheever brothers, Conway, and, briefly, Douglass, however, stood by Cleveland. While they opposed Lincoln as a means to achieve further reform, they had grown fixated upon defeating him at all costs. They became blinded to the looming consequences of their myopic actions—the self-destructive damage to their influence Smalley had predicted. As James Brewer Stewart has illustrated, they now embraced Frémont as a third-party candidate, ignoring warnings that he could cleave the loyal vote in the unrealistic belief he could win. In a letter to the Radical Democracy convention, a name chosen to reflect the party's bifurcated blocs, Phillips urged it to adopt his egalitarian agenda. Yet he also acquiesced to the reality that Cochrane would never sanction such an unadulterated platform. As he acknowledged, "if some of these points are not covered, I shall still support" the Cleveland party should it nominate Frémont. The general, he declared, had to take on Lincoln as a third-party candidate to "save us from another such three years as we have seen." In order to remove this intolerable evil, Phillips prepared in advance to compromise—to accept his dangerous new partners alongside a weakened party platform.[40]

In attending the convention, Pillsbury, Stephen Foster, and Henry Cheever likewise accepted a Copperhead-skewed platform that was far from their egalitarian expectations. Serving on the resolutions committee, Foster and Pillsbury fought for planks endorsing the redistribution of land to freed slaves as well as a constitutional amendment for abolition and Black equality before the law. But the Cochrane men controlled the proceedings by weakening any antislavery resolutions beyond recognition. They diluted the confiscation plank into a purposefully vague call for the distribution of confiscated rebel land "among soldiers and actual settlers." They also transfigured the amendment plank into a resolution that the "Rebellion has destroyed slavery, and the Constitution should be amended to prohibit its re-establishment, and to secure all men absolute equality before the law." This color-blind call for equality met abolitionists' demands in name but not in substance, especially after Pillsbury failed to secure a corollary on Black suffrage. Foster also denounced as "a lie" the misleading imputation that slavery was already dead, adding that it would "take away [a] principle argument against Lincoln": that he had not gone far enough on abolition. The War Democrats prevailed nonetheless. They also appealed to Copperheads by passing a plank that the "rights of free speech, free press, and habeas corpus be held indivisible." Yet even as this contradictory platform realized Pillsbury's fears, he, Foster, and Cheever accepted it, twisting themselves into morally perilous configurations as they sought to best Lincoln.[41]

The loyal press and pro-Lincoln abolitionists denounced the Cleveland convention as a Copperhead-backed scheme. The *New York Times* scathed that such disloyal forces "hope by means of it to make a breach in the Union lines," by either wreaking havoc as a third party or uniting with the rest of the Democrats. Frémont's letter accepting his nomination, in which he disavowed the convention's confiscation plank while stressing Lincoln's "violation of personal liberty," reinforced his receptivity to the latter possibility. "The affection which the Copperheads have recently manifested for him is more than justified. It is amorously reciprocated," Garrison blared in the *Liberator*. He proceeded to mock the Cleveland abolitionists with vitriolic relish, asking, "Is this the lofty moral and anti-slavery platform" they had promised? Garrison could not "find a word of the necessity of recognizing the colored man as a citizen, or giving him the right to vote." Phillips, he implied, had compromised his moral integrity for a rotten cause.[42]

Yet Garrison was no stranger to compromise. Though he invoked Black rights to deride his opponents, he had long since disregarded the issue to make total emancipation his mission—and Lincoln his instrument. Garrison ensconced himself deeper in the president's orbit in June by attending the Baltimore convention. He crowed that its emancipatory platform was "radically anti-slavery," ignoring that it, too, omitted Black suffrage. Afterward, the government welcomed him to Washington as a loyal ally. Garrison had resented not being invited to the capital in 1862. Now, Secretary of War Stanton, declaring Garrison the "one person whom he wished to see before he died," joined Republican senators to invite him as a guest of honor. Garrison met with Stanton and greeted politicians on the Senate floor, where his presence caused "quite a sensation," as he relayed home. His trip culminated in two "very satisfactory"

meetings with Lincoln. Recalling the convivial exchanges, Garrison corrobo-
rated "Mr. Lincoln's desire . . . to uproot slavery." Altogether, he concluded,
his sojourn "confirm[ed] the cheerful view I take" of the abolitionist cause,
affirming that Lincoln would secure his moral goals.[43]

Over the first half of 1864, pro- and anti-Lincoln abolitionists came to
blows over clashing candidates. Garrison and Child looked to Lincoln as the
moral guarantor of abolition, seeking his victory at all costs. Phillips, Conway, Cheever, the Fosters, Pillsbury, and, briefly, Douglass viewed him as an
irredeemable enemy, striving to dethrone him through various plots and candidates. As their hell-bent resolves to reelect or defeat the president clouded
their judgments, their clashes and compromises would worsen, with serious
repercussions for abolitionism. As would become clear, the moral dangers of
immediatists' wartime political submersion cut both ways. The narrow interventionist Garrison prepared to settle for his moderated moral mission and
abandon organized activism. The broad interventionists and moral purists leading the rival faction—the above figures save Conway—instead remained committed to the cause, never wavering from their evolved, politicized visions of
an egalitarian morally transformed Union. Yet they would harm their prestige
by plunging further into quasi-Faustian means which were counterproductive
to this end, ultimately weakening their long-term sway.

CHAPTER ELEVEN

The Perils of Abolitionist Politicking,
June–December 1864

As he returned from the Cleveland convention in June, Parker Pillsbury found himself at a moral crossroads. He had gone to the convention to secure an expansive platform, only to accede to far less. In its wake, he debated whether he should reject John C. Frémont's Radical Democracy Party, which was now controlled by the "smallest specimens of manhood" he had "ever attempted to cooperate with." In reporting on the convention to Phillips, Pillsbury admitted that the "hardest agony was on the construction of the platform." The result was "unsatisfactory . . . [though] all I could possibly get." Yet as he concluded, Cleveland was the only political vehicle capable of defeating Lincoln, who grew "more and more repulsive" by the day. Pillsbury thus reaffirmed his dedication to the party, rationalizing that its weakened planks on equality and land confiscation were prideworthy. "This is the beginning of my political pilgrimage," he resolved, banishing any unease as he steeped himself deeper in partisanship.[1]

Over the summer of 1864, pro- and anti-Lincoln abolitionists waged electoral warfare with abandon, pursuing partisan tactics that inadvertently enfeebled immediatism. Following the Cleveland and Baltimore conventions, Child and the pro-Lincoln faction entreated the anti-Lincoln immediatists to fall in line, warning that proslavery Copperheads controlled Cleveland. But while Douglass deserted Frémont, Pillsbury, the Fosters, the Cheever brothers, Phillips, and Conway assuaged their doubts to carry on in support of the third-party movement. These remaining anti-Lincoln, or pro-Frémont, immediatists also exacerbated the abolitionist civil war by sparring with Oliver Johnson and Garrison, destroying Phillips's relationships with both.

Over the ensuing months, the two factions lost any sense of perspective regarding the election. In their rush to reelect the president, the narrow interventionists who directed the pro-Lincoln faction sacrificed what remained of their moderated beliefs. As Garrison endorsed once-loathed officials with antiegalitarian values such as Nathaniel P. Banks and Postmaster General Montgomery Blair, he explicitly disavowed his original dedication to Black rights as a fundamental component of the abolitionist crusade. While the broad interventionists and purists who led the opposing faction spurned Lincoln to aspire for egalitarian perfection, they had grown obsessed with beating him. Now, they endorsed rhetoric and pacts further at odds with their lofty missions. George Cheever intensified his Copperhead-like attacks on Lincoln as a budding despot. Pillsbury, Conway, and Phillips, meanwhile, sought to merge Cleveland with the Democratic Party, deluding themselves that they could do so on an antislavery platform. Through such reckless politicking, both factions damaged abolitionism's long-term power—and compounded the tragedy of wartime abolitionism.

By late summer, the now-disenchanted Cheever brothers, Conway, and Douglass began to pursue alternatives to Cleveland, dragging all save Douglass into further compromises. As a stagnating military situation endangered Lincoln's reelection, leading Radical Republicans and Gotham elites inaugurated the Cincinnati movement—a campaign to displace both Lincoln and Frémont. The Cheever brothers, having grown weary of Cleveland's flaws, helped lead this new effort. Yet it, too, quickly diluted its antislavery agenda to broaden its appeal. As he parried blows from Garrison, meanwhile, Conway reconceived his late offer to James Mason as genuine, warming to the antiegalitarian idea of a slaveless Confederacy. Douglass instead returned to his old position of tolerating Lincoln as a necessary evil, supporting his reelection. But he also joined other Black activists in channeling their discontent over the government's failures on enlistment, total emancipation, and Black rights into a reform convention. Over the fall, these conventioneers chartered the National Equal Rights League (NERL) to seek change through loyal, nonpartisan means.

Two events in late August and September upended the election: George B. McClellan's nomination at the Democratic convention on a propeace platform and the Union's capture of Atlanta. As Lincoln gained momentum, the Cincinnati movement collapsed, forcing a reluctant George Cheever into backing the president. Yet even as Frémont withdrew from the race, Phillips, Pillsbury, and Conway continued to resist Lincoln as a singular villain. Only after Lincoln's victory did Phillips seek peace with his jubilant rivals, holding out the illusory hope that abolitionists could move past their infighting and pursue antislavery reform in unison.

THE AFTERMATH OF THE CLEVELAND AND BALTIMORE CONVENTIONS

As the summer began, abolitionists labored to process the fallout from the Cleveland and Baltimore conventions. In recent weeks, Theodore Tilton, Franklin B. Sanborn, and other former supporters of Salmon P. Chase had abandoned the anti-Lincoln faction and reluctantly bowed anew to Lincoln as a necessary evil. Now, they condemned Cleveland as a perfidious plot to rend the loyal vote or combine with the Democrats. "I will not be a party to any alliance with Copperheads," Tilton vowed in June. "It is a misfortune" that Lincoln was the Republican candidate, "but it cannot now be helped." Lincoln was the only loyal choice—and the only antislavery one. The Baltimore delegates had endorsed total emancipation, Tilton noted, while Frémont's contradictory platform had proven itself "unworthy of those good men" like Phillips who supported him.[2]

Though they stood apart from both warring factions and their unrestrained partisanship, these nonfactional immediatists especially begged pro-Frémont abolitionists to stand down. Upon learning that Conway was drafting an anti-Lincoln tract, Sanborn moved to dissuade him. The election "will be fought on the old issue" of slavery, he argued, "with Lincoln representing . . . the antislavery men" and the Democrats a proslavery peace. Frémont courted the latter, "tak[ing] ground much worse than Lincoln's." By supporting Cleveland, Conway was splitting the field. "Of all evils we should avoid throwing power into the hands of the Peace Democrats," Sanborn asserted. "As bad as Lincoln is, he is better than [Fernando] Wood," the New York Copperhead. Conway, he advised, had to accept Lincoln for the nation's sake.[3]

Alongside these begrudging backers of the president, fervent pro-Lincoln factional partisans also urged the Cleveland supporters to abandon their corrupted party. Frémont "reveals his want of principle, playing into the hands of the Copperheads!" Child averred. Phillips, she asserted, "[should] feel in a very false position standing by him." As she understood, Phillips had to exit the "sliding plane of politics. Moral giants have died from the effects of that slide!" Yet even as she sought to stop Phillips from campaigning, Child continued to politick for Lincoln. The president "has a hearty abhorrence of slavery," she praised, perpetuating the rival factions' tendencies to decry their opponents as political animals while overlooking their own actions.[4]

Oliver Johnson also prodded anti-Lincoln abolitionists to come to terms with the president's candidacy. Before the Cleveland convention, Phillips had asked Johnson to advertise the event in the *National Anti-Slavery Standard*. Though Johnson had agreed to do so, space constraints had ultimately stayed his hand. Phillips had responded by insisting that he print the notice in the next issue alongside commentary welcoming Cleveland's "radical and true politics." Johnson had declined this "unreasonable request," bristling that it indicated a "state of mind . . . to be lamented." When George Cheever sought to publish his own pro-Frémont articles in the paper in June, Johnson accordingly erupted. "However pure may be the motives" of its immediatist adherents, he scathed, Cleveland was doing the bidding of Jefferson Davis, "its Copperheadism conspicuous." As Johnson chastised Cheever, "What delusion has fallen upon . . . yourself, that you can lend your support to such a movement?" Appealing to Cheever's noble, if misguided, intentions, Johnson urged him to reject the "disgusting alliance" and return to the "right path."[5]

Despite such pleas, most pro-Frémont abolitionists persevered in their partisanship. Of all who had endorsed Cleveland before its convention, only Douglass backed away afterward from its compromised planks. In June, Phillips reflected on his letter to the convention advocating Black legislative equality by affirming his impartial dedication to righteousness "in these days of exclusive devotion to . . . expediency." By restaking his claim to the moral high ground over his pro-Lincoln rivals, Phillips also justified his continuing commitment to Cleveland—and disregarded Frémont's catering to base elements. Pillsbury acknowledged the flaws of the Cleveland platform, protesting in July against its plank which declared slavery dead. Yet he, too, threw himself further into this campaign as his anti-Lincoln fixation overcame any moral hesitance.[6]

The Cheever brothers likewise pushed past their own misgivings. "It was well . . . you were not there," Henry Cheever informed George about the convention. "You would not have liked the elements." But rather than abandon the Frémont party, he aimed to regain influence over it by "supply[ing], if possible, to the new party the high-toned principles by which . . . God may control it— make it a power." By publicly articulating the antislavery case against Lincoln, the siblings could right the Cleveland ship and sway public opinion toward it. Yet their quixotic strategy of "political campaign management" also allowed them to rationalize away their guilt over settling still for a flawed vessel to defeat Lincoln. "Watch yourself narrowly lest the same bitter party spirit does not control you, as always seems to rule in the mass of politicians," their sister, Elizabeth, warned about their unfettered politicking.[7]

In June, the brothers initiated their plan. At a speech in Worcester, Massachusetts, George Cheever reviewed Lincoln's unwillingness to initiate emancipation early in the war. "God is alienated from us," he thundered, thanks to the "vacillating, shuffling president." He ended his high-minded appeal by extolling Frémont as the "Pathfinder of Justice," overlooking in the process the general's overtures to the Copperheads. That same month, Henry Cheever led Stephen Foster and the Worcester Freedom Club in assailing Lincoln as a "politician, whose only pilot is shifting expediency." Yet they, too, paired this invocation of principle with a "cordial acceptance" of the Cleveland platform, itself an unwieldy product of political expediency. In practical terms, the Cheever brothers' quest to uplift Cleveland sustained their support of its existing form.[8]

From Britain, meanwhile, Conway churned out columns in the *Commonwealth* lambasting Lincoln and his conspicuous supporter Garrison. Through his proxy Banks, Conway reiterated, the president made "serfs of all the free negroes" in Louisiana. Turning to the execution of William Walker, the Black sergeant who had protested for equal pay, Conway argued that "the man under whom that could happen can never be the President" again. Why, he asked, was "the *Liberator* silent" on such matters? "If the things now done . . . had been done under [James] Buchanan," he averred, "would not the *Liberator* have thundered until the White House trembled?" Yet "veteran abolitionists, whose whole life had been an appeal that men should not wait to do right . . . [now] justif[ied] Lincoln" and tolerated his unsettling policies. Conway refused to behave likewise, vowing to overcome Lincoln and Garrison alike.[9]

Conway, having endorsed Cleveland right before its convention, now became its fierce partisan. As he sought to promote Frémont as the righteous alternative to Lincoln, Conway once again showcased his superficial facade of support for expansive Black rights. Though the Republicans supported total emancipation, Conway explained in the *Commonwealth* that African Americans also required "full and equal rights" beyond emancipation. Only Cleveland "demands absolute equality before the law," he averred, oversimplifying its platform. The Union war "must be referred to a higher plane than that of Liberty. It is a war for Equality," Conway repeated in *Testimonies Concerning Slavery*, a book released to acclaim in Britain.[10]

Yet Conway's thin conceit still masked his longstanding worldview—a narrow, Anglo-Saxon supremacist vision of a morally transformed Union that shot through his invocations of equality. In his *Testimonies,* Conway enumerated the damages which slavery inflicted upon Black and white southerners to refute the British theorist James Hunt, a prominent believer in the innate inferiority of the Black race. In condemning Hunt's scientific racism, he countered that a lack of equal opportunity, rather than biology, laid Blacks low. Conway anticipated their elevation, even endorsing the prospect of racial amalgamation. Underlying this ostensibly egalitarian paean, however, was his paternalistic belief in romantic racialism. "Each race is stronger in some direction," he explained. Anglo-Saxons possessed superior intellects. Blacks, though "weaker in the direction of the understanding," prevailed in terms of their "simple goodness"—their emotive piety and moral sensibility. Through amalgamation, Conway hoped to "evolve a more complete character than the unmitigated Anglo-Saxon," breeding in desirable Black qualities. He sought racial mixing not in rejection of natural racial difference, but because of it. Moreover, he still imagined Blacks' postwar rights as that of a plantation underclass. "Free-labor gets twice as much cotton from the acre as slave-labor," he assured readers. Beneath cosmetic gestures to equality, Conway thereby perpetuated his vision of a socioeconomically antiegalitarian Reconstruction.[11]

As they affirmed their fealty to Frémont, anti-Lincoln immediatists rejoined their rivals in the abolitionist civil war with scorched-earth ferocity. Susan B. Anthony, her pen dripping with sarcasm, derided in June that the loyal press was lauding "all of Garrison's eulogies on Lincoln. In their eyes, Mr. Garrison is now a sound philosopher and wise statesman." Though Pillsbury wished a "ten Pharaoh-power plague on Lincoln," he likewise focused his scorn upon Garrison. The nation, he explained to Tilton, "has no polar star but the *uncompromising antislavery movement.*" But Garrison betrayed that mandate. "Until the abolitionists restore themselves to their former integrity, and demand liberty instead of Lincoln . . . we shall continue to fail," Pillsbury scathed. Yet the Garrison faction refused to "rebuke [the] shortcomings" of politicians and advocate post-emancipation Black rights. They had become tainted partisans, losing their moral footing. "The *Standard* and *Liberator* must attend to the Politics. Mine is, in my view, a higher work," Pillsbury averred. Even as he grasped that narrow interventionists were cutting back their moral missions, Pillsbury overlooked the dangers of his own political experimenting.[12]

Though Garrison resented such accusations, he took greater offense at the assaults of his estranged friend Phillips. As James Brewer Stewart has shown, deep philosophical differences inflected their political bickering. Garrison promoted his interest in freedmen's aid as proof of his rectitude and investment in a post-emancipation future. But Phillips recognized freedmen's aid as a paternalistic "old clothes movement"—a pale imitation of abolitionism's mission to empower former slaves. Garrison hoped for a détente despite these disparities, anticipating that Phillips would cease campaigning "in view of the farcical character of the Cleveland Convention." Yet upon paying Phillips a personal visit in June, Garrison found him "more impassioned . . . in his opposition to the President." When Garrison chided him that "the loyal men had gone to Baltimore," Phillips replied by impugning Garrison's credentials as a reformer. The real "loyal men"—those faithful to abolitionist principles—"were at Cleveland," he countered. Garrison and Phillips thus left their relationship in tatters, with each convinced that the other had lost his way.[13]

Phillips also extended this feud to include Johnson. Citing Johnson's refusal to publicize the Cleveland convention as proof that his *Standard* was a "partisan Lincoln sheet," Phillips demanded that Garrison convene the AASS's executive committee to discuss disciplinary measures. Though Garrison protested that Phillips "compelled a fair and friendly defense of the President by his partisan appeals for Fremont [*sic*]," he acceded. "Our Society is to be rent asunder," he lamented to Johnson. "We are so much divided, that separation or dissolution threatens to be the only alternative." Phillips, he argued, was tearing apart abolitionism at the very moment when it should have been celebrating its imminent triumph. Ahead of the late June hearing, Johnson acknowledged that he favored Lincoln, but "only because . . . he was a thorough antislavery man." Principle, not politics, drove his actions. Should Phillips impose his will upon the committee, Johnson vowed to resign rather than "set the *Standard* in opposition to Lincoln." Garrison's forces, however, prevailed in this skirmish by acquitting Johnson.[14]

Following his exoneration, Johnson pursued peace with Phillips on his own terms. "I have cherished for you . . . the sincerest admiration," he wrote, praying that "our differences may not degenerate into personal unkindness." Yet he resented Phillips's attacks on his status as a right-minded reformer. Johnson portrayed himself not as a "partisan of Lincoln," but as an activist whose "moral intuition" impelled him to denounce Frémont as a "base man, in affiliation with other base men, and therefore unworthy of anti-slavery support." Johnson deflected scrutiny from himself onto Phillips by begging his interlocutor to renounce Cleveland as a "transparent swindle." Phillips, however, ignored this olive branch. "How can he open a quarrel against a lifelong friend, and then neglect to respond to such a letter as mine?" Johnson subsequently complained to a friend. The embittered editor would abandon any sense of civility going forward.[15]

The other narrow interventionists who led the pro-Lincoln faction alongside Garrison and Johnson soon joined the fray. In June, James Miller McKim derided Frémont supporters like "Jean Baptiste Pillsbury and Jean Paul Foster" as Jacobin revolutionaries. "The American Anti-Slavery Society has accomplished its mission," he asserted, echoing Johnson. Yet anti-Lincoln abolitionists upended its emancipatory victory lap. In straining to advance beyond the free-labor Union the president offered, they risked bargains with figures who could undo their significant wartime achievements. When Phillips proclaimed to McKim that he would never choose between two evils, McKim hence rejoined, "but you do . . . [and] you choose unwisely." Unlike McKim, Edmund Quincy recognized that the anti-Lincoln faction was not alone in its compromises. Garrison, he averred, was "unconscious of being in a state of political partisanship." He had "felt the stimulating effect of politics" and was caught unaware in its grasp. Quincy nevertheless sided with Garrison over Phillips, who was himself "too far gone to be accusing." As this factional infighting spread like wildfire across abolitionism, the AASS was soon forced to cancel its annual Fourth of July and First of August gatherings.[16]

A CAUSE DAMAGED

As they waged war deep into the summer, the two factions landed blows not only against each other but also against abolitionism's postwar power. Each side contributed to this tragedy of wartime abolitionism in its own way. Garrison and his fellow narrow interventionists atop the pro-Lincoln faction had pruned their missions over the past year by implicitly excising post-emancipation Black rights from their agendas. Now, they explicitly renounced this issue as being beyond their concern. Garrison, in particular, began to cultivate partnerships with officials who opposed Black rights as he parried attacks from the British anti-Lincoln abolitionist Francis Newman. Newman, a classics scholar who had become Conway's confidante in London, blamed Garrison for enabling Lincoln to remain in power. As long as Garrison "side[s] with Lincoln, the North will not learn that they might have a better man," he wrote Conway in June. Newman soon appealed directly to Garrison. "From the day that I knew [you had] ... become [a] unionist," he explained in July, he had backed the Union war. Yet the flaws of the Union emancipation process, especially in Nathaniel P. Banks's Louisiana, shook his faith. Newman therefore demanded that Garrison leverage his "moral weight" as the "patriarch of freedom" to speak out. "A great responsibility now rests on you to use this power," he averred.[17]

As Newman wielded Banks as a cudgel against Lincoln, Garrison aligned himself with the general. Reflecting his uncertainty about pursuing such a course, he forwarded anti-Lincoln abolitionists' critiques over Banks's regressive wage-labor regime and his failure to implement Black suffrage to the general. Garrison glossed over the latter issue but fretted over the former, asking Banks, "Are there not some of the features of serfdom" in Louisiana? But as he worked single-mindedly to rebut his rivals and bolster Lincoln, Garrison resolved to defend Banks and his "grand achievements." In two July public letters to Newman, Garrison emphasized the general's dedication to meeting the material needs of freed slaves. Banks also executed Lincoln's commitment to total emancipation, bringing nearer the "day of jubilee." Turning to the issue of suffrage, Garrison seized on the standard of the politically possible. Lincoln, he declared, had to abide by the dictates of his office rather than the "abstract principles of justice." Neither the president nor Banks could reach beyond practical precedent to implement Black political equality alongside abolition. Garrison thereby used this standard to judge Banks. After the *North American Review* approached him to write an article about Union-occupied Louisiana, Garrison similarly agreed to do so according to the "possibilities of statesmanship." While he vowed to "maintain, uncompromisingly, all the principles I have advocated for the last thirty years," he also had to be "just to all men ... [in] the new order of things." By defending administration officials, Garrison affirmed, he was bowing to political realities without moderating his mission.[18]

Yet Garrison had long since embraced Lincoln not just as the practical choice but as his personal paragon, adopting the standard of the possible as his internal imperative. He regarded total emancipation not as a feasible objective for now, but as his moral endpoint. He reinforced this dynamic by allying with another official: the colonizationist postmaster general Montgomery Blair. Though he had impugned Blair as a racist in 1862, Garrison now praised him in the *Liberator*. In response, Franklin B. Sanborn decried in the *Commonwealth* that "Garrison's zeal for Lincoln" had prompted his lurch to the "diabolical"

Blair. Rather than backtrack, Garrison tied himself closer to Blair by soliciting the latter's position on emancipation and then publishing his encouraging reply. Garrison proclaimed that the "most cruel injustice has been done to Mr. Blair," touting his "friendliness to the cause of emancipation." Blair remained a colonizationist, which "we strongly reprobate." But Garrison downplayed the significance of his bigotry relative to their aligned missions—their convergence in a mainstream that distinguished emancipation from equality. "If [Blair] will advocate the emancipation of all," he declared, "time will tell whether freedom and equality are possible for masses of blacks and whites in the same community." Moderating his original purposes beyond recognition, Garrison proclaimed that Black rights in general were irrelevant to his moral vision of a Republican-guided and emancipatory nation.[19]

Garrison was effectively rewriting his "Declaration of Sentiments," which had made Black inclusion a concurrent and co-equal demand of abolitionism alongside emancipation. Now, he expunged it from his agendas past and present, especially singling out the idea of Black suffrage. Suffrage, he informed Newman, "is a conventional, not a natural right," with no place in his mission. Freedom "is one thing . . . the elective franchise is quite another," Garrison added in the *Liberator*. In protesting the suffering of slaves, he claimed, "no abolitionist has ever alluded to their exclusion from the ballot-box," nor proven the necessity of "granting [suffrage] in immediate connection" with abolition. Garrison was not opposed to "ultimate social, civil and political equality," albeit through "educational development, and not by any arbitrary mandate," such as legislation. But whereas broad interventionists portrayed such equality as the glue of a reconstructed nation, signifying a substantive freedom that purged slavery's effects, he explicitly disavowed it as a secondary issue for others to sort out in the indeterminate future. Though he yearned to celebrate emancipation "without . . . the imputation of lowering the standard of equal and exact justice," he had lowered it. He prepared to end his activism and settle for far less than his original aims, thereby shattering abolitionism's strength as the prime instigator of its tragedy.[20]

Nonfactional abolitionists denigrated Garrison's positions throughout the summer. "Shame on Garrison . . . to turn from philanthropist to politician," accused one such immediatist. In the *Commonwealth,* Sanborn labeled Garrison Lincoln's "eulogist-in-chief." Abolitionists, he affirmed, possessed providential roles as prophets leading the people to perfection. While politicians abided by the constraints of the possible, this did not make it "any less the duty" of immediatists "to keep up a constant fire upon them." But to "oblige his new friend," Garrison threw away any semblance of integrity, forsaking the "principle that justice . . . should always be immediate." He could not "escape the criticism of those whom he thus deserts in the very crisis of the battle," Sanborn proclaimed in regard to suffrage. Lamenting how Garrison was ruining his reputation even as he readied to retire in triumph, Sanborn declared him a prophet no more.[21]

Garrison's factional rivals likewise assailed his attenuated mission. "The *Liberator* and *Standard* are gone stark mad," marveled Susan B. Anthony in July. Unlike Garrison, broad interventionists such as herself had deepened their moral visions over the course of the war by developing a lasting and politics-laced vision of a morally transformed Union grounded in Black legislative equality. Yet their political submersion, too, had its downside. In order to achieve "entire freedom and perfect equality," the broad interventionists and moral purists who helmed the anti-Lincoln faction partook in further myopic compromises, diminishing their sway over postwar affairs. In early July, George Cheever reiterated at his New York church that Lincoln, by seeking to "exclude [Blacks] from the rights of citizens" and prevent true freedom, was the paramount obstacle to his moral mission. He further legitimized abolitionists' use of Copperhead-inspired tactics to unseat the president by portraying Lincoln as a wanton violator of civil liberties with the "powers of Military Dictator." He also affirmed his fealty to Frémont as the "representative of heroism [and] justice," even as he vied without success to control the Cleveland movement.[22]

While pro-Frémont abolitionists had embraced Cleveland as a divisive third party, they now laid the groundwork for an even more troubling move: merging Cleveland with the Democratic Party. In recent months, Pillsbury had ceased to acknowledge that prowar Republicans were lesser evils relative to the Democrats. "The slaves . . . have [no] worse enemy on earth than Lincoln," he declared to Phillips in August. As a result, he cast his gaze toward Lincoln's own enemies. "Between Baltimore past, and Chicago prospective, to me, there is no difference," he argued about the Republican and Democratic conventions. The Republicans were in no way morally superior to the Democrats. If abolitionists could partner with the former, they could just as easily join with the latter to achieve their "divinely ordained mission." Pillsbury's reading of politics was warped, in that it ignored the clear-cut differences between the parties over slavery. Yet as Conway agreed, the Democrats could not "do us more harm than we are now enduring." In their desperation to defeat Lincoln for their greater good, these abolitionists broached a once-unfathomable alliance.[23]

Phillips took Pillsbury's and Conway's ideas a step further. He advocated an alliance with the Democrats on antislavery terms, seeking to win over the "sound portion of the Democratic party" to Frémont. The party's prowar wing, he theorized in July, would "see that there is no hope but in a pure antislavery position ... [and] embrace the Cleveland Platform in its full sense." To "subdue the Administration," Phillips pinned his hopes on pragmatists within the party. "Far better to lift the Democrat[s] higher" than accept "those miserable Republicans," agreed Elizabeth Cady Stanton. Yet this strategy contravened broad interventionists' larger mission. Even antislavery War Democrats like Daniel S. Dickinson ignored Black rights. Moreover, such figures had long since flocked to Lincoln, leaving proslavery Copperheads to dominate the remainder of the Democratic Party. In their illogical attempts to foment radical change by partnering with regressive forces, these immediatists were losing touch with political reality.[24]

In justifying his actions, Phillips waded into a bitter debate with Theodore Tilton that further endangered his moral prestige. As Tilton delineated the chasm between the vacuous Cleveland planks and Phillips's own vision in *The Independent,* Phillips affirmed in a public letter that he was "proud to be identified with such a movement." Looking to Reconstruction, he argued that "there can be no possible salvation for the Union" without Black civil, political, and socioeconomic rights—true legislative equality. The Cleveland platform, which endorsed parity before the law, represented the "high-water mark of American politics"—a "full loaf" compared to Republicans' emancipatory "half loaf." When Tilton replied that the president was a necessary evil relative to the Democrats, Phillips countered that he would not "fil[e] down my protests" against Lincoln's "pandering to negrophobia." He had given the government "generous confidence for three years," only to see it "wreck the nation." Phillips therefore refused to do so again. He welcomed a pact between Cleveland and "any Democrat, who will join me in securing a union" free of slavery and racism, thereby reiterating how far he would travel to dethrone Lincoln.[25]

As expected, Phillips's pro-Lincoln factional rivals decried his compromises. Samuel May Jr. comforted Tilton by lambasting Phillips's "political defilements of a very gross sort." Another pro-Lincoln abolitionist mocked that "if Phillips drank I could account" for his flirtations with Democrats. A still-seething Oliver Johnson declared in August that "we may have erred in making him an idol ... the revelation of the last three months may be just what we needed to correct our estimate of his character." If he could make Phillips "rather than

Lincoln President," Johnson concluded, "I would not do it." Reflecting their own estrangement, Garrison also gave a "severe talk against Phillips" at a private gathering. "It is sad to see the bitterness which old friends nurse so carefully," Garrison's son Willie noted mournfully.[26]

Reinforcing how Phillips was tarnishing his reputation, nonfactional abolitionists also assailed his uninhibited partisanship. Immediatists had long extolled him as a pillar of virtue—a "moral physician" treating the nation's ills. Now, those who, like Tilton, accepted Lincoln only reluctantly concluded that Phillips had lost his senses alongside Garrison. "Nothing can take from the immense value of your criticisms on Lincoln except an undue entanglement with Fremont [sic]," one reformer wrote, begging Phillips not to "follow Garrison's abnegation of the old independent abolitionist." In July, Lucy Stone, a broad interventionist and women's rights activist, remarked of Garrison and his narrowing mission that "one who has battled bravely for the right should die before his time in triumph [rather] than live to make himself a fool." Yet she also chided Phillips for "touch[ing] the Cleveland people." He belonged "outside of all parties—an advocate of great principles," Stone argued. "The tools of politicians are dead weights in our hands." As George W. Smalley had warned, Phillips's political dalliances were eroding his esteem.[27]

Phillips's star fell the farthest in the estimation of Wendell Phillips Garrison. Unlike his father, the nonfactional younger Garrison had sought to deprive Lincoln of the Republican nomination before acceding to his candidacy. Now, he rebuked Phillips over the *Independent* fracas. "To you, more than any other man besides my father, I owe what I am," he began. Phillips had mentored his namesake, even paying his way through Harvard. But in joining Cleveland, Phillips surrendered his "independent position for a paltry equivalent. Your wand was broken and your prestige destroyed by leveling yourself with politicians." Though Phillips had once spoken with the "unchallenged sight" of moral objectivity, he had "left Olympus for a caucus chamber—from a god become as one of us." Condemning his "coquetry to win the votes of the Democrat[s]," the young Garrison begged him to cease his politicking. Yet Phillips dismissed this plea, replying that "no man criticizing me now ... would on his present mood have been an abolitionist in 1835." The young Garrison thus turned against Phillips, sighing that "I shall dread to hear or even meet him." Even as Phillips unswervingly advocated his evolved moral vision, his self-destructive tactics sapped his power—and that of the movement he would help lead into the postwar future.[28]

PURSUING ALTERNATIVES TO CLEVELAND

Many anti-Lincoln abolitionists nonetheless began to tire of Cleveland—and of their own rationalizations—by the late summer. In late July, Phillips met with Frémont to gain reassurances about the general's commitment to emancipation and egalitarianism. Frémont, however, merely affirmed his support of the convoluted Cleveland platform. "I wish I had some more influence with [Frémont]," Phillips admitted to Elizabeth Cady Stanton as his enthusiasm flagged. He also fretted about military affairs, as the Army of the Potomac led a seemingly interminable siege of Petersburg, Virginia. Union morale was plummeting alongside Lincoln's popularity, increasing the chances that the Democrats would select George B. McClellan on a Copperhead platform. Should they do so, Phillips admitted that he might have to favor the Republicans. Yet such equivocations aside, he, Pillsbury, and Stephen Foster ultimately stood by Frémont to the end.[29]

The Cheever brothers, by contrast, abandoned Cleveland for a new anti-Lincoln group: the Cincinnati movement. This initiative emerged after Lincoln's July pocket veto of the Wade-Davis bill, which sought through such measures as a federally mandated emancipation to impose a harsh Reconstruction upon the South. The bill's sponsors, Benjamin Wade and Maryland congressman Henry Winter Davis, lambasted Lincoln for overruling congressional prerogative. Though George Cheever had once denounced the bill for omitting Black suffrage, the president's veto outraged him even more. "Had he signed this bill, there would have been an end to slavery," Cheever lamented. He thus proved receptive when Davis wrote him in late July, averring that Lincoln had "destroy[ed] what little confidence is still felt in [him]." Politicos also feared that the military situation rendered Lincoln unelectable. His chances "are getting smaller every day," one plotter noted. Rather than turn to the corrupted Cleveland movement, Davis sought a new coalition to "en masse desert Lincoln and demand a new candidate," while inducing Frémont "to step aside." The loyal North could then coalesce around this single candidate. Cheever, desperate in his desire to find an uncompromising means to ensure total emancipation and legislative equality, embraced this project. "An election of Lincoln is the choice of war up to exhaustion, and compromise," he declared, while Frémont, too, had failed. He thus advised Davis to craft a call for a new convention, offering the names of "leading men" who might also be amenable.[30]

By August, the Cincinnati movement had attracted a wide swath of recruits. Motivated by antislavery anger and electoral anxiety, Radical Republicans like Davis and John Andrew, New York antislavery conservatives and business elites like Dickinson, David Dudley Field, and John Austin Stevens Jr., and nonfactional abolitionists like Tilton joined the Cheever brothers in the plot. These figures soon agreed to organize a new convention in Cincinnati in September. As new recruits swelled their ranks, they put their plans into motion. James Stone and other abolitionist officers of the Emancipation League asked Frémont to bow out of the race, to which the general assented on the condition that Lincoln also withdrew. The newspapermen Horace Greeley and Parke Godwin, however, failed to wring a similar commitment from Lincoln. Greeley, Godwin, and Tilton also mailed a questionnaire to loyal northern governors. In the name of "a body of influential unionists," they solicited governors' opinions about whether the president could be reelected, whether their states would vote for him, and whether the "Union party . . . require[d] the substitution of another candidate," throwing them a political lifeline to escape Lincoln's sinking ship. Finally, a committee drafted the convention call proposing an alternative to the "apathy which depress[es] the friends of the Union." The Cincinnati men looked to go public after the Democratic convention in late August, confident that loyal voters would rally to their side.[31]

Though the Cheever brothers had spurned Cleveland for Cincinnati as a purer antislavery vessel, this movement also watered down its ideals to garner as wide a constituency as possible. Despite the antislavery impulses of its animators, the call omitted any reference to emancipation. In order to popularize the movement, moreover, Republican John Jay proposed a strategy that contravened his antislavery beliefs. As he argued, Cincinnati needed the aid of War Democrats to succeed. The Baltimore platform had alienated this bloc by adopting "abolition not as a means but an end." In endorsing the Thirteenth Amendment, it had transformed emancipation from an expedient weapon of war into its chief aim. To win over War Democrats, Jay advised Stevens to attack Lincoln as too radically antislavery for "chang[ing] the issue of the war." These new anti-Lincoln plotters thus moved in the same compromising direction as their Cleveland forerunners.[32]

By the late summer, Conway, too, wavered in his commitment to Frémont. "I own myself disappointed in Fremont's [sic] friends . . . and somewhat in him," he confessed. While he stood by Cleveland for now, a flurry of attacks from

Johnson and the elder Garrison nudged him toward an even more impolitic method of opposition to Lincoln. As Conway and Francis Newman challenged their self-ascribed roles as unmarred reformers, Johnson and Garrison moved to discredit the still exiled Virginian. Though the previous year's Mason affair had since fallen out of discussion, they now resurrected public scrutiny of it. In June, Johnson blared in the *Standard* that Conway's disastrous offer to James Mason should have taught him to be "sparing in his rebukes of other abolitionists." In his public replies to Newman, Garrison likewise argued that "certain ill-balanced, erratic American minds"—namely Conway—"affect your imagination." In the "impulsive, eccentric" Conway "you will not find a safe counsellor," Garrison warned. His "unwarrantable correspondence" with Mason illustrated that, despite his "pretensions to superior vigilance . . . he is not specially competent to call into question the antislavery integrity" of others. Garrison thereby rendered Conway into an unprincipled abolitionist apostate.[33]

Conway's friends reacted to this smear campaign with outrage. Sanborn protested that Garrison's attack was "uncalled for, not to say malicious," while Phillips scolded Johnson for his "unnecessary . . . and cruel" rehashing of the Mason affair. "These taunts proceed" from Johnson's base resentment of "our Anti-Lincoln attitude" and therefore held no moral bearing, he comforted Conway. Conway himself returned fire in August, wondering again in the *Commonwealth* why Garrison had not upbraided Lincoln over the state of affairs in Louisiana. "The Garrison I last saw in America would surely have [done so]. I trust he is not dead," he decried. With Lincoln gaining Garrison's "hearty support . . . where, in heaven's name, is any *pressure* to come to make him do the rest of his work?" Conway asked. Garrison had "surrendered the chief fortress" of abolitionism by accepting Lincoln's own goals rather than agitating for more. He "finished *his* course" of reform, leaving others to "take up the burthen for the legal and social equality of the negro." Keeping up his illusory appearance of favoring sweeping post-emancipation Black rights, Conway vowed to fight on when Garrison would not.[34]

As his critics revived the Mason affair, Conway retroactively reframed his feigned offer of support for a slaveless Confederacy as real. As he had made clear the previous summer, he had embraced the logic behind his trick: that immediatists should pursue any avenue to their righteous ends rather than adhere blindly to Lincoln's war. The backlash against his proposal had hence appalled him. "It had never occurred to me before [then] that I had given the Abolitionists too high credit in saying that they would not support a cruel war except for a principle," he recalled in August—that, "should the issue of Freedom . . . be out of the way," they would oppose a war for empire. Yet the "demoralization which this infernal Administration has introduced into the ranks of the Abolitionists" had since become even clearer. "I have lived to see a political canvass silence the protest of the *Liberator*," he bemoaned. Garrison was "forcing upon the people" an "irredeemable Kentuckian" whose reelection would suck the war's moral potential dry. Conway now wrote his current hatred of Lincoln back into his late offer by claiming that he had made Mason a genuine proposal to advance the "cause of emancipation." For now, Conway would resist the president by fighting "heart and soul" for Frémont. But should Lincoln win, he would consider more drastic approaches, such as actually championing a free Confederacy.[35]

Douglass, having long since abandoned Cleveland, resorted instead to countenancing Lincoln as a necessary evil once again. As David W. Blight has illustrated, a second White House meeting with the president in August helped shape his decision. Lincoln, fearing that the Democrats would win the election and reverse military emancipation, enlisted Douglass to draft a contingency plan to "[bring] within our lines" as many slaves as possible before he left office. Moved by the president's dedication to abolition, Douglass consulted with other Black activists to outline the proposal. When Garrison published Douglass's springtime critiques of the president the following month, intimating that he remained an anti-Lincoln partisan, Douglass responded by endorsing Lincoln. In a public reply to Garrison, he stressed that he still did not share Garrison's conception of Lincoln as an unadulterated paragon. Over the spring, he had sought to nominate a man of "more decided anti-slavery convictions and a firmer faith in the immediate necessity of . . . justice and equality for all men" than Lincoln. But "that possibility is no longer conceivable." In a zero-sum contest between the president and the "slavery perpetuating" Democrats, Douglass had to support Lincoln as the loyal candidate.[36]

Yet Douglass also sought to push beyond Lincoln's goals. Though he and other Black activists had stifled their frustrations on becoming recruiters, their anger had since boiled over. Abolition remained incomplete. The government was finally moving to provide equal pay and advancement to Black soldiers, but this process, too, unfurled slowly. And post-emancipation Black rights still went unaddressed. Black abolitionists had thus decided to direct their discontent into a reform convention. Rather than spurn their agencies through electoral resistance to Lincoln, they would pressure him to enact their goals through nonpartisan agitation. Henry Highland Garnet, Robert Hamilton, and others began to plan the convention in earnest in July, aiming to transcend differences of ideology and "appear as united as possible." They and other delegates, including Douglass, William Wells Brown, George T. Downing, and James W. C. Pennington, then assembled in Syracuse in October for the National Convention of Colored Men.[37]

There, these activists issued a clarion call for their politicized vision of a morally transformed Union. Douglass, who was elected the convention's president, devoted his soaring address to proposing a national renewal. "When great and terrible calamities are abroad . . . men are said to learn righteousness," he began. By achieving the golden moment, abolitionists had expected to precipitate such a moral revolution. Their national metamorphosis, however, had not truly materialized. "Powerful influences . . . [remain] to defeat our just hopes," he observed, manifesting still in the formal institution of slavery and its auxiliary, prejudice. The delegates had experienced the latter arriving in Syracuse, as mobs chanted "here comes the nigger . . . they can't have any convention here." And white allies like Garrison, in declining to "ask for the enfranchisement of colored men," shirked from combating this persistent phenomenon. Douglass thereby rallied Black activists to do the work themselves—to transition their wartime intervention into high political lobbying and complete the nation's perfection by promoting an agenda of total emancipation, fair military treatment, and legislative equality. As he detailed, only a substantive freedom that both abolished slavery and enabled Blacks to defend themselves and the "ark of federal Liberty" in the South would ensure national "unity . . . and [the] highest welfare." The Union also owed Black soldiers as much. "Are we good enough to use bullets, and not . . . a ballot?" Douglass queried. "All we ask is equal opportunities and equal rights," summed up a fellow activist. In the name of necessity and moral obligation, the conventioneers thus demanded Black political advancement.[38]

The delegates concurrently gave form to such demands by launching a new political pressure group: the National Equal Rights League (NERL). Its inaugural president, the pioneering African American officeholder John Mercer Langston, introduced the organization the following month. As he explained, the current moment, with African Americans serving in Union blue by the hundreds of thousands, represented their ideal opportunity to request equality before the law "as American citizens." He vowed to secure "all those rights, natural and political, which belong to us as men" and Americans, utilizing the lessons of abolitionists' wartime political educations to do so.[39]

THE END OF AN ELECTION

By the time the conventioneers met, two events had all but assured Lincoln's victory. In late August, the Democrats nominated George B. McClellan on a propeace platform, dashing anti-Lincoln abolitionists' fusion hopes. Days later, Union forces captured the rebel hub of Atlanta, renewing public faith in the war and its prosecutor. "How splendid is our prospect now!" crowed Oliver Johnson, confident that his vision of a Lincoln-led, emancipatory morally transformed Union was secure—and that his rivals had "wasted their power in foolish faction" for naught.[40]

The Cincinnati movement quickly collapsed under the weight of these developments. In returning their questionnaires in September, northern governors agreed that "any attempt now to substitute another candidate would result in disaster." As John Austin Stevens Jr. admitted, "our call was based upon the ... impossibility of electing Mr. Lincoln—but now all this is changed." The plotters thus canceled their plans. Though the Cheever brothers briefly resisted the pull of fate, they, too, ultimately grasped that their "opportunity to strike for God and justice" was lost. With reluctance, they abandoned their anti-Lincoln crusade. In sober recognition of political realities, George Cheever began campaigning for Lincoln as the lesser evil against McClellan.[41]

In its own death throes Cincinnati also brought down Cleveland, as James Stone prevailed on Frémont to withdraw. Yet the remaining pro-Frémont abolitionists refused to move past their all-consuming opposition to the president as the paramount threat to an egalitarian Reconstruction. "I shall be the inflexible foe of Abraham Lincoln," Pillsbury proclaimed to Phillips, citing Lincoln's veto of the Wade-Davis bill as his casus belli. "I'd cut off both hands before ... doing anything to elect [McClellan], and one hand before doing the same for Lincoln," agreed Phillips. Speaking in October, Phillips reiterated that "there can be no real peace ... except based on the suffrage and equality of all men." Such a "substantial freedom" would empower Blacks to reconstruct the South into a bastion of democracy. But Lincoln would stop still at a formal freedom that left the region's aristocratic power structures intact. Phillips therefore declined to support the president against the far worse McClellan, opting instead to "agitate, till I bayonet him and his party into justice." He would never settle for Lincoln again. Unlike "some of you," he berated one pro-Lincoln abolitionist, "I still remain reformer and not politician . . . on the old platform" of undeterred righteousness, even as his own politicking cut through such pretensions.[42]

Conway likewise refused to yield against Lincoln—or Garrison. He and Garrison battled over the past by disputing whether Garrison had granted him diplomatic authority for his 1863 mission to Britain. Conway linked this feud to his anti-Lincoln crusade, informing Phillips in November that "Garrison was the cause of Mr. Lincoln's renomination—if he said no when he said yes . . . Baltimore must have yielded." He thereby blamed Garrison for Lincoln's imminent victory, which he now framed in dire terms. The president, as he began to claim, would not only obstruct post-emancipation Black rights but also reverse emancipation itself. "The South will propose negotiation if Lincoln is re-elected," Conway predicted, and Lincoln would "compromise with slavery" and restore the Union of old. Such a contention was unfounded: Lincoln would soon press Congress to pass the Thirteenth Amendment. In order to avert an imagined proslavery reunion, however, Conway returned to his idea of last resort. "May we not . . . contemplate offering the South independence for abolition?" he asked Phillips. Only by becoming "disunionists yet again" and supporting sectional separation, he asserted, could activists kill slavery before Lincoln saved it.[43]

Conway soon publicized this idea in a British periodical. Echoing his Mason proposal, he declared that abolitionists should "offer the South independence whenever it is willing to concede independence to those whom it binds." As Conway stressed, he endorsed a free Confederacy only as a hopeless gesture of desperation. "I fear the reelection of Lincoln will prove fatal" to immediatists' moral project, he confessed to Phillips. As the prospects of a Union redeemed and reunited vanished, he sought to salvage what progress he could from the war. Yet his plan was both far-fetched and antiegalitarian. "You struggle to make things far worse than Lincoln . . . solely because he does not do them as well as we wish," scolded Francis Newman. Conway would secure Blacks a nominal freedom at best under the "absolute control" in practice of Jefferson Davis, reinforcing the superficiality of his commitment to expansive Black rights.[44]

Unlike Conway, Lincoln's partisans rejoiced when he prevailed on election day. "Our republican form of government rests on secure foundations," glowed

Child. Phillips, meanwhile, conceded his electoral failure. "We have got Mr. Lincoln and his principles for four years more," he acknowledged, rendering any further "quarrel with" the president futile. He thus changed tack by seeking to reunify abolitionists around a concerted push for equality. He subsequently prodded Conway to cease his feuding with Garrison, explaining that abolitionists' partisan infighting had placed a "tremendous strain on our machinery" when it was needed the most. Immediatists had "very hard work to do," he asserted, and "need every atom of our strength." Only by remaining "as much a unit as possible" could they force Lincoln into sanctioning an egalitarian morally transformed Union. In eyeing this fight ahead, Phillips strove to heal over the scars of the recent canvass.[45]

Yet immediatists had fought over far more than Lincoln. Inflecting such brawling was a fundamental rift over the purpose of abolitionism and the contours of the antislavery millennium. The narrow interventionists like Garrison who steered the pro-Lincoln faction had rallied to the president to guarantee their emancipatory endgame. The broad interventionists and purists like Phillips, George Cheever, Pillsbury, the Fosters, and, briefly, Douglass who led the rival faction had opposed Lincoln to advance post-abolition equality. After the election, this division would realign wartime abolitionism a third time into a battle over the movement's very continuation.

The scars of the election would haunt this final stage of the abolitionist civil war. By journeying to electoral extremes, immediatists had marred their moral esteem. Garrison allied with officials like Banks and Blair while avowing that Black rights lay outside the abolitionist mission. Even as his opponents decried his behavior, they corroded their own influence by mimicking Copperhead rhetoric and making overtures to Democrats. As abolitionist partisans lost legitimacy in each other's eyes, observers lamented their reckless compromises— and the wider repercussions of such compromises. As his resolve to abandon organized antislavery reform hardened, Garrison would move to shut down the entire movement. Though broad-minded immediatists would hold out for expansive ends, their politicking had sapped their wherewithal to help achieve such changes. Over the election season, abolitionists had thereby aggravated their tragic inability to build on their emancipatory successes in the post-emancipation future.

CHAPTER TWELVE

The End of Wartime Abolitionism, January–May 1865

In April 1865, Secretary of War Stanton organized a seminal event to mark the Union's imminent defeat of the Confederacy: the reraising of the federal flag over Fort Sumter. Alongside the distinguished officers and politicos whom he invited to the ceremony was another guest: Garrison. The symbolism of such an invitation was not lost on Garrison's narrow interventionist associates. For decades, as Samuel May Jr. averred in the *Liberator,* the country had banished Garrison into the wilderness. Over the past four years, however, the war, and abolitionists, had wrought such changes as they could "hardly comprehend." Garrison had become "no longer a proscribed, but an honored man" who was now ushered to Charleston "as the nation's guest." Much like Garrison himself, his friends interpreted his celebrity as proof of abolitionism's total triumph. "It tells of a regenerated public sentiment, of a new moral purpose," May glowed. The nation was "no longer at variance with Garrison," its moral revolution purportedly complete. Garrison thus had "no desire to be . . . at variance with the nation" either. He could relinquish his identity as a reformer and disappear into the American ether, his work concluded.[1]

As he wrote home, Garrison reflected on the significance of his journey. He had long since converged with the northern mainstream around the goal of an emancipatory and victorious Union helmed by Lincoln. Over the last few months, the country had fulfilled his moderated criteria for its salvation. Following his reelection, Lincoln had pressured the House into passing the Thirteenth Amendment. As he commenced his April trip, moreover, Garrison learned that Robert E. Lee had surrendered at Appomattox Court House, all but ending the war. "The rebellion is indeed washed," he declared, "and slavery with it." Garrison's voyage, and the generous reception accorded him, reinforced how his morally transformed Union had arrived. "Nothing more satisfies me that slavery is annihilated beyond any hope of resurrection," he crowed, "than the deference, kindness, and congratulations extended to me by . . . unerring representatives of public opinion." Garrison hence joined his friends in pronouncing the nation redeemed—and the immediatist crusade completed. The AASS "may reasonably conclude that its specific mission is ended," he averred, determined not only to cease his own participation in abolitionism, but also to disband the movement altogether.[2]

Wartime abolitionism barreled into the final phase of its civil war in early 1865, as the electoral battle over Lincoln gave way to the disagreements that had largely motivated it over the purpose and trajectory of organized antislavery reform. What had been a partisan row between pro- and anti-Lincoln immediatists became an unvarnished ideological struggle between narrow interventionists on the one hand and broad interventionists and moral purists on the other over the movement's continuation. Garrison led the narrow interventionists in proclaiming that the Thirteenth Amendment and the Union's victory capped their lifelong missions. They moved to dissolve abolitionism into a supposedly redeemed North, framing Black rights as a desirable but superfluous issue—one best left up to progress and the people. Broad interventionists and purists, including Phillips, the Fosters, Pillsbury, George Cheever, Douglass, Forten, and Child, countered that the movement had to press beyond the formal emancipation of the Thirteenth Amendment to obtain a substantive freedom that cemented Black legislative equality. As they argued, abolitionists' sacred duty was to push a still-unredeemed North toward an expansive morally transformed Union. After months of sparring, Garrison and his anticontinuation clique tried but failed to shutter the AASS at its May meeting. They then retired, abandoning abolitionism to a small, procontinuation remnant.[3]

After the war, narrow interventionists like Garrison and Conway dabbled in the continued fight for justice. Yet Garrison largely preoccupied himself not with contemporary activism but with securing his own historical legacy. Conway, meanwhile, shed all pretense to endorse a white supremacist social order in the South. The work of postwar reform fell to the abolitionist remnant, as Phillips, the Fosters, Pillsbury, Douglass, Forten, Cheever, and Child labored on for their evolved visions of moral perfection as transformative agents of political change. They deployed the Phillips-led AASS, the Cheever-led CASS, and the Black-led NERL as modern political interest groups during Reconstruction, using pressure tactics to help shape and pass the Fifteenth Amendment. Such success, however, proved to be but a silver lining to a dispiriting arc of overall failure. These persevering activists lacked the influence of a united movement after Garrison's withdrawal, and carried still the scars of their late electioneering. They proved powerless to buttress Reconstruction as it grew politically unpalatable before ultimately collapsing in the 1870s. The tragedy of wartime abolitionism thus became fully apparent: its intervention to help achieve military emancipation ultimately precluded its ability to help achieve post-emancipation equality.

THE FIGHT OVER CONTINUATION

Even as the partisan heat of the election dissipated in early 1865, immediatists remained still at each other's throats. A referendum on Lincoln morphed into one on their movement's future, pitting anticontinuation narrow interventionists against procontinuation broad interventionists and purists in the third realignment of wartime abolitionism. The former had long since adopted a narrowed definition of antislavery triumph based on the formal abolition of slavery and Union victory, looking to Lincoln to complete the nation's perfection. In January, Garrison wrote the president to evince "faith in your integrity of purpose" in ensuring the House's passage of the Thirteenth Amendment. As he explained through biblical metaphor, the amendment was the "rod of Moses to swallow all the rods of the magicians"—the missing piece of his morally transformed Union.[4]

After the House passed the amendment at Lincoln's urging on January 31, Garrison commemorated the end of the abolitionist crusade as he now saw it. As he mounted the rostrum at a celebration in Boston, he basked in the glow of public adulation. Journals across the North were pouring praise upon him, deeming emancipation his "personal triumph." As Garrison affirmed, "friends and strangers stop me in the street, daily, to congratulate me." Once again, he equated his vindication in the nation's eyes with the victory of the "Anti-Slavery phalanx." After years of tireless advocacy to remake the Union along the lines of the Declaration of Independence, abolitionists had seen that "Declaration Constitutionalized—made the supreme law of the land." The Constitution was no longer a "covenant with death . . . [but] with life," in a nation where "we are all abolitionists." By "throw[ing] off this terrible incubus" of slavery, he declared, the Union could rise from its role as a global pariah and assume its rightful destiny as "world-wide propagandists in the cause of human liberty." As formal freedom took root, Garrison proclaimed the nation "thus redeemed, thus qualified to lead"—and thus no longer requiring the guidance of abolitionist prophets.[5]

At least implicitly, Conway joined these other narrow interventionists in disclaiming an expansive postwar abolitionist mission. Superficially, he continued to stand with racial egalitarians like Phillips by belittling the claim of his bête noire, Garrison, of a mission fulfilled. In February, Conway penned in the *Commonwealth* that "now is the time for our watchword—equality." Abolitionists, he informed Phillips, could not "lay aside their armor until . . . every negro has an equal right to vote with the white man," albeit one restricted by literacy—a qualification that spurred outcry from such friends as the Italian revolutionary Giuseppe Mazzini. Yet beneath such posturing, Conway nourished still his true, and far more limited, vision of post-emancipation America. Throughout the new year he advocated his antiegalitarian idea of a slaveless Confederacy. "It would be a glorious end" to the war if peace came by the "North conceding its Uniolatry and the South its much worse Slaveolatry," he wrote in a March article. Conway had once looked to the Union to redeem the South from the blight of slavery. Now, he asked white southerners to save themselves from that "evil weed," enabling them to grow and prosper on the backs of freed but still-subjugated Black laborers. While his plan came to naught, its white supremacist inflections would shape his postwar dissociation from antislavery reform.[6]

As narrow interventionists laid the groundwork for ending abolitionism, moral purists and broad interventionists urged its prolongation. Pillsbury protested Garrison's push for the movement to "commit suicide," demanding that it fulfill its founding commitment to Black rights in addition to emancipation. Until then, its mission remained unfinished—and its distinctive role in society vital. Whereas Garrison deemed the white North and political mainstream already perfected, Phillips retorted that they were only "half educated to the demands of the hour." Most Republicans strove still for a white, free-labor Union, "believ[ing] in getting rid of chattelism but go[ing] no farther." They accepted a technical freedom, but not a substantive one that equipped Blacks with "all the privileges that belong to a white man." While Radical Republicans favored the latter goal, even some of them still shied away from it as too impolitic for the time being. Phillips had lobbied Congress on the issue of Black suffrage in late 1864, only to find Henry Winter Davis "sneer at [its] impracticality." Yet

Davis's political reticence was understandable: as Pillsbury detailed, a white North that had endorsed emancipation for its own survival, rather than for justice, rejected "negro equality . . . [as] beyond all reason." Prominent antislavery conservatives like George Bancroft declined to pursue any measures that would not benefit them, including Black rights in general. Abolitionists thus had to press on and shove an unwilling nation higher.[7]

In making the case for continuation, these immediatists emphasized their vision of a sweeping morally transformed Union and the goal at its heart: legislative equality. In a late 1864 speech, Phillips called upon his idea of constructing a "real and durable nationality," stitching the war-torn land back together through the New England values of democratic citizenship. "Massachusetts ideas must kiss the Gulf before we can be truly one and truly great," he asserted. Despite what Garrison believed, the Thirteenth Amendment would not seal this national regeneration. Alone, it was "mere parchment"—a flimsy half-measure in the struggle against slavery and its effects. As Phillips explained, conniving ex-rebels would abuse its definition of formal freedom to keep Blacks "in a condition . . . hardly better than slavery." The amendment, moreover, was "too narrow for us to stand on." Abolitionists needed to elevate a populace not yet "raised enough to be trusted with reconstruction" to their own level through further legislation. The nation, he reiterated, required another amendment banning "any distinction . . . on account of race, color or nationality" to combat prejudice. Phillips, recognizing the need to act "before our convulsion ends" and ex-rebel states returned to the Union, also entreated Congress to make "negro suffrage an indispensable condition of [their] readmission." Taken alongside his earlier demands for Black education and civil and socioeconomic as well as political rights, Phillips proposed a panoramic package for legislative equality in the name of "universal justice" and national safety.[8]

While Phillips downplayed the significance of the Thirteenth Amendment, Stephen Foster and George Cheever declared their outright opposition to it. Foster had campaigned for just such an amendment back in 1863. But in a willfully provocative speech, he now labeled it a "deceitful device, and a pro-slavery measure," which enabled the peculiar institution to persist by another name. African Americans required rights beyond nominal freedom, but "Jefferson Davis would sooner recognize the manhood and equality of the negro than Lincoln." As Foster concluded, Garrison "betrayed the cause" by supporting the amendment. Cheever, meanwhile, invoked his antebellum belief in an antislavery Constitution to critique the amendment as counterproductive. In a petition which he entrusted to Charles Sumner, he asked Congress to "act out a constitution already adequate" by legislating abolition, rather than impugn the spirit of a charter that "needs no amendment." Yet such differences aside, procontinuation immediatists shared a common understanding of their movement's future. As Cheever's brother, Henry, avowed before the CASS, "our duty as a Society is by no means done, nor its mission ended." Abolitionism, George added, must continue "until the same rights . . . have been secured for black men that we claim for ourselves." Without "negro suffrage, we are a slave republic still," he averred.[9]

Douglass, too, campaigned throughout the new year for suffrage. "I see little advantage in emancipation" without the vote, he affirmed to Child, since the returning rebel states could exploit the lacunae of the Thirteenth Amendment. As David W. Blight has discussed, Douglass subsequently traversed the North, dipping into his wellspring of biblical imagery to offer a rhapsodic vision of his envisioned national renewal. At one lecture in Boston, he invoked the parable of Lazarus, the impoverished beggar spurned by a rich neighbor. Their fortunes had reversed after death, as Lazarus rose to heaven and the wealthy man plummeted to hell. Blacks, Douglass declared, had been the "Lazaruses of the South," abused by aristocratic slaveholders. But now, the "negro is coming up—he is rising." Blacks had become "citizens in war," winning whites' respect through martial sacrifice. Whites had to respond in kind by making Blacks "fully and entirely . . . citizens in peace." Enfranchised Blacks could then bind the nation together, raising it into the heights of Elysium as slavery perished in the flames of damnation.[10]

In less lyrical but equally decisive terms, Forten vowed to secure expansive Black rights through the abolitionist movement. In a demonstration of her wartime maturation into a soaring champion of equality, she co-wrote an AASS subscription call asserting that the "negro, even if technically free, is still a slave, while destitute of civil and political rights." The Union, she warned, should not readmit the rebels "without securing land or the ballot to the negro." These were vital "elements of [Black] self-defense," without which any freedom on paper would be an "absurd sham." Abolitionism thus had to fight on for a "real emancipation." It "becomes the Abolitionists, it is a solemn pledge imposed upon them . . . to rally public opinion" to a higher plane, Forten concluded in an implicit rebuke of Garrison. Without them, no one would.[11]

While Child had opposed her fellow broad interventionists during the election, she now joined them to support the continuation of organized reform. Though she retained her fervent faith in Lincoln, Child confessed that she was "far from feeling secure about a safe and judicious reconstruction." In March she cited her detailed knowledge of West Indian emancipation to warn Garrison that "slaveholders here will doubtless behave as they did in Jamaica. They will do their utmost to make the system of free labor a failure." Should they maintain their political power and "haughty oligarchies with a monopoly of land," they would keep the nation "in commotion for years." As Child concluded, there could be "no security for the Republic without negro suffrage" or the redistribution of confiscated land to freed slaves.[12]

As she sought to light the path ahead for abolitionists, Child drew on their recent past advocating the war power. Interventionists had realized early in the war that northerners would sanction emancipation not for "justice, or by conversion to liberal principles," but only for expediency. She welcomed such self-interested motives, noting that "all great revolutions . . . would look mean and meagre, if examined in details." Yet the moral revolution that interventionists had expected after the onset of military emancipation, which would wash away iniquity and usher in the antislavery millennium, had not come to pass. Echoing Phillips, Child explained to Garrison that many white northerners were only "half converted" to immediatist principles. They continued to distinguish emancipation from equality by endorsing freedom while still "despis[ing] the colored people." But just as abolitionists had popularized military emancipation as a means to win the war, they might push racist northerners to support postwar legislative equality to keep "[ex]-rebel voters . . . held in check," hopefully purifying the nation in the end. Adopting a unique tack, Child called for immediatists to disband their antislavery societies and "reorganize [them] as protection societies." While Garrison was "no longer needed as a *Liberator,* [he] will be needed as a *Protector.*" But in whatever form, abolitionists had to remain the "vigilant watchmen on the towers" in order to ensure Black rights.[13]

As they staked out diametric interpretations of abolitionism, pro- and anticontinuation immediatists quickly came to blows. While Phillips had been hoping for abolitionist unity following the election, the January meeting of the MASS quashed this dream. At the session, Douglass dismantled the argument that the abolitionist mission was complete. Immediatism, he reiterated, was "based on two principles": emancipation and Black rights. He celebrated formal abolition as a remarkable milestone. Yet without suffrage, "liberty is a mockery; without this, you might as well almost retain the old name of slavery," since the freed slave would have "no means of protecting himself." Abolitionists could not abnegate their remaining responsibility. Where, he asked, could the "black man look . . . for the assertion of his right, if [not] to the MASS?" Like Child, Douglass stressed that "this is the hour" to strike. With the war ending, the North seemed ripe for arguments portraying enfranchised Blacks as "counter-balance[s]" to the ex-rebels. "If abolitionists fail to press now," he warned, "we may not see, for centuries, the same disposition that exists at this moment." They had to secure an egalitarian Reconstruction while they still could.[14]

Other like-minded abolitionists complemented Douglass's call for contin-uation. Phillips resolved that "the end is not yet, that real and complete success is not achieved, and that the slave's cause needs yet our most devoted efforts." As he elaborated, there remained "one question for abolitionists . . . the terms of reconstruction." While Lincoln championed as his model the "so-called freedom of Louisiana" under Nathaniel P. Banks, Phillips scathed that "it is no freedom for me." He sought an "effectual emancipation . . . something that can maintain and vindicate itself." In practical terms, Abby Kelley Foster clarified that the Union should recognize "every man as free and equal, under the law, in making any reconstruction." When one abolitionist downplayed this goal as not pressing, Phillips rejoined that it was the "essence of the present anti-slavery opportunity." As he detailed, the "best blood of the North" had carried the Union into the South. In order to keep it there and integrate the region as a true "part of the nation," the Union needed to "have out of Carolina, not the parchment form of justice, but its very substance." Immediatists had to fight with urgency for Black rights as the "only pathway to safety and empire" as well as a moral imperative.[15]

Garrison, meanwhile, formally made his case for disbandment. After Ste-phen Foster denounced him for making a "compromise with the devil" by supporting Banks, Garrison countered by announcing his support of Black political rights. Congress, he resolved, should "lose no time" in crafting an amendment "making the electoral law uniform in all of the states, without regard to complexional distinctions." Yet he still framed this demand not as an essential target in the antislavery fight, but as an extraneous one. Garrison disputed Douglass's assertion that abolition without suffrage was meaningless, jibing that "surely, Mr. Douglass did not think so when he burst his fetters" to flee bondage. Suffrage, he reiterated, was a "conventional right of society . . . not to be confounded with the natural right" of liberty. As such, it lay beyond the scope of immediatism and its mission of total emancipation, which Garrison deemed the "all in all for the redemption of the colored man." He therefore countered Phillips's resolution for continuation by resolving that the MASS, whose "labors . . . were rapidly coming to a close," should "terminate its existence" after the passage of the Thirteenth Amendment—a proposal which was voted down only after vicious debate.[16]

Later, Garrison again attempted to defend his position—and his moral integrity. Bristling at any implication that "I had fallen into the rear, and [Phillips] was now the leader," Garrison denied that "he precedes me . . . [in] superior fidelity to the anti-slavery cause." Yet as an observer noted, the "two men were looking at entirely different objects" regarding what that cause meant. Whereas Phillips held out for more than abolition, Garrison believed that "anti-slavery, as such, dies the moment slavery dies." With the "work of abolitionism" accomplished, its members could "mingle with the great mass of the people . . . and unite with them in carrying forward the struggle for equal political privileges." As Garrison elaborated, the immediatist movement had no "great importance . . . in this altered state of things." The North had "passed the Rubicon . . . entirely changed, in spirit and feeling, towards us and the cause of the oppressed." As waves of progress swept over the land, racism would "soon pass away." Rather than retain their distinctiveness as upright activists, abolitionists could disperse into a regenerated populace and pass the torch of activism onto the people and the momentum of fate.[17]

In response, procontinuation immediatists assailed Garrison's view as both morally adulterated and an unrealistic depiction of the northern racial landscape. George T. Downing recited the AASS's "Declaration of Sentiments" to ask how Garrison "reconciles his position" with its promise to achieve emancipation alongside post-emancipation Black rights. But Garrison managed only a muddled reply, warping the intent behind his original mission statement by claiming that "I never supposed that, after the abolition of slavery, we should . . . perpetuate our anti-slavery organizations." Instead of leading a continuing crusade for justice, Phillips accordingly decried, he would "fold [his] arms and trust Lincoln to consummate a perfect victory." Yet abolitionists could not "let the helm of the cause go out of [their] hands" and into those of mainstream party politicians and the people, whose racial limitations Garrison obscured. "We must rely on men who are more than anti-slavery, in a narrow and technical sense," Phillips argued—who opposed bondage but not inequality. Rather than shed their providential roles, abolitionists had still to guide the nation as its prophets if they hoped to see an egalitarian future.[18]

THE ROAD TO THE AASS

Following their initial skirmish, warring activists girded themselves for the main battle: the May meeting of the preeminent abolitionist organization, the AASS. Dismissing his rivals' pleas as "a farce," Garrison assembled the AASS executive committee in March to endorse his plan to disband the Society at its coming anniversary. In doing so, he outpaced even his closest colleagues, such as Oliver Johnson. Like Garrison, Johnson disregarded the arguments of the procontinuation side. Sustaining the animosities which had burst forth during the election, he especially derided Phillips's points as "pure clap-trap." In the *Liberator,* Johnson explained that abolitionists had successfully "purif[ied] by long moral agitation" the public mind. As a result, the "cause of the Negro has far transcended . . . any voluntary association. It is the nation's work" now, and to the nation they could consign it. Yet as he confessed in March, he feared that "Phillips will show himself . . . at the head of a party of sore-heads" and turn the AASS meeting into a melee. In order to avoid such a spectacle, he proposed keeping the AASS and its organ, the *National Anti-Slavery Standard,* "alive till the consummation of the great Amendment." Its final ratification, he hoped, would enable the AASS to dissolve without incident.[19]

Despite his reservations, Johnson soon fell in line with Garrison's call for disbandment, which would be put to a vote at the anniversary. In April, he learned that Garrison would "refuse to take office in the [AASS] for another year" should he lose this referendum. With Garrison "going out, I shall certainly not stay" in the AASS, Johnson concluded. Nor did he want its machinery to fall into the hands of their opponents. "The advantages of a nominal existence for another year would be light compared with the evils that would follow from a new administration" led by Phillips, he argued. Johnson hence decided to "vote for dissolution" the next month, despite the "scene of strife" that doubtless awaited. "I am solicitous that on our side there shall be nothing to provoke . . . what I so much fear from the other," he fretted, citing the "temper of Phillips." He also began to whip votes in the weeks before the meeting, calling on members to "make an end and [be] done with it." Other narrow interventionists, from James Miller McKim to Edmund Quincy, also rallied to Garrison's side. "If anybody wants to keep up an Anti-Slavery Society after slavery is abolished, they may for all we care," quipped Quincy.[20]

In the midst of such preparations, Garrison ventured to Fort Sumter. Following the April 14 flag-raising ceremony, he marched in a Black procession through Charleston. Speaking at a banquet that evening, Garrison distilled his recumbent sense of satisfaction. He contrasted his days fleeing mobs in Boston to his current place as a guest in the cradle of secession, affirming that "we are living in altered times." Garrison praised Lincoln as his coadjutor in this "transition from death to life," declaring that the president either "has become a Garrisonian Abolitionist or I have become a Lincoln Emancipationist, for . . . we blend together, like kindred drops." In his telling, immediatism and the political mainstream had become one. Yet as broad interventionists recognized, the gap between the abolitionist mission as originally conceived and the mind-set of the still-imperfect North remained wide. In ignoring these differences, Garrison spoke to his own moderation as much as to the public's progression. He used his invitation to Charleston not as an opportunity to demand further reform but as his personal victory lap, thanking Secretary of War Stanton for validating "my labors to secure universal emancipation." Garrison portrayed the nation's—and his own—success as absolute, thereby minimizing the unfinished struggle against racial oppression.[21]

While Garrison feasted in Charleston, John Wilkes Booth fired a bullet in Washington that shook the nation. As he began his second term, Lincoln hinted at his deepening moral evolution. He started to shed his party's racially constrictive vision of a free-labor Union in favor of a burgeoning interest in post-emancipation Black rights. Surpassing Phillips's low expectations of his leadership, he endorsed voting rights for Black soldiers in Louisiana in his last speech. Yet his death on April 15 cut short such growth, leaving his ultimate destination unknown.[22]

As they took in this shocking news, immediatists filtered Lincoln's assassination through their own agendas. Garrison eulogized that Lincoln had redeemed the nation, rendering the Union "imperishable on the basis of universal liberty." Conway, advised by Franklin B. Sanborn not "to speak with censure" of a leader now hailed as a martyr across the North, claimed in a British magazine that "I had rarely . . . known a man whom I could more admire" than Lincoln. Procontinuation abolitionists instead warned that slavery had killed Lincoln, proving the need to wage further war against it. Rather than critique the fallen leader, Phillips highlighted the "lesson God teaches us in [his] blood." Booth's "deed is but the result . . . of the system in whose defense it was done," he argued. "With all his shortcomings," Phillips noted, Lincoln had still overseen a war against slavery—and was felled because of it. Even in its seeming last gasps, added Pillsbury, "the monster is not dead." As Douglass summed up, the Union had to remove "any vestige of slavery" and enshrine Black equality in a radical Reconstruction to avenge its fallen captain.[23]

In the weeks preceding the AASS anniversary, Phillips doubted whether his side would prevail. "[He] thinks the society will dissolve," reported Sanborn. Yet he underrated his chances. Broad interventionists and moral purists from across the movement sought to sustain the AASS, reflecting its role as the leading expression of organized abolitionism. His fellow egalitarians within the Garrisonian society, such as Susan B. Anthony, urged its continuation with "Phillips in the chair." Only it could purge from the land the spirit of slavery, which still "lives in terrible power in the hearts of the people." The non-Garrisonian Douglass agreed. In early May, he led a meeting of Black New Yorkers in resolving that the AASS could not dissolve "without a violation of assumed honorable trust," because its mission remained undone. As a final rallying cry, Phillips pled in the *Liberator* for abolitionists to remember the pledges "we have held for thirty years" and persist at their posts. "To dissolve when the mere abolition of chattelism is accomplished is practically surrender," he declared to all who might heed his call.[24]

Days later, immediatists gathered for their climactic showdown in New York. Alongside the gathered Garrisonians, non-Garrisonians like Douglass and Downing were also in attendance. In unison, procontinuation activists reiterated that abolitionists could not rest until they achieved legislative equality. Phillips stressed that immediatists had to "give effect to the parchment recognition of liberty" of the Thirteenth Amendment. Their purpose was to force a "reformation of the elements of the state," redistributing power into the "hands of the people" through "Land and the Ballot." Only when "we have ... put the negro into the full enjoyment of his liberty," thereby shielding Blacks and the nation from the Slave Power's grasp, could they rest. As Douglass contended, "the work of Abolitionists is not done." In some "new skin this old snake" of slavery would rise anew to keep Blacks down. Immediatists had to help cut out this cancer of chattelism by empowering freed slaves—an endeavor that could not succeed without the moral pull and machinery of the AASS. Who, Douglass asked, would help Blacks if a "Society that has survived mobs, and martyrdom ... shall all at once subside?" Only such a "time-approved organization," Stephen Foster added, could "imprint the law of justice upon the American heart," implementing what Abby Kelley Foster termed a "deep and radical regeneration" that expunged slavery in spirit and in name. As Pillsbury concluded, "we can never lay down our distinctive apostleship until all those high purposes are fully accomplished" and a true morally transformed Union unleashed.[25]

As his opponents contested his depiction of a mission consummated, Garrison held his ground. "My vocation, as an Abolitionist . . . is ended," he declared early in the meeting. "Four years ago, there was not a single city, town, or hamlet . . . that would not have voted down the abolition enterprise." But now, all such locales desired the "everlasting emancipation of those in bondage." Garrison disputed Pillsbury by claiming once again that "abolitionism has ceased to be distinctive . . . we are one people united." Immediatists, he argued, could spike their guns and "mingle with . . . our fellow-countrymen," who "seem prepared to do full justice" and elevate Blacks to political parity. As expected, Garrison therefore proposed that the AASS should disband.[26]

What one observer called Garrison's "dictatorial tone" in moving to dismantle the AASS provoked dissent. Black activist Charles Lenox Remond invoked its "Declaration of Sentiments" to assert that Black rights were "within the purposes of this Society." Yet "our white friends" like Garrison, he asserted, failed "to understand the black man's case in this nation." Chiding Garrison, Remond denied that "anti-slavery, according to this platform"—meaning "full recognition of the colored man's equality"—was "the order of the day." Northerners were far from perfected, as Remond, who had endured a barrage of slurs in transit to New York, knew. They opposed Black suffrage "ten to one." In the face of this grim reality, Remond warned against any "betrayal of our movement." Why, he asked, would Garrison not only curtail his own mission but also bring down the entire AASS with him "in a way that shall cause great harm to our cause, and . . . to the colored people?" In response, Garrison bristled that "I do not ask the Society to permit me to retire." Remond's assertion of persisting prejudice, he argued, was a "caricature of the nation." As he claimed, disbandment was neither premature nor an abridgment of abolitionism. "We organized expressly for the abolition of slavery," Garrison maintained, in yet another distortion of his 1833 manifesto. "The other work was incidental . . . to [that] grand object"—a secondary consideration all along.[27]

Phillips soon rose to protest Garrison's interpretation of abolitionism. The two questions facing immediatists, he argued, were these: "Have we got anything to do, and are we better able to do it as members of this Society?" Regarding the first query, he echoed Remond's point that the AASS had always dedicated itself to making the "negro an equal with the white." Turning to the second, Phillips denied that the government was "so thoroughly impregnated with the idea of justice" that abolitionists could stand down. Nor, he added, had immediatists "fused and melted into the general public." They could not "give up the prestige of [the Society's] name, earned by thirty years of labor." In addition to its monetary resources and networks, the AASS's reputation "increases our influence a hundred-fold." As Phillips elaborated, "we keep together, because we want the country to understand that there is work to be done." Northerners "see the pressure and personal influence standing behind" such societies, prodding them higher than they would otherwise go. Abolitionists should therefore "well the flood on which the state shall float into a safe harbor," remaining organized to achieve equality rather than surrender their material and symbolic moral power.[28]

As the personification of the push for disbandment, Garrison defended himself as much as his arguments in rebutting his critics. Yet he now offered little of substance beyond repeating that "this is no death-bed scene . . . it is a day of jubilee." Instead, he proceeded to wonder why old rivals of the AASS like Douglass "have suddenly become greatly interested in [its] preservation." When Stephen Foster objected, Garrison retorted that neither he nor Phillips "has been a friend of the [AASS] . . . for some time past," refashioning even AASS stalwarts into its sworn enemies. "If he had fired a pistol . . . it could not have startled the house more," noted an observer. Thanks in part to such comments, Garrison lost the dissolution vote. Though the victors asked him to remain at the head of the AASS, he and his cadre chose to resign. "It grieves me . . . that he who has stood first and foremost in this fight should retire before the battle is ended," lamented Foster. The diminished AASS appointed Phillips as president in Garrison's place, while Abby Kelley Foster joined its executive committee. The non-Garrisonian George Cheever became one of its vice presidents, reinforcing the collaboration among procontinuation activists.[29]

ABOLITIONISM IN THE ERA OF RECONSTRUCTION

In the days following the anniversary, procontinuation immediatists rejoiced at their triumph. "Old society sustained!" crowed Pillsbury, who replaced Johnson as the *Standard*'s editor. Yet their victory was bittersweet. While Garrison vowed in retiring that "I shall work with" the Phillips-led AASS, he and his anticontinuation followers revealed the emptiness behind this promise by disavowing the postwar abolitionist remnant as an illegitimate successor to the original movement. "I regard the whole thing as ridiculous," Garrison seethed after the meeting. "This determination to go on is not the result of any conviction ... but arises from personal pique." The rump AASS, Johnson ridiculed, was a "small clique masquerading in the old clothes of the [AASS]." Rather than succor it from afar, Garrison led a failed campaign the following year to disband its leading affiliate, the MASS. "The whole thing is a farce, and I care nothing for it," he fumed, emphasizing his acrimonious divorce from organized abolitionism.[30]

During the postwar years, Garrison at times voiced support for the struggle for equality as well as for freedmen's aid. As James M. McPherson has noted, he sporadically spoke and wrote in favor of Black suffrage. In 1866, he thanked George W. Julian for fighting to give Blacks "all the rights and immunities which belong to citizenship." But Garrison was more enthused about the freedmen's aid movement, whose paternalistic quest to provide freed slaves with education and material needs increasingly contravened the abolitionist crusade for Black ennoblement. As Garrison explained, it now aimed to "fit [former slaves] for the enjoyment of liberty," preparing them to be good Americans by, as one of its leaders added, "teaching them how to work." The abolitionist remnant rejected this condescending vision of Black servility. "If that is the only goal you have reached, if that is your estimate of the black race," scathed Phillips, "I don't belong to you." But Garrison did belong to it, if only casually. He intermittently attended meetings of the American Freedmen's Aid Commission and represented it at the global Anti-Slavery Conference held in Paris in 1867. He also sued Phillips over a fund which the late activist Francis Jackson had bequeathed to the AASS in 1861, claiming it for freedmen's aid while Phillips, supported by Child and Forten, sought it for the rump AASS. After the Massachusetts Supreme Court ruled for Garrison, Phillips excoriated his "gross perversion of the fund." In response, Garrison decried Phillips's own "network of fallacies"—and further relegated their friendship to the past.[31]

Garrison increasingly devoted his own labors to the past as well, straining in his waning years to secure his historical legacy as the protagonist of a finished abolitionist struggle. As he stressed, his career as a reformer—and the cause of immediatism—was complete. "I withdrew from the lecturing field ... and I have no thought or expectation of again entering it," he informed one interlocutor, as he consigned the work of organizing on the ground to the abolitionist remnant. Garrison implicitly downplayed the importance of such work by claiming that the immediatist movement had already achieved absolute victory. "To what class of reformers . . . [did] God ever before accord such a triumph?" he marveled in mid-1865. Abolition, he later added, was "so marvelous a change as to make whatever else of evil remains comparatively trivial"—an inconsequential drop in the national bucket relative to the tidal wave which he had helped precipitate.[32]

Instead of contemporary activism, Garrison fixated on burnishing his image in the arena of antislavery memory. In 1866, he declined requests from freedmen's aid leaders to embark on a lecturing tour, opting rather to "write a history of the Anti-Slavery struggle" featuring himself front and center. Omitting himself from such a narrative, he noted, would be akin to "leaving Hamlet out of the play." While Garrison never completed his magnum opus, he policed the myriad memoirs written by other antislavery veterans to ensure his rightful place in history. Among others, he chided Republican Henry Wilson for failing to "do entire justice to the Garrisonian[s]" in his antislavery chronicle. Garrison's efforts soon bore fruit: in 1866, his loyal clique joined with national figures from Salmon P. Chase to Frederick Law Olmstead to organize a testimonial in his honor, commemorating the "man who must be regarded in all future time as the visible leader" in the "accomplishment of the Great Work of Emancipation." His appearance in Paris as guest of honor, culminating a victory tour through Europe where he was hailed as the "liberator of the slaves," solidified Garrison's apotheosis into the pantheon of national saviors.[33]

As John D'Entremont has shown, Conway, too, advocated equality at times. Yet he ultimately discarded this egalitarian facade to champion his harsh vision of Black rights that enshrined white southern supremacy. In 1875, he returned to Virginia and reconciled with his family after decades of estrangement. Democrats had retaken control of the state, ensuring Anglo-Saxon racial dominance there. Far from protesting this outcome, Conway marveled at how his state was "free from the curse of slavery—the white and the black dwelling kindly together." Finally, Virginia had redeemed itself. In dooming freed slaves to be plantation wage laborers, free but unequal, it had answered his prayers. "Every society must have domestic and farm servants, and kindliness will make the negroes the best of servants," he affirmed. Conway "hope[d] [that] the negro will somehow disappear from American politics," abandoning talk of a substantive form of freedom—and of Reconstruction itself. He instead awaited Virginia's return to primacy as first among antiegalitarian equals, leading the reunited nation by its paternalistic example.[34]

The abolitionist remnant, by contrast, remained at its post to pursue Black legislative equality. Broad interventionists and purists like Phillips, Douglass, Forten, Child, Cheever, Pillsbury, and the Fosters emerged from the war as sophisticated interest group strategists who had enriched their understandings of what a morally transformed Union signified. The war, Phillips averred, had rendered their fight for Black rights "deeper . . . than [what] our movement first contemplated." These immediatists had integrated political sensibilities into their moral frameworks, harnessing pressure politics where Garrison had let it consume him. Rather than "go to Europe with Mr. Garrison," jibed Abby Kelley Foster, they fought on. They strove, as Susan B. Anthony argued, to "lift the entire nation into the practical realization of the republican idea"—to create a multiracial democracy. "I do not dare to call the revolution complete," Pillsbury added, "until every black man is as free as I am," wholly liberated through the political power of citizenship, suffrage, and land. "Political rights . . . [are] justice, and justice will not yield one inch," agreed Cheever.[35]

As these remaining abolitionists knew, Reconstruction represented their final opportunity to fulfill their refined moral visions. They thus drew on their wartime political educations to craft a persuasive argument for legislative equality. Speaking in late 1865, John Mercer Langston stressed that the dictates of justice and the martial sacrifices of Black veterans compelled the nation into action. But above all, he crystallized a point that Phillips, Douglass, and others had introduced during the war: expansive Black rights offered a practical means to subdue the South and prevent future warfare. Since then, the fight for equality had migrated from the battlefield into Congress. Just as during the war "military necessity brought us emancipation," Langston now asserted that "political necessity may yet bring us enfranchisement"—a renewed appeal to utility and national self-interest that took hold across the persevering movement.[36]

Yet a formidable obstacle stood in abolitionists' way: Andrew Johnson. Shortly after he assumed office in 1865, Johnson commenced reinstating ex-rebels to power in the South. His "infatuation [is to] restore as much as possible the Union as it was," seethed Phillips. But as Eric Foner has shown, Johnson's blatantly prosouthern policies, and ex-Confederates' resulting resurgence, provided Radical Republicans with the capital to take up their long-sought, but long politically circumscribed, aim of elevating Blacks. As Xi Wang has proven, they combined principle and pragmatism as they seized control of Reconstruction and promoted former slaves as keys to a Republican power base in the South. The rest of their party and much of the northern public supported this initiative, as Johnson radicalized them into stepping beyond the confines of a free-labor Union.[37]

Immediatists pounced on this opening by inserting themselves into Reconstruction, commencing a pressure campaign to enshrine expansive Black rights in the Constitution. In a concerted strategy, the remaining abolitionists deployed their societies, such as Phillips's AASS, the Cheever brothers' CASS, and Langston's NERL, as politicized interest groups. They acted as what James Brewer Stewart has called the "Republican party conscience," using articles, speeches, and lobbying to harry Congress into action. In the *Standard,* Phillips kept up pressure on Republicans to enact "measures indispensable for the nation's safety," of which "suffrage [was] the nucleus." George Cheever addressed Congress throughout 1866 on the urgency of Black voting. And Douglass appealed to Republicans not to be "enemies of that wise, just and necessary measure" that same year.[38]

Douglass also joined other Black activists in continuing their own political organizing through the NERL, drawing upon abolitionists' war-forged political playbook. On Downing's urging, the NERL and affiliated groups appointed Douglass, Langston, and himself as lobbyists to "engage the attention of every member of Congress" in early 1866. These delegates proceeded to pen petitions importuning the White House and Congress to accord Blacks the "right[s] which every American citizen should enjoy." The NERL's powerful Pennsylvania affiliate soon undertook its own trip to interview leading Republicans and present a memorial for manhood suffrage. "The mission was eminently successful," reported one of its officers. The group engaged in a media blitz thereafter, distributing its memorial to editors across the North.[39]

Abolitionists were outraged when Congress granted Blacks citizenship but not suffrage through the Fourteenth Amendment. Phillips decried the measure as a "total surrender" to the South. Yet this setback only heightened immediatists' advocacy for more—an endeavor Republicans warmed to after retaking the White House in 1868. The abolitionist remnant subsequently helped to form and pass the signal achievement of Reconstruction, the Fifteenth Amendment. In early 1869, Wilson confided to Abby Kelley Foster his "grave doubts" that an amendment enfranchising Black men could succeed without abolitionists' help in "bringing up the public sentiment to a higher level." The rump AASS answered his call, spurring higher the public and politicians alike through editorials and lobbying trips that "[plied] every shaky member with such arguments as shall bring him up to the point of duty." Black activists orchestrated their own push at an 1869 convention. Under the gaze of invited Republicans, they called on Congress to grant Blacks "universal suffrage" and "throw open public lands in the South" for their use. Though the NERL had fallen into disrepair, the delegates inaugurated a new group in its place: the National Executive Committee of Colored Men. Its officers, including Downing, Langston, and Lewis Douglass, soon launched a lobbying effort to compel Congress into action.[40]

By February, the House and Senate had drafted competing amendments, with the former prohibiting the denial of suffrage on the basis of race and the latter additionally banning property and educational requirements—a provision that would also outlaw many northern states' own voting restrictions. After the House balked, Phillips urged senators in the *Standard* "to be a little more *politicians*—and a little less *reformers*"—to rethink their too-impolitic draft. His plea rallied both chambers around the more moderate House version. As one Republican admitted, Phillips "saved the amendment." These persevering immediatists, however, had done more than seal its passage. Their evolved visions of Black rights had inspired it in the first place by laying the ideological groundwork for the radical language of Reconstruction. They had helped to ensure that the Constitution embodied their democratic ideas of citizenship and representation—a codification which was left woefully unenforced in their own time, but which, as Foner argued, nevertheless provided a framework for future civil rights advances. At least in part, these activists shaped a document whose transformational legacy would reverberate into the ages.[41]

Yet this milestone proved to be the remnant's high-water mark. As became clear, the abolitionist movement had become an enfeebled shell of its former self, helpless to prevent its expansive mission from perishing alongside Reconstruction. The figures who had once helmed its power structures, from Garrison of the AASS to Oliver Johnson of the *Standard* to Edmund Quincy, who had led the MASS, had deserted immediatism, taking their resources and clout with them—and shearing the movement of the sway it had commanded at its wartime height. "[We], weakened by the splitting of our ranks, have no single dollar to spend in anything not absolutely needed," admitted Phillips. Garrison "left us in the ground . . . crippl[ing] our resources and cramp[ing] our operations," agreed Abby Kelley Foster. Aggravating this problem, Phillips and other leaders of the remnant had marred their reputations during the election of 1864. "Phillips has lost influence [since then] at a rapid rate," smirked Johnson about his rival's depleted moral pull.[42]

Making matters worse, the abolitionist remnant failed to maintain its own internal cohesion. While most remaining immediatists advocated suffrage for women as well as for Black men, they clashed in the late 1860s over the Fifteenth Amendment's omission of the former. As Stacey M. Robertson has shown, Phillips, Douglass, and Abby Kelley Foster accepted Black male suffrage as their priority, while Pillsbury and Stephen Foster joined Anthony and Elizabeth Cady Stanton in rejecting the amendment as an unholy compromise. This infighting soon intensified, leading Pillsbury to "turn on Phillips and condemn him for narrowness." He and both Fosters dissented further when Phillips, with Douglass's blessing, disbanded the AASS following the ratification of the Fifteenth Amendment in 1870. Abolitionism's work, they protested, remained still incomplete.[43]

Unlike Garrison when he had tried to dissolve the AASS in 1865, Phillips understood that its struggle lay unfinished. "Our long crusade is not . . . fully ended," he admitted. As he knew, the abolitionist remnant had not secured its goal of legislative equality, which encompassed Black socioeconomic as well as political rights. For decades, immediatism had been the only organized bloc in the nation dedicated to racial justice irrespective of party-political considerations. It had been the backbone of this struggle, throwing its weight around to great effect during the war. But its power ultimately lay in its ability, whether through public pressure or direct lobbying, to hold policymakers' feet to the fire—to "direct the Republican party up to the radicalism of its own ranks," as Phillips affirmed. Now, after desertions, old wounds, and further strife had enervated its strength, it could no longer do so. By 1870, as Stewart has argued, Phillips grasped that abolitionists could nudge most Republicans no further—that essential reforms like land redistribution were unattainable. As he recognized with increasing fatalism, the fate of Black rights depended almost entirely upon the whims of a self-interested and unreceptive mainstream. Phillips therefore wound up the AASS not in celebration, but in resignation at its limitations—its powerlessness to realize the expansive morally transformed Union of which he dreamed.[44]

Without the bulwark of a strong abolitionist movement to advocate Black rights in the face of mainstream resistance, Reconstruction could not survive the shifting political headwinds of the 1870s. As historians have shown, the tide of public opinion turned against Blacks in a changing North that was both weary of conflict and increasingly preoccupied with newer struggles over labor and immigration. Most white northerners continued to separate still the concepts of emancipation and equality, even as self-interest had propelled their qualified support for the latter. Now, they readily moved on from Reconstruction. George Cheever, deprived of the flocks that had lapped up his wartime sermons, was forced to close his church. As Black rights lost its political appeal and economic luster, mainstream politicos shed their commitments to it. All now retreated, from Republicans, including Radicals like Julian, to antislavery businessmen like John Murray Forbes, a latecomer to the fight for suffrage. Though Douglass and other Black activists fought on, abolitionists could do little as Reconstruction fell by 1877 under the combined weight of northern apathy and southern terrorism. Alongside such larger causes, the weakening of immediatism was a minor factor in this collapse. It left African Americans at the mercy of a people nowhere near ready to accept their expansive rights—but more than ready to doom them to another century of horrific oppression.[45]

× × ×

Writing in 1878, Child reflected on the woeful state of the reconstructed Union. Phillips, she recorded, had mentioned the possibility of mob violence while conversing with a young man in Boston. "Oh, they never have mobs in Boston," the youth had replied. When Phillips recalled his own experiences to the contrary, his companion had queried, "What were the mobs about? I have never heard of them." In relaying this episode, Child could hardly contain her indignation. "To say *that* to Mr. Phillips, of all men!" she bristled. Yet it only reinforced "how completely the anti-slavery struggle is forgotten by the people," its ideals "sinking into oblivion" as northerners strode blithely into the future. Awash in lamentation, Child revised her earlier assessment of the concept of expediency. In 1865, she had welcomed abolitionists' wartime use of this tactic. Though the onset of military emancipation as an expedient war measure had not bathed the North in a purifying revolution, she had remained confident that such imperfect means could yet produce perfect ends. Now, she regretted that "emancipation was not the result of a popular moral sentiment, but of a miserable military necessity. It was not the fruit of righteousness, and therefore it is not peace." A populace that had acted from self-preservation had never internalized the need for justice, leaving it hostile still to a genuinely inclusive morally transformed Union. By utilizing such tactics, she argued, abolitionism had faltered in its mission.[46]

Despite Child's despondency, immediatists bore far from the full blame for the death of their egalitarian dreams. As she recognized, abolitionists had proved unable to guide the political mainstream into accepting Blacks as full citizens. Yet wartime northerners had never seemed amenable to this possibility in the first place, time and again rejecting any allusions to the subject. They moved according to the rhythms of political and economic expediency, over which immediatists held no power. The Union's closing of the door on expansive Black rights represented not so much abolitionists' failure as that of the larger, noninclusive nation.

The deeper tragedy of wartime immediatism lay not in the effects of its intervention on the public, but on itself. Entering the war precipitated both interventionists' greatest success, as they helped attain military emancipation at the conflict's height, and greatest failure, as they destroyed their power to help secure lasting equality in its aftermath. In consecrating their movement and its millennial project of a morally transformed Union, abolitionists had dedicated themselves to emancipation and post-emancipation Black rights. When war broke out in 1861, Garrison, Phillips, Douglass, Forten, Cheever, Conway, and Child sensed an opportunity and banded together to achieve the former, more immediate—and far from inevitable—objective. Even while managing their resulting ambivalence, they gained the unprecedented influence and political capital necessary to help ensure the Emancipation Proclamation. They defied the predictions of purists like Pillsbury and the Fosters to play critical roles in realizing their emancipatory golden moment, their agonizing efforts climaxing in a stunning high in 1863.

Yet abolitionists won this breathtaking victory only at the cost of their movement's ultimate defeat. Though they had misjudged the possibility of military emancipation, purists had prophesied the dangers of their counterparts' interventions—the terrible cost of their embracing of expedient tactics and mingling with imperfect allies. Garrison, having submerged himself in the mainstream, drowned in its depths. He assumed not the role of Hamlet the conquering hero, but of Hamlet the prime mover of an overarching tragedy. Alongside Conway, he left broad interventionists and purists in the lurch as the war ended, stifling their continued quest for legislative equality. The weakened movement, its heyday long past, could not prevent a postwar settlement that guaranteed Blacks expansive rights in name only. By intervening in the war, abolitionists had engendered their fate of accomplishing both so much and so little in terms of advancing racial justice. The immediatist movement had made itself heard with a bang in the wartime struggle for emancipation but ended with a whimper as Reconstruction died alongside the dream of multiracial democracy, its tragic saga complete.

NOTES

ABBREVIATIONS

AASS   American Anti-Slavery Society

AD   Anna Dickinson Papers, Library of Congress

AKF   Abby Kelley Foster

AL   Abraham Lincoln Papers, Library of Congress

BAP   C. Peter Ripley et al., eds., *The Black Abolitionist Papers*

BPL   Anti-Slavery Collection, Boston Public Library

CC   Patricia G. Holland et al., eds., *The Collected Correspondence of Lydia Maria Child, 1817–1880*

CF   Charlotte Forten

CFP   Cheever Family Papers, American Antiquarian Society

CHI   Lydia Maria Francis Child Correspondence, Library of Congress

COR   Samuel J. May Anti-Slavery Collection, Cornell University

CS   Charles Sumner

CU   Moncure Conway Papers, Rare Book and Manuscript Library, Columbia University

CW   Cheever-Wheeler Family Papers, American Antiquarian Society

DIC   Conway Family Papers, Archives and Special Collections, Dickinson College

DM   *Douglass' Monthly*

ECS   Elizabeth Cady Stanton Papers, Library of Congress

EQ   Edmund Quincy

FD   Frederick Douglass

FRED   Frederick Douglass Papers, Library of Congress

GBC   George B. Cheever

GER   Gerrit Smith Papers, Special Collections Research Center, Syracuse University

GWJ   George W. Julian

HC   Henry Cheever

HOU   Wendell Phillips Papers, Houghton Library, Harvard University

JAS   John Austin Stevens Papers, New-York Historical Society

JMM   James Miller McKim

JUL   Joshua R. Giddings and George Washington Julian Papers, Library of Congress

LMC   Lydia Maria Child

MDC   Moncure D. Conway

MER   Walter M. Merrill and Louis Ruchames, eds., *Let the Oppressed Go Free: The Letters of William Lloyd Garrison,* vol. 5

NASS   *National Anti-Slavery Standard*

NYPL   Maloney Collection of McKim-Garrison Family Papers, New York Public Library

NYHS   Parker Pillsbury Letters to Theodore Tilton, New-York Historical Society

OJ   Oliver Johnson

PP   Parker Pillsbury

QUIN   Quincy, Wendell, Holmes, and Upham Family Papers, Massachusetts Historical Society

RAD   Alma Lutz Collection of Documents by and about Abolitionists and Women's Rights Activists, Schlesinger Library, Radcliffe Institute, Harvard University

ROC   Frederick Douglass Papers, Rare Books, Special Collections and Preservation, River Campus Libraries, University of Rochester

RUB   Parker Pillsbury Diaries, David M. Rubenstein Rare Book and Manuscript Library, Duke University

SHG   Sydney Howard Gay Papers, Rare Book and Manuscript Library, Columbia University

SMJ   Samuel May Jr.

SSF   Stephen Symonds Foster

SUM   Charles Sumner Papers, Houghton Library, Harvard University

TILT   Theodore Tilton Correspondence, New-York Historical Society

TT   Theodore Tilton

VHS   Oliver Johnson Papers, Vermont Historical Society

WAA   *Weekly Anglo-African*

WLG   William Lloyd Garrison

WP   Wendell Phillips

WPG   Wendell Phillips Garrison Correspondence, Houghton Library, Harvard University

INTRODUCTION

1. Ann Phillips to WP, March, March 20, April 3, 1862, HOU. See James Brewer Stewart, *Wendell Phillips: Liberty's Hero* (Baton Rouge: Louisiana State Univ. Press, 1986), 231–33.

2. Works on immediatism include Ronald G. Walters, *The Antislavery Appeal: American Abolitionism after 1830* (Baton Rouge: Louisiana State Univ. Press, 1978); Peter Walker, *Moral Choices: Memory, Desire, and Imagination in Nineteenth-Century American Abolition* (Baton Rouge: Louisiana State Univ. Press, 1978); R. J. M. Blackett, *Building an Antislavery Wall: Black Americans in the Atlantic Abolitionist Movement, 1830–1860* (Baton Rouge: Louisiana State Univ. Press, 1983); Edward Rugemer, *The Problem of Emancipation: The Caribbean Roots of the American Civil War* (Baton Rouge: Louisiana State Univ. Press, 2008); James Brewer Stewart, *Holy Warriors: The Abolitionists and American Slavery* (1976; reprint, New York: Hill and Wang, 1997); Richard S. Newman, *The Transformation of American Abolitionism: Fighting Slavery in the Early*

Republic (Chapel Hill: Univ. of North Carolina Press, 2002); James M. McPherson, *The Struggle for Equality: Abolitionists and the Negro in the Civil War and Reconstruction* (1967; reprint, Princeton: Princeton Univ. Press, 2014); Manisha Sinha, *The Slave's Cause: A History of Abolition* (New Haven: Yale Univ. Press, 2016); Corey M. Brooks, *Liberty Power: Antislavery Third Parties and the Transformation of American Politics* (Chicago: Univ. of Chicago Press, 2016); Stanley Harrold, *American Abolitionism: Its Direct Political Impact from Colonial Times into Reconstruction* (Charlottesville: Univ. of Virginia Press, 2019). For its origins and antecedents, see Newman, *American Abolitionism;* Paul J. Polgar, *Standard-Bearers of Equality: America's First Abolition Movement* (Chapel Hill: Univ. of North Carolina Press, 2019).

3. WLG, *Selections from the Writings and Speeches of W.L. Garrison* (Boston: R. F. Wallcut, 1852), 69–71.

4. GBC, *God Against Slavery* (New York: Joseph H. Ladd, 1857), 217–18, 222. For national trends, see Melinda Lawson, *Patriot Fires: Forging a New American Nationalism in the American Civil War* (Lawrence: Univ. Press of Kansas, 2002); Nicholas Guyatt, *Providence and the Intervention of the United States, 1607–1876* (New York: Cambridge Univ. Press, 2007); Andrew F. Lang, *A Contest of Civilizations: Exposing the Crisis of American Exceptionalism in the Civil War Era* (Chapel Hill: Univ. of North Carolina Press, 2021). For moral revolution, see Merton L. Dillon, "The Failure of the American Abolitionists," *Journal of Southern History* 25, no. 2 (May 1959): 159–77.

5. GBC, *God Against Slavery,* 217; LMC to Parke Godwin, November 18, 1856, Bryant-Godwin Papers, New York Public Library.

6. Works discussing abolitionist millennialism include David W. Blight, *Frederick Douglass' Civil War: Keeping Faith in Jubilee* (Baton Rouge: Louisiana State Univ. Press, 1989); Mark Voss-Hubbard, "The Political Culture of Emancipation: Morality, Politics, and the State in Garrisonian Abolitionism, 1854–1863," *Journal of American Studies* 29, no. 2 (August 1995): 159–84; Rogan Kersh, *Dreams of a More Perfect Union* (Ithaca: Cornell Univ. Press, 2001); W. Caleb McDaniel, *The Problem of Democracy in the Age of Slavery: Garrisonian Abolitionists and Transatlantic Reform* (Baton Rouge: Louisiana State Univ. Press, 2013); Graham Peck, *Making an Antislavery Nation: Lincoln, Douglas, and the Battle over Freedom* (Champaign: Univ. of Illinois Press, 2017); David W. Blight, *Frederick Douglass: Prophet of Freedom* (New York: Simon and Schuster, 2018); Ben Wright, *Bonds of Salvation: How Christianity Inspired and Limited American Abolitionism* (Baton Rouge: Louisiana State Univ. Press, 2020); Peter Wirzbicki, *Fighting for the Higher Law: Black and White Transcendentalists Against Slavery* (Philadelphia: Univ. of Pennsylvania Press, 2021). For transatlantic abolitionism, see Blackett, *Antislavery Wall;* Rugemer, *Problem of Emancipation;* Hannah-Rose Murray, *Advocates of Freedom: African American Transatlantic Abolitionism in the British Isles* (Cambridge: Cambridge Univ. Press, 2020).

7. WLG and Maria Weston Chapman to David Lee Child, May 14, 1843, David Lee Child Correspondence, New-York Historical Society; Susan B. Anthony, July 1862, Susan Brownell Anthony Papers, Schlesinger Library, Radcliffe Institute, Harvard University. For pan-abolitionist saintliness, see Lawrence Jacob Friedman, *Gregarious Saints: Self and Community in American Abolitionism, 1830–1870* (Cambridge: Cambridge Univ. Press, 1982). For tactics, see Aileen S. Kraditor, *Means and Ends in American Abolitionism: Garrison and His Critics on Strategy and Tactics, 1834–1850* (Chicago: Ivan S. Dee, 1989).

8. MDC, "Where There Is No Vision the People Perish," 1857, CU. See Carolyn L. Karcher, *First Woman in the Republic: A Cultural Biography of Lydia Maria Child* (Durham, N.C.: Duke Univ. Press, 1994); Zachary Lechner, "'Are We Ready for the Conflict?' Black Abolitionist Response to the Kansas Crisis, 1854–1856," *Kansas History* 31 (spring 2008): 14–31; Kellie Carter Jackson, *Force and Freedom: Black Abolitionists and the Politics of Violence* (Philadelphia: Univ. of Pennsylvania Press, 2020).

9. FD, *Two Speeches, by Frederick Douglass* (Rochester, N.Y.: C. P. Dewey, 1857), 6, 22. See Blight, *Frederick Douglass' Civil War,* chapter 1.

10. See Kate Masur, *Until Justice Be Done: America's First Civil Rights Movement to Reconstruction* (New York: W. W. Norton, 2021), chapters 7–8, For white northern distinctions of slavery and race, see Paul D. Escott, *The Worst Passions of Human Nature: White Supremacy in the Civil War North* (Charlottesville: Univ. of Virginia Press, 2020). Also see Eric Foner, *Free Soil, Free Labor, Free Men: The Ideology of the Republican Party before the Civil War* (New York: Oxford Univ. Press, 1995); Joanne Pope Melish, *Disowning Slavery: Gradual Emancipation and "Race" in New England, 1780–1860* (Ithaca: Cornell Univ. Press, 1998); James Brewer Stewart, "Modernizing 'Difference': The Political Meanings of Color in the Free States, 1776–1840," *Journal of the Early Republic* 19, no. 4 (winter 1999): 691–712; Paul D. Escott, *Lincoln's Dilemma: Blair, Sumner, and the Republican Struggle over Racism and Equality in the Civil War Era* (Charlottesville: Univ. of Virginia Press, 2014); Adam I. P. Smith, *The Stormy Present: Conservatism and the Problem of Slavery in Northern Politics, 1846–1865* (Chapel Hill: Univ. of North Carolina Press, 2017).

11. *Liberator,* February 4, 1859; *DM,* June, September 1860; *Liberator,* June 22, 1860. See McPherson, *Struggle for Equality,* chapter 1; Blight, *Frederick Douglass,* chapter 16; Henry Mayer, *All on Fire: William Lloyd Garrison and the Abolition of Slavery* (New York: W. W. Norton, 2008), 452–53.

12. LMC to CS, April 4, 1860, SUM; *Liberator,* February 4, 1859. See Voss-Hubbard, "Political Culture"; James Oakes, *The Crooked Path to Abolition: Abraham Lincoln and the Antislavery Constitution* (New York: W. W. Norton, 2021), chapter 3.

13. AKF to WP, March 29, 1856, HOU; AKF to SSF, n.d., Abby Kelley Foster Papers, American Antiquarian Society; *Liberator,* February 4, 1859, June 6, 1856. See Dorothy Sterling, *Ahead of Her Time: Abby Kelley and the Politics of Antislavery* (New York: W. W. Norton, 1991), chapter 16; Stacey M. Robertson, *Parker Pillsbury: Radical Abolitionist, Male Feminist* (Ithaca: Cornell Univ. Press, 2000), 115–21.

14. *Liberator,* February 4, 1859; Maria Weston Chapman to WP, n.d., HOU; AKF to WLG, July 22, 1859, RAD; WLG to AKF, July 25, September 8, 1859, BPL; SMJ to WP, August 6, 1859, HOU.

15. Works on individuals or factions include Stewart, *Liberty's Hero;* Karcher, *First Woman;* Robertson, *Parker Pillsbury;* McDaniel, *Problem of Democracy;* Blight, *Frederick Douglass.*

16. Studies of wartime abolitionism include McPherson, *Struggle for Equality;* A. J. Aiséirithe, "Piloting the Car of Human Freedom: Abolitionism, Woman Suffrage, and Radical Reform, 1860–1870" (Ph.D. diss., Univ. of Chicago, 2007); Harrold, *American Abolitionism.* Works on wartime nation-building include Lawson, *Patriot Fires;* Matthew Gallman, *Defining Duty in the Civil War: Personal Choice, Popular Culture, and the Union Home Front* (Chapel Hill: Univ. of North Carolina Press, 2015); Lang, *Contest of Civilizations.*

17. Andrew Delbanco, *The Abolitionist Imagination* (Cambridge: Harvard Univ. Press, 2012). Works on abolitionists' dynamism include Louis S. Gerteis, *Morality and Utility in American Antislavery Reform* (Chapel Hill: Univ. of North Carolina Press, 2000); Brooks, *Liberty Power;* Sinha, *Slave's Cause;* R. J. M. Blackett, *The Captive's Quest for Freedom: Fugitive Slaves, the 1850 Fugitive Slave Law, and the Politics of Slavery* (New York: Cambridge Univ. Press, 2018); Harrold, *American Abolitionism;* Wirzbicki, *Fighting for the Higher Law;* Van Gosse, *The First Reconstruction: Black Politics in America from the Revolution to the Civil War* (Chapel Hill: Univ. of North Carolina Press, 2021); Masur, *Until Justice,* chapter 5.

18. Studies overemphasizing the antislavery determinations of Lincoln, his party, and the white North include Allen C. Guelzo, *Lincoln's Emancipation Proclamation: The End of Slavery in America* (New York: Simon and Schuster, 2006); Chandra Manning, *What This Cruel War Was Over: Soldiers, Slavery, and the Civil War* (New York: Vintage Books, 2008); James Oakes, *Freedom National: The Destruction of Slavery in the United States, 1861–1865* (New York: W. W. Norton, 2012); Adam Goodheart, *1861: The Civil War Awakening* (New York: Vintage Books, 2011); Sean Wilentz, *No Property in Man: Slavery and Antislavery at the Nation's Founding* (Cambridge: Harvard Univ. Press, 2018); Oakes, *Crooked Path;* Masur, *Until Justice.*

19. Studies stressing Lincoln's reliance on necessity and pragmatism include Richard Carwardine, *Lincoln: A Life of Purpose and Power* (New York: Vintage Books, 2003); James Oakes, *The Radical and the Republican: Frederick Douglass, Abraham Lincoln, and the Triumph of Antislavery* (New York: W. W. Norton, 2007); Eric Foner, *The Fiery Trial: Abraham Lincoln and American Slavery* (New York: W. W. Norton, 2010); Escott, *Lincoln's Dilemma;* Daniel W. Crofts, *Lincoln and the Politics of Slavery: The Other Thirteenth Amendment and the Struggle to Save the Union* (Chapel Hill: Univ. of North Carolina Press, 2016); William W. Freehling, *Becoming Lincoln* (Charlottesville: Univ. of Virginia Press, 2018). On public motivations, see Gary W. Gallagher, *The Union War* (Cambridge: Harvard Univ. Press, 2012); Smith, *Stormy Present;* Escott, *Worst Passions.* Studies on the contingency of emancipation include Glenn Brasher, *The Peninsula Campaign and the Necessity of Emancipation: African Americans and the Fight for Freedom* (Chapel Hill: Univ. of North Carolina Press, 2012); Gallagher, *Union War;* Crofts, *Politics of Slavery;* Smith, *Stormy Present;* Amy Murrell Taylor, *Embattled Freedom: Journeys through the Civil War's Slave Refugee Camps* (Chapel Hill: Univ. of North Carolina Press, 2018); Elizabeth R. Varon, *Armies of Deliverance: A New History of the Civil War* (New York: Oxford Univ. Press, 2019); Joseph P. Reidy, *Illusions of Emancipation: The Pursuit of Freedom and Equality in the Twilight of Slavery* (Chapel Hill: Univ. of North Carolina Press, 2019).

20. See George M. Fredrickson, *The Inner Civil War: Northern Intellectuals and the Crisis of the Union* (Champaign: Univ. of Illinois Press, 1993).

21. Masur, *Until Justice.* On northerners' disinterest in equality, see Gallagher, *Union War;* Richard S. Newman, "The Grammar of Emancipation: Putting Final Freedom in Context," in *Beyond Freedom: Disrupting the History of Emancipation,* ed. David W. Blight and Jim Downs (Athens: Univ. of Georgia Press, 2017), 11–25; Jack Furniss, "States of the Union: The Rise and Fall of the Political Center in the Civil War North" (Ph.D. diss., Univ. of Virginia, 2017); Smith, *Stormy Present;* Daniel W. Crofts, "Ending Slavery and Limiting Democracy: Sidney George Fisher and the American Civil War," *Pennsylvania Magazine of History and Biography* 144, no. 1 (January 2020): 29–60; Escott, *Worst Passions.*

22. Works on nineteenth-century Black activism include Blight, *Frederick Douglass' Civil War;* Stephen Kantrowitz, *More Than Freedom: Fighting for Black Citizenship in a White Republic, 1829–1889* (New York: Penguin Press, 2012); Chandra Manning, *Troubled Refuge: Struggling for Freedom in the Civil War* (New York: Knopf, 2016); Martha S. Jones, *Birthright Citizens: A History of Race and Rights in Antebellum America* (New York: Cambridge Univ. Press, 2018); Christopher Bonner, *Remaking the Republic: Black Politics and the Creation of American Citizenship* (Philadelphia: Univ. of Pennsylvania Press, 2020); Brian M. Taylor, *Fighting for Citizenship: Black Northerners and the Debate over Military Service in the Civil War* (Chapel Hill: Univ. of North Carolina Press, 2020); Gosse, *First Reconstruction.*

23. See William Gillette, *Retreat from Reconstruction, 1869–1879* (Baton Rouge: Louisiana State Univ. Press, 1979); Eric Foner, *Reconstruction: America's Finished Revolution, 1863–1877* (New York: Harper Perennial Modern Classics, 1988); Heather Cox Richardson, *The Death of Reconstruction: Race, Labor, and Politics in the Post-Civil War North, 1865–1901* (Cambridge: Harvard Univ. Press, 2001); Andrew W. Slap, *The Doom of Reconstruction: The Liberal Republicans in the Civil War Era* (New York: Fordham Univ. Press, 2006).

24. Sinha, *Slave's Cause.* For a tragic bent, see Dillon, "American Abolitionists"; Harrold, *American Abolitionism,* "Conclusion."

25. For Garrison, see James Brewer Stewart, *William Lloyd Garrison and the Challenge of Emancipation* (Arlington Heights, Ill.: Harlan Davidson, 1992); Mayer, *All on Fire;* Enrico Dal Lago, *William Lloyd Garrison and Giuseppe Mazzini: Abolition, Democracy, and Radical Reform* (Baton Rouge: Louisiana State Univ. Press, 2013). For Phillips, see Stewart, *Liberty's Hero;* A. J. Aiséirithe and Donald Yacovone, eds., *Wendell Phillips, Social Justice, and the Power of the Past* (Baton Rouge: Louisiana State Univ. Press, 2016). For the Fosters, see Sterling, *Ahead of Her Time.* For Pillsbury, see Robertson, *Parker Pillsbury.*

26. For Child, see Karcher, *First Woman.* For Conway, see John D'Entremont, *Southern Emancipator: Moncure Conway: The American Years, 1832–1865* (New York: Oxford Univ. Press, 1987). For Forten, see Brenda E. Stevenson, "Considering the War from Home and the Front: Charlotte Forten's Civil War Entry Diaries," in *Civil War Writing: New Perspectives on Iconic Texts,* ed. Gary W. Gallagher and Stephen Cushman (Baton Rouge: Louisiana State Univ. Press, 2019), 171–200.

27. For Douglass, see Blight, *Frederick Douglass' Civil War;* Oakes, *The Radical and the Republican;* Blight, *Frederick Douglass.* For Cheever, see John R. McKivigan, *The War Against Proslavery Religion: Abolitionism and the Northern Churches, 1830–1865* (Ithaca: Cornell Univ. Press, 1984).

PRELUDE: THE DILEMMA OF THE SECESSION WINTER

1. SSF to Elizabeth Cady Stanton, ECS; AKF to WP, December 9, 1860, HOU.

2. LMC to Francis Shaw, January 8, 1861, *CC;* MDC, "Life in Washington," circa 1860, CU; *Liberator,* March 8, 1861; *DM,* April 1861. See Crofts, *Politics of Slavery.*

3. See McPherson, *Struggle for Equality,* chapter 2.

4. *Liberator,* April 5, 1861; Angelina Grimké Weld to Theodore Grimké Weld, December 12, 1860, Weld-Grimké Family Papers, William L. Clements Library, University of Michigan; MDC, "Secession," circa 1861, CU; *Anti-Slavery Bugle,* November 17, 1860; WP, January 20, 1861, in

Speeches, Lectures, and Letters by Wendell Phillips, ed. James Redpath (Boston: James Redpath, 1863), 343–70.

5. WP, April 9, 1861, in George Lowell Austin, *Life and Times of Wendell Phillips* (Boston: Lee and Shepard, 1888), 206–9. See Mayer, *All on Fire,* 452; Stewart, *Liberty's Hero,* 211–13.

6. *DM,* January 1861; diary of GBC, January 22, February 15, 1861, CFP.

7. *Liberator,* February 8, 1861; Thomas Gold Appleton to Nathan Appleton, 1861, Appleton Family Papers, Massachusetts Historical Society; MDC, "Secession," 1861, CU.

8. Diary of Charles Frederick Winslow, June 18, 1861, Charles Frederick Winslow Papers, Massachusetts Historical Society. See McPherson, *Struggle for Equality,* 3–8, 90.

1. THE ONSET OF CIVIL WAR, APRIL–MAY 1861

1. George W. Smalley, *Anglo-American Memories,* Series I (New York: Putnam's Sons, 1911), 108–12.

2. EQ to Edmund Quincy, April 23, 1861, QUIN; *DM,* May 1861. See Russell McClintock, *Lincoln and the Decision for War* (Chapel Hill: Univ. of North Carolina Press, 2008); Gallagher, *Union War.*

3. AASS Circular, May 9, 1861, VHS; *Anti-Slavery Bugle,* May 4, 1861; *Liberator,* July 5, 1861. For abolitionists and public relations, see Newman, *American Abolitionism.*

4. WLG to OJ, April 19, 1861, BPL; diary of GBC, May 1861, CFP; *DM,* June 1861. See Mayer, *All on Fire,* 518–21.

5. WLG to WP, April 19, 1861, HOU; WLG to OJ, April 19, 1861, BPL; *Proceedings of the Yearly Meeting of Congregational Friends (Waterloo Meeting)* (Cortland, N.Y.: Van Slyck and Ford's, 1861), 7, 24. See Mayer, *All on Fire,* 523–24.

6. Susan B. Anthony to WP, April 28, 29, 1861, HOU; FD to Gerrit Smith, August 12, 1861, GER. See Richard S. Newman, "The Rise and Fall of the Abolitionist Republic," in *Massachusetts and the Civil War: The Commonwealth and National Disunion,* ed. Matthew Mason et al. (Amherst: Univ. of Massachusetts Press, 2015), 103–35.

7. *Liberator,* June 28, May 24, 1861.

8. *Liberator,* May 10, 1861; LMC to Henrietta Sargent, July 26, 1861, *CC.*

9. *Liberator,* May 31, July 12, 1861.

10. *DM,* May 1861; GBC to Elizabeth Cheever, June 21, 1861, CFP; WLG to WP, April 19, 1861, HOU; WLG to James S. Gibbons, April 28, 1861, *MER,* 19; LMC to Henrietta Sargent, August 24, 1861, COR.

11. WP, April 21, 1861, in Redpath, *Speeches,* 396–414; WLG to George T. Downing, May 13, 1861, *MER,* 25.

12. See Stewart, *Liberty's Hero,* 223–24; James Brewer Stewart, "Comfortable in His Own Skin: Wendell Phillips and Racial Egalitarianism," in Aiséirithe and Yacovone, eds., *Wendell Phillips,* 111–32.

13. See this book's introduction, note 22.

14. See James Brewer Stewart, "Garrison, Phillips, and the Symmetry of Autobiography: Charisma and Character of Abolitionist Leadership," in *The Moment of Decision: Biographical*

Essays on American Character and Regional Identity, ed. Randall M. Miller and John R. McKivigan (Westport, Conn.: Greenwood Press, 1994), 117–33.

15. Mary Livermore, *My Story of the War: A Woman's Narrative of Four Years' Personal Experience* (Hartford, Conn.: A. D. Worthington, 1896), 98–99.

16. MDC, *Autobiography: Memories and Experiences of Moncure Daniel Conway,* vol. 1 (Boston: Houghton, Mifflin and Company, 1904), 327.

17. *DM,* May 1861. See Brasher, *Peninsula Campaign.*

18. Diary of GBC, June 12, 1861, CFP; LMC to Lucy Osgood, May 7, 1861, *CC; DM,* July, June 1861.

19. HC to Elizabeth Cheever, August 2, 1861, HC, "Second Annual Report to the Church Anti-Slavery Society," May 1861, CFP; *Liberator,* July 12, August 30, 1861.

20. *Liberator,* April 26, 1861; *WAA,* September 28, 1861.

21. *WAA,* May 4, 1861.

22. *Liberator,* April 19, 1861. See McPherson, *Struggle for Equality,* 47–51.

23. WLG to OJ, April 19, 1861, BPL; George William Brown, *Baltimore and the Nineteenth of April 1861: A Study of the War,* vol. 3 (Baltimore: N. Murray, 1886), 26.

24. OJ to SMJ, April 15, 1861, OJ to SMJ, May 1861, VHS; Elizabeth Gay to Sarah Pugh, April 13, 1861, SHG.

25. WP, April 21, 1861, in Redpath, *Speeches,* 396–414; WLG to WP, 1861, OJ to WP, May 9, 1861, HOU. See Lawson, *Patriot Fires,* 132–41.

26. *DM,* May 1861. See Oakes, *The Radical and the Republican,* 159–61; Blight, *Frederick Douglass,* chapters 17, 19.

27. *WAA,* May 4, 1861. See Taylor, *Fighting for Citizenship,* chapter 1.

28. William Parham to Jacob C. White, October 12, 1861, Jacob C. White Collection, Moorland-Spingarn Research Center, Howard University. See Taylor, *Fighting for Citizenship,* 49–50.

29. Diary of GBC, April 28, May 30, 1861, CFP. See R. J. M. Blackett, *Divided Hearts: Britain and the American Civil War* (Baton Rouge: Louisiana State Univ. Press, 2001), chapter 1.

30. MDC, *Autobiography,* 324–39; MDC to Abraham Lincoln, May 7, 1861, AL. See D'Entremont, *Southern Emancipator,* 153–54.

31. LMC to Sarah Blake Shaw, May 5, 1861, LMC to OJ, June 3, 1861, *CC.* See Karcher, *First Woman,* chapter 18.

32. Edward Gilbert to WP, May 8, 1861, HOU; LMC to OJ, June 3, 1861, *CC.*

33. EQ to Sydney Howard Gay, April 19, 1861, SHG; WLG to OJ, April 19, 1861, BPL; *Liberator,* April 19, 1861. See Lewis Perry, *Radical Abolitionism: Anarchy and the Government of God in Antislavery Thought* (Ithaca: Cornell Univ. Press, 1973).

34. WLG to OJ, April 19, 1861, BPL; EQ to Sydney Howard Gay, April 19, 1861, SHG.

35. *Liberator,* April 5, 1861; WLG quoted in Francis Jackson Garrison and Wendell Phillips Garrison, *William Lloyd Garrison, 1805–1879: The Story of His Life Told by His Children,* vol. 4 (New York: Century, 1889), 20–21; WLG to Aaron Macy Powell, May 14, 1861, *MER,* 27–28; C. J. Warren to HC, April 24, 1861, CW. See McPherson, *Struggle for Equality,* 55–57.

36. C. J. Warren to HC, April 24, 1861, WP to HC, May 21, 1861, CW.

37. MDC, *Autobiography*, 337. McPherson, *Struggle for Equality*, downplays the antiwar faction's importance.

38. Lucretia Mott to Martha Wright, August 18, 1861, Mott Manuscripts, Friends Historical Library, Swarthmore College; diary of Alfred Love, April 28, 1861, Peace Collection, Swarthmore College; *Liberator*, June 7, 1861. See Thomas Curran, *Soldiers of Peace: Civil War Pacifism and the Postwar Radical Peace Movement* (New York: Fordham Univ. Press, 2003).

39. *Anti-Slavery Bugle*, April 27, 1861. See Sterling, *Ahead of Her Time*, chapter 17; Robertson, *Parker Pillsbury*, 123–28.

40. PP to WP, May 1, 1861, HOU; *Anti-Slavery Bugle*, April 27, 1861.

41. *Anti-Slavery Bugle*, May 4, March 16, 1861; PP to WP, May 1, 1861, HOU.

42. *Liberator*, August 16, 1861; PP quoted in Robertson, *Parker Pillsbury*, 129; *Anti-Slavery Bugle*, May 4, 1861.

43. PP to WP, May 1, 1861, HOU.

44. George Bassett, *A Discourse on the Wickedness and Folly of the Present War* (Ottawa, Ill.: n.p., 1861); *Liberator*, May 24, 1861.

45. *Liberator*, May 10, 1861; *Waterloo Meeting*, 27, 38.

46. WLG to OJ, May 9, 1861, BPL; WP to PP, May 5, 1861, Parker Pillsbury Family Papers, Cleveland Colby Colgate Archives, Colby-Sawyer College.

47. *Liberator*, April 19, May 10, 1861. See McPherson, *Struggle for Equality*, 57–61.

2. AN INTERVENTIONIST STRATEGY EMERGES, JUNE–MID-JULY 1861

1. *DM*, June 1861. For Butler, see Elizabeth D. Leonard, *Benjamin Franklin Butler: A Noisy, Fearless Life* (Chapel Hill: Univ. of North Carolina Press, 2022).

2. This book employs the political science terms *political interest group* and *political pressure group* interchangeably. See Anthony J. Nownes, *Interest Groups in American Politics* (New York: Routledge, 2013).

3. See Voss-Hubbard, "Political Culture." In recentering politics in the history of abolitionism, this book aligns with James Brewer Stewart, "Reconsidering the Abolitionists in an Age of Fundamentalist Politics," *Journal of the Early Republic* 26, no. 1 (spring 2006): 1–24; W. Caleb McDaniel, "The Bonds and Boundaries of Antislavery," *Journal of the Civil War Era* 4, no. 1 (March 2014): 84–105; Corey M. Brooks, "Reconsidering Politics in the Study of American Abolitionists," *Journal of the Civil War Era* 8, no. 2 (June 2018): 291–317.

4. McPherson, *Struggle for Equality*, overlooks the early formation of an antislavery alliance.

5. See Blackett, *Divided Hearts*, chapter 1; McDaniel, *Problem of Democracy*, chapter 9.

6. *Liberator*, July 19, 26, August 16, 23, 1861. See McPherson, *Struggle for Equality*, 61–69.

7. *Liberator*, August 9, 16, 1861.

8. LMC to Sarah Blake Shaw, August 11, 1861, COR; *DM*, June 1861. See Karcher, *First Woman*, 448.

9. *Liberator*, July 12, 1861.

10. GBC quoted in *Echoes of Harper's Ferry,* ed. James Redpath (Boston: Thayer and Eldridge, 1860), 170.

11. Rochester Ladies' Anti-Slavery Society, Tenth Annual Report, October 1861, Rochester Ladies' Anti-Slavery Society Collection, William L. Clements Library, University of Michigan. Oakes, *Freedom National,* mischaracterizes northerners as already-willing emancipators.

12. WLG to HC, September 9, 1861, CFP. See Mayer, *All on Fire,* 525–26.

13. See Brasher, *Peninsula Campaign,* chapter 3.

14. WLG to WP, April 21, 1861, HOU; WLG, *The Spirit of the South towards Northern Freemen and Soldiers Defending the American Flag against Traitors of the Deepest Dye* (Boston: R. F. Wallcut, 1861).

15. *Liberator,* May 3, 1861; *DM,* August 1861. See McPherson, *Struggle for Equality,* chapter 3.

16. WLG, *The War and Slavery; or, Victory Only Through Emancipation* (Boston: R. F. Wallcut, 1861), 3–7; *DM,* May 1861.

17. WLG, *War and Slavery,* 3–7.

18. *Liberator,* May 3, 1861; WLG, *War and Slavery,* 3–7; *Liberator,* August 16, 1861.

19. *DM,* July 1861; *Liberator,* May 3, 1861.

20. *Liberator,* June 28, July 12, August 16, 1861; WLG, *Emancipation under the War Power* (Boston: R. F. Wallcut, 1861); *DM,* August 1861; GBC quoted in Abijah Marvin, *History of Worcester in the War of the Rebellion* (Worcester: Self-published, 1870), 93; Elizur Wright to Salmon P. Chase, May 4, 1861, Elizur Wright Papers, Library of Congress. See McPherson, *Struggle for Equality,* 61–69, 93. Oakes, *Freedom National,* portrays the war power as accepted administration doctrine by 1861, eliding these axioms' importance.

21. *DM,* July 1861; OJ to HC, June 11, 1861, CW.

22. OJ to HC, June 11, 1861, CW; *Liberator,* July 19, 1861.

23. OJ to SMJ, July 31, 1861, VHS.

24. OJ to HC, August 30, 1861, CW.

25. FD to Elizabeth Cady Stanton, August 25, 1860, ECS; WLG to Samuel J. May, September 28, 1860, BPL. See Mayer, *All on Fire;* Blight, *Frederick Douglass.*

26. *DM,* June 1861, March 1862; WLG to Samuel J. May, December 6, 1861, BPL. See McPherson, *Struggle for Equality,* 104–6.

27. *DM,* February 1862; WLG to Helen Garrison, May 14, 1863, BPL.

28. *Liberator,* July 12, 1861.

29. Ibid.

30. *DM,* April 1855; WLG quoted in Garrison, *William Lloyd Garrison,* 24–25. See Stewart, *Holy Warriors,* 103–4; Brooks, *Liberty Power.*

31. *Liberator,* July 12, 1861.

32. GBC to Elizabeth Cheever, June 21, 1861, CFP.

33. MDC, *Autobiography,* 353; MDC to Ellen Conway, n.d. [June 1861], July 2, 1861, CU. See D'Entremont, *Southern Emancipator,* 155.

34. *Liberator,* July 12, 1861.

35. Ibid.

36. Ibid.

37. Ibid.

38. Ibid.; *Liberator,* July 19, 1861.

39. *Liberator,* May 31, 1861. See McDaniel, *Problem of Democracy,* chapter 9; Murray, *Advocates of Freedom,* chapter 6.

40. *Liberator,* July 26, 1861; Richard Davis Webb to Anne Weston, July 16, 1861, BPL.

41. Richard Davis Webb to Anne Weston, July 16, 1861, Webb to SMJ, May 25, 1861, BPL; *Liberator,* June 21, 1861.

42. *Liberator,* May 31, 1861.

43. *Liberator,* June 21, 28, 1861.

44. Mrs. Beriah Green to Clara, November 28, 1861, Elizur Wright Papers, Library of Congress; *Liberator,* August 30, 1861.

45. John Bright to Lewis Tappan, April 2, 1863, Lewis Tappan Papers, Library of Congress; Richard Cobden to John Bright, January 9, 1862, in *The Letters of Richard Cobden,* vol. 4, *1860–1865,* ed. Anthony Howe and Simon Morgan (Oxford: Oxford Univ. Press, 2015), 251–52; *Liberator,* August 30, June 28, 1861. See McDaniel, *Problem of Democracy,* chapter 9.

46. *Liberator,* June 28, 1861. See Mayer, *All on Fire,* 535–36.

3. THE IMPACT OF BULL RUN, LATE JULY–AUGUST 1861

1. MDC, *Autobiography,* 330; MDC to CS, August 22, 1861, SUM; CS to WP, September 17, 1861, HOU; Walker, Wise, and Co. to CS, September 23, 1861, SUM; MDC to CS, 1861, HOU; MDC to CS, October 5, 1861, SUM.

2. McPherson, *Struggle for Equality,* overlooks abolitionists' true motives, and thus their internal agonies.

3. For Ashley, see Rebecca E. Zietlow, *The Forgotten Emancipator: James Mitchell Ashley and the Ideological Origins of Reconstruction* (New York: Cambridge Univ. Press, 2017).

4. McPherson, *Struggle for Equality,* overlooks this emergence of a concerted alliance.

5. MDC, *Autobiography,* 334; WLG, *War and Slavery,* 5, 7–8.

6. *Liberator,* August 9, 1861.

7. *Liberator,* August 9, 30, 1861.

8. Ibid. For this evolution, see W. Caleb McDaniel, "The Transatlantic Mind of Wendell Phillips and the Problem of Democracy in America," in Aiséirithe and Yacovone, eds., *Wendell Phillips,* 50–72; Peter Wirzbicki, "Wendell Phillips and Transatlantic Radicalism," in Aiséirithe and Yacovone, eds., *Wendell Phillips,* 155–80.

9. FD to Samuel J. May, August 30, 1861, ROC.

10. *DM,* September 1861. See Oakes, *The Radical and the Republican,* 161–62; Blight, *Frederick Douglass,* 350.

11. *WAA,* March 30, 1861.

12. James McCune Smith to Gerrit Smith, August 22, 1861, *BAP,* 5:113. For Smith, see Leslie M. Alexander, *African or American? Identity and Political Activism in New York City, 1784–1861* (Champaign: Univ. of Illinois Press, 2008).

13. *WAA,* August 10, 17, 1861. See Debra Jackson, "A Black Journalist in Civil War Virginia: Robert Hamilton and the 'Anglo-African,'" *Virginia Magazine of History and Biography* 116, no. 1 (2008): 42–72.

14. *WAA,* August 24, 1861. See Taylor, *Fighting for Citizenship,* chapter 3.

15. FD to Samuel J. May, August 30, 1861, ROC. To an extent, Douglass vacillated regarding enlistment over the next year. See Taylor, *Fighting for Citizenship,* 62.

16. MDC to Ellen Conway, July 20, 1861, CU.

17. HC to Elizabeth Cheever, July 28, 1861, CFP; Angelina Grimké Weld to Mr. Cutler, July 29, 1861, Weld-Grimké Family Papers, William L. Clements Library, University of Michigan; EQ to Edmund Quincy, July 22, 1861, QUIN.

18. *DM,* August 1861; William Lloyd Garrison Jr. to Fanny Garrison, August 22, 1861, Fanny Garrison Villard Correspondence, Houghton Library, Harvard University.

19. MDC to Ellen Conway, July 23, 1861, CU; MDC, *The Rejected Stone; or, Insurrection vs. Resurrection in America* (Boston: Walker, Wise, 1861), 65–67. See McPherson, *Struggle for Equality,* 70–71.

20. LMC to Henrietta Sargent, July 26, 1861, *CC.*

21. Ibid.; LMC to Lucy Searle, August 22, 1861, *CC.* See Karcher, *First Woman,* 443–56.

22. Diary of GBC, May 1861, CFP.

23. For Radical Republicans and expediency, see Frederick J. Blue, *No Taint of Compromise: Crusaders in Antislavery Politics* (Baton Rouge: Louisiana State Univ. Press, 2005); Hans L. Trefousse, *The Radical Republicans: Lincoln's Vanguard for Racial Justice* (1968; reprint, New York: Knopf, 2014).

24. Diary of Charles Frederick Winslow, June 18, 1861, Charles Frederick Winslow Papers, Massachusetts Historical Society; *Liberator,* August 9, 1861. See McPherson, *Struggle for Equality,* 90. For the differences between abolitionists and Radicals, see Brooks, *Liberty Power,* 44–45. Masur, *Until Justice,* downplays this distinction.

25. Diary of Charles Frederick Winslow, June 18, 1861, Charles Frederick Winslow Papers, Massachusetts Historical Society.

26. OJ to WP, May 9, 1861, HOU; WP to CS, July 15, 1861, HC to CS, July 8, 1861, SUM; HC to Department of State, June 6, 1861, AL. See McKivigan, *The War Against Proslavery Religion,* 191.

27. James Ashley to JMM, July 29, 1861, NYPL; CS to SP, August 3, 8, 1861, HOU; CS to WP, August 8, 1861, SUM. See Escott, *Lincoln's Dilemma.* Radical Republicans were already receptive to the war power argument. See Oakes, *Crooked Path,* 137–41.

28. CS to WP, August 8, 1861, HOU. For antebellum precedents, see Brooks, *Liberty Power,* chapter 2; Sinha, *Slave's Cause,* chapter 14.

29. MDC to CS, 1861, HOU; WP to CS, September 17, 1861, SUM; MDC, *Autobiography,* 338.

30. David Lee Child, *Rights and Duties of the United States Relative to Slavery Under the Laws of War* (Boston: R. F. Wallcut, 1861); Walker, Wise, and Co. to CS, September 23, 1861, MDC to CS, September 1861, SUM; MDC, *Rejected Stone,* 1. See D'Entremont, *Southern Emancipator,* 157–59; Wirzbicki, *Fighting for the Higher Law,* 236–37.

31. MDC, *Rejected Stone,* 10–13, 21.

32. Ibid., 29–30, 81–84.

33. Ibid., 86–88, 103–8.

34. Ibid., 108, 117.

35. Ibid., 127–28. See Rugemer, *Problem of Emancipation,* chapters 4–5.

36. Ibid. For white abolitionist antiegalitarianism, see McPherson, *Struggle for Equality,* chapter 6; George M. Fredrickson, *The Black Image in the White Mind: The Debate on Afro-American Character and Destiny, 1817–1914* (New York: Harper and Row, 1971); Melish, *Disowning Slavery;* Joanne Pope Melish, "The 'Condition' Debate and Racial Discourse in the Antebellum North," *Journal of the Early Republic* 19, no. 4 (winter 1999): 651–72; Bruce Laurie, *Beyond Garrison: Antislavery and Social Reform* (New York: Cambridge Univ. Press, 2005); John Frederick Bell, *Degrees of Equality: Abolitionist Colleges and the Politics of Race* (Baton Rouge: Louisiana State Univ. Press, 2022).

37. CS to WP, August 3, 1861, HOU.

38. CS, "Union and Peace! How They Shall Be Restored," October 1, 1861, Charles Sumner Correspondence, Library of Congress; MDC to CS, October 5, 1861, SUM. See Trefousse, *Radical Republicans;* Jane Anne Moore and William F. Moore, *Owen Lovejoy and the Coalition for Equality: Clergy, African Americans, and Women United for Abolition* (Champaign: Univ. of Illinois Press, 2019), chapter 8; Bruce Levine, *Thaddeus Stevens: Civil War Revolutionary, Fighter for Racial Justice* (New York: Simon and Schuster, 2021).

39. *Liberator,* August 30, 1861. See Silvana R. Siddali, *From Property to Person: Slavery and the Confiscation Acts, 1861–1862* (Baton Rouge: Louisiana State Univ. Press, 2005).

40. Benjamin Butler and Simon Cameron quoted in Foner, *Fiery Trial,* 175; WLG quoted in Garrison, *William Lloyd Garrison,* 32.

41. LMC to John Greenleaf Whittier, September 10, 1861, CHI; LMC to James Freeman Clarke, December 15, 1861, Lydia Maria Child Correspondence and Story, New-York Historical Society; MDC to WP, December 9, 1861, HOU. See Wirzbicki, *Fighting for the Higher Law,* chapter 6.

42. *Liberator,* July 26, August 16, 1861; Tenth Annual Report, October 1861, Rochester Ladies' Anti-Slavery Society Collection, William L. Clements Library, University of Michigan; *Liberator,* September 6, 1861. See Gallagher, *Union War.*

43. *Liberator,* August 30, 1861.

44. *Christian Recorder,* August 24, 1861; William Lloyd Garrison Jr. to AKF, August 7, 1861, Abby Kelley Foster Papers, American Antiquarian Society; *Liberator,* August 16, 1861; Bradford Wood to John Bright, August 14, 1861, John Bright Papers, British Library.

45. SSF to WP, November 8, 1861, HOU.

46. Ibid.

47. Ibid.

48. *Liberator,* June 6, 1862.

49. William Lloyd Garrison Jr. to AKF, August 7, 1861, AKF to William Lloyd Garrison Jr., August 14, 1861, Abby Kelley Foster Papers, American Antiquarian Society. See Sterling, *Ahead of Her Time,* chapter 17.

50. PP to the *NASS,* August 24, 1861, RAD; *DM,* August 1861; *Liberator,* August 16, 1861.

51. *Liberator,* August 16, 1861; PP to Sydney Howard Gay, November 21, 1861, SHG; *Liberator,* November 21, 1861. See Robertson, *Parker Pillsbury,* chapter 7.

52. *Liberator,* August 16, 1861.

53. Ibid.; PP to the *NASS,* August 24, 1861, RAD.

54. *Liberator,* August 16, 1861.

4. THE RISE OF THE EMANCIPATION LEAGUE, SEPTEMBER–DECEMBER 1861

1. LMC to John Greenleaf Whittier, September 10, 1861, CHI. See Karcher, *First Woman*, 447–48.

2. Works overlooking the League's significance as an extension of the antislavery alliance include McPherson, *Struggle for Equality;* John Stauffer, "The Union of Abolitionists and Emancipationists in Civil War-Era Massachusetts," in Mason et al., eds., *Massachusetts and the Civil War,* 9–46.

3. Edward Morris Davis to Sydney Howard Gay, September 1, 1861, SHG; WLG to Helen Garrison, October 29, 1861, BPL; Wendell Phillips Garrison to WLG, October 31, 1861, WPG. See McPherson, *Struggle for Equality,* 72.

4. *DM,* October 1861; LMC to George W. Curtis, September 1, 1861, Lydia Maria Child Papers, Rare Book and Manuscript Library, Columbia University; LMC to John Greenleaf Whittier, September 22, 1861, CHI; WLG to Gerrit Smith, September 5, 1861, GER.

5. See James Oakes, "Reluctant to Emancipate? Another Look at the First Confiscation Act," *Journal of the Civil War Era* 3, no. 4 (December 2013): 458–66. For Lincoln's pragmatism, see Oakes, *The Radical and the Republican,* 151–52; Foner, *Fiery Trial.*

6. Harriet Martineau to CS, November 14, 1861, SUM.

7. *DM,* October, November 1861; *Liberator,* September 20, 1861. See McPherson, *Struggle for Equality,* 73–74.

8. LMC to John Greenleaf Whittier, September 22, 1861, CHI; LMC to Lucy Osgood, October 11, 1861, COR.

9. WP to CS, September 17, 1861, SUM; WLG to OJ, October 7, December 26, 1861, BPL.

10. HC to Jane Cheever, October 10, 1861, CW; HC to Elizabeth Cheever, January 16, 1862, CFP; FD to Gerrit Smith, December 22, 1861, GER.

11. LMC to unknown, December 1861, Lydia Maria Child Papers, Rare Book and Manuscript Library, Columbia University.

12. WLG to HC, September 9, 1861, CFP.

13. Ibid. See McPherson, *Struggle for Equality,* chapter 4.

14. Ibid.; George Luther Stearns to Lysander Spooner, October 1, 1861, Lysander Spooner Papers, New-York Historical Society; James M. Stone to Caroline Dall, October 10, 1861, Caroline Wells Healey Dall Papers, Massachusetts Historical Society; Frank Stearns, *The Life and Public Service of George Luther Stearns* (Philadelphia: J. B. Lippincott, 1907), 256–57.

15. *DM,* December 1861; *WAA,* September 21, 1861.

16. WLG to HC, September 9, 1861, CFP; WLG to CS, December 20, 1861, SUM. See Harrold, *American Abolitionism,* chapter 8. For antebellum petitions, see Stanley Harrold, *Subversives: Antislavery Community in Washington, D.C., 1828–1865* (Baton Rouge: Louisiana State Univ. Press, 2003).

17. *Liberator,* September 27, 1861; WLG to HC, September 9, 1861, CFP. See Mayer, *All on Fire,* 529.

18. *DM,* April 1862. See Oakes, *The Radical and the Republican,* 162.

19. MDC to CS, September 23, 1861, SUM; MDC to WP, October 7, 1861, HOU.

20. MDC to WP, October 7, 1861, HOU.

21. Aaron Macy Powell to WLG, October 7, 1861, BPL; WP to EQ, October 1, 1861, QUIN; *Liberator,* November 29, 1861. See Stewart, *Liberty's Hero,* 231–32.

22. George Luther Stearns to Lysander Spooner, October 1, 1861, Lysander Spooner Papers, New-York Historical Society; *Commonwealth,* May 29, 1863; James M. Stone to John Andrew, November 12, December 14, 1861, John A. Andrew Papers, Massachusetts Historical Society; James M. Stone to Elizur Wright, November 26, 1861, Elizur Wright Papers, Library of Congress; *Liberator,* December 20, 1861. See McPherson, *Struggle for Equality,* chapter 4; Richard H. Abbott, *Cotton and Capital: Businessmen and Antislavery Reform, 1854–1868* (Amherst: Univ. of Massachusetts Press, 1991), 77.

23. *Liberator,* December 13, 1861; *Commonwealth,* May 29, 1863.

24. See Bruce Tap, *Over Lincoln's Shoulder: The Joint Committee on the Conduct of the War* (Lawrence: Univ. Press of Kansas, 1998).

25. OJ to WLG, December 5, 1861, BPL.

26. WP to CS, October 12, 1861, SUM. Abolitionists had long cultivated ties with Radical Republicans, though the level of wartime coordination was unprecedented. See Stewart, *Holy Warriors,* chapter 7.

27. See Stewart, *Liberty's Hero,* 212–13; Matthew Mason, *Apostle of Union: A Political Biography of Edward Everett* (Chapel Hill: Univ. of North Carolina Press, 2016), chapter 10.

28. WP to EQ, October 1, 1861, QUIN.

29. *Liberator,* December 13, 1861; diary of Caroline Dall, November 27, 1861, Caroline Wells Healey Dall Papers, Massachusetts Historical Society. Stauffer, "Union of Abolitionists," overstates antislavery conservatives' embrace of abolitionists' racial agenda. For nineteenth-century conservatism, see Mason, *Apostle of Union,* chapter 10; Newman, "Grammar of Emancipation"; Smith, *Stormy Present,* 220–25; Joshua A. Lynn, *Preserving the White Man's Republic: Jacksonian Democracy, Race, and the Transformation of American Conservatism* (Charlottesville: Univ. of Virginia Press, 2019); Crofts, "Ending Slavery and Limiting Democracy"; Frank Towers and Andrew Wiley, eds., Special Issue on Civil War-Era Conservatism, *Civil War History* 66, no. 3 (September 2020); Escott, *Worst Passions,* chapter 1.

30. Maria Weston Chapman to John Jay, September 7, 1861, John Jay II Papers, Rare Book and Manuscript Library, Columbia University; Chapman to JMM, October 1861, BPL; *Liberator,* December 13, 1861. See McPherson, *Struggle for Equality,* 78.

31. Edward Atkinson, "Is Cotton Our King?," *Continental Monthly* 1, no. 3 (March 1862): 247–56. See Susan Schulten, *Mapping the Nation: History and Cartography in Nineteenth-Century America* (Chicago: Univ. of Chicago Press, 2012), 152–54.

32. Jesse Hamel to John Austin Stevens Jr., February 1, 1863; William Haskell to John Austin Stevens Jr., November 30, 1862, JAS. See Abbott, *Cotton and Capital,* 77–81; William C. Harris, *With Charity for All: Lincoln and the Restoration of the Union* (Lexington: Univ. Press of Kentucky, 1997), chapter 4.

33. John Murray Forbes quoted in Abbott, *Cotton and Capital,* 75; *Liberator,* December 20, 27, 1861. See Abbott, *Cotton and Capital,* 75–76.

34. Maria Weston Chapman to JMM, October 1861, BPL; journal of Lewis Tappan, September 12, 1861, Lewis Tappan Papers, Library of Congress; *New York Times,* September 24, 1861; John

Jay to George W. Bancroft, September 16, 1861, John Jay II Papers, Rare Book and Manuscript Library, Columbia University. See McPherson, *Struggle for Equality,* 77–78.

35. *Liberator,* December 27, 1861. See McPherson, *Struggle for Equality,* 82.

36. *Liberator,* March 21, 1862; G. G. Walker to Franklin B. Sanborn, March 19, 1862, F. B. Sanborn Correspondence and Essays, Library of Congress; Report of SMJ, May 1862, BPL.

37. William Croffut, *An American Procession, 1855–1914: A Personal Chronicle of Famous Men* (Boston: Little, Brown and Company, 1931), 56–61. See Michael F. Conlin, "The Smithsonian Abolition Lecture Controversy: The Clash of Antislavery Politics with American Science in Wartime Washington," *Civil War History* 46, no. 4 (2000): 301–23.

38. Croffut, *American Procession,* 57–66; William Croffut to GBC, November 25, 1861, CW; MDC to CS, December 12, 1861, SUM; Croffut to MDC, January 5, 1862, CU.

39. Croffut, *American Procession,* 64–69.

40. *Commonwealth,* May 29, 1863; MDC to Ellen Conway, March 16, 1862, CU; MDC to CS, April 22, 1862, SUM.

41. JMM to Sydney Howard Gay, October 18, 1861, SHG; JMM to EQ, January 1, 1862, QUIN; JMM to Anna Dickinson, 1861, AD.

42. WLG to Helen Garrison, October 21, 1861, BPL; Rosine Draz to FD, November 13, 1861, FRED.

43. GBC to Elizabeth Cheever, December 31, 1861, CW; GBC to FD, April 4, 1862, FRED; GBC, *The Salvation of the Country Secured by Immediate Emancipation* (New York: John A. Gray, 1861), 4, 10.

44. GBC, *Salvation of the Country,* 15.

45. WLG to CS, December 20, 1861, SUM; WLG to OJ, December 6, 1861, BPL. See Stewart, *Garrison,* 176–77.

46. *Liberator,* December 6, 1861, February 7, 1862.

47. WLG to TT, December 22, 1861, William Lloyd Garrison Papers, New-York Historical Society; OJ to WP, December 20, 1861, HOU; *New York Times,* January 15, 1862. See Mayer, *All on Fire,* 531–32.

48. *New York Times,* January 15, 1862.

49. *Liberator,* December 6, 1861; WLG to CS, December 20, 1861, SUM.

50. WP, December 1861, in Redpath, *Speeches,* 415–47.

51. Ibid. See Stewart, *Liberty's Hero,* 223–42; McDaniel, "Transatlantic Mind."

52. *DM,* February 1862. See Blight, *Frederick Douglass' Civil War,* 101–21.

53. *DM,* March 1862.

54. Ibid. See Blight, *Frederick Douglass' Civil War,* 115–21.

5. ON TO WASHINGTON, JANUARY–MARCH 1862

1. Walker, Wise, and Co. to CS, March 25, 1862, SUM; MDC to Ellen Conway, March 13, 16, 23, 1862, CU.

2. See Stewart, "Symmetry of Autobiography."

3. Stauffer, "Union of Abolitionists," mischaracterizes emancipationists as dedicated to Black rights.

4. William Pippey to brother, March 28, July 31, 1862, William T. Pippey Letters, David M. Rubenstein Rare Book and Manuscript Library, Duke University. See Gallagher, *Union War.*

5. SMJ to Richard Davis Webb, 1862, BPL; *Liberator,* January 31, 1862. See Escott, *Worst Passions,* chapters 1–2.

6. *Liberator,* January 31, February 7, 1862.

7. Susan B. Anthony to Martha Coffin Wright, February 9, 1862, ECS.

8. *DM,* February, March 1862. See Blight, *Frederick Douglass,* 361–63.

9. LMC John Greenleaf Whittier, January 21, 1862, CHI; MDC to Ellen Conway, January 24, 1862, CU; Report by SMJ, 1862, BPL. See D'Entremont, *Southern Emancipator,* 159–63.

10. JMM to Anna Dickinson, October 1861, Anna Dickinson to WLG, March 16, 1861, AD; OJ to WLG, March 20, 1862, BPL; WLG to Anna Dickinson, March 22, 1862, AD; WLG to OJ, March 30, 1862, BPL. See McPherson, *Struggle for Equality,* 128–29; J. Matthew Gallman, *America's Joan of Arc: The Life of Anna Elizabeth Dickinson* (New York: Oxford Univ. Press, 2006).

11. *Liberator,* April 4, 18, 1862; Anna Dickinson to Susan Dickinson, April 28, 1862, AD; *Liberator,* May 2, 1862.

12. James Harlan to GBC, August 2, 1862, CFP; *Liberator,* February 28, 1862; GWJ to GBC, January 27, 1862, CFP; GWJ to WLG, January 19, 1862, BPL; OJ to SMJ, February 6, 1862, VHS.

13. LMC to GWJ, January 30, 1862, GBC to GWJ, January 23, 1862, WLG to GWJ, January 31, 1862, JUL; *Liberator,* February 28, 1862; OJ to GWJ, January 28, 1862, Cephas Brainerd to GWJ, February 11, 1862, WLG to GWJ, April 13, 1862, JUL. See Blue, *No Taint of Compromise,* chapter 8.

14. Gordon Berry et al. to GBC, January 14, 1862, CFP.

15. Gordon Berry to GBC, January 23, 1862, HC to Elizabeth Cheever, January 26, 1862, CFP; William Goodell to GWJ, January 22, 1862, JUL.

16. Aaron Macy Powell to GBC, March 5, 1862, CFP; *NASS,* March 29, 1862.

17. *Liberator,* February 28, 1862; Croffut, *American Procession,* 68; CS to WP, December 8, 1861, Martin Conway to WP, December 27, 1861, HOU. See McPherson, *Struggle for Equality,* 82–86.

18. Croffut, *American Procession,* 71; GWJ, *Political Recollections, 1840 to 1872* (Chicago: Jansen, McClurg, 1884), 369–70.

19. *DM,* February 1862; GWJ, *Political Recollections,* 370; John Geyser to GBC, January 15, 1862, CFP. See Guyatt, *Providence,* 281–82.

20. James Ashley et al. to GBC, January 14, 1862, CFP; Octavius Brooks Frothingham, ed., *Memoir of William Henry Channing* (Boston: Houghton, Mifflin and Company, 1886), 323–24; William Croffut to GBC, March 5, 1862, CFP. See Wirzbicki, *Fighting for the Higher Law,* 234–35.

21. MDC to Ellen Conway, January 15, 16, 1862, CU; Croffut, *American Procession,* 72–73; MDC, *Autobiography,* 344–45.

22. MDC, *Autobiography,* 345–47.

23. See Guyatt, *Providence,* 281–83.

24. MDC to Ellen Conway, March 6, 8, 17, 1862, CU; MDC, *The Golden Hour* (Boston: Ticknor and Fields, 1862), 128–29.

25. MDC, *Autobiography,* 353; MDC to CS, April 22, 30, 1862, WP to CS, May 1862, SUM.

26. LMC to John Greenleaf Whittier, January 21, 1862, CHI; GBC to GWJ, January 23, 1862, JUL.

27. Ann Phillips to WP, March 1862, HOU.

28. J. K. Herbert to GWJ, June 23, 1862, JUL; J. K. Herbert to Sydney Howard Gay, October 28, 1863, SHG.

29. Ann Phillips to WLG, March 24, 1862, BPL; Ann Phillips to WP, March 1862, HOU; WLG to GWJ, April 13, 1862, JUL; GWJ to WLG, April 16, 1862, BPL.

30. Fanny Garrison to TT, April 6, 1862, TILT; Croffut, *American Procession,* 67–68. See Stewart, *Liberty's Hero,* 177–96, 234–35; McDaniel, "Transatlantic Mind."

31. WP to Ann Phillips, March 31, 1862, HOU; Croffut, *American Procession,* 78.

32. WP to Ann Phillips, March 1862, BPL. See Stewart, *Liberty's Hero,* 235–36.

33. MDC to Ellen Conway, March 8, 1862, CU; *Liberator,* March 14, 1862. See Stewart, *Liberty's Hero,* 235–36.

34. EQ to Emma Weston, March 23, 1862; EQ to Mary Quincy, March 27, 31, 1862, QUIN; OJ to CS, June 13, 1862, WP to CS, March 27, 1862, SUM; WLG to GWJ, April 13, 1862, JUL; WLG to OJ, March 30, 1862, BPL. See Stewart, *Liberty's Hero,* 237–38.

35. Maria Weston Chapman to Anne Dicey, November 22, 1862, BPL; John Austin Stevens Jr., "Organization of a Corps of Turcos," June 1862, William Haskell to John Austin Stevens Jr., November 30, 1862, JAS. See William Leeman, "George Bancroft's Civil War: Slavery, Abraham Lincoln, and the Course of History," *New England Quarterly* 81, no. 3 (September 2008): 462–88; Harris, *With Charity for All,* chapter 4.

36. *DM,* February 1862; *NASS,* January 11, 1862.

37. John Kelly to George Bancroft, March 9, 1862, George Bancroft Papers, Massachusetts Historical Society; *Liberator,* March 7, 14, 1862; *New York Times,* March 7, 1862.

38. *Liberator,* March 14, 1862. For Blair, see Escott, *Lincoln's Dilemma.*

39. "Our War and Our Want," *Continental Monthly* 1, no. 2 (February 1862): 113–17; "Editor's Table," *Continental Monthly* 1, no. 1 (January 1862): 95–100. See McPherson, *Struggle for Equality,* 91–93; David Brown, *Southern Outcast: Hinton Rowan Helper and the Impending Crisis of the South* (Baton Rouge: Louisiana State Univ. Press, 2006); Brian P. Luskey, *Men Is Cheap: Exposing the Frauds of Free Labor in Civil War America* (Chapel Hill: Univ. of North Carolina Press, 2020), chapters 3–4; Escott, *Worst Passions,* chapters 4–5.

40. Ibid.

41. "Literary Notices," *Continental Monthly* 1, no. 1 (January 1862): 91–92; "What To Do With the Darkies," *Continental Monthly* 1, no. 1 (January 1862): 84–86.

42. LMC to Lucy Osgood, January 3, 1862, COR; *Liberator,* February 28, 1862.

43. *Liberator,* February 14, May 23, 1862.

44. SSF to George Thompson, March 16, 1862, Abby Kelley Foster Papers, American Antiquarian Society. See Robertson, *Parker Pillsbury,* chapter 7; Sterling, *Ahead of Her Time,* chapter 17.

45. *Liberator,* January 10, 31, 1862.

46. Ibid.

47. PP to GBC, March 11, 1862, CW; *Liberator,* March 7, 1862. See Robertson, *Parker Pillsbury,* chapter 7.

48. *Liberator,* March 7, 1862.

49. Susan B. Anthony to Martha Coffin Wright, February 9, 1862, ECS; SSF to George Thompson, March 16, 1862, Abby Kelley Foster Papers, American Antiquarian Society.

50. *Liberator,* January 31, March 7, 1862. See McPherson, *Struggle for Equality,* 99–104.

51. *Liberator,* February 21, 1862; William Robson to Francis Jackson Garrison, December 7, 1861, BPL. See McDaniel, *Problem of Democracy,* chapter 9.

52. Samuel J. May to WLG, February 13, 1862, BPL; *Liberator,* January 31, February 7, 1862.

53. SMJ to Richard Davis Webb, November 21, 1861, June 30, 1862, BPL; *Liberator,* February 21, 28, March 7, 1862.

54. *Liberator,* February 21, 28, March 7, 1862. See McDaniel, *Problem of Democracy.*

55. LMC to Lucy Yearle, January 3, 1862, LMC to Lucy Osgood, January 3, 1862, COR; EQ to Richard Davis Webb, February 24, 1862, QUIN.

6. IMAGINING RECONSTRUCTIONS, MARCH–SEPTEMBER 1862

1. LMC to Lewis Tappan, March 23, 1862, Lewis Tappan Papers, Library of Congress.

2. LMC to GWJ, June 16, 1862, JUL. See Karcher, *First Woman,* 457–62.

3. McPherson, *Struggle for Equality,* and Harrold, *American Abolitionism,* portray abolitionists as factors in emancipation.

4. For Phillips, see Stewart, *Liberty's Hero,* chapter 10.

5. See Willie Lee Rose, *Rehearsal for Reconstruction: The Port Royal Experiment* (Athens: Univ. of Georgia Press, 1999).

6. See Aiséirithe, "Piloting the Car," chapter 5.

7. *Liberator,* March 14, 1862; LMC, *The Right Way the Safe Way* (New York: n.p., 1862); LMC to Lewis Tappan, March 23, 1862, Lewis Tappan Papers, Library of Congress. See Rugemer, *Problem of Emancipation,* 133–36, 290; Karcher, *First Woman,* 430–32; McPherson, *Struggle for Equality,* 96–97.

8. LMC to Sarah Blake Shaw, May 18, 1862, Shaw Family Correspondence, New York Public Library; LMC to CS, June 22, 1862, *CC.* See Eric Burin, *Slavery and the Peculiar Solution: A History of the American Colonization Society* (Gainesville: Univ. of Florida Press, 2008).

9. WLG to GWJ, April 13, 1862, JUL; LMC to Lucy Osgood, April 20, 1862, COR; *Christian Recorder,* April 26, 1862. See Kate Masur, *An Example for All the Land: Emancipation and the Struggle over Equality in Washington, D.C.* (Chapel Hill: Univ. of North Carolina Press, 2010).

10. Mary Grew to Helen Garrison, June 20, 1862, BPL; *DM,* May 1862.

11. WLG to Charles Sedgwick, May 20, 1862, Charles B. Sedgwick Papers, Special Collections Research Center, Syracuse University; OJ to WP, March 31, 1862, HOU; *American Missionary,* September 1862.

12. Abraham Lincoln, "Proclamation Revoking General Hunter's Order," May 19, 1862, in *The Collected Works of Abraham Lincoln,* ed. Roy P. Basler (New Brunswick: Rutgers Univ. Press, 1953), 5:222. See Oakes, *The Radical and the Republican,* chapter 5; Gary W. Gallagher, ed., *The Richmond Campaign of 1862: The Peninsula and the Seven Days* (Chapel Hill: Univ. of North Carolina Press, 2000).

13. *Liberator,* April 11, 1862; LMC to Sarah Blake Shaw, June 9, 1862, Shaw Family Correspondence, New York Public Library; Sarah Grimké to Mr. Talman, May 3, 1862, Weld-Grimké Family Papers, William L. Clements Library, University of Michigan.

14. See Gallagher, *Richmond Campaign;* Brasher, *Peninsula Campaign,* 81–83; Foner, *Fiery Trial,* chapter 7.

15. Coates Kinney to GWJ, June 27, 1862, JUL. See Foner, *Fiery Trial,* chapter 7; Varon, *Armies of Deliverance.*

16. LMC to Lucy Osgood, June 9, 1862, COR; LMC to GWJ, June 16, 1862, JUL. See McPherson, *Struggle for Equality,* 107–9.

17. *Liberator,* June 6, 1862; editorial of Philip A. Bell, June 14, 1862, *BAP,* 5:143.

18. *Liberator,* May 23, 16, April 25, 1862. See Stewart, *Liberty's Hero,* 235–40.

19. WP to CS, May 1862, SUM.

20. WP to CS, June 27, 1862, SUM; *Liberator,* June 6, July 11, 1862.

21. *Liberator,* June 6, 1862.

22. WP to CS, June 7, 29, 1862, SUM. See Stewart, *Liberty's Hero,* 235–40.

23. MDC, "The Southern Mote and Northern Beam," February 23, 1862, CU.

24. Ibid.

25. MDC, *Golden Hour,* 14, 58–62, 128–29, 160.

26. GBC to CS, March 5, 1862, SUM. See McPherson, *Struggle for Equality,* 239.

27. PP to SMJ, June 28, 1859, BPL; *Liberator,* March 7, 1862; PP to GBC, March 11, 1862, CW; GBC to PP, March 21, 1862, Parker Pillsbury Family Papers, Cleveland Colby Colgate Archives, Colby-Sawyer College. See Robertson, *Parker Pillsbury,* chapter 7.

28. *Principia,* July 5, May 29, February 27, June 5, 1862.

29. GBC to Elizabeth Cheever, June 3, June 1862, HC to Elizabeth Cheever, July 3, 10, 1862, CFP.

30. *DM,* June 1862. See Blight, *Frederick Douglass' Civil War,* chapter 7. Wirzbicki, *Fighting for the Higher Law,* chapter 6, and McPherson, *Struggle for Equality,* chapter 11, present abolitionists' fight for egalitarianism as a unifying endeavor, not one dividing the movement.

31. FD to GBC, April 5, 1862, CFP; *DM,* March 1862.

32. *DM,* March, April, August 1862. See Blight, *Frederick Douglass,* chapter 18.

33. *WAA,* November 23, 30, 1861. See Blight, *Frederick Douglass,* 426.

34. *Liberator,* January 31, May 23, 1862. See Stewart, *Liberty's Hero,* 229–31; McDaniel, *Problem of Democracy,* 237–45.

35. *Liberator,* May 23, June 6, 1862. See Lawson, *Patriot Fires.*

36. *Liberator,* June 6, 1862. See Stewart, *Liberty's Hero,* 223–24, 246–58.

37. CF, *The Journal of Charlotte Forten* (New York: Dryden Press, 1953), 116–87; CF, "Life on the Sea Islands, Part I," *The Atlantic Monthly* 13 (May 1864), 587–96. See Rose, *Rehearsal for Reconstruction;* Stevenson, "Considering the War."

38. FD to JMM, March 2, 1865, COR. See McPherson, *Struggle for Equality,* chapter 7; Blight, *Frederick Douglass' Civil War,* 177–79; Aiséirithe, "Piloting the Car."

39. JMM to Sarah McKim, June 19, 1862, NYPL; *Liberator,* May 9, 29, 1862. See McPherson, *Struggle for Equality,* 160–66.

40. *Liberator,* July 25, 1862. See Abbott, *Cotton and Capital,* chapters 4, 7; McPherson, *Struggle for Equality,* 249–52.

41. MDC, *Golden Hour,* 125–27.

42. MDC, "Then and Now in the Old Dominion," *The Atlantic Monthly* 9 (April 1862), 493–502. See D'Entremont, *Southern Emancipator,* 165–66.

43. Mildred Conway March to MDC, July 11, 1862, CU; MDC, *Autobiography,* 357–63. See D'Entremont, *Southern Emancipator,* 167–71.

44. MDC, *Autobiography,* 362–63; *Commonwealth,* July 17, 1863; MDC, *Testimonies Concerning Slavery* (London: Chapman and Hall, 1864), 114; MDC, *North and South, and Slavery* (Manchester: Henry Pitman, 1863), 233. See Fredrickson, *Black Image.*

45. *Liberator,* May 16, 1862.

46. *Liberator,* June 6, 1862.

47. Ibid. See Sterling, *Ahead of Her Time,* 335; Robertson, *Parker Pillsbury,* chapter 7.

48. Ibid.

49. SMJ to Richard Davis Webb, June 30, 1862, BPL; JMM to EQ, January 1, 1862, QUIN.

50. *Liberator,* July 11, 1862; PP to TT, September 16, 1862, NYHS.

51. *Liberator,* July 25, 1862; *DM,* October 1862. See Foner, *Fiery Trial,* 215.

52. *DM,* September, August 1862. See Blight, *Frederick Douglass' Civil War,* 137–47; Varon, *Armies of Deliverance,* 114–18.

53. *Liberator,* August 8, 1862; WLG to OJ, September 9, 1862, BPL; FD to Gerrit Smith, September 8, 1862, GER. See Mayer, *All on Fire,* 538–39.

54. WLG to Aaron Macy Powell, June 10, 1862, Gilder Lehrman Collection; WLG to OJ, September 9, 1862, BPL; "Meeting of Loyal Citizens," 1862, JAS.

55. *Commonwealth,* September 6, 13, 1862. See D'Entremont, *Southern Emancipator,* 172–74; Wirzbicki, *Fighting for the Higher Law,* 237–38.

56. LMC to Lucy Osgood, August 10, 21, 1862, COR; LMC to CS, June 22, 1862, *CC;* LMC, "Mrs. L. Maria Child to the President," August 29, 1862, COR. See Karcher, *First Woman,* 459–61.

57. LMC to William Cutler, July 10, 1862, Lydia Maria Child Papers, William L. Clements Library, University of Michigan; LMC to Sarah Blake Shaw, June 9, 1862, Shaw Family Correspondence, New York Public Library. See Karcher, *First Woman,* 443–56.

58. WP, August 16, 1862, in Redpath, *Speeches,* 464–94; Joseph A. Wright to Abraham Lincoln, August 18, 1862, AL. See Stewart, *Liberty's Hero,* 239–41.

59. WP, August 1, 1862, in Redpath, *Speeches,* 448–63; WP to Sydney Howard Gay, September 2, 1862, SHG; WP to unknown, August 28, 1862, Wendell Phillips Letters, New-York Historical Society. See Stewart, *Liberty's Hero,* 239–41; McPherson, *Struggle for Equality,* 110–17.

7. THE AFTERGLOW OF EMANCIPATION, SEPTEMBER 1862–JANUARY 1863

1. *Liberator,* January 9, 1863. See Mayer, *All on Fire,* 545–47.

2. *Liberator,* January 2, 1863.

3. Reidy, *Illusions of Emancipation,* details the emancipation process as gradual and incomplete.

4. Abraham Lincoln, "Preliminary Emancipation Proclamation," September 22, 1862, in Basler, ed., *Collected Works,* 5:433–36. See Guelzo, *Lincoln's Emancipation,* 200–7.

5. *DM,* January 1863; LMC to CS, October 3, 1862, *CC;* LMC to Eliza Scudder, November 1, 1862, COR. See Karcher, *First Woman,* 463.

6. *Liberator,* December 19, 1862; Fanny Garrison to Anna Dickinson, October 12, 1862, AD; *DM,* January 1863; *Commonwealth,* October 11, 1862.

7. *Liberator,* September 26, 1862. See Mayer, *All on Fire,* 135–37.

8. *DM,* October 1862, January 1863. See Blight, *Frederick Douglass,* 378–80.

9. *Liberator,* September 26, 1862; LMC to Henrietta Sargent, September 30, 1862, COR.

10. *Liberator,* November 28, 1862. See Stewart, *Liberty's Hero,* 241–42.

11. GBC to Elizabeth Cheever, September 29, 1862, CFP. See McKivigan, *The War Against Proslavery Religion,* 192–93.

12. GBC to Abraham Lincoln, November 22, 1862, AL.

13. Ibid.

14. *Liberator,* December 12, 1862; PP to TT, December 12, 1862, NYHS; *Liberator,* December 12, 1862. See Robertson, *Parker Pillsbury,* chapter 7.

15. FD to TT, October 21, 1862, Frederick Douglass Letters, New-York Historical Society; TT to WP, November 8, 1862, HOU. See Smith, *Stormy Present,* chapter 6.

16. *Commonwealth,* December 6, 1862; *Liberator,* December 12, 1862. See McPherson, *Struggle for Equality,* 119–20.

17. *Liberator,* December 5, 1862. See Mayer, *All on Fire,* 543.

18. GBC to Elizabeth Washburn, December 10, 1862, James Harlan to GBC, December 12, 1862, James Ashley to GBC, December 23, 1862, CFP.

19. *DM,* January 1863; Julia Crofts to FD, December 5, 1862, FRED; Lewis Douglass to Helen Loguen, November 20, 1862, Walter O. Evans Collection of Douglass Family Papers, Beinecke Rare Book and Manuscript Library, Yale University. See Blight, *Frederick Douglass,* 380–82.

20. Abraham Lincoln, "Emancipation Proclamation," January 1, 1863, in Basler, ed., *Collected Works,* 6:28–31. For Lincoln's growth, see Oakes, *The Radical and the Republican;* Foner, *Fiery Trial;* Freehling, *Becoming Lincoln.*

21. *Liberator,* January 9, 1863; WP to P. A. Comstock, January 1863, Wendell Phillips Papers, Library of Congress; diary of MDC, January 2, 7, 1863, CU; *DM,* March 1863.

22. Diary of Thomas Bradford Drew, January 1, 1863, Thomas Bradford Drew Diaries, Massachusetts Historical Society; EQ to Emma Weston, January 27, 1863, QUIN; *Liberator,* February 6, 1863.

23. *Liberator,* February 13, January 16, 1863.

24. EQ to Emma Weston, January 27, 1863, QUIN; John Parkman to Sarah Blake Shaw, January 13, 1863, John Parkman Papers, Massachusetts Historical Society; *Commonwealth,* March 20, 1863; *DM,* March 1863; *Liberator,* January 16, 1863. See McPherson, *Struggle for Equality,* 120–22; Gallagher, *Union War.*

25. *Liberator,* February 6, 1863. See Stewart, *Garrison,* 181.

26. Ibid. Fredrickson, *Inner Civil War,* 122–29, overgeneralizes this trend.

27. *Liberator,* January 16, 1863; *Commonwealth,* January 4, 1863; *Liberator,* January 30, 1863. See Blight, *Frederick Douglass' Civil War,* 106–9; Stewart, *Liberty's Hero,* 241–44.

28. CF, *The Journal of Charlotte Forten*, 122–61; *Liberator*, December 12, 1862. For uplift, see Patrick Rael, *Black Identity and Black Protest in the Antebellum North* (Chapel Hill: Univ. of North Carolina Press, 2003).

29. *Liberator*, December 12, 1862; CF, *The Journal of Charlotte Forten*, 133, 157. See Wirzbicki, *Fighting for the Higher Law*, 247–48.

30. *Liberator*, February 6, 1863.

31. LMC quoted in Karcher, *First Woman*, 464. See Karcher, *First Woman*, 464–66.

32. *Liberator*, January 9, 1863. See Stewart, *Liberty's Hero*, 241–44.

33. *Commonwealth*, January 4, 1863; *Liberator*, February 13, 1863.

34. *WAA*, January 10, 1863; GBC to HC, February 26, 1863, CFP; "Discourse," February 15, 1863, CFP.

35. *Commonwealth*, January 10, 1863. See D'Entremont, *Southern Emancipator*, 177–79.

36. *Liberator*, February 13, 1863. See Robertson, *Parker Pillsbury*, chapter 7.

37. Beriah Green to Clara, January 15, 1863, Elizur Wright Papers, Library of Congress; *Liberator*, February 6, 1863.

38. *Liberator*, February 27, January 30, 1863. See Blackett, *Divided Hearts*, 75–88.

39. *New York Times*, April 21, 1863; *Proceedings of the Convention of Loyal Leagues* (New York: W. C. Bryant, 1863), 52. See Abbott, *Cotton and Capital*, chapter 5; Adam I. P. Smith, *No Party Now: Politics in the Civil War North* (New York: Oxford Univ. Press, 2006), chapter 4; Paul Taylor, *The Most Complete Political Machine Ever Known: The North's Union Leagues in the American Civil War* (Kent: Kent State Univ. Press, 2018).

40. Loyal National League to Sydney Howard Gay, June 19, 1863, SHG; Benjamin Prescott to Anna Dickinson, May 11, 1863, AD; JMM to Charles Gibbon, February 12, 1863, NYPL; John Forbes to John Austin Stevens Jr., April 18, 1863, JAS. See Abbott, *Cotton and Capital*, 101–5.

41. Benjamin Prescott to Anna Dickinson, February 11, 12, 18, April 2, May 11, October 1863, SMJ to Anna Dickinson, January 13, March 30, 1863, Unknown to Benjamin Prescott, February 27, 28, 1863, AD; *Keene Sentinel*, March 20, 1863. See McPherson, *Struggle for Equality*, 129–31.

42. *Liberator*, January 16, 1863. See Blight, *Frederick Douglass' Civil War*, 106–9; Oakes, *The Radical and the Republican*, 201–5; McPherson, *Struggle for Equality*, chapter 9.

43. Ibid.; *WAA*, January 17, 1863. See Taylor, *Fighting for Citizenship*, chapter 3.

44. George Ward Nichols to John C. Frémont, June 5, 1863, George Ward Nichols Papers, New-York Historical Society; *Liberator*, July 3, 1863; Andrew Jackson Hamilton, *Letter of Gen. A. J. Hamilton* (New York: Loyal Publication Society, 1863), JAS; John Forbes to Abraham Lincoln, August 24, 1863, James Morrison MacKaye Papers, Library of Congress. See McPherson, *Struggle for Equality*, 206–7; Abbott, *Cotton and Capital*, chapter 6; Mason, *Apostle of Union*, chapter 10; Luskey, *Men Is Cheap*, chapter 5.

45. John Austin Stevens Jr. to Salmon P. Chase, April 18, 1863, JAS; Benjamin Prescott to Anna Dickinson, December 31, 1863, AD.

46. See Escott, *Lincoln's Dilemma*. Oakes, *Crooked Path*, portrays Lincoln as moving toward total emancipation from January.

47. GBC to HC, February 26, 1863, CFP; *Principia*, January 1, 1863. See Steve Gowler, "Radical Orthodoxy: William Goodell and the Abolition of American Slavery," *New England Quarterly* 4, no. 91 (December 2018): 592–625.

48. *Commonwealth,* January 10, 1863.

49. *Commonwealth,* February 22, 1863; Emancipation League, *Facts Concerning the Freedmen: Their Capacity and Their Destiny* (Boston: Commercial Publishing House, 1863). See McPherson, *Struggle for Equality,* 178–81.

50. MASS to Abraham Lincoln, January 29, 1863, AL; *Commonwealth,* January 31, 1863.

51. Diary of MDC, January 25, 1863, CU; MDC, *Autobiography,* 378–82. See Stewart, *Liberty's Hero,* 246; D'Entremont, *Southern Emancipator,* 179–80.

52. Diary of MDC, January 26, 1863, CU.

53. PP to TT, January 31, 1863, NYHS.

54. JMM to Frank Bird, December 23, 1862, JMM to Sydney Howard Gay, January 3, 1863, CS to JMM, January 2, 1863, JMM to William Furness, April 3, 1863, CS to JMM, January 18, 1863, NYPL; JMM to CS, January 20, 1863, SUM. See McPherson, *Struggle for Equality,* 181–82.

55. JMM to CS, March 21, 23, 1863, JMM to William Furness, April 3, 1863, NYPL; John Andrew to CS, December 10, 1862, HOU; JMM to Miss Weston, September 18, 1863, JMM to Edward Pierce, September 8, 1863, NYPL.

56. Croffut, *American Procession,* 80–81. See McPherson, *Struggle for Equality,* 182–86.

8. THE STIRRINGS OF REALIGNMENT, FEBRUARY–JUNE 1863

1. *WAA,* May 9, 1863; *Liberator,* May 22, 1863.

2. *Liberator,* May 22, 29, 1863. See Kantrowitz, *More Than Freedom,* chapter 7; Bonner, *Remaking the Republic,* chapter 6.

3. McPherson, *Struggle for Equality,* overlooks the moral ideological roots of abolitionists' fight over Lincoln.

4. FD to Gerrit Smith, March 9, June 19, 1863, GER. See McPherson, *Struggle for Equality,* 204–8; Gallman, *Defining Duty,* 236–44; Blight, *Frederick Douglass,* chapter 19; Taylor, *Fighting for Citizenship,* chapter 3; Masur, *Until Justice,* chapter 8.

5. GWJ to unknown, January 19, 1864, George T. Downing Papers, Moorland-Spingarn Research Center, Howard University; Laz Noble, Special Orders of the State of Indiana, August 15, 1864, Mary Ann Shadd Cary Papers, Moorland-Spingarn Research Center, Howard University; William Parham to Jacob C. White, March 28, August 7, 1863, Jacob C. White Collection, Moorland-Spingarn Research Center, Howard University; American Freedmen's Friend Society, Broadsides, 1863, James Morrison MacKaye Papers, Library of Congress. For Cary, see Elena K. Abbott, *Beacons of Liberty: International Free Soil and the Fight for Racial Justice in Antebellum America* (Cambridge: Cambridge Univ. Press, 2021).

6. CF to Thomas W. Higginson, May 14, 1863, Military Order of the Loyal Legion of the United States Commandery of the State of Massachusetts Civil War Collection, Houghton Library, Harvard University; CF, *The Journal of Charlotte Forten,* 156, 172–75.

7. *Liberator,* July 6, 1863; "Men of Color, to Arms!," 1863, FRED; *DM,* April 1863. See Blight, *Frederick Douglass' Civil War,* 148–73; A. Kristen Foster, "'We Are Men!' Frederick Douglass and the Fault Lines of Gendered Citizenship," *Journal of the Civil War Era* 1, no. 2 (June 2011): 143–75.

8. *WAA,* February 28, 1863; *Liberator,* May 29, 1863; *WAA,* May 16, January 10, 1863. See Taylor, *Fighting for Citizenship,* chapter 3.

9. *Liberator,* May 29, 1863; *WAA,* February 28, 1863. For Garnet, see Alexander, *African or American?*

10. FD to Gerrit Smith, March 6, 1863, GER; MDC to Ellen Conway, July 14, 1863, CU. See Blight, *Frederick Douglass' Civil War,* 162.

11. *Liberator,* May 29, 1863; George E. Stephens to *WAA,* April 2, 1863, *BAP,* 5:197–201.

12. *WAA,* February 28, 1863; *DM,* March 1863; *Liberator,* June 5, 1863.

13. *WAA,* June 20, 1863; *Liberator,* July 6, 1863.

14. Masur, *Until Justice,* discounts how most northerners maintained an unfavorable view of equality, restricting Lincoln. See Escott, *Worst Passions,* chapters 4–6; Smith, *No Party Now,* 187–91.

15. See Fredrickson, *Black Image,* 126–27; Aiséirithe, "Piloting the Car."

16. *Liberator,* May 29, 1863.

17. See Dal Lago, *William Lloyd Garrison and Giuseppe Mazzini,* chapter 7.

18. *New York Times,* May 12, 1863.

19. WLG to John Andrew, April 6, 1863, John A. Andrew Papers, Massachusetts Historical Society.

20. *Liberator,* June 5, 1863. See Mayer, *All on Fire,* 550–51. While McDaniel, *Problem of Democracy,* argues that Garrison settled only in resignation at the war's limitations, his later actions reinforced how he had curtailed his mission.

21. WLG to Helen Garrison, May 14, 1863, WLG to OJ, May 5, 1863, BPL. See Stewart, "Symmetry of Autobiography."

22. *New York Times,* May 12, 1863; *Liberator,* May 29, 1863.

23. JMM to Charles Gibbon, February 12, 1863, NYPL; *Liberator,* May 29, 1863.

24. WLG to TT, March 10, 16, 1863, William Lloyd Garrison Papers, New-York Historical Society. See Stewart, *Garrison,* 83–85.

25. LMC to William Lloyd Garrison Haskins, April 30, 1863, *CC;* Mary Stearns to WP, [1863], HOU; LMC to Henrietta Sargent, February 11, 1864, COR; LMC to Elizabeth Cady Stanton, May 24, 1863, ECS.

26. LMC to Elizabeth Cady Stanton, May 24, 1863, ECS; LMC to Eliza Scudder, n.d., COR. See Karcher, *First Woman,* 464–87.

27. *DM,* April 1863.

28. Ibid.; *DM,* June 1863. See McPherson, *Struggle for Equality,* 287–91; Blight, *Frederick Douglass' Civil War,* 176–78; Eric Foner, *Nothing but Freedom: Emancipation and Its Legacy* (Baton Rouge: Louisiana State Univ. Press, 2007).

29. *DM,* June 1863; *Liberator,* June 5, 1863. See Blight, *Frederick Douglass,* chapter 19; John David Smith, *Lincoln and the U.S. Colored Troops* (Carbondale: Southern Illinois Univ. Press, 2013).

30. Elizabeth Remond to WP, December 17, 1863, HOU; *DM,* March 1863; *WAA,* February 28, 1863. For Phillips's problematic arguments, see Taylor, *Fighting for Citizenship,* 77–79.

31. WP, May 11, 1863, in Redpath, *Speeches,* 524–62.

32. *Liberator,* July 10, 1863. See Stewart, *Liberty's Hero,* 257–95.

33. Ibid.

34. Maria Weston Chapman to Elizabeth Laugel, May 15, 1863, BPL; George W. Smalley to Sydney Howard Gay, June 27, 28, 1862, SHG.

35. "Church Anti-Slavery Society," May 1863, CFP.

36. GBC to HC, April 23, 1863, CFP.

37. MDC to Sydney Howard Gay, January 17, 1863, SHG; *Commonwealth,* May 29, 1863.

38. MDC, "Benjamin Banneker," *The Atlantic Monthly* 11 (January 1863), 79–83; *Commonwealth,* January 17, 1863.

39. WLG to WP, February 22, 1863, HOU; WLG to OJ, March 10, 1863, BPL. See D'Entremont, *Southern Emancipator,* 181–82.

40. MDC to Sydney Howard Gay, March 30, 1863, SHG; *New-York Daily Tribune,* April 1, 1863; Sydney Howard Gay to John Austin Stevens Jr., March 1863, MDC to John Austin Stevens Jr., March 30, April 4, 1863, John Austin Stevens Jr. to MDC, April 1863, JAS; George Thompson to MDC, April 29, 1863, NYPL; WLG to Andrew Paton, April 10, 1863, Miscellaneous Manuscripts, Dickinson College; WP to Richard Davis Webb, April 7, 1863, CU; EQ to Anne Weston, July 3, 1863, QUIN.

41. *Commonwealth,* June 5, 1863; MDC, *North and South,* 230–31. See D'Entremont, *Southern Emancipator;* Blackett, *Divided Hearts,* 187–95.

42. Ibid.

43. *Liberator,* June 5, 1863.

44. Ibid.; *Liberator,* July 10, 1863. See Sterling, *Ahead of Her Time,* chapter 17; Robertson, *Parker Pillsbury,* 131–33.

9. THE COLLAPSE OF THE INTERVENTIONISTS, JUNE–DECEMBER 1863

1. *Liberator,* July 10, 1863.

2. D'Entremont, *Southern Emancipator,* mischaracterizes Conway's offer as genuine.

3. GBC to Elizabeth Cheever, August 5, 1863, HC to Elizabeth Cheever, July 15, 1863, CFP; GBC to Salmon P. Chase, August 7, 1863, Salmon P. Chase Papers, Library of Congress. See Iver Bernstein, *The New York City Draft Riots: Their Significance for American Society and Politics in the Age of the Civil War* (New York: Oxford Univ. Press, 1990).

4. GBC to Elizabeth Cheever, August 5, 1863, CFP; GBC to Salmon P. Chase, August 7, 1863, Salmon P. Chase Papers, Library of Congress; Salmon P. Chase to GBC, October 17, 1863, CFP. For Chase, see Frederick J. Blue, *Salmon P. Chase: A Life in Politics* (Kent: Kent State Univ. Press, 1987).

5. WLG to OJ, July 14, 1863, BPL; Wendell Phillips Garrison to William Lloyd Garrison Jr., August 2, 1863, WPG. See Mayer, *All on Fire,* 551–56.

6. CF, *The Journal of Charlotte Forten,* 195–96; LMC to Samuel Sewall, July 28, 1863, *CC.*

7. LMC to Sarah Blake Shaw, July 25, 1863, *CC;* LMC to unknown, August 9, 1863, Ellis Gray Loring Family Papers, Schlesinger Library, Radcliffe Institute, Harvard University; LMC to Lucy Osgood, December 18, 1863, COR. See Karcher, *First Woman,* 471–72.

8. *Commonwealth,* July 10, 1863. See Blackett, *Divided Hearts,* 160–61.

9. *Liberator,* July 10, 1863; George Thompson to Richard Davis Webb, June 23, 1863, BPL.

10. MDC to James Mason, June 14, 1863, CU; *Liberator,* July 10, 1863. See D'Entremont, *Southern Emancipator,* 190–93.

11. Maria Martineau to Richard Davis Webb, June 20, 1863, George Thompson to Richard Davis Webb, June 23, 1863, Richard Davis Webb to Caroline Weston, June 25, 1863, BPL; *Liberator,* July 10, 1863; Conway, *Autobiography,* 374–76. Certain British immediatists partly inspired Conway's plan. See Conway, *Autobiography,* 367–68.

12. *Commonwealth,* July 10, 1863; MDC to Ellen Conway, June 23, 1863, CU.

13. WP to Ellen Conway, July 1, 1863, NYPL; WLG to OJ, July 14, 1863, BPL.

14. *Liberator,* July 3, 17, 1863.

15. *Liberator,* July 3, 10, 1863.

16. *Liberator,* July 10, 1863. See Aiséirithe, "Piloting the Car," 131–32.

17. *Liberator,* July 3, 10, 1863; SMJ to Richard Davis Webb, July 1, 1863, BPL.

18. *Commonwealth,* July 3, 1863; WP to Ellen Conway, July 1, 1863, NYPL.

19. WP to Ellen Conway, July 1, 1863, NYPL; *Liberator,* July 10, 1863.

20. *Commonwealth,* July 3, 1863.

21. Elizabeth Cady Stanton to WP, September 29, 1863, HOU. See Stewart, *Liberty's Hero,* 244–46.

22. Franklin B. Sanborn to MDC, July 23, 1863, CU; Franklin B. Sanborn to MDC, August 16, 1863, DIC.

23. MDC to Ellen Conway, July 14, 22, 1863, CU; Franklin B. Sanborn to MDC, August 16, 1863, DIC; MDC, *Autobiography,* 379–80. See D'Entremont, *Southern Emancipator,* 198–99.

24. MDC to Ellen Conway, July 6, 14, 1863, CU.

25. Diary of MDC, September 23, 1863, MDC to Franklin B. Sanborn, September 23, 1863, CU; *Commonwealth,* June 5, 1863; *Liberator,* September 18, 1863; MDC to Edmund Beales, October 13, 1863, BPL; MDC to Ellen Conway, July 14, 1863, CU.

26. *DM,* August 1863. See Kantrowitz, *More Than Freedom,* chapter 7.

27. *DM,* August 1863. See Blight, *Frederick Douglass' Civil War,* 165–68.

28. FD to George Luther Stearns, August 12, 1863, Frederick Douglass Papers Additions Part II, Library of Congress; *Proceedings of the American Anti-Slavery Society at Its Third Decade* (New York: American Anti-Slavery Society, 1864), 110–18; *DM,* August 1863; C. W. Foster to FD, August 21, 1863, FRED. See Oakes, *The Radical and the Republican,* 208–15; Blight, *Frederick Douglass,* 407–11.

29. *WAA,* September 26, 12, 1863. See Jackson, "Black Journalist."

30. *WAA,* September 26, 1863.

31. *WAA,* August 8, October 3, September 19, 1863. For separatism, see Mia Bay, *The White Image in the Black Mind: African-American Ideas about White People, 1830–1925* (New York: Oxford Univ. Press, 2000).

32. *Liberator,* October 16, November 13, 1863; Susan B. Anthony to Elizabeth Cady Stanton, October 10, 1863, ECS. See Robertson, *Parker Pillsbury,* chapter 7; Michael Vorenberg, *Final Freedom: The Civil War, the Abolition of Slavery, and the Thirteenth Amendment* (Cambridge: Cambridge Univ. Press, 2001), chapter 2; Harrold, *American Abolitionism,* chapter 8.

33. WLG to GWJ, November 12, 1863, JUL; JMM to WLG, October 26, 1863, BPL. See Mayer, *All on Fire,* 558–61.

34. JMM to WLG, October 26, 1863, JMM to WLG, October 17, 1863, CS to WLG, December 1, 1863, BPL; *Proceedings of the American Anti-Slavery Society at Its Third Decade.*

35. JMM to WLG, October 17, 1863, WLG to OJ, November 22, 1863, WLG to JMM, November 19, 1863, BPL.

36. *Proceedings of the American Anti-Slavery Society at Its Third Decade,* 4–5, 21–28.

37. Ibid., 56–59.

38. Ibid., 70–73. See Sterling, *Ahead of Her Time,* 338–40.

39. Ibid., 69, 75, 87–89.

40. Ibid., 73, 79–81.

41. Ibid., 110–17. See Blight, *Frederick Douglass,* 416–24; Stewart, *Liberty's Hero,* 243–44.

42. Ibid. See Escott, *Worst Passions,* chapter 6.

43. *Liberator,* December 18, 1863; Wendell Phillips Garrison to Helen Garrison, December 15, 1863, WPG. See Oakes, *The Radical and the Republican,* 222–23; Foner, *Fiery Trial,* 273–74; Escott, *Lincoln's Dilemma.*

44. *New York Times,* December 23, 1863.

45. Ibid. See McPherson, *Struggle for Equality,* chapter 11; Stewart, *Liberty's Hero,* 246–48.

10. THE COMPETING CONVENTIONS, JANUARY–JUNE 1864

1. WLG to Helen Garrison, June 8, 1864, BPL; *New York Times,* June 9, 1864. See Stewart, *Garrison,* 186–88.

2. McPherson, *Struggle for Equality,* chapters 12–13; McDaniel, *Problem of Democracy,* chapter 10; and Sinha, *Slave's Cause,* epilogue, ground this clash between abolitionists in misunderstandings or differing interpretations of public opinion and political action, not incompatible moral visions.

3. See McPherson, *Struggle for Equality,* chapter 12; Vorenberg, *Final Freedom,* 116–21; Aiséirithe, "Piloting the Car," chapter 4; Harrold, *American Abolitionism,* chapter 8.

4. *Commonwealth,* February 19, 1864; *Liberator,* February 5, 1864. See Stewart, *Liberty's Hero,* 248–49; Vorenberg, *Final Freedom,* 121–27; Oakes, *Crooked Path,* chapter 6.

5. *Commonwealth,* February 19, March 4, May 27, 1864; WP to Adam Gurowski, March 13, 1864, Gilder Lehrman Collection. See Stewart, *Liberty's Hero,* 245–51; Foner, *Fiery Trial,* 282–83; James G. Hollandsworth Jr., *Pretense of Glory: The Life of General Nathaniel P. Banks* (Baton Rouge: Louisiana State Univ. Press, 1998), chapter 12.

6. Franklin B. Sanborn to MDC, March 31, 1864, WP to MDC, March 16, 1864, CU.

7. *Commonwealth,* March 11, 25, April 22, 1864.

8. SSF and AKF to WP, February 1, 1864, PP to WP, March 8, 17, 1864, HOU.

9. *Liberator,* February 5, January 8, 1864; PP to WP, March 17, 1864, HOU; *Liberator,* June 3, May 20, 1864. See Sterling, *Ahead of Her Time,* 340–42; Robertson, *Parker Pillsbury,* 127–28.

10. PP to WP, April 21, 1864, HOU; diary of PP, January 11, 1864, RUB.

11. *Liberator,* January 8, April 15, June 3, 1864.

12. "Sixth Annual Meeting of the Church Anti-Slavery Society," May 26, 1864, CFP; A. L. Stimson to Abraham Lincoln, May 9, 1864, AL.

13. John Austin Stevens Jr. to John Jay, July 21, August 6, 11, 1863, Salmon P. Chase to John Austin Stevens Jr., February 12, 1862, August 17, 1863, John Austin Stevens Jr. to Salmon P. Chase, August 11, December 31, 1863, John Austin Stevens Jr. to Roscoe Conkling, March 29, 1864, JAS; Thomas Webster to FD, January 31, 1864, FRED; Samuel Pomeroy to Anna Dickinson, February 1864, AD. See Masur, *Until Justice;* Abbott, *Cotton and Capital,* 107–8; Foner, *Fiery Trial,* chapter 9; Trefousse, *Radical Republicans,* 285–91; Vorenberg, *Final Freedom,* chapter 4; Escott, *Worst Passions,* chapters 6–7.

14. Ann Harlan to GBC, March 22, 1864, GBC to Elizabeth Cheever, May 29, 1864, CFP; GBC, *Rights of the Coloured Race to Citizenship and Representation* (New York: Francis and Loutrel, 1864), COR.

15. GBC to Elizabeth Cheever, May 31, 1864, CFP. See McPherson, *Struggle for Equality,* 261–64.

16. FD, "The Mission of the War," 1863, FRED; *Commonwealth,* April 29, 1864. See Blight, *Frederick Douglass,* 416–25.

17. *WAA,* April 23, 1864; John S. Rock to George T. Downing, April 19, 1864, Ruffin Family Papers, Moorland-Spingarn Research Center, Howard University. See Kantrowitz, *More Than Freedom,* chapters 7–8; Taylor, *Fighting for Citizenship,* chapter 4; Masur, *Until Justice,* chapter 8; P. Gabrielle Foreman et al., eds., *The Colored Conventions Movement: Black Organizing in the Nineteenth Century* (Chapel Hill: Univ. of North Carolina Press, 2021).

18. CF, "Life on the Sea Islands, Part I," *The Atlantic Monthly* 13 (May 1864), 587–96; CF, "Life on the Sea Islands, Part II," *The Atlantic Monthly* 13 (June 1864), 666–76.

19. *Commonwealth,* April 29, 1864; WLG to OJ, May 6, 1864, BPL.

20. WLG to JMM, March 14, 1864, COR; WLG to OJ, March 14, 1864, BPL; *Liberator,* March 18, 1864; Benjamin Prescott to Anna Dickinson, May 29, 1864, AD; George William Curtis to WLG, May 7, 1864, BPL. See Mayer, *All on Fire,* 562–65; McPherson, *Struggle for Equality,* 266–67.

21. *Commonwealth,* February 19, 1864; WLG to OJ, February 16, March 14, 1864, BPL; James Ashley to Abraham Lincoln, March 1, 1864, AL.

22. WLG to OJ, March 14, 1864, BPL; *Commonwealth,* April 29, 1864; William Channing to GBC, April 1, 1864, CFP; autograph entry of George Thompson, December 8, 1864, Jacob Heaton Scrapbook, Morgan Library and Museum.

23. *NASS,* April 22, 1865; LMC to GWJ, March 27, 1864, JUL. See Karcher, *First Woman,* 479–81; McPherson, *Struggle for Equality,* 255–57.

24. LMC to Lucy Osgood, June 19, 1864, COR; *Liberator,* February 19, 1864; LMC to Henrietta Sargent, May 15, 1864, COR. See Karcher, *First Woman,* 475–77.

25. *Liberator,* February 5, 1864. See Stewart, *Liberty's Hero,* 248–49; Stewart, *Garrison,* 183–84.

26. Ibid.

27. Ibid.; *Liberator,* February 26, 1864. See Stewart, *Liberty's Hero,* 248–51; McPherson, *Struggle for Equality,* 260–62.

28. *Liberator,* May 20, 1864; WLG to Helen Garrison, May 13, 1864, BPL. See McPherson, *Struggle for Equality,* 268.

29. *Liberator,* June 3, 1864.

30. Diary of Caroline Dall, May 26, 27, 1864, Caroline Wells Healey Dall Papers, Massachusetts Historical Society; WLG to James Yerrinton, June 29, 1864, BPL; PP to WP, July 6, 1864, HOU; *Liberator,* July 8, 1864.

31. Diary of PP, February 10, 1864, RUB; Edward Gilbert to WP, February 10, 1864, Jacob Muller to WP, January 28, 1864, HOU. See McPherson, *Struggle for Equality,* 264–66; Aiséirithe, "Piloting the Car"; Mischa Honeck, *We Are the Revolutionists: German-Speaking Immigrants and American Abolitionists after 1848* (Athens: Univ. of Georgia Press, 2011), chapter 5.

32. Edward Morris Davis to WP, March 10, 1864, Edward Gilbert to WP, February 10, 1864, HOU.

33. Diary of PP, March 12, 18, 19, 1864, RUB; *Liberator,* March 25, 1864; PP to WP, March 8, 1864, Edward Morris Davis to WP, March 10, 1864, HOU. See McPherson, *Struggle for Equality,* 265; Aiséirithe, "Piloting the Car," chapter 4.

34. George W. Smalley to WP, March 15, 1864, HOU; WP to Elizabeth Cady Stanton, April 25, 1864, RAD. See Aiséirithe, "Piloting the Car," chapter 4.

35. Leonidas Haskell to PP, April 18, 1864, PP to WP, May 3, 1864, HOU.

36. *Commonwealth,* May 13, 1864; *Principia,* June 2, May 26, 1864; *New York Times,* May 6, 1864. See McPherson, *Struggle for Equality,* 267–68.

37. MDC to William Dean Howells, May 16, 1864, Howells Family Papers, Houghton Library, Harvard University; *Liberator,* September 16, 1864; *New York Times,* May 27, 1864. See Blight, *Frederick Douglass,* 429–32.

38. *New York Times,* March 21, 1863; *New-York Daily Tribune,* May 18, 1864. See McPherson, *Struggle for Equality,* 78, 193, 270–74.

39. Daniel S. Dickinson, Printed Correspondence, June 1864, AL; Franklin B. Sanborn to MDC, June 3, 1864, DIC. See Smith, *No Party Now,* chapters 6–7; Mason, *Apostle of Union,* 292–94; Abbott, *Cotton and Capital,* 107; McPherson, *Struggle for Equality,* 265–66.

40. *Commonwealth,* June 10, 1864. See Stewart, *Liberty's Hero,* 250–53.

41. *New-York Daily Tribune,* June 1, 1864; *Liberator,* June 3, 1864. See McPherson, *Struggle for Equality,* 269–71.

42. *New York Times,* June 3, 6, 1864; *Liberator,* July 1, June 3, 1864. See McPherson, *Struggle for Equality,* 272–74.

43. WLG to SMJ, June 17, 1864, Henry Wilson to WLG, February 11, 22, 1864, WLG to Helen Garrison, June 6, 9, 11, 1864, BPL. See Mayer, *All on Fire,* 567–69.

11. THE PERILS OF ABOLITIONIST POLITICKING, JUNE–DECEMBER 1864

1. Aaron Macy Powell to WP, June 25, 1864, PP to WP, June 1, 22, 1864, HOU. See Robertson, *Parker Pillsbury,* 127–28.

2. TT to Anna Dickinson, June 30, July 13, 1864, AD; *Independent,* June 23, 1864.

3. Franklin B. Sanborn to MDC, June 20, 1864, DIC; Franklin B. Sanborn to MDC, July 10, 1864, CU. See McPherson, *Struggle for Equality,* 273–75.

4. LMC to Mrs. Samuel Sewall, July 3, 1864, *CC;* LMC to Lucy Osgood, June 19, 1864, COR; LMC to John Greenleaf Whittier, July 3, 1864, CHI. See Karcher, *First Woman,* 466–67.

5. OJ to SMJ, May 20, 1864, VHS; OJ to GBC, June 16, 1864, CFP.

6. WP to Mr. Chalmers, June 1864, Wendell Phillips Papers, Library of Congress, Washington, D.C. See Blight, *Frederick Douglass' Civil War,* 183.

7. *Liberator,* July 8, 1864; HC to GBC, June 8, 1864, Elizabeth Washburn to GBC, June 25, 1864, CFP.

8. HC to Anna Dickinson, June 8, 1864, CFP; *Commonwealth,* July 8, 1864; *Principia,* July 14, 1864.

9. *Commonwealth,* June 10, 24, August 12, 1864.

10. Ibid.; MDC, *Testimonies,* 131–32; "Mr. Conway's Testimonies," August 26, 1864, Scrapbooks Compiled by Thompson and Chesson, Library of Congress.

11. MDC, *Testimonies,* 71–77, 124–25. See D'Entremont, *Southern Emancipator,* 202–7; Murray, *Advocates of Freedom,* chapter 6.

12. Susan B. Anthony to Elizabeth Cady Stanton, June 12, 1864, ECS; PP to TT, May 22, 1864, NYHS; PP to WP, May 23, 1864, HOU; PP to unknown, July 17, 1864, BPL. See McPherson, *Struggle for Equality,* 272.

13. WLG to SMJ, June 17, 1864, BPL; diary of Caroline Dall, June 21, 1864, Caroline Wells Healey Dall Papers, Massachusetts Historical Society; *Liberator,* February 5, 1864. See Stewart, *Liberty's Hero,* 248–54; Stewart, *Garrison,* 185–86.

14. WLG to OJ, June 17, 20, 1864, OJ to WLG, June 20, 1864, BPL. See McPherson, *Struggle for Equality,* 278–79; Stewart, *Liberty's Hero,* 253.

15. OJ to WP, June 22, 1864, HOU; OJ to SMJ, June 30, 1864, BPL.

16. JMM to Caroline Weston, June 2, 1864, BPL; JMM to WP, July 12, 1864, HOU; EQ to unknown, June 21, 1864, QUIN; *Liberator,* June 24, July 22, 1864.

17. Francis Newman to MDC, June 28, 1864, Francis William Newman Papers, Syracuse University; *Commonwealth,* July 1, 1864.

18. WLG to Nathaniel P. Banks, January 21, 1865, *MER,* 252–53; *True Daily Delta,* December 3, 1864; *Liberator,* July 15, 22, 1864; WLG to Charles Eliot Norton, January 13, 1865, Charles Eliot Norton Papers, Houghton Library, Harvard University. See McPherson, *Struggle for Equality,* 207, 290–95; McDaniel, *Problem of Democracy,* 246–48.

19. *Commonwealth,* June 17, 1864; Montgomery Blair to WLG, June 22, 1864, BPL; *Liberator,* July 1, 1864. See McPherson, *Struggle for Equality,* 290–93.

20. *Liberator,* January 13, 1865, July 22, 1864. See McPherson, *Struggle for Equality,* 297.

21. Orson Murray to Benjamin F. Wade, September 6, 1864, B. F. Wade Papers, Library of Congress; *Commonwealth,* August 19, July 22, August 5, 1864. See McPherson, *Struggle for Equality,* 295.

22. Susan B. Anthony to Anna Dickinson, July 1, 1864, AD; *Principia,* July 24, August 4, 1864. See McPherson, *Struggle for Equality,* 274–75.

23. PP to WP, August 14, 24, 1864, HOU; PP to TT, July 10, 1864, NYHS; *Commonwealth,* June 24, 1864.

24. WP to Elizabeth Cady Stanton, August 22, 1864, ECS; WP to MDC, July 16, 1864, NYPL; Stanton to WP, July 3, 1864, HOU.

25. *Independent,* June 30, 1864; *Liberator,* July 15, 1864. See McPherson, *Struggle for Equality,* 275–78.

26. SMJ to TT, July 15, 1864, Samuel May Jr. Letters, New-York Historical Society; R. J. Matthews to TT, July 6, 1864, TILT; OJ to SMJ, August 9, 1864, VHS; Lucretia Mott to Martha Wright, October 31, 1864, Mott Manuscripts, Friends Historical Library, Swarthmore College; William Lloyd Garrison Jr. to Wendell Phillips Garrison, August 13, 1864, Garrison Family Papers, Houghton Library, Harvard University.

27. Francis Jackson to Sydney Howard Gay, December 31, 1860, SHG; Thomas Wentworth Higginson to WP, July 11, 1864, HOU; Lucy Stone to Susan B. Anthony, July 12, 1864, Blackwell Family Papers, Library of Congress. See Aiséirithe, "Piloting the Car," 189–94.

28. Wendell Phillips Garrison to WP, June 30, 1864, HOU; WP to WLG, September 12, 1855, Garrison Family Papers, Houghton Library, Harvard University; WP to Wendell Phillips Garrison, July 12, 1864, HOU; Wendell Phillips Garrison to Helen Garrison, October 6, 1864, WPG.

29. *Commonwealth,* August 5, 1864; WP to Elizabeth Cady Stanton, August 22, 1864, ECS. See McPherson, *Struggle for Equality,* 279–80.

30. GBC to unknown, 1864, Henry Winter Davis to GBC, July 21, 31, 1864, Smith Regnas to GBC, July 25, 1864, CFP; GBC to TT, August 1864, TILT. See Vorenberg, *Final Freedom,* 150–52; Trefousse, *Radical Republicans,* 285–95.

31. John Austin Stevens Jr., Account of Meeting, Resolutions, August 1864, Daniel S. Dickinson to John Austin Stevens Jr., August 26, 1864, JAS; *Commonwealth,* August 26, 1864; William Alfred Buckingham to TT, Horace Greeley, and Parke Godwin, September 3, 1864, TILT; John Austin Stevens Jr., printed call, August 1864, JAS; John Austin Stevens Jr. to GBC, August 25, 1864, CFP. See McPherson, *Struggle for Equality,* 280–82.

32. John Jay to WP, August 10, 1864, John Jay II Papers, Rare Book and Manuscript Library, Columbia University; John Jay to John Austin Stevens Jr., August 29, 1864, JAS.

33. MDC to J. McClintock, July 21, 1864, DIC; *NASS,* June 25, 1864; *Liberator,* July 15, 1864. See D'Entremont, *Southern Emancipator,* 207–16.

34. *Commonwealth,* July 22, 1864; OJ to WP, July 22, 1864, HOU; WP to MDC, July 16, 1864, NYPL; *Commonwealth,* August 12, 26, 1864.

35. *NASS,* August 27, 1864.

36. FD to Abraham Lincoln, August 29, 1864, AL; FD to WLG, September 17, 1864, FRED. See Oakes, *The Radical and the Republican,* 229–34; Blight, *Frederick Douglass,* 432–37.

37. John S. Rock to Henry Highland Garnet et al., July 15, 23, 1864, Ruffin Family Papers, Moorland-Spingarn Research Center, Howard University. See Taylor, *Fighting for Citizenship,* 121–23.

38. *Proceedings of the National Convention of Colored Men* (Boston: J. S. Rock and Geo. L. Ruffin, 1864), 23, 43–61; George Ruffin, Report, October 1864, Ruffin Family Papers, Moorland-Spingarn Research Center, Howard University. See Kantrowitz, *More Than Freedom,* chapter 8; Wirzbicki, *Fighting for the Higher Law,* chapter 6; Blight, *Frederick Douglass,* 440–43.

39. *National Convention,* 18–19; *Liberator,* December 23, 1864. See William and Aimee Lee Check, *John Mercer Langston and the Fight for Black Freedom, 1829–65* (Champaign: Univ. of Illinois Press, 1989); Hugh Davis, *"We Will Be Satisfied with Nothing Less": The African American*

Struggle for Equal Rights in the North During Reconstruction (Ithaca: Cornell Univ. Press, 2011), chapter 1.

40. OJ to Anna Dickinson, September 22, 1864, AD. See Gallagher, *Union War*, 96.

41. Austin Blair to TT, September 11, 1864, TILT; John Austin Stevens Jr. to HC, September 14, 1864, CFP; Worcester Freedom Club Resolutions, September 1864, JAS; GBC to Elizabeth Washburn, September 10, 1864, CFP; Francis Newman to unknown, October 12, 1864, BPL. See McPherson, *Struggle for Equality*, 282–84.

42. PP to WP, September 11, 1864, HOU; WP to SMJ, September 19, 1864, BPL; *Liberator*, October 28, 1864. See McPherson, *Struggle for Equality*, 284–85.

43. *Liberator*, January 20, 1865; MDC to WP, November 5, 10, 1864, HOU; MDC to William Dean Howells, October 18, 1864, Howells Family Papers, Houghton Library, Harvard University. See Vorenberg, *Final Freedom*, chapter 7.

44. MDC to WP, January 21, 1865, HOU; MDC, "President Lincoln," *Fraser's Magazine* 71 (January 1865): 1–21; Francis Newman to MDC, January 25, 1865, Francis William Newman Papers, Syracuse University. See D'Entremont, *Southern Emancipator*, 216–17.

45. *Commonwealth*, December 10, 1864; LMC to Eliza Scudder, November 14, 1864, COR; WP to MDC, January 18, 1865, NYPL. See Stewart, *Liberty's Hero*, 254; Karcher, *First Woman*, 476–77.

12. THE END OF WARTIME ABOLITIONISM, JANUARY–MAY 1865

1. *Liberator*, April 14, 1865; SMJ to Richard Davis Webb, April 14, 1865, BPL.

2. WLG to Helen Garrison, April 7, 1865, BPL. See Stewart, *Garrison*, 190–92.

3. McPherson, *Struggle for Equality*, 297–307, and McDaniel, *Problem of Democracy*, chapter 10 and epilogue, downplay the ideological roots of this continuation struggle.

4. WLG to Abraham Lincoln, January 21, 1865, AL; WLG to John Forbes, January 21, 1865, BPL.

5. *Liberator*, February 10, 17, 1865. See Vorenberg, *Final Freedom*, chapter 7; Stewart, *Garrison*, 189–90; Dal Lago, *William Lloyd Garrison and Giuseppe Mazzini*, 179–83.

6. *Commonwealth*, February 11, 1865; MDC to WP, April 21, 1865, HOU; Giuseppe Mazzini to MDC, October 30, 1865, CU; *Commonwealth*, February 18, 1865; MDC, "Virginia, First and Last," *Fraser's Magazine* 71 (March 1865), 277–94. For suffrage restrictions, see McDaniel, *Problem of Democracy*, chapter 10; McPherson, *Struggle for Equality*, 327–28.

7. PP to WP, February 27, April 6, 1865, HOU; *Commonwealth*, December 10, 1864; WP to GWJ, March 27, 1865, JUL; *Liberator*, January 27, 1865; WP to MDC, n.d., NYPL. See Escott, *Worst Passions*, chapter 8; Leeman, "George Bancroft's Civil War"; Furniss, "States of the Union"; Smith, *Stormy Present*.

8. *Commonwealth*, December 10, 1864; WP to MDC, January 18, 1865, NYPL; *New York Times*, December 29, 1864. See McPherson, *Struggle for Equality*, 298; Stewart, *Liberty's Hero*, 254–55.

9. *Liberator,* January 27, 1865; GBC et al., "The Privilege and Dignity," December 1864, CFP; CS to HC, January 6, 1865, CFP; *Liberator,* June 9, 1865; *New York Times,* May 8, 1865.

10. FD to LMC, July 30, 1865, ROC; *Liberator,* April 7, 1865. See Blight, *Frederick Douglass,* 453–57.

11. *Liberator,* December 22, 1865.

12. LMC to GWJ, April 8, 1865, JUL; *Liberator,* March 24, 1865; LMC to Lucy Osgood, April 13, 1865, LMC to Henrietta Sargent, June 18, 1865, COR. See Karcher, *First Woman,* chapter 18.

13. LMC to GWJ, April 8, 1865, JUL; *Liberator,* March 24, 1865. See Escott, *Worst Passions,* chapter 8.

14. *Liberator,* February 3, 10, 17, 1865.

15. Ibid. See Stewart, *Liberty's Hero,* 254–55.

16. Ibid. See McPherson, *Struggle for Equality,* 297–99.

17. Ibid.; Caroline Dall to unknown, January 28, 1865, Caroline Wells Healey Dall Papers, Massachusetts Historical Society.

18. *Liberator,* February 17, 1865.

19. WLG to Fanny Garrison, January 27, 1865, WLG to Henry C. Wright, March 14, 1865, BPL; OJ to SMJ, February 9, March 17, 1865, VHS; *Liberator,* April 28, 1865; OJ to SMJ, March 2, 13, 1865, BPL. See McPherson, *Struggle for Equality,* 301–2.

20. OJ to unknown, April 6, 1865, OJ to SMJ, March 31, April 24, 1865, VHS; EQ to Mary Quincy, May 15, 1865, QUIN. See McPherson, *Struggle for Equality,* 301–2.

21. WLG to Helen Garrison, April 7, 15, 1865, BPL; *Liberator,* April 12, 1865; WLG to Edwin M. Stanton, September 15, 1865, Edwin McMaster Stanton Papers, Library of Congress.

22. See Oakes, *The Radical and the Republican,* chapters 6–7; Foner, *Fiery Trial;* Escott, *Lincoln's Dilemma,* chapters 19–20.

23. WLG, "Eulogy of Abraham Lincoln," November 1865, William Lloyd Garrison Papers, Massachusetts Historical Society; Franklin B. Sanborn to MDC, April 20, 1865, CU; MDC, "Personal Recollections of President Lincoln," *Fortnightly Review* 1, no. 1 (May 1865): 56–65; *Commonwealth,* April 29, 1865; PP to GBC, April 27, 1865, CW; *New York Times,* April 20, 1865. See Stewart, *Liberty's Hero,* 264–65; Oakes, *The Radical and the Republican,* 255–64; Blight, *Frederick Douglass,* 460–62.

24. Franklin B. Sanborn to MDC, February 17, 1865, DIC; Susan B. Anthony to WP, April 19, 1865, HOU; *New York Times,* May 3, 1865; *Liberator,* April 28, 1865. See McPherson, *Struggle for Equality,* 302–3.

25. *Liberator,* May 19, May 26, June 2, 1865. See McPherson, *Struggle for Equality,* 303–7; Stewart, *Liberty's Hero,* 264–65; Blight, *Frederick Douglass,* 468–69.

26. *Liberator,* May 19, May 26, June 2, 1865.

27. *Commonwealth,* May 13, 1865; *Liberator,* May 26, 1865.

28. *Liberator,* May 26, June 2, 1865. See Stewart, *Liberty's Hero,* 264–65.

29. *Liberator,* May 26, June 2, 1865. *Commonwealth,* May 20, 1865. See Sterling, *Ahead of Her Time,* 341–42.

30. Diary of PP, May 10, 1865, RUB; *Liberator,* June 2, 1865; WLG to Helen Garrison, May 10, 1865, BPL; OJ to SMJ, June 23, 1865, VHS; WLG to Fanny Garrison, January 27, 1866, BPL. See Robertson, *Parker Pillsbury,* 132–33.

31. WLG to GWJ, February 11, 1866, JUL; *Sacramento Daily Union,* December 25, 1865; *New York Times,* May 10, 1865; *Liberator,* May 26, 1865; WLG to Elizabeth Pease Nichol, October 9, 1865, WLG to SMJ, April 5, 1867, WLG to Wendell Phillips Garrison, March 6, 1868, BPL; LMC to Samuel Sewall, March 21, 1868, *CC;* CF to WP, October 30, 1868, HOU. See McPherson, *Struggle for Equality,* chapters 17–18; Stewart, *Liberty's Hero,* 248–53; Guyatt, *Providence,* 320–22.

32. WLG to Sylvanus Cadwallader, January 30, 1873, Sylvanus Cadwallader Papers, Library of Congress; WLG to Benjamin Chase, July 24, 1865, February 28, 1876, African American History Collection, William L. Clements Library, University of Michigan.

33. WLG to JMM, March 31, 1866, NYPL; WLG to Henry Villard, September 12, 1865, WLG to Henry Wilson, May 2, 1872, BPL; "National Testimonial," April 25, 1866, John A. Andrew Papers, Massachusetts Historical Society; *Proceedings at the Public Breakfast Held in Honour of William Lloyd Garrison* (London: William Tweedie, 1868); *Special Report of the Anti-Slavery Conference* (London: British and Foreign Anti-Slavery Society, 1868). See Julie Roy Jeffrey, *Abolitionists Remember: Antislavery Autobiographies and the Unfinished Work of Emancipation* (Chapel Hill: Univ. of North Carolina Press, 2008); Wirzbicki, *Fighting for the Higher Law,* epilogue.

34. MDC, "Letter from Virginia," circa 1875, CU; MDC to Walter Conway, January 1, 1877, DIC. See Fredrickson, *Inner Civil War,* 124–25; D'Entremont, *Southern Emancipator,* 218–19.

35. *NASS,* December 8, 1866, June 15, 1867; Susan B. Anthony to James Freeman Clarke, November 12, 1866, Perry-Clarke Collection, Massachusetts Historical Society; GBC, *Impartial Suffrage a Right* (New York: Robert J. Johnston, 1866); PP to Prince Crowell, September 27, 1866, Crowell Family Collection, Dennis Historical Society. See McPherson, *Struggle for Equality,* chapters 15–16, 18; Stewart, *Liberty's Hero,* chapter 12; Sterling, *Ahead of Her Time,* chapter 17.

36. Speech of John Mercer Langston, October 25, 1865, *BAP,* 5:374–90.

37. WP to MDC, September 12, 1865, NYPL. See Trefousse, *Radical Republicans,* chapters 9–10, 12; Foner, *Reconstruction;* Xi Wang, *The Trial of Democracy: Black Suffrage and Northern Republicans, 1860–1910* (Athens: Univ. of Georgia Press, 2012); Paul D. Escott, *Black Suffrage: Lincoln's Last Goal* (Charlottesville: Univ. of Virginia Press, 2022).

38. *NASS,* December 8, 1866; WP to Henry C. Wright, n.d., BPL; GBC to WP, April 21, 1866, HOU; FD to Henry Wilson, September 12, 1866, FRED. See McPherson, *Struggle for Equality,* chapters 15–16, 18; Stewart, *Liberty's Hero,* 279; Guyatt, *Providence,* 311–12; Blight, *Frederick Douglass,* chapters 22–26.

39. George T. Downing to Robert Hamilton, October 20, 1865, *BAP,* 5:372–73; Downing to FD, January 8, 1866, FRED; William Nesbit to the Executive Board, March 5, 1866, Jacob C. White Collection, Moorland-Spingarn Research Center, Howard University. See Bonner, *Remaking the Republic,* chapter 6; Davis, *"We Will Be Satisfied with Nothing Less,"* chapter 2.

40. WP to Thaddeus Stevens, April 30, 1866, Thaddeus Stevens Papers, Library of Congress; AKF to Gerrit Smith, January 13, 1869, GER; *Proceedings of the National Convention of the Colored Men of America* (Washington, D.C.: Great Republic Book and Job Printing Establishment, 1869). See McPherson, *Struggle for Equality,* chapters 15, 18; Kantrowitz, *More Than Freedom,* 348–50; Davis, *"We Will Be Satisfied with Nothing Less,"* chapter 2.

41. *NASS,* February 20, 1869; George S. Boutwell, *Reminiscences of Sixty Years in Public Affairs,* vol. 2 (New York: McClure, Phillips, 1902), 46. See McPherson, *Struggle for Equality,* 425–26; Stewart, *Liberty's Hero,* chapter 12. For the Reconstruction Amendments, see Richard-

son, *Death of Reconstruction;* Eric Foner, *Second Founding: How the Civil War and Reconstruction Remade the Constitution* (New York: W. W. Norton, 2019).

42. WP to Sydney Howard Gay, May 19, 1866, SHG; AKF to Gerrit Smith, January 13, 1869, GER; OJ to SMJ, June 23, 1865, VHS. See Stewart, *Liberty's Hero,* chapter 12; McPherson, *Struggle for Equality,* 430–32.

43. SMJ to Samuel J. May, March 26, 1868, BPL. See Robertson, *Parker Pillsbury,* 142–57; McDaniel, *Problem of Democracy,* epilogue; Blight, *Frederick Douglass,* 488–93.

44. *NASS,* April 16, 1870. See Stewart, *Liberty's Hero,* chapter 12.

45. For Reconstruction, see this book's introduction, note 23. For emancipation versus equality, see Caroline E. Janney, *Remembering the Civil War: Reunion and the Limits of Reconciliation* (Chapel Hill: Univ. of North Carolina Press, 2013); Escott, *Worst Passions.* For Cheever, see Guyatt, *Providence,* 311–12. For businessmen, see Abbott, *Cotton and Capital,* chapter 10, epilogue. For Black activism, see Davis, *"We Will Be Satisfied with Nothing Less,"* chapters 4–5.

46. LMC to GWJ, September 28, 1878, JUL. See Dillon, "American Abolitionists"; Robert S. Levine, *The Failed Promise: Reconstruction, Frederick Douglass, and the Impeachment of Andrew Johnson* (New York: W. W. Norton, 2021).

INDEX

Printed in the USA
CPSIA information can be obtained
at www.ICGtesting.com
LVHW041925041223
765468LV00004B/170